T5-AST-428

RESEARCH METHODS AND STATISTICS

RESEARCH METHODS AND STATISTICS

A Primer for Criminal Justice & Related Sciences

Ronald J. Hy
Department of Political Science
University of Mississippi

Douglas G. Feig
Department of Political Science
Mississippi State University

Robert M. Regoli
Department of Sociology
University of Colorado, Boulder

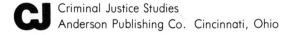 Criminal Justice Studies
Anderson Publishing Co. Cincinnati, Ohio

RESEARCH METHODS AND STATISTICS
A Primer for Criminal Justice & Related Sciences

Library of Congress Cataloging in Publication Data
Hy, Ronald John.
    Research methods and statistics.

    1. Criminal statistics.   I. Feig, Douglas.
II. Regoli, Robert M. III. Title.
HV7415.H9   1983   364'.072   83-3810
ISBN 0-87084-357-5

Rick Adams, Publisher's Staff Editor
Cover design by Steve Faske

Criminal Justice Studies
Anderson Publishing Co./Cincinnati, Ohio

TO OUR WIVES AND CHILDREN

Table Of Contents

Preface

Today, as never before researchers are using research methods and statistics to help them make decisions. This approach to problem solving has become so popular that research and statistics courses are now being taught to undergraduate and graduate criminal justice students. A major problem for many criminal justice instructors, however, is that there are not many research methods books which use criminal justice examples. Instead, instructors have to rely on research methods books from the social sciences, many of which are too complex for beginners to comprehend.

This text is intended for use in a beginning criminal justice course. It introduces the subjects of research methods and statistics as painlessly as possible. Yet enough information is presented to allow readers to answer the following questions: What are the basic assumptions behind each method and statistic? What are the primary computations underlying each solution? When and how should a method and statistic be applied? How is the statistical solution interpreted? What are the utilities and the limitations of the method and the statistic?

Since most research methods and statistics books are either too complex or rely solely on examples unfamiliar to most criminal justice students, this text stresses only those research methods and statistics which are most useful. While the volume illustrates how to compute problems, it does not focus primarily on the algorithms. Mathematical computations are introduced only when they enhance the understanding and the application of the statistics.

The book's emphasis is on application rather than on computation and derivation.

This text uses criminal justice illustrations for two obvious reasons. First, such examples help readers understand the utility and applicability of research methods and statistics, since it is far easier to comprehend these techniques when they are peppered with illustrations explicitly related to the readers' future or present employment. Second, the use of criminal justice examples unambiguously demonstrates the generality of the research methods and statistics presented in this volume. The objective of this text, then, is to introduce the principal elements of the research process and some of the most frequently used statistics. This knowledge is presented in such a way that the reader does not need a quantitative background.

The basics or research methods and statistics must be mastered for two reasons. First, a high proportion of the published work in criminal justice is empirical and quantitative, frequently using sophisticated statistical techniques. To read published works intelligently, one must be able to understand how a research question is formulated and how the data are collected and analyzed. While this book cannot possibly discuss all research methods and statistics, it does provide a guide to those which are used most frequently. A second, and in some ways a more important, reason for needing to understand research methods and statistics is that they are extremely marketable skills.

This book has three authors. Ronald John Hy wrote Chapters 2, 9, and 13, and contributed to Chapters 4 and 6. Douglas Feig wrote Chapters 7, 8, 10, 11, and 12. Robert M. Regoli wrote Chapters 1, 3, 4, 5, and 6. However, we all benefited immensely from each other's comments and critiques.

Many persons helped us prepare this book. Although it is impossible to cite each individually, a few deserve special thanks. We are particularly indebted to Herbert Watzer, Gary Brooks, and Jeff Schrink. We are also indebted to Roy Lotz (who provided some materials for some chapters), Leroy Alford (who assisted in developing many of the sample problems), and to our students at the University of Mississippi, Mississippi State University, and the University of Colorado, whose blank stares during our lectures pointed us in the right direction. We also would like to thank Rick Adams of Anderson Publishing Company for his support and criticisms of the manuscript. Finally, this book is dedicated to our families as a way of thanking them for their understanding, patience, help, and love.

Chapter 1
Science:
Elements and Explanation

Learning Objectives

After completing this chapter, the reader should be able to:
1. Distinguish between science and common sense explanations
2. Discuss the four methods of knowing
3. Identify the basic elements of the scientific research process
4. Describe scientific research as a developmental process
5. Recognize the impact of researchers on scientific studies

Introduction

Scientific explanation is an attempt to justify statements by utilizing either direct or indirect empirical observation. Scientific explanation seeks to go beyond merely collecting data. It attempts to organize information in such a way that generalizations can be made; that is, scientific explanation uses theories and concepts to help researchers arrange and organize observable data in a way that enables them to make generalizations.

Scientific explanation differs from common sense explanation in one important aspect. Scientific explanation uses theories and concepts to help researchers collect, arrange, and organize data. Researchers deduce hypotheses from acceptable theories and subject those hypotheses to rigorous empirical tests. Although common sense explanations can test hypotheses, they often rely only on evidence that supports a hypothesis and often ignore information that negates it.

Scientific explanation tests an assumed relationship through systematic procedures which require, among other things, that one specifies exactly what is being tested and how it is defined, measured, and operationalized. Scientific investigations make extensive use of controlling for extraneous variables. *Controlling* entails the use of a set of procedures which allows scientists to rule out variables that are not part of the relationship.

Science as a Way of Knowing

Science is a way of knowing, but it is only one of four distinguishable methods of knowing: (1) method of tenacity, (2) method of authority, (3) *a priori* method, and (4) method of science (Kerlinger, 1973). *Knowing by the method of tenacity* means that persons know something is true because they hold firmly to it — "they believe it with all their heart." *Knowing by method of authority* means that persons know through established belief. Many persons believe, for example, that something is true if it is written in the Bible; others may believe something is true because a government official has said it is true. *Knowing by the a priori method* means persons know because certain propositions are considered to be self-evident; some persons, for example, seem to know that punishment deters misbehavior. *Knowing by the scientific method* means that persons know on the basis of probability statements founded on systematic observations. Science possesses one characteristic none of the other methods does — the ability to self-correct. When a scientist detects an error in an explanation, it is possible to determine what went wrong and why. Even when a relationship seems obvious, scientists continue to examine alternative explanations.

If science does not prove relationships absolutely, what is the function of scientific explanation? The question cannot be answered easily. This text, however, subscribes to the purpose stated by Braithwaite (1953, p. 1):

> The function of science . . . is to establish general laws covering the behavior of the empirical events or objects with which the science in question is concerned, and thereby enable us to connect together our knowledge of the separately known events, and to make reliable predictions of events as yet unknown. This function of establishing general laws is . . . characteristic also of those parts of psychology and of the social sciences which would ordinarily be called scientific. . . .

According to this view the function of science is the formulation of theoretical statements (theory). Theory is the basic aim of scientific inquiry under which all other aims can be subsumed (Kerlinger, 1973).

Elements of the Scientific Research Process

The distinctive elements of the scientific research process are concepts, definitions, variables, hypotheses, and theories. Each is discussed below.

Concepts

Concepts are mental abstractions, representing mental constructions of reality, and as such, they are abstracted from the physical/material world.

Consider the term *delinquent*. What does it mean? For some, it may mean a 13 or 17 year old gang member who wears a black jacket and blue jeans and who terrorizes respectable citizens. For others *delinquent* may bring to mind visions of a misfortunate child, a victim of bad luck, spending time in a state correctional institution because his or her family is no longer willing to care for him or her.

The point here is that the concept *delinquent* has different meanings, depending on the context in which it is used. The meanings of scientific concepts also vary.

Definitions

Definitions are statements of what something is. Definitions used in scientific research take one of two forms; they are either nominal or operational. *Nominal definitions* are those that describe a concept in terms of another concept. *Operational definitions* are nominal definitions that are stated in measurable terms. Usually the nominal definition of a concept is stated first and then the operational definition is given.

It is critical that both the nominal and the operational definition of a concept be explicit; there is no room for ambiguity. An illustration is in order. Consider the term *police officer*. In nominal terms, *police officer* may be defined as "a member of a police force." The definition is nominal because it uses another concept to define police officer. In operational terms, *police officer* may be defined in other ways. For example, only persons holding a rank of corporal or below may be considered police officers; persons holding a rank higher than corporal might be termed *administrators*. Because a concept like *police officer* can have various meanings, researchers must specify its precise operational meaning; that is, how it was observed — then other researchers can know exactly how to replicate and extend previous studies.

Variables

A *variable* is an operationalized concept that takes on different values or meanings. Age, for example, is a variable. People's ages vary. Social class is also a variable. Researchers, for example, can differentiate between persons being in a lower, middle, or an upper class. A variable, then, is a concept which generates more than one category.

In the research process, there are three types of variables: dependent, independent, and control. *Dependent variables* are those derived from theory or hypotheses and are the ones researchers are trying to explain, understand, or predict. *Independent variables* are those that are assumed to influence the dependent variable. Independent variables generally are those researchers manipulate (or change). *Control variables* are those which are neither independent nor dependent. Using a control variable is much like sifting out its influences on the dependent and independent variables. While many research studies begin by examining the relation between independent and dependent variables, they usually include at least one control variable. The inclusion of control variables often facilitates a more indepth understanding of the bivariate (two variable) relation.

An example will make these terms more clear. One hundred youths are sampled. *Social class* is operationally defined as a dichotomous variable (i.e., a variable consisting of only two categories). Youths from families earning less than $10,000 per year are placed in one category, and youths from families earning $10,000 per year or more are put in another category. *Delinquent behavior* is operationally defined as the frequency with which a child had committed an act punishable by the state's juvenile statutes during the previous six months. Children committing five or fewer infractions are called *nondelinquents;* children committing more than five infractions are labelled *delinquent.* Respondents' sex is assessed by self-identification; that is, respondents simply indicate whether they are male or female.

The data are presented in Tables 1.1 and 1.2. Table 1.1 shows that lower class children from families earning less than $10,000 per year tend to be more delinquent than children from families earning more than $10,000 per year.

Table 1.1   Frequency of Delinquent Behavior by Social Class (N = 100)

	Family Income < $10,000 (n = 50)	Family Income ≥ $10,000 (n = 50)
Low Delinquency	20	40
High Delinquency	30	10

Or so it seems. Table 1.2 presents a different picture.

Table 1.2   Frequency of Delinquent Behavior by Social Class Controlling for Sex (N = 100)

	Male (N = 50)		Female (N = 50)	
	< $10,000	≥ $10,000	< $10,000	≥ $10,000
Low Delinquency	0	25	20	15
High Delinquency	25	0	5	10

In Table 1.2, sex is introduced as a control variable. The table illustrates the separate effects of the independent variable (family income) on the dependent variable (delinquent behavior) controlling for sex. Table 1.2 presents three noteworthy findings: (1) male youths from families earning less than $10,000 are the most delinquent, (2) females from families earning less than $10,000 are less delinquent than those from families earning more than $10,000 per year, and (3) males from families earning more than $10,000 are the least delinquent group.

Hypotheses

Hypotheses are statements suggesting the relationship researchers believe will help explain some phenomenon. They generally deal only with a portion of reality. *Delinquent behavior is related to family income of youths aged 11 to 16 years* is a hypothesis.

Research is based on testing the hypothesis. Actually a hypothesis consists of two hypotheses: the research hypothesis and the null hypothesis. The *research hypothesis* states what one expects to find. The research hypothesis is the one researchers want to confirm. The *null hypothesis* is a contradiction of the research hypothesis. It is the null hypothesis which is actually tested. For the above stated research hypothesis, the null hypothesis would read: Delinquent behavior *is not* related to the family income of youths aged 11 to 16 years old. (Research and null hypotheses will be discussed in greater detail in Chapter 2.)

In order to test a hypothesis, the key concepts must be operationalized. *Operationalization* is a process whereby specific empirical observations (variables) are used to indicate the existence or the nonexistence of a particular concept. Operationalizing concepts is a complex and difficult task, primarily because there is always a variety of variables that can be used to measure any one concept. Therefore, when selecting variables to operationalize a concept, two basic rules must be remembered. The variables used to measure the concept should (1) fit its commonly accepted meaning and (2) provide the most accurate measurement available.

To insure that these two rules are satisfied, all variables must be both as reliable and as valid as possible. *Reliability* refers to the extent to which a measurement instrument yields consistent results on repeated applications. *Validity* is the extent to which a measurement instrument corresponds to the concept being measured. With respect to the concept *delinquent behavior,* for example, researchers must demonstrate whether the way they operationalized the term is both reliable and valid; that is, will the operationalized term (i.e., a child who has committed an act punishable by the state's juvenile statutes during the previous six months) offer both consistent results (reliability) and correspond to the concept being measured (validity). (These, and related issues are explored in Chapter 4.)

Theory

A *theory* is a set of logically interrelated statements that are empirically meaningful. There are three dimensions to theory: (1) the logical structure, (2) the propositions concerning the interrelationships in the empirical world, and (3) the assumptions made regarding the scientific method and data (Sjoberg and Nett, 1968). This definition is more encompassing than most, but it is necessary. After all, theory is more than a classificatory, logico-deductive scheme. It includes the assumptions researchers make concerning their method and data. Theory affects not only what is studied, but how it is studied.

The basic goal of science is to validate theory and subsequently advance scientific laws (Labovitz and Hagedorn, 1976). Exactly what does that mean? Theory is a form of explanation, but unlike all other explanatory forms, theory allows for prediction. Without theory, relationships between variables can only be assumed. Because theory permits prediction, hypotheses can be tested. While it is true that hypotheses can be tested in the absence of theory, such testing would not allow for the development of generalizations. In other words, theory is the substance from which hypotheses are culled. Finally, theory allows researchers to find their errors. Suppose, for example, that a particular hypothesis is tested, and the results are different than expected (a common occurrence). How are such findings accounted for? If the hypothesis has been theoretically derived, it is possible to assess what went wrong and why.

Theories also have other functions; for example, they facilitate the generation of new knowledge, help explain the causes of past as well as present events, and offer an intuitively pleasing explanation for when, where, how, and why events occur. Theory is science's most powerful tool.

The Scientific Research Process: Operationalized

Until now, the scientific research process has been dealt with in a static fashion. This was necessary to familarize readers with the terminology involved. However, scientific research is not static; it is a very dynamic enterprise.

When adapting scientific explanation to a particular subject matter (e.g., criminal justice), one integrates five interrelated concepts: theories, hypotheses, methodology, observations, and empirical generalizations. Sometimes it is difficult to tell where one concept ends and another begins.

In other words, there are many shaded (or gray) areas where it is impossible to state something in unquestionable terms.

Insofar as these components can be distinguished from one another, they may vary internally, particularly in their degree of formalization. This means that for any given criminal justice research study, for example, the theory may only be hinted at, while the hypotheses and methodology are stated explicitly. However, in all research, these five components are present. The difference among studies is the degree to which they are present. It is improper to identify some research as atheoretical (i.e., without theory) and others as theoretical. Rather, some research is only more explicit in its coverage than are others.

To make matters a bit less confusing, Wallace (1969, p. ix) has developed a model designed to show these relationships more clearly. It is presented in Figure 1.1. Examing this figure closely, one notes that science

Figure 1.1   The Scientific Research Process

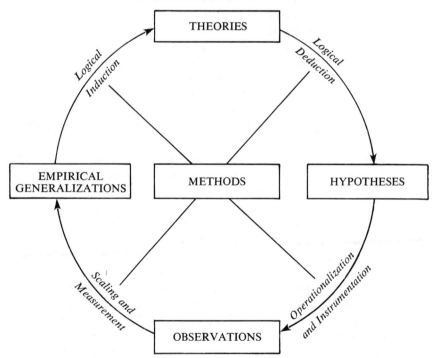

Source: Walter Wallace, *Sociological Theory*. Chicago: Aldine Publishing Company, 1969, p. ix.

is perceived as a succession of manipulations of information, each with its own kind of methodology. *Methodology* is the logic of scientific procedure

(Merton, 1968, p. 140), or the recipe for getting things done. In science, "getting things done" suggests logical induction and deduction. The set of methods labelled in Figure 1.1 *Scaling and Measurement* governs the manipulations involved in transforming observations into empirical generalizations; the method called *Logical Induction* controls the transformation of empirical generalizations into theories, and so on in a clockwise fashion.

No doubt an example from the literature will help in understanding the scientific research process as it is presented here. In Durkheim's now classic study of suicide (1966; 1897), he challenged the existing belief that suicide was an individualistic phenomenon. Durkheim argued that suicide possessed a social quality. While there are a variety of ways to address this issue, a seemingly logical place to start was with direct observations of the background of persons who committed suicide. Simultaneously, one could count and compute suicide rates for various subcategories of persons (e.g., Catholics, men, and Italians). These observations could then be transformed into empirical generalizations.

One empirical generalization which emerged in *Suicide* was that Protestants have a higher suicide rate than Catholics. To make the next transformation, from empirical generalization to theory via logical induction (the method), required Durkheim to answer two questions: (1) Are there distinctive characteristics that persons possess because they are either Catholic or Protestant and do these characteristics explain differences in the suicide rates? and (2) If suicide rates do vary according to specific individual characteristics, how can they be accounted for? (Wallace, 1969, p. ix).

Together these questions ask, Can the phenomenon-that-explains (religious affiliation) and the phenomenon-to-be-explained (in suicide) be inductively generalized (i.e., can they add to scientific knowledge)? One way to express answers yielded by this transformation might be in terms of theoretical statements; i.e., *suicide rates vary inversely with degree of social integration* and *acts of personal disorganization vary inversely with degree of social integration.* When the theory is coupled with the fact that unmarried persons experience less social integration, the following hypothesis can be deduced: *Unmarried persons are more likely to commit suicide.*

The validity of this hypothesis can be tested by observations. If upheld, it can be incorporated into the theory by logical induction. So it goes; as research study upon research study is completed, theoretical statements become increasingly refined and subsequently help researchers make predictions.

Summary

There are a variety of ways persons acquire knowledge. This text subscribes to the belief that the scientific method is the most valid one for understanding the world around us.

Sometimes researchers can influence outcomes by having certain expectations about the study's results. The research literature is filled with studies demonstrating how researchers' expectations alter or distort both their perceptions of events and their results (Rosenthal, 1976). (See Chapter 5.)

At this point it suffices to say that researchers must be aware of the potential effect they have on a study's outcome. Researchers must be cognizant not only of their values and how these affect the relationships being examined but also of their impact on the interpretation of the data. Subsequent chapters intend to sensitize readers to these and related issues, all in an endeavor to demonstrate the utility of scientific explanation for criminal justice research.

Review Questions

1. Define the following terms and ideas:
    a. science
    b. concept
    c. nominal definition
    d. operational definition
    e. variable
    f. hypothesis
    g. theory
2. Identify the different "methods of knowing."
3. Develop a nominal definition for the concept *education*.
4. Write an operational definition for the following terms:
    a. police officer
    b. authoritarian
    c. criminal offender
    d. poverty
    e. juvenile delinquent
5. Explain the difference between a research hypothesis and a null hypothesis.
6. Explain the operationalization of the scientific research process.

References

Braithwaite, Richard. *Scientific Explanation.* Cambridge, MA: Cambridge University Press, 1953.

Durkheim, Emile. *Suicide.* Translated by John Spaulding and George Simpson. New York: The Free Press, 1966 (1897).

Kerlinger, Fred. *Foundations of Behavioral Research.* 2nd ed. New York: Holt, Rinehart & Winston, 1973.

Labovitz, Sanford and Hagedorn, Robert. *Introduction to Social Research.* 2nd ed. New York: McGraw-Hill Book Co., 1976.

Merton, Robert K. *Social Theory and Social Structure.* New York: The Free Press, 1968.

Rosenthal, Robert. *Experimenter Effects in Behavioral Research.* New York: Irvington Publishers, Inc., 1976.

Sjoberg, Gideon and Nett, Roger. *A Methodology for Social Research,* New York: Harper & Row, Publishers, Inc., 1968.

Wallace, Walter, ed., *Sociological Theory.* Chicago: Aldine Publishing Company, 1969.

Chapter 2

Hypothesis Testing

Learning Objectives

After completing this chapter, the reader should be able to:

1. Formulate a hypothesis
2. Construct a directional and a nondirectional research hypothesis
3. Know how to ascertain the permissible level of error (significance)
4. Explain the difference between a Type I error and a Type II error
5. Define a sampling distribution and the critical region

Introduction

While all research is not concerned with formally testing hypotheses, much of it is. *Hypothesis testing* primarily involves making statistical inferences about a population based on the characteristics found in a sample drawn from that population. Hypothesis testing uses inferential statistics to ascertain how much of a mistake is being made *(level of error)* when making inferences about a population from a sample of data. This chapter describes the strategy of hypothesis testing.

A hypothesis is stated in terms of independent and dependent variables. An *independent variable* is the element one thinks will explain changes in the *dependent variable*.

For example, if a police department implements a burglary prevention program designed to urge municipal residents to lock their houses and automobiles, the department might hypothesize (speculate) that the number of burglaries will decline after the program is implemented. The research hypothesis is: *The burglary reduction program decreases the number of burglaries occurring in the city.* The burglary reduction program is the independent variable, and the number of burglaries is the dependent variable.

After each sample is selected and the hypothesis is formulated, the level of error is set, and the hypothesis is tested. Figure 2.1 shows how this is generally done. It should be remembered, however, that even though these steps are usually followed in sequence, this is not always the case. Each step may have to be modified in light of various constraints.

Formulating a Hypothesis[1]

A hypothesis actually consists of two hypotheses: a research hypothesis (denoted by the symbol H_a) and a null hypothesis (indicated by the symbol H_o). The *research hypothesis* is the one which researchers would like to substantiate. The null hypothesis is a contradiction of the research hypothesis, hence the hypothesis that should be rejected. For example, if the research hypothesis is: *The burglary prevention program decreases the number of burglaries occurring in the city,* the null hypothesis is: *The burglary prevention program does not decrease the number of burglaries occurring in the city.*

Figure 2.1   Steps for Hypothesis Testing

```
    1.  Select the sample.

    2.  Formulate a hypothesis.

    3.  Set the level of error.

    4.  Test the hypothesis.
```

It is exceedingly important to remember that the null hypothesis is the one which is tested directly. It is assumed to be true unless the sampled data suggest otherwise. When the null hypothesis, being a contradiction of the research hypothesis, is rejected, it can be assumed that the research hypothesis *may be* true and thus accepted. The null hypothesis only is rejected or not rejected. As a result of such reasoning, researchers can decide either that the null hypothesis is false and reject it, thereby suggesting that the research hypothesis *may be* true; or they cannot reject the null hypothesis (Elzey, 1976, p. 109).

There are two types of hypotheses: nondirectional and directional. A *nondirectional hypothesis* merely suggests that there either is or is not a difference. An illustration of a nondirectional null hypothesis is: *An arrest technique training program does not affect the quality of arrests.*[2] The nondirectional research hypothesis, then, must be: *An arrest technique training program does affect the quality of arrests.*

The two hypotheses are stated as follows:

$$\text{H}_o\!: \mu_1 = \mu_2$$
$$\text{H}_a\!: \mu_1 \neq \mu_2$$

where:

> μ_1 = the mean (average) quality of arrests *before* implementation of the arrest technique training program
>
> μ_2 = the mean (average) quality of arrests *after* implementation of the arrest technique training program
>
> $\neq$ = does not equal

In this example, the null hypothesis is rejected if either (1) the mean quality of arrests decreases after the program is implemented or (2) the mean quality of arrests increases after program implementation; that is, the null hypothesis is rejected as long as there is a difference between the mean quality of arrests before and after program implementation, regardless of the direction of that difference.

A *directional hypothesis* stipulates the direction of the speculated difference in "greater than" or "less than" terms. For instance, a directional null hypothesis is: *The arrest technique training program does not improve the quality of arrests.* The directional research hypothesis is: *The arrest technique training program does improve the quality of arrests.*

The two hypotheses are stated in the following manner:

$$\text{H}_o\!: \mu_1 \geq \mu_2$$
$$\text{H}_a\!: \mu_1 < \mu_2$$

where:

> μ_1 = the mean quality of arrests *before* implementation of the arrest technique training program
>
> μ_2 = the mean quality of arrests *after* implementation of the arrest technique training program
>
> $\geq$ = greater than or equal to
>
> $<$ = less than

When such a directional hypothesis is used, the null hypothesis is rejected only if there is an increase in the mean quality of arrests after a program is implemented.

In summary, a hypothesis based on common sense, personal experience, indirect experience, a review of similar projects, and/or a theoretical perspective must be developed. After that, the hypothesis must be converted into a null hypothesis and research hypothesis in order to test it.

Logic of Hypothesis Testing

Once the hypothesis is stated, it can be tested. Hypothesis testing answers two simple questions: (1) What is the probability that the difference between the samples is significant? and (2) Are there adequate grounds for concluding that each sample represents the population from which it was drawn? Figure 2.2 illustrates these two questions.

Figure 2.2   **Hypothesis Testing Questions**

		Probability That the Difference Is Significant	
		High	Low
Grounds for Concluding That the Sample(s) Represents the Population(s)	Adequate	Reject H_o	Do Not Reject H_o
	Inadequate	Do Not Reject H_o	Do Not Reject H_o

When there is a high probability that the difference is significant and adequate grounds exist for assuming that each sample represents the population from which it was drawn, *it can be concluded that the difference probably did not occur because of chance, and therefore the null hypothesis should be rejected in favor of the research hypothesis.*

The logic of hypothesis testing is based on a method that is analogous to proof by contradiction. This line of reasoning is similar to that used in a court trial (Mendenhall, 1978, p. 172). When trying a person for theft, the court assumes the accused is not guilty until proven guilty. The prosecution, therefore, has to present evidence to contradict the not-guilty plea in order to obtain a conviction. Holding that a person is not guilty is analogous to hypothesizing that an independent variable has no effect (null hypothesis). In a court of law the prosecution demonstrates that a not-guilty plea is incorrect by presenting evidence which refutes such a plea. Therefore, when the evidence suggests that a not-guilty plea is incorrect, the court changes its mind and concludes that the accused is guilty. Likewise, researchers start with the assumption that the independent variable does not have the desired impact, and then they proceed to try to refute that claim by presenting evidence which shows that such an assumption is incorrect. When the assumption that an independent variable does not have the desired impact is refuted, it can be assumed the opposite is true — the independent variable does have an impact.

The null hypothesis, as mentioned before, is rejected and the research hypothesis is accepted when there is a difference between the samples, and this difference could not have occurred by chance. On the other hand, if the difference could have occurred by chance, that difference is assumed not to be significant.

Setting the Level of Error

Researchers, of course, *can never be absolutely certain* which of the two hypotheses — the null or the research — is correct, principally because the difference between the samples may be the result of chance occurrence rather than a result of the independent variable. They, however, can estimate the probability (level) of making an error (and thus determine the probability of being wrong) when deciding to reject the null hypothesis.

The level of error (often called the *level of significance*) is the probability of making an incorrect decision when rejecting the null hypothesis in favor of the research hypothesis. The level of error is measured by appropriate *test statistics* which compare the samples. When the variations are large, it can no longer be assumed that the difference between the samples is attributable to chance alone. When this situation occurs, researchers may assume with little probability of error that the null hypothesis actually is false and, therefore, should be rejected. By using test statistics to determine the precise level of error, researchers can determine the probability of making a wrong decision when rejecting or not rejecting the null hypothesis. Thus, with the aid of test statistics the correct decision can be made most of the time.

Types of Errors

There are two inversely related types of error that can be made when deciding to reject or not to reject a null hypothesis — a Type I error or a Type II error. A *Type I error* is committed when a true null hypothesis is rejected. Thus, a Type I error is made when there is a difference shown between the samples, but one does not really exist. To put it another way, a Type I error occurs when the research hypothesis is accepted, even though that conclusion is incorrect.

A *Type II error* is committed when a false null hypothesis is not rejected. Therefore, a Type II error is made when there is no difference shown between samples, but there actually is. Figure 2.3 presents the four possible decision making alternatives.

Since the two types of errors are inversely related, one is caught in an inescapable predicament: reducing the probability of making a Type I error increases the probability of committing a Type II error, and vice versa. Figure 2.4 illustrates the relationship between the probable occurrence of Type I and Type II errors. As the figure shows, it is impossible to, simultaneously, eliminate the risk of making both types of errors.

Figure 2.3   Decisionmaking Alternatives

	True State of Affairs	
Decision	Null Hypothesis Is True	Null Hypothesis Is False
Reject null hypothesis	Type I Error	No Error
Do not reject null hypothesis	No Error	Type II Error

Figure 2.4   Relationship Between Type I and Type II Errors

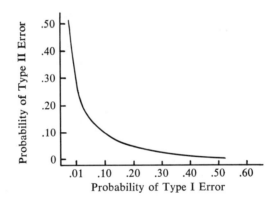

Source: Janet P. Moursund, *Evaluation: An Introduction to Research Design.* Monterey, California: Brooks/Cole Publishing Company, 1973, p. 111.

The following example best illustrates Type I and Type II errors. When deciding whether to parole a prisoner, a parole board can make one of two types of errors. A parole board could release a prisoner who subsequently commits a crime (Type I error); or a parole board could refuse to release a prisoner who actually would not have committed a crime if he or she had been paroled (Type II error). The problem, of course, is that these two errors are related. The parole board could reduce the chances of making a Type I error (releasing prisoners who will subsequently commit a crime) by refusing to parole anybody. If the board does, it increases the chance of making a Type II error (failing to release prisoners who will not subsequently commit a crime).

The type of error that one chooses to risk making depends upon which error is perceived as leading to the most undesirable consequences. A parole board generally prefers to make a Type II error rather than a Type I error because it is more concerned with protecting public safety than with successful rehabilitation (Levine et al., 1980, p. 424).

Setting the Permissible Level of Error

It is an arduous task to determine the level of error one is willing to accept and still be able to feel confident about rejecting the null hypothesis and accepting the research hypothesis. Not only is such a decision based on absolutely no rules and few guidelines but it also is founded on the amount of risk one is willing to take, a purely subjective judgment. Put as simply and concisely as possible, ascertaining the permissible level of error is somewhat, though not entirely, arbitrary. However, convention does, as shown in Figure 2.5, offer some guidelines.[3]

Figure 2.5   Guidelines for Selecting the Permissible Level of Error

1. .01 is used with large samples (i.e., more than 100)

2. .05 is used with moderate size samples (i.e., 30-100)

3. .10 is used with unavoidably small samples (i.e., fewer than 30)

Achieving a level of .01 means that the probability of committing a Type I error is 1 percent or less. Attaining a level of .05 means that the probability of making a Type I error is 5 percent or less. Finally, and it should be obvious by now, reaching a level of .10 means one has a 10 percent or less chance of making an incorrect decision and at least a 90 percent chance of making a correct decision.

At this point a note of caution is necessary. These guidelines are merely a matter of convention and convenience and are by no means universal. The guidelines have been developed by statisticians as rules of thumb to determine the amount of statistical risk one should be willing to take when rejecting a null hypothesis. These rules of thumb can and should be adjusted according to the consequences of making an incorrect decision.

In summary, the probability of making a Type I error should not be set too low, for this will result in increasing the probability of committing a Type II error. *Similar studies should be reviewed to see the permissible level of error other experts are using.* When such studies are not available, one should depend on the guidelines suggested in Figure 2.5. Moreover, *as large a sample as fiscal and human resources allow should be used.* The reason for this statement is that the most satisfactory way to reduce the probability of making a Type I error without increasing the probability of committing a Type II error is to increase the size of the sample.

Testing the Hypothesis

After the sample is selected, the hypothesis formulated, and the level of error set, the hypothesis needs to be tested. Such a hypothesis is tested by first calculating the appropriate test statistic and then seeing how the value of that statistic relates to an appropriate sampling distribution. When the test statistic falls into an extreme portion of the sampling distribution (called the *critical region*), the null hypothesis is rejected, and the research hypothesis is accepted. Using these two sampling constructs — the sampling distribution and the critical region — researchers can determine precisely the level (probability) of making a Type I error when rejecting the null hypothesis in favor of accepting the research hypothesis.

Since persons who are neither mathematically inclined nor versed in probability theory are likely to find the concepts of sampling distribution and critical region difficult to understand, this section will explain these two statistical concepts verbally rather than mathematically. While such an approach inevitably is subject to some criticism, verbal rather than mathematical explanations are the only way such complex concepts can be introduced to persons unfamiliar with probability theory.

Sampling Distribution

A *sampling distribution* is a hypothetical frequency distribution constructed for a given sample statistic (e.g., mean or standard deviation) from a large number of sample frequency distributions which are drawn from the same population. Such a distribution is actually a theoretical probability distribution — a mathematical construct derived from deductive probability theory — and as such does not depict actual data. A sampling distribution, in other words, is a myriad of frequency distributions — one for each possible sample size — based not on empirical data but deduced from probability theory.

Such a deductive process is based on the statistical assumption that when a large number of samples are drawn randomly from the same population, the average sample statistic approximates the corresponding population statistic. Put more concretely, the arithmetic mean of several hundred sample means is a close approximation of the population mean. By drawing a large number of samples from the same population, statisticians can approximate a population statistic without knowing its actual value. Thus, one can draw a sample, calculate a statistic, and compare it to a sampling distribution to determine how closely the sample statistic represents the population statistic.

Statisticians can assume that several hundred sample statistics approximate a population statistic because such an inference is based on the *Central Limit Theorem.* The theorem postulates that:

1. Regardless of the number of units in each sample, a statistic (e.g., mean or standard deviation) from a sample drawn from a normally distributed population is normally distributed.
2. A statistic from a large sample is more likely to be normally distributed than is a statistic from a small sample.
3. A statistic from a normally distributed sample is a close approximation of a population statistic.

Due to the wide acceptance of the *Central Limit Theorem,* conclusions about the population can be reached by examining a sample statistic and comparing it to an appropriate sampling distribution. If a sample statistic falls into the part of the sampling distribution called the critical region, the likelihood is that the difference between samples is not due to chance but is actual. Therefore, the null hypothesis can be rejected in favor of the alternative hypothesis.

Knowing how to calculate myriad sampling distributions to test a null hypothesis is not necessary because statisticians have generated tables for each type of the most frequently used sampling distributions. (These tables appear in the appendices.) Consequently, the typical procedure for deciding whether or not to reject a null hypothesis is to draw a random sample (or samples), compute an appropriate test statistic from the sampled data, and compare the value generated by the test statistic to the sampling distribution to see if the value falls within the critical region. When the value of the test statistic falls within the critical region of the sampling distribution, the null hypothesis is rejected. Conversely, when the value of the test statistic does not fall within the critical region, the null hypothesis is not rejected.

Critical Region

The *critical region* is the extreme end(s) of a sampling distribution. The probability of the value of a test statistic falling within either one or both of these extreme ends is so small that when it does occur, it can be concluded that the probability of making an error when rejecting the null hypothesis is low. The size of the critical region is not fixed; it varies with the permissible level of error. When the level of error is set at .10, the critical region includes the extreme 10 percent of the sampling distribution. When the level of error is set at .05, the critical region comprises the extreme 5 percent of the sampling distribution. When the level of error is set at .01, the critical region consists of the extreme 1 percent of the sampling distribution.

If the calculated value of the test statistic is equal to or greater than the value associated with the critical region of a sampling distribution, the null hypothesis is rejected with a known probability of making a Type I error. When the calculated value of the test statistic is smaller than the value associated with the critical region, the null hypothesis is not rejected because there is a possibility that the difference between the samples could have occurred by chance.

The critical region is best understood when the sampling distribution is viewed as a continuous distribution of occurrences placed under the area of a curve. The exact shape of a sampling distribution depends on a number of factors, chiefly the sample size. However, regardless of its shape, the area under each sampling distribution always is 100 percent. Figure 2.6 visually represents a sampling distribution, a critical region, and a test statistic value.

Figure 2.6   Representation Of A Sampling Distribution, Critical Region, And Test Statistic

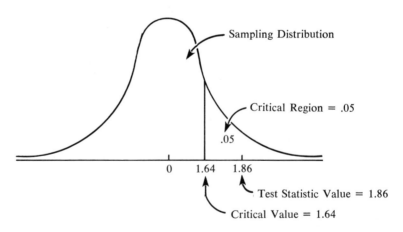

Note: Since the value of the test statistic (1.86) falls within the critical region (1.64), the null hypothesis is rejected.

A test statistic is a measure based on sample observations that compares a sample statistic to a sampling distribution to ascertain the degree of risk involved in rejecting a null hypothesis. A test statistic normally has no descriptive power. It is used only to ascertain whether to reject the null hypothesis.

Summary

This chapter has introduced and discussed a number of extremely important concepts. These concepts will appear repeatedly in subsequent chapters.

First of all, *hypothesis testing* is a technique used to reach conclusions about a population on the basis of sampled data. Hypothesis testing requires *two* hypotheses: a *research hypothesis* and a *null hypothesis*. A research hypothesis is the hypothesis believed to be true. A null hypothesis is the exact opposite of the research hypothesis. Thus, only one of these hypotheses can be true. In hypothesis testing, it is the null hypothesis which is actually tested.

These two hypotheses are either *nondirectional* or *directional*. Nondirectional hypotheses assert that two samples of data are either *alike* or *different* in some respect. Directional hypotheses state that one sample is *greater than* or *less than* another sample in some respect.

There are two types of errors that can be made when conducting hypothesis tests. When a true null hypothesis is mistakenly rejected, a Type I error is made. When a false null hypothesis is mistakenly not rejected, a Type II error is made. Furthermore, these two types of error are inversely related. Efforts to minimize the risk of making a Type I error increase the risk of making a Type II error, and vice versa. This "risk" is called the *level of error*.

Hypothesis testing requires that a *test statistic* be computed. The computed test statistic then is examined in order to see where it fits in the *sampling distribution*. If the test statistic falls in the part of the sampling distribution called the *critical region,* the null hypothesis is rejected in favor of the research hypothesis. If the test statistic does not fall into the critical region, the null hypothesis is not rejected. The size of the critical region and, hence, the likelihood of rejoicing the null hypothesis, depends solely upon the level of error mentioned earlier.

In this chapter, these important concepts have been discussed rather abstractly. The following chapters will introduce several commonly used hypothesis tests and will make use of these central concepts while discussing the most frequently used hypothesis tests. As these subsequent chapters are read and understood, readers should develop a greater understanding both of what these concepts mean and how they are used. This chapter has provided readers with a sort of tourist's road map which identifies the major points of interest and shows how they are connected.

Notes

[1]The way a hypothesis is formulated depends upon the number of samples and/or the number of variables being used. For instance, a one sample hypothesis is formulated somewhat differently from a two-sample hypothesis. Since this chapter focuses on developing a brief understanding of the theoretical basis of hypothesis testing, the examples used will focus on hypothesis formulation for a two-sample test. This type of example does not limit the understanding of the theory behind the use of statistics since the hypothesis formulation procedure for other types of hypotheses is merely a variation of the examples presented. Moreover, the other hypothesis tests will be formulated in the appropriate chapters.

[2]Quality of arrests usually is operationalized by an index consisting of the percentage of felony arrests passing either a preliminary court hearing or a grand jury and the percentage of arrests leading to conviction or treatment.

[3]These guidelines should be viewed as maximums; that is, one would be elated to calculate a lower level of error than the permissible one. For instance, if the permissible level of error were set at .05 and the calculated level of error is .002, researchers would be overjoyed since the probability of making a correct decision when rejecting the null hypothesis is 99.8 percent instead of 95 percent.

Review Questions

1. Explain the meaning and significance of the following terms and ideas:
   a. research hypothesis
   b. level of error
   c. directional and nondirectional hypotheses
   d. Type I and Type II errors
   e. .05 level of error
   f. dependent and independent variables
   g. logic of hypothesis testing
   h. sampling distribution
   i. critical region
   j. test statistic

2. Explain why the null hypothesis is not rejected when the computed test statistic does not fall within the critical region.

3. Under what conditions would researchers stipulate a high permissible level of error?

4. An evaluation team is testing the following hypotheses:

   H_o: The drug is not safe.

   H_a: The drug is safe.

   Regarding this statistical hypothesis, which type of error (Type I or Type II) has the most potential danger?

References

Elzey, Freeman F. *An Introduction to Statistical Methods in the Behavioral Sciences*. Monterey, CA: Brooks/Cole Publishing Company, 1976.

Levine, James P. et al. *Criminal Justice: A Public Policy Approach:* New York: Harcourt Brace Jovanovich, Inc., 1980.

Mendenhall, William, and Reinmuth, James. *Statistics for Management and Economics*. 3rd ed. North Scituate, MA: Duxbury Press, 1978.

Chapter 3
Research Design

Learning Objectives
After completing this chapter, the reader should be able to:
1. Identify the types of units of analysis
2. Comprehend the association between variables and relationships
3. Differentiate among experimental and cross-sectional research designs
4. Discuss the concept *internal validity*
5. Distinguish between internal and external validity
6. Explain how to control for a third variable
7. Describe experimental and nonexperimental designs
8. Define the concept *model*
9. Differentiate among accounting, implications, and process models

Introduction
Once the problem has been formulated, the theoretical statements developed, the hypotheses advanced, and the variables defined and operationalized, an execution plan must be advanced. The execution plan or *research design* guides the research endeavor in the testing of the hypotheses. In many ways, the research design is a model that permits subsequent inferences to be made about the causal relationships among the variables.

This chapter discusses research designs in two ways. First, specific types of research designs are presented. Second, the pattern is conceived through modeling. These designs are categorized as either experimental or nonexperimental. The advantages and disadvantages of each design are also mentioned. Finally the key issues relating to the research design are discussed.

Relationships and Variables
A *relationship* involves an association between at least two variables. There

cannot be a relationship when only one variable is examined. The existence of a relationship requires that the values of one variable vary jointly with the values of a second variable. The more variation between the values, the stronger the relationship.

The requirement that at least two variables are needed for a relationship is so fundamental that it hardly deserves to be mentioned, but the fact is the rule is often violated. Table 3.1 is used to show how a person might unwittingly break this rule. The table is designed to answer the question, Is the South an especially violent region of the United States?

Table 3.1   Rate of Violent Crime in the South

Area	Population (in thousands)	Violent crimes per 100,000 inhabitants
South	74,767	568.7
A. South Atlantic (including D.C.)	36,552	663.7
1. Delaware	594	474.8
2. Florida	9,567	983.5
3. Georgia	5,400	555.3
4. Maryland	4,192	852.4
5. North Carolina	5,843	455.0
6. South Carolina	3,064	660.0
7. Virginia	5,323	307.2
8. West Virginia	1,930	183.7
B. East South Central	14,560	387.7
1. Alabama	3,861	448.5
2. Kentucky	3,641	266.7
3. Mississippi	2,511	341.9
4. Tennessee	4,545	458.1
C. West South Central	23,654	533.3
1. Arkansas	2,284	335.2
2. Louisiana	4,199	665.0
3. Oklahoma	3,001	419.5
4. Texas	14,169	550.3

Source: William H. Webster, *Crime in the United States 1980*. Washington, D.C.: U.S. Department of Justice, 1981, pp. 44-46.

After reading Table 3.1 the research question still cannot be answered. The reason is simple: it cannot be determined from these data whether the South is higher, lower, or about the same as other regions in its rate of violent crime because the table provides no data on these other regions. Only the official rates of violent crime in one region are known.

A relationship cannot be assumed to exist. Experience has demonstrated the folly of *assuming* certain relationships. The literature is filled with widely held beliefs which do not stand up in the face of research. Consider the following two examples:

1. *Assumption:* "Criminals and delinquents can be rehabilitated." Martinson (1974) surveyed all the evaluative reports addressing such an assumption. He depicted these as an endless procession of failures and disappointments. Academic training, vocational training, individual psychotherapy and counseling, group counseling, transforming the institutional environment as a whole, and dealing with the convicted by taking them outside the institution and into the community — all of these have proved to be failures except in rare and isolated instances. In other words, the stated assumption is problematical at best.

Consider an alternative assumption:

2. *Assumption:* "Persons with emotional troubles are almost invariably cured if they are given psychotherapy. Without such treatment, few if any can be expected to recover." What kind of evidence exists to indicate the accuracy of Assumption 2? Two noted therapists, Carkhuff and Berenson (1967, p. 13) have stated:

> When we look at the data, we find that troubled people, both children and adults, are as likely to be rehabilitated if they are left alone as if they are treated in professional counseling and psychotherapy.

Other researchers (Eysenck, 1952, 1960, 1965; Levitt, 1957, 1963) support this finding.

The point is that while many assumptions, cherished beliefs, and unexamined opinions are correct, many others are not. Unfortunately, it is seldom known when a theory is accurate. The accuracy of a theory cannot be assessed without testing at least parts of the theory. The research process is designed to expose an unsupported theory or parts of a theory and to determine its credibility. Another part of the research task is to point out which theory is most compatible with the available findings.

Internal Validity

Internal validity is concerned with the question of whether the independent variable (X) does indeed cause variation in, or the existence of, the dependent variable (Y). One way to determine internal validity is to eliminate plausible *rival hypothesis* (Campbell and Stanley, 1963). The more rival hypotheses that can be shown to be unsupported, the more faith one can put in the research hypothesis. As rival hypotheses are eliminated, internal validity is enhanced.

For instance, in order to establish the conclusion that X causes Y, several types of rival hypotheses must first be discredited. The first of these rival hypotheses that must be proven false is that Y causes X. If Y causes X, the values of Y are determined before the values of X. Sometimes this possibility can easily be ruled out on the grounds of temporal order. If X is gender (sex) of the person convicted and Y is the severity of sentence, researchers can reason that getting a severe or a mild sentence cannot affect one's being male or female, since gender is determined before sentencing and is notoriously resistant to change. Of course, the temporal order between variables is often less clearcut than it is in this example.

When working with variables whose temporal ordering is not clear, researchers can conduct experiments to alter the values of variable X in order to determine what effects such changes have on variable Y. Then the procedure can be reversed: alter the values of Y to see whether X is affected. Consider the hypothesis that one's social status within a primary group (X) increases one's bowling scores (Y) (Whyte, 1943). Whyte has shown that the two variables definitely are related, but a rival hypothesis could be that bowling performance affects one's status within a group. The two hypotheses can be tested.

If X does not change when Y is manipulated, but Y changes when X is manipulated, researchers have good evidence to claim that Y does not cause X. Eliminating that hypothesis increases the credibility of the hypothesis that X causes Y. *It does not prove X causes Y.* While a hypothesis can be dismissed, it can never be proved. This seems convoluted but such is the way of research.

After ruling out the rival hypothesis that Y causes X, at least one more plausible alternative must be considered: X and Y are associated only because they are *both* affected by another variable. In such a situation, the relationship between X and Y is called a *spurious relationship*; that is, a third unknown variable affects the relationship between X and Y.

Generally, it is not known if some third variable causes both X and Y. Even when there is such a third variable, it may be difficult to identify and isolate it. The only recourse is to list several possible variables and then check each one to see if it is affecting the X-Y relationship. Such a variable must precede X and Y in time.

The following is an example of a spurious relationship. It is widely believed that collective protest causes either violence or bloodshed. Some downtrodden groups rise up in a collective frenzy, and this often leads to a violent attack on some ostensible enemy. But is this so? Some contemporary commentators would suggest that both variables are instead caused by a third variable, repression, a term which is admittedly imprecise. In the prison conflict at Attica, New York, in 1971, for example, official repression seems to have triggered both the protest and the violence. The protest apparently grew out of repressive conditions such as overcrowding, frequent searches, use of solitary confinement, censorship of mail, lack of showers, and religious persecution, among other conditions. The violence was triggered by the State of New York after it refused to negotiate seriously the demands of the prisoners.

> Six minutes after [the helicopter] had dropped its load of CS gas over D-yard, the firing stopped. To most of the D-yard [inmates] it had seemed like hours. At the end, they lay . . . dead, wounded, bleeding, choking, and crying from gas, shock, pain, and fear. . . . Two hostages [prison guards] had been seriously injured by inmates; several other hostages had suffered minor injuries from inmates. Ten hostages were dead or dying, 29 inmates were dead or dying, three hostages, 85 inmates, and one trooper had been wounded — all by guns in the hands of state police and corrections officers (Wicker, 1975, p. 364).

This sobering account includes only one case, so it is at best suggestive. However, if a relationship between X and Y is assumed, Figure 3.2 suggests that rival hypotheses are plausible: X (protest) and Y (violence) are related spuriously because both of them are affected by Z (repression of prisoners).

Figure 3.2   Basic Hypothesis and Rival Hypotheses

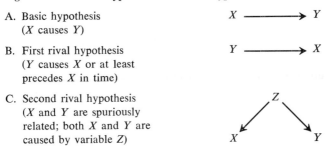

A. Basic hypothesis
   (X causes Y) $X \longrightarrow Y$

B. First rival hypothesis
   (Y causes X or at least
   precedes X in time) $Y \longrightarrow X$

C. Second rival hypothesis
   (X and Y are spuriously
   related; both X and Y are
   caused by variable Z) $X \nearrow^{Z} \searrow Y$

If the first rival hypothesis can be effectively eliminated and, after a valiant effort, no spurious relationship is found, more confidence can be placed in the research hypothesis. Again, this is not to say that the research hypothesis is proven. There are several other plausible rival hypotheses that have not been ruled out and even after ruling those out the research hypothesis still will not be proven — but it will be more believable.

External Validity

External validity is the extent to which a hypothesized relationship between variables can be generalized to other settings, conditions, populations, or time periods. Whenever a hypothesis is supported by only one study using only one population from one setting at one time, it lacks external validity. Most research designs are susceptible to criticisms of external validity.

External validity can be assessed by conducting similar studies under different conditions, different settings, and/or using different populations. If the same results continue to emerge from each repetition, the external validity of the hypothesis is enhanced.

External validity can also be estimated from a single study. Durkheim's (1966; 1897) *Suicide* is a case in point. He hypothesized that integration in domestic society caused a decrease in suicides. He found that adult married persons are less likely to commit suicide. The Durkheim study also showed that:

1. The finding occurred not only in 19th century France (Durkheim's home country) but also in Italy, Prussia and Württenberg.
2. The finding did *not* apply to men who married early, between ages 15 and 20 (in France, Oldenburg, and Sweden).
3. The effect of marriage on suicide rate was greater for men than for women (in France).
4. Women who marry but have no children are more likely to commit suicide than those who do not marry; women who marry and have children are least likely to commit suicide.
5. Men who are not married are most likely to commit suicide; least likely are men who marry and have children.

All five of the above findings contribute to the external validity of Durkheim's hypothesis. Point 1 shows the hypothesis can be generalized to other countries or provinces. Point 2 shows that there is one part of the population to which the hypothesis cannot be generalized — young men. Points 3, 4, and 5 show that it applies more strongly to some subgroups of the population than it does to others.

Usually, a study's subjects can be broken down into different genders, ages, areas, family sizes, or other categories. If the same finding emerges from each of these subgroups, external validity is enhanced considerably. It is eminently possible, however, that the finding will apply to some subgroups and not to others. In any event, it is always in the researchers' interest to determine the limits to which they may generalize from their findings.

Controlling for a Third Variable

One may occasionally hear comments like "all other things being equal" or "holding that constant" preceding some statement about the relationship between two variables. These are just two ways of saying that one or more variables should be controlled. There are a variety of ways to control for other variables.

The most widely accepted form of control appears in experimental designs. To see what effect X has on Y, researchers try to eliminate all other unwanted influences. This is accomplished by trying to make the experimental group the same as the control group except for the experimental stimulus. This can be accomplished in various ways, among them: random assignment, matching, homogeneous sampling, and division into homogeneous subgroups.

Random assignment is the allocation of subjects or respondents, usually to two groups (an experimental group, which receives the treatment, and a control group, which does not) on a random basis. Subjects thus do not choose which group they shall be in, nor do researchers get to use their discretion to assign them. Instead, assignment is done by chance. Random assignment means that whatever unknown variable affects the dependent variable will do so randomly. Of course, random assignment usually is feasible only in laboratory experiments.

Matching involves (1) dividing units into pairs that are similar and (2) assigning one member of each pair to the experimental group and the other to the control group. While on the surface, matching seems to be an eminently suitable form of control, in practice it is often unsuitable because it can be misused. How might this be done? One way is by matching *after* the stimulus is administered. Another way is by matching according to variables that are not crucial and not matching crucial variables (i.e., those which have an important impact on the dependent variable). Matching is an effective control technique only when a person cannot influence the assignment of cases to the experimental and control groups. For this reason, researchers generally regard matching as a methodologically respectable control technique only when it is combined with random assignment; that is, when cases are divided into pairs that are similar and then one member of each pair is assigned randomly either to the experimental group or to the control group. Matching is not useful with nonexperimental designs.

Homogeneous sampling is one way to look at the relationship between X and Y while controlling for variable Z. It involves selecting only those units which are equal in terms of Z. If Z does not vary, it cannot affect the dependent variable. For instance, researchers may hypothesize that a person's height affects his/her chance of promotion. They may also want to make sure that the influence of another variable, say each person's professional productivity, is eliminated. This can be done by homogeneous sampling. The population is divided into groups according to their level of productivity, and then units are selected from only one of these groups. The cases will still differ a little on productivity, but probably not enough to influence the results. The relationship between X and Y then is assumed to be free from any influence of Z.

Division into homogeneous subgroups requires researchers to divide the units into several subgroups before looking at the relationship between X and Y. If Z is the variable to be controlled, researchers can divide the units into various levels of Z. Then they can look at the relationship between X and Y *within each different level of Z*. This greatly reduces the effect of Z on the other variables.

Experimental and Nonexperimental Design

While many research design issues have been addressed, the types of research designs have not. Deciding on whether to use an experimental or nonexperimental design is no easy task. It depends primarily on the relationship being studied. Rosenberg (1968), for example, distinguishes between stimulus-response and property-disposition relationships. The former identifies relationships having an external, well-defined independent variable and a dependent variable, while the latter is a relationship between some property (e.g., respondent background characteristic) and a disposition (e.g., attitude or value). Each type of relationship is best studied through a particular type of research design. Stimulus-response relationships are best studied via experimental designs. Property-disposition relationships, which study people or processes and do not permit researchers to manipulate the independent variable(s), are best tested by means of nonexperimental designs.

Not every experimental or nonexperimental design that has been developed is discussed here. Only those most frequently used are mentioned. (Readers seeking further information on both types of designs should read Campbell and Stanley, 1963.)

Classical Experimental Designs

A *classical experimental design* requires the random assignment of subjects into experimental and control groups. Meeting this condition allows for the manipulation of the independent variable while observing changes, if any, in the dependent variable. The classical experimental design is shown in Figure 3.3, where X designates the independent variable and O designates observed values of the dependent variable. If the difference between pretest and posttest values is statistically significant, the difference is attributed to the independent variable.

Figure 3.3   Classical Experimental Design

	Before		After
R	O_1	X	O_2
R	O_3	- - -	O_4

R = randomization of subjects
O_1 and O_2 = experimental groups
O_3 and O_4 = control groups
X = independent variable
- - - = no independent variable

Research assessing the effect of alcohol on vehicle-braking reaction time lends itself to being examined by this design. Subjects can be randomly assigned to either a control or an experimental group, asked to perform the vehicle-braking task (the pretest), after which, alcohol (the independent variable) is given to the experimental group, and then all subjects would repeat the task (the posttest). Any differences detected would be attributed to the ingestion of alcohol.

Posttest-Only Control Group Design

As shown in Figure 3.4, the *posttest-only control group design,* unlike the classical experimental design, omits pretesting the control and the experimental groups. Subjects are randomly assigned to either the control or the experimental group and are measured after introduction of the independent variable. The difference between the groups indicates the impact of the independent variable since both groups are exposed to the same external events and processes.

Figure 3.4   Posttest-Only Control Group Design

R	X	O_1
R	---	O_2

R = randomization of subjects
O_1 = experimental group
O_2 = control group
X = independent variable

In the alcohol and vehicle-braking study, one would randomly assign subjects to either a control or an experimental group, introduce the independent variable (alcohol) and measure group differences in reaction times. Again, differences would be attributed to the independent variable. (Omitting the pretesting assumes that both the control and experimental group are similar.)

Solomon Four-Group Design

Besides the classical experimental or posttest-only control group designs, the *Solomon Four-Group design* offers an attractive alternative. This design, depicted in Figure 3.5, combines the strengths of the two previously mentioned designs into a single design which permits direct pretest measurement. This is the best feature of the Solomon Four-Group design. Not only does this design allow for comparisons between control and experimental groups, but it also allows for comparisons between experimental groups (O_2 and O_5) and control groups (O_4 and O_6). These latter comparisons reveal whether or not the independent variable (X) has an effect on subjects not sensitized by a pretest. When the differences within experimental and/or control groups are small, it can be concluded that the independent variable does not have much of an effect.

Applying the Solomon Four-Group design to the alcohol and vehicle-braking reaction time study requires the random assignment of subjects into one of four groups. Group 1 is pretested on their reaction time, given alcohol, and is posttested; Group 2 is pretested on their reaction time, *not* given alcohol, and is posttested; Group 3 is *not* pretested on the task, is given alcohol, and is posttested; Group 4 is not pretested on the task, is *not* given alcohol, but is posttested. By comparing reaction time differences among groups, researchers can determine the effect of the pre-test and of introduction of the independent variable.

Figure 3.5   Solomon Four-Group Design

		Before		After
R		O_1	X	O_2
R		O_3	- - -	O_4
R			X	O_5
R			- - -	O_6

R = randomization of subjects
O_1, O_2, and O_5 = experimental groups
O_3, O_4, and O_6 = control groups
- - - = no independent variable
X = independent variable

Nonexperimental Designs

Nonexperimental designs do not permit either random assignment or the manipulation of subjects. Compared to experimental designs, non-experimental designs often seem primitive. Nevertheless, the uses of non-experimental designs are many. The presentation below distinguishes between cross-sectional and longitudinal designs. For cross-sectional designs, the one-shot study and correlational designs are discussed; for the longitudinal designs, the one-group pretest-posttest and static-group comparison designs are presented.

Cross-Sectional Designs:
One-Shot Study and Correlational Designs

All cross-sectional designs observe a single group at one point in time. The most elementary cross-sectional design is the *one-shot study*. As shown in Figure 3.6, it is an observation of what exists only at the time of the study. An example of a one-shot study design is illustrated by the investigator who institutionalizes himself for a one-week period in a prison. He then reports on the social organization within the prison.

Figure 3.6   One-Shot Study

Before	After
X	Posttest

X = independent variable

Not too surprisingly, the one-shot study is severely limited. One cannot manipulate the independent variable, and the subjects are not randomly assigned. Moreover, the results from one-shot studies cannot be generalized. Consequently, casual relations cannot be tested.

However, the one-shot study design does have merit. One-shot studies are especially well-suited for exploratory research. Often, exploratory research leads to more systematic study and eventually to testable hypotheses and more predictive theoretical statements.

A *correlational design,* being slightly more sophisticated than a one-shot design, is the most frequently used research design. As illustrated in Figure 3.7, a correlational design compares the control and experimental groups statistically. A correlational design tries to approximate the posttest-only control group design by using various statistical techniques to make comparisons between the two groups. (These techniques are discussed in Chapter 12.)

Figure 3.7   Correlational Design

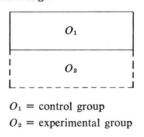

O_1 = control group
O_2 = experimental group

Correlational designs can be misleading because persons often confuse correlation with causality. The two are very different. Just because two variables are correlated does not mean they are causally related. Correlation, in other words, is only a necessary, but not a sufficient, condition for causality (Smith, 1975).

Longitudinal Designs: One-Group Pretest-Posttest and Static-Group Comparison Designs

Longitudinal designs make observations of one or more groups at more than a one-time interval. The most popular longitudinal designs are the *one-group pretest-posttest design* and the *static-group comparison design*.

The *one-group pretest-posttest design* requires pretesting a group, introducing the independent variable, and posttesting the *same* group. As shown in Figure 3.8, the design incorporates the before-after condition found in some experimental designs. For instance, researchers studying the effects of school integration on racial attitudes might use this design. A person's racial attitudes could be tapped prior to school integration and then again after integration has taken place. As in all nonexperimental

Figure 3.8   One-Group Pretest-Posttest Design

Before		After
O_1	X	O_2

X = independent variable
O_1 = pretested group
O_2 = posttested group

designs, subjects are not randomly assigned. Herein lies the design's most serious shortcoming — making certain that subjects are representative of some larger population unit. The design only assumes subject representativeness. This design also has other pertinent limitations. Often subjects drop out of the research study. Moreover, there are many interaction effects among variables, and this design tends to ignore them.

The *static-group comparison design,* depicted in Figure 3.9, uses equivalent samples. A static-group comparison design, like the one-group pretest-posttest design, suffers from a lack of randomization procedures.

The principal uses of a static-group comparison design are for research studies comparing changes of a gradual nature (e.g., attitude changes). Its most salient drawback is its failure to control for effects stemming from *history* and *instrumentation*. Historical events, for example, occurring during the study period often alter subjects' attitudes. Also, instrumentation effects occur if there have been changes in how and what data are produced. Researchers using the *Uniform Crime Report,* for example, must be sensitive to potential instrumentation effects when comparing crime report data across decades. Unfortunately, static-group comparison designs do not contain any built-in mechanism to alleviate these potential hazards.

Figure 3.9   Static-Group Comparison Design

Before		After
O_1	X	O_3
O_2	- - -	O_4

X = independent variable
O_1 and O_3 = experimental group
O_2 and O_4 = control group

Comparing Experimental and Nonexperimental Designs

One type of design is not always better to use than another type. Rather, each type of design, experimental or nonexperimental, possesses its own advantages and disadvantages. Experimental designs are typically best for answering questions relating to whether or not the study's methods had any effect on the results obtained. In other words, would alternative methods yield different results? Nonexperimental designs, on the other hand, are best for addressing issues examining a study's generalizability; that is, nonexperimental designs are assumed to produce data that are more representative of a larger population than are data produced with experimental designs. The differences between the two, however, can be summed up by saying that experimental designs are stronger on control (internal validity) but weaker on representativeness (external validity) than are nonexperimental designs.

Because experiments exert such strong control and often produce valid causal inferences, many persons believe that only experimental designs should be used. But "all that glitters is not gold"! Experiments are plagued with limitations. Most notably, experiments are often performed in laboratories. Can social life be replicated in a laboratory? Scientists do not agree on the answer to this question. Sometimes experiments find their way out of the laboratory and into the "real world." Consider for a moment, the Kansas City Police Department's Proactive-Reactive Patrol

Deployment Project (Kelling, 1972). This project, designed experimentally (Caldwell and Nardini, 1977, p. 69), tried to determine whether there were any significant differences in the uses of "types" of patrol practices in reducing crime and delivering services. To test this idea, three similar geographical areas were identified and a different patrol strategy was used in each one. In geographical Area 1, police were totally committed to answering citizen calls for help as quickly as possible; geographical Area 2 saw police likewise responding to citizens' call but also using aggressive patrol techniques; and geographical Area 3 had their police operating as usual.

The Kansas City experiment was not an experiment in the true meaning of that concept. Clearly, while designed as an experiment, the fact that the project was implemented in the real world reduced considerably the amount of control the researchers had over the variables examined. While it is likely the Kansas City experiment yielded more generalizable data, it is equally likely that the data derived was less internally valid than data which would have evolved in a laboratory.

The bottom line is this: one cannot say with certainty that one type of design is always better than another type. As the introductory pages to this section stated, whether one uses an experimental or a nonexperimental design is contingent upon the type of relationship being studied. Stimulus-response relationships are best studied through experimental designs; property-disposition relationships are best examined through nonexperimental designs.

Models

Models are illustrations which show the structured pattern of relationships among a study's variables. Three types of models are discussed here: accounting, implications, and process models.

The *accounting model* uses one dependent variable, and the task is to locate and identify the independent variables that are most likely to influence it. Finding *all* of these crucial variables obviously could be an endless and fruitless undertaking. The result would probably be a long list of independent variables with no coherent pattern among them, no interpretation of the relationships, and no link to more general theory. Such mechanical research may be tempting, but it advances the state of knowledge very little. The accounting model allows researchers to search for more general concepts that link several variables together.

An example of an accounting model that does *not* contain an endless list of disparate variables is Hirschi's (1969) study of the causes of delinquency. He used a small number of general concepts to summarize a much larger number of more specific variables. These general concepts are *attachment, commitment, involvement,* and *belief. Attachment* alone included about 12 different variables, ranging from a mother's supervision to respect for the opinions of one's friends. Instead of an unwieldy collection of variables which stretch beyond the reader's threshold for boredom, Hirschi provided a well organized and small set of key influential variables.

Hirschi's accounting model of delinquency is based upon his understanding of control theory, which claims that young people will not be as likely to become delinquent if they are strongly integrated into societal institutions. Such integration assumes that they feel an attachment to conventional activities and accept conventional beliefs. The Hirschi delinquency model, shown in Figure 3.10, is an excellent example of an accounting model.

Figure 3.10   An Accounting Model: Hirschi's Control Theory

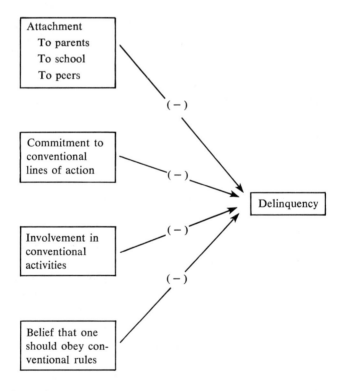

Note: Each arrow has a negative sign attached to it. This is to show that the relationship is negative. For example, as attachment increases, delinquency decreases.

An *implications model* is the opposite of an accounting model. It includes a single independent variable and a number of dependent variables. The questions it attempts to answer are: (1) What will happen to the dependent variables when the independent variable is changed? and (2) What consequences, if any, does the independent variable have? Sometimes these questions produce interesting answers — variables occasionally have unintended effects. Urban renewal, once considered a panacea for problems from delinquency to rat control, apparently has instead fostered dislocation and shattered interpersonal ties among youths, leading to more violence and force because youths need to gain a reputation for toughness in a new, unstable environment. Figure 3.11 depicts an implications model.

Figure 3.11   An Implications Model: The Impact of Religious Commitment

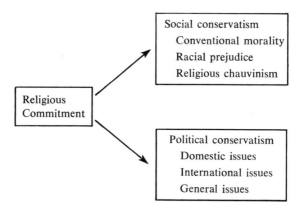

Like the accounting model, an implications model can turn into a disjointed or interminable list of variables, but this is again unnecessary, since boundaries can be put on the kind of dependent variables researchers might wish to consider before beginning their footwork. Imagine that religious commitment is chosen as an independent variable in an implications model. The variables to be considered might be grouped first under the general umbrella term *conservatism*; then conservatism can be subdivided into social and political aspects. These concepts, in turn, can be further subdivided as shown in Figure 3.11.

A *process model* focuses on one independent variable, one dependent variable, and one or more intervening variables. This model assumes that the independent and dependent variables are indeed related. What remains unknown is why they are related. What is the intervening variable stimulating this relationship?

Suppose that previous research has shown that organizations whose personnel are assigned a large amount of boring, dangerous, offensive, and publicly scorned work tend to be organizations with a rather pronounced elitist ideology. One thinks of examples such as the police force and the Marine Corps. The basic question is: What is the mechanism or variable that links this type of work to organizational elitism?

Perhaps it is a question of morale. Organizations whose personnel are assigned such tasks must worry about their people becoming cynical and demoralized. Not wanting these morale problems, organizations may try to give workers a new image as highly committed professionals doing a job that is honorable, vitally necessary, and highly demanding. Hence, they turn to slogans such as "the thin blue line," "the nation's finest," and "the Marines need a few good men."

Organizations with personnel who are assigned mostly "dirty work" may soon find that they have low morale. Organizations respond to this problem by trying to recast the image of the work, proclaiming that less is more, sacrifice builds character, or poverty is honorable. (Police and Marines emphasize their indispensability, as well.) Figure 3.12 illustrates this process model.

Figure 3.12   A Process Model

Dirtiness of Work ⟶ Morale Problems ⟶ Elitist Ideology

Another variation of the process model has been posited by Bell (1953). In his rather journalistic account of organized crime, a reader cannot find terms like *independent, intervening,* or *dependent variables,* but such variables can be extracted from Bell's article. It is summarized below:

1. Increasing organization in society's legitimate spheres leads to increasing organization and rationality in its illegitimate spheres: societal organization causes criminal organization.
2. Increasing organization and rationality in criminal networks produce greater financial success for such networks: organization increases success.
3. If the criminal network succeeds, its members (most of whom begin as impoverished immigrants) move up the ladder of social status (e.g., gain more wealth, better reputations): organizational success leads to upward social mobility.
4. Respected and wealthy leaders make the networks more rational, efficient, and organized.

These statements can be placed into a model by adding one new element, *a feedback loop.* This loop simply indicates that a dependent variable "comes back" to affect one of the independent or intervening variables. The Bell thesis is presented in Figure 3.13. This example con-

Figure 3.13   The Bell Thesis: An Example of a Feedback Loop

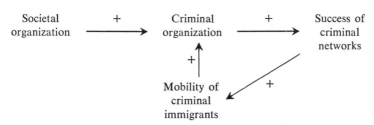

tains a *positive* feedback, implying that the system is unstable because criminal organization and success increase (or decrease) until they reach extreme levels and some part of the system breaks down. If there were a *negative* feedback loop (if one of the arrows linking criminal organization and success were negative), the system would tend to maintain a relatively steady state ("stasis") like the relationship between thermostat and temperature: as temperature increases, the thermostat's recording device increases, and this in turn shuts off the heating mechanism, so that temperature then decreases.

An element other than the feedback loop is sometimes required when relationships among variables are diagrammed. This is *statistical interaction,* the peculiar effect produced by the combination of two independent variables.

At this point, a few cautionary comments are in order. First of all, these three prototypical models (accounting, implications, and process) are not useful for research describing kinship, friendship, or organizational *networks.* Social anthropologists are the leading exponents of such research, and they make little use of these models. Some of the most recent and interesting research using these models deals with interlocking directorates and the persons who occupy positions on the boards of directors of several corporations simultaneously.

Second, these models are not useful when tracing items, persons, or products through a series of agents, distributors, or stages. If researchers wished to trace the passage of heroin, they might discover that it passes from importer to kilo connection, from weight to street dealer, from dealer to juggler (or pusher), and on to the user-addict (Preble and Casey, 1969). These stages, however, are not variables — they are stages of distribution — so researchers cannot compute the degree of relationship between any of them. However, investigators might consider the degree or amount of dilution or impurities added at each stage, or the danger of being caught by police authorities at each stage, but no one tries to relate such variables (danger and dilution) to each other.

Third, these models are not appropriate for those who plan to produce data merely to generalize from the findings on the sampled group to characteristics of a much larger group. When George Gallup's researchers poll a few thousand citizens about their attitudes toward presidential candidates, these data are adequate for making reasonably accurate judgments about the attitudes toward these candidates held by the entire adult population in the United States. This sort of information is rarely fitted into models because there is little interest in relationships between variables. However, they *could* be used in this way.

Summary

Conducting research is not so simple as it sometimes appears. Once it is determined what will be studied and how it will be studied, an "execution plan," called the research design, must be developed. The research design specifies relationships among variables. Then researchers must rule out alternative rival hypotheses.

After other hypotheses have been ruled out, questions about external validity can be addressed; that is, to what other settings, conditions, and populations does the hypothesis apply? There are also numerous ways to control for the effect of unwanted variables. These include random assignment, matching, experimental techniques, and nonexperimental techniques.

To analyze the relationships between and among variables, researchers must design a plan to test their hypotheses. They must choose among a variety of experimental and nonexperimental designs. Each design has its own advantages, and selecting the most appropriate is contingent upon the relationship being studied.

Once the study is executed, the next step is to look more closely at the relationships among variables, using one of three models. An *accounting model* looks at the impact of one or more independent variables on a single dependent variable. An *implications model* examines the effects of a single independent variable on one or more dependent variables. A *process model* traces the relationship between independent and dependent variables by locating linking or intervening variables.

Review Questions

1. Explain the meaning and significance of the following terms and ideas:
    a. research design

    b. relationship
    c. internal validity
    d. external validity
    e. cross-sectional study
    f. spurious relationship
    g. randomization
    h. matching
    i. homogeneous sampling
    j. models
    k. experimental group
    l. control group

2. Explain how the Bell thesis is an example of a feedback loop.
3. Discuss what conditions would make a strong relationship.
4. Explain the steps investigators can take to be more certain that "all other things are equal."
5. Differentiate between experimental and nonexperimental designs.
6. Construct examples illustrating an accounting model, an implications model, and a process model.

References

Bell, Daniel. "Crime as an American Way of Life." *Antioch Review* 13 (1953): 131-154.

Caldwell, Robert G. and Nardini, William. *Foundation of Law Enforcement and Criminal Justice.* Indianapolis, IN: The Bobbs-Merrill Educational Publishing Co., 1977.

Campbell, Donald and Stanley, Julian. *Experimental and Quasi-Experimental Designs for Research.* Chicago: Rand-McNally, 1963.

Carkhuff, Robert and Berenson, Bernard. *Beyond Counseling and Therapy.* New York: Holt, Rinehart and Winston, 1967.

Durkheim, Emile. *Suicide.* Translated by John Spaulding and George Simpson. New York: The Free Press, 1966 (1897).

Eysenck, H. J. "The Effects of Psychotherapy: An Evaluation." *Journal of Consulting Psychology* 16 (1952): 319-324.

——————. "The Effects of Psychotherapy." In *The Handbook of Abnormal Psychology.* Edited by H. J. Eysench. New York: Basic Books, 1960.

——————. "The Effects of Psychotherapy." *International Journal of Psychotherapy* 1 (1965): 99-178.

Hirschi, Travis. *Causes of Delinquency*. Berkeley, CA: University of California Press, 1969.

Kelling, George L. *Kansas City South Patrol Division: Proactive-Reactive Patrol Deployment Project*. Washington, D.C.: Police Foundation, 1972.

Levitt, E. E. "The Results of Psychotherapy with Children." *Journal of Consulting Psychology* 21 (1957): 189-196.

——————. "Psychotherapy with Children: A Further Evaluation." *Behavior Research and Therapy* 1 (1963): 45-51.

Martinson, Robert. "What Works? Questions and Answers about Prison Reform." *Public Interest* 35 (1974): 22-54.

Preble, Edward and Casey, John. "Taking Care of Business — The Heroin User's Life on the Street." *International Journal of the Addictions* 4 (1969): 1-24.

Rosenberg, Morris. *The Logic of Survey Analysis*. New York: Basic Books, 1968.

Smith, H. W. *Strategies of Social Research*. Englewood Cliffs, NJ; Prentice-Hall, Inc., 1975.

Webster, William H. *Crime in the United States* 1980. Washington, D.C.: United States Government Printing Office, 1981.

Whyte, William. *Street Corner Society*. 2nd ed. Chicago: University of Chicago Press, 1955.

Wicker, Tom. *A Time to Die*. New York: Quadrangle Books, 1975.

Wilson, James. *Varieties of Police Behavior*. Cambridge, MA: Harvard University Press, 1968.

Chapter 4
Measurement

Learning Objectives

After completing this chapter, the reader should be able to:
1. Distinguish among the types of measures
2. Discuss measurement error
3. Differentiate among several methods for assessing reliability and validity
4. Comprehend the distinction between the ecological fallacy and the atomistic fallacy

Introduction

Measurement is a collection of rules for assigning numbers to variables to represent quantities of attributes (Nunnally, 1968). This definition includes several key terms. *Rules* are procedures for assigning meaning and must be explicitly formulated. *Attribute* refers to a particular feature of a variable. Attributes frequently refer to characteristics of persons or things, whereas variables specify the logical groupings of attributes (Babbie, 1975). *Numbers* represent quantities of an attribute; they specify how much of an attribute is present.

Measurement is a vital component of the scientific research process. There are good reasons for this. The use of standardized measures facilitates objectivity, quantification, communication, and economy (Nunnally, 1968). Standardized measures enhance objectivity because they take the guess-work out of scientific observation. An elementary scientific principle requires that any hypothesis be verifiable. Therefore, researchers must first agree on how to measure variables. Theoretical statements can be tested only if unambiguous measures are used.

Quantification refers to the numerical results derived from standardized measures. The advantages of quantification are twofold. First, it permits reporting research results more precisely than could otherwise be accomplished. Thermometers, for example, make it possible to report nearly exact amounts of increases or decreases in temperature instead of recording only that the temperature increased or decreased. A second advantage of quantification is that it facilitates mathematical analysis, and mathematical analysis is usually the only practical way to handle large amounts of data and make precise deductions for subsequent research.

Measurement facilitates *communication* among researchers. Whenever a research project is designed, the findings of other researchers are almost always incorporated in the proposed study. Consequently, it is critical to have standardized measures; otherwise it would be impossible to verify previous findings and difficult to advance theoretical knowledge.

Economy is also a feature of quantification. While it takes considerable time to develop standardized measures, once they are developed, the amount of time saved by using them is immeasurable. Imagine that no standardized IQ test had been developed. The amount of time clinical psychologists alone would have to spend assessing characteristics would be enormous. By having standardized measures, researchers are freed to pursue other lines of scientific inquiry.

Measurement Levels

Variables are attributes of persons or things which take on different values. They are the building blocks of both theory and research. Although there exists an infinite variety of variables, they tend to fall into certain distinct categories. These categories normally are defined by the method of measurement; that is, categories of measurement are derived from mathematical properties of the variables. There are four categories of measurement: nominal, ordinal, interval, and ratio.

Nominal Measures

Nominal measures are categorized information having no numerical order. There is no logical basis for performing any arithmetic operation with them, except counting. The numerical values that are assigned to the categories are purely arbitrary. Occupation is a nominal variable often used in criminal justice research. There is a variety of ways numbers can be assigned to occupation. One might classify respondents as being police officers, prison guards, or probation officers. Then the number "1" might be assigned to a police officer, the number "2" to a prison guard, and the number "3" to a probation officer. A separate value would be assigned to each occupational group, but these values are merely differences in *kind*. No claim is made that being a police officer, for example, is a *better* or *worse* occupation than being a prison guard or a probation officer. One can say only that these numerical values are *different*. When, as in the above example, the values of a variable differ in kind and not in degree, the variable is called *nominal*. This is the simplest type of variable to consider.

Ordinal Measures

Ordinal measures are categorized information that can be arranged in less-than and greater-than terms, but they lack known intervals. The numerical values assigned to each category indicate some ranking scheme; for instance, instead of talking about occupation, one can discuss *occupational prestige*. This variable, occupational prestige, takes on different values such as *very high, high, medium, low,* and *very low.* Occupations can now be assigned numbers in order from *most* to *least.* Table 4.1 presents an occupational ranking from the highest to the lowest prestige for 15 occupations in Czechoslovakia.

Table 4.1   Rankings of Prestige of Occupations (Czechoslovakia)

Occupation	Prestige Ranking
Doctor	1st (Highest)
Collective farmer	2nd
Scientist	3rd
Miner	4th
High school teacher	5th
Engineer	6th
University professor	7th
Architect	8th
Mason	9th
Agronomist	10th
Locomotive driver	11th
Writer	12th
Cabinet minister	13th
Actor	14th
Cabinet maker	15th (Lowest)

Source: Roger Penn, "Occupational Prestige in Hierarchies: A Great Empirical Invariant?" *Social Forces* 54 (1975), p. 355.

Although ordinal measures can be ranked, the distance between the values is unknown. An analogy may be made to a horse race. The second place finisher runs a faster race than does a third place horse, but the difference might be anywhere from a nose to ten lengths. In other words, knowing the order in which the horses finished tells one very little about the distance between the horses.

Ratio and Interval Measures

Ratio measures are data categorized in standard units of measurement in such a way that the exact distance between units can be determined. In addition, the zero point in a ratio scale means the absence of a particular attribute. Income is an example of a ratio measure. The exact distance between ten dollars and five dollars is and always will be five dollars; and zero dollars indicates the absence of income.

Interval measures are ratio measures that have an *arbitrary* zero point; that is, the zero point does not indicate the absence of an attribute. The Fahrenheit scale for measuring temperature is an interval measure. The exact difference between 75 degrees and 80 degrees is and always will be five degrees, but zero degrees does not indicate the absence of heat.

Measurement Levels: Mathematical Operations

Although nominal measures hardly seem like measures at all, certain arithmetic techniques can be applied to them. Each category can be counted, ratios between categories can be computed, and percentages in any category can be calculated. Two nominal scores, however, cannot be added, subtracted, multiplied, divided, or used in greater-than or less-than terms.

Any operation that can be applied to nominal measures can be applied to ordinal measures. Cases can be counted, and ratios and percentages can be calculated. Although two ordinal scores cannot be added, subtracted, multiplied, or divided, greater-than and less-than comparisons can be made between ordinal data.

Interval and ratio measurements can be added, subtracted, multiplied, divided, and used in greater-than or less-than comparisons. Since most of the statistical techniques discussed in later chapters require adding, subtracting, multiplying, and dividing, the most appropriate level of data used is either interval or ratio data. Interval and ratio measures also permit more mathematical manipulations, an important advantage when analyzing variables. Moreover, a good deal of information may be lost when data are measured nominally and ordinally. Even though it is sometimes necessary to measure data either nominally or ordinally, it is wise to use interval or ratio measures whenever possible.

Measurement Error: Reliability and Validity

Any time variables are measured an error can be made. The objective of a sound measurement process is to insure that errors are not made. If errors cannot be eliminated, they must be kept minimal.

Errors occur in two forms; they are either systematic or random. *Systematic error* occurs when the same error is made consistently. For instance, the chemist who uses only one thermometer, which consistently registers one degree lower than it should, may commit a systematic error. *Random error,* on the other hand, occurs when the error is made inconsistently.

Frequently, systematic error may not be terribly critical; in studies of individual differences, systematic bias contributes to the mean (average) score of *all* respondents. On the other hand, because random errors tend to attenuate relationships, they are important to minimize (Nunnally, 1968). To the extent that systematic and random errors are minimized, the measuring process is said to be reliable and valid.

Reliability is the extent to which an operational definition yields similar results on repeated applications. *Validity* is the extent to which an operational definition measures the concept. The question validity asks is, Does an operational definition measure what it is intended to measure?

Figure 4.1   Relationship Between Reliability and Validity

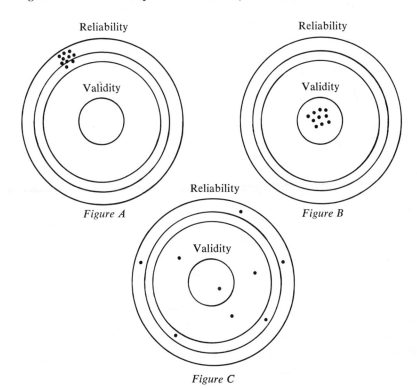

Figure A

Figure B

Figure C

The relationship between reliability and validity is illustrated in Figure 4.1. When interpreting the figures, one should realize that as the observations move toward the center of the circle, a more valid instrument si implied. Figure A illustrates test results using a reliable, but not a valid, measuring instrument. An example might be an IQ test which does not measure IQ. Figure B presents results obtained using a valid instrument. These data might be produced by having 100 people measure the length of a piece of wood with a yardstick. More than likely, little variation in the reported length would be detected. Figure B demonstrates that valid instruments are always reliable. Figure C reports test results from an instrument that is neither reliable nor valid.

Assessing Reliability

An operational definition usually is very complex. For this reason, it is difficult to estimate just how reliable an operational definition may be. For any single operational definition, it is possible to compute several reliability coefficients. Most often, however, only one reliability coefficient is computed per operational definition. Which reliability coefficient is computed depends upon the way data are collected. Several reliability coefficients are discussed below: the coefficient of stability, the coefficient of equivalence, and the coefficient of internal consistency. Regardless of which coefficient is calculated, the objective is the same — to estimate the degree to which the measuring instrument offers the same measurement in successive uses.

Test-Retest Method

Estimating reliability by the test-retest method requires giving the same test twice to the same group of persons. The results derived from the first test are correlated with the results from the second test, resulting in a *coefficient of stability*.

Imagine that the cynicism level among prison guards is being investigated. A questionnaire is designed to tap this attitude. Determining the questionnaire's reliability via the test-retest method requires that it be administered to a sample of prison guards, each officer's score computed, and then the test be readministered to the same prison guards. The scale's coefficient of stability would be the correlation between the officers' scores on the first and second questionnaires. If each prison guard scored the same on both questionnaires, the coefficient of stability would be 1.00, which is a perfect correlation. Conversely, if the two scores were completely unrelated, the coefficient of stability would be .00, or no reliability. Generally, the coefficient of stability lies somewhere between the two extremes. Figure 4.2 illustrates possible relationships.

Figure 4.2   Relationship Between Two Variables

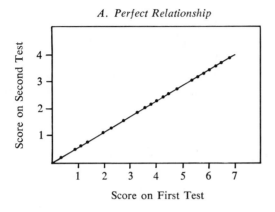

A. Perfect Relationship

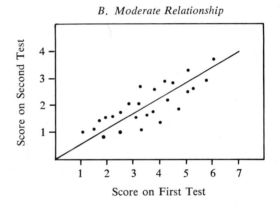

B. Moderate Relationship

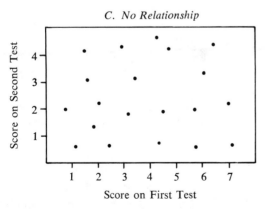

C. No Relationship

Even though the test-retest method is widely used for computing reliability coefficients, there are some problems with it. The primary problem is carry-over effect which influences the results obtained on the second administration of the test. *Carry-over effect* implies that respondents learned something from the test's initial administration and altered their performances accordingly. Using the prison guard cynicism study as an example, if the first questionnaires were administered on Wednesday at 4:00 P.M. and the second were given one hour later at 5:00 P.M., the coefficient between the results probably would be higher than if the second questionnaire were administered on Wednesday at 4:00 P.M. of the following week. This occurs because after only a one-hour waiting period the respondents probably would recall their answers from the first questionnaire and repeat them on the second questionnaire. In this case, the coefficient of stability would yield an artificially high correlation coefficient. On the other hand, respondents might intentionally answer the items exactly in the opposite way. When this happens, the coefficient of stability would be smaller than it really is. What is actually derived, therefore, is a correlation which underestimates *or* overestimates the true value. The problem is that it is not possible to determine the true coefficient of stability of an operational definition. *Difficulties like these arise when sufficient time is not allowed between the test administrations.*

These shortcomings cannot necessarily be overcome simply by increasing the time between administering questionnaires. Other factors may also affect the coefficient of stability. For example, if the time between administering the questionnaires is too long, the respondent's attitudes may change. Suppose that two years passed between the administration of the questionnaires and that the coefficient of stability was very low. What does this mean? Does it mean that the test is a poor indicator of prison guard cynicism? Not necessarily. Nor does it necessarily mean that the instrument is a good indicator of cynicism. It cannot be determined exactly what the results mean. When an operational definition is extended to an attitude like cynicism, long delays between its administration sometimes result in a low coefficient of stability.

The length of time between test and retest is critical. A short delay generally results in a coefficient of stability that reflects respondents' memory. Long delays affect the coefficient of stability by allowing respondents time to change their attitudes. Exactly how the length of the interval between testing affects the coefficient of stability is unknown.

Although coefficients of stability are often used, their usefulness in criminal justice research is limited. For one reason, criminal justice research generally measures traits that are susceptible to carry-over effect. When such traits are considered, the coefficient of stability is difficult to compute. *It is best to calculate coefficients of stability for instruments measuring sensory or muscle discrimination tasks,* e.g., the effect, if any, that varying amounts of alcohol have on specific motor coordination tasks like braking when driving an automobile.

Equivalent-Forms Method

A test's reliability can also be estimated by means of the coefficient of equivalence. The *coefficient of equivalence* is generated by administering in close succession two parallel (or equivalent) forms of the same instrument to the same group of persons. The results from the two instruments are compared and a correlation coefficient is again computed. Realistically, however, it is nearly impossible to determine if two measuring instruments are parallel. Therefore, this coefficient actually represents a correlation between *alternate* forms of an instrument. The difference between alternate and parallel forms is that the latter are "any two test forms that have been constructed in an effort to make them parallel" (Allen and Yen, 1979, p. 78).

Using alternate forms of an instrument is quite simple. The method is like the test-retest method except that two different, but similar, operational definitions are administered and correlated. Because it resembles the test-retest method, the shortcomings (e.g., carry-over effects) are similar, too.

Split-Half Method

Reliability also can be estimated from a single form of an operational definition. The coefficient, called a *coefficient of internal consistency,* is computed by dividing the definition's items into equal halves. For each half, a score is calculated. The two scores are correlated; the result is the coefficient of internal consistency.

The split-half method is used more often than either the test-retest or equivalent-form methods because the coefficient of internal consistency is easier to compute and carry-over effect is minimal. However, the coefficient of internal consistency is usually larger than other reliability coefficients since the split-half method requires that the instrument's halves be parallel — a condition difficult to satisfy.

Besides the parallel forms requirement, another problem is determining how to divide the instrument's items. One of three methods is usually used: the odd/even method, the ordered method, and the matched-random method. Of the three, the odd/even and ordered methods are the simplest to implement, but they both produce less reliable halves than does the matched-random method.

Kuder-Richardson Method

Reliability coefficients can be derived via the *Kuder-Richardson method* (Thorndike, 1971). Like the split-half method, the Kuder-Richardson method estimates internal consistency, but unlike the split-half method, the Kuder-Richardson procedure does not require splitting an operational definition into halves. While there are several Kuder-Richardson reliability coefficient techniques, the simplest and most often used is KR21. KR21 can be applied to any measuring instrument that has been scored on the basis of the number of correct answers.

Assessing Validity

Validity is the extent to which an operational definition corresponds to the concept being measured. Validity is basically a matter of degree. Some operational definitions are more valid, or less valid, than are others. Validity can be assessed only through empirical testing; it cannot be assumed. Subsequent paragraphs discuss different types of validity; criterion-related validity, content validity, and construct validity.

Criterion-Related Validity

Criterion-related validity occurs when an operational definition is used to estimate some behavior (i.e., quality of arrest rate). The two variables by which criterion-related validity is determined are called the *predictor variable* (independent variable) and the *criterion variable* (dependent variable). There are two types of criterion-related validity: predictive and concurrent.

Predictive Validity. Predictive validity is concerned with how well the scores of an operational definition predict some future criterion. This is the most common use of criterion-related validity. Imagine that a criminal justice department at a midwestern university developed a test to predict each graduating student's overall grade point average (GPA). To ascertain the test's predictive validity, the subsequent steps would be followed:

1. All incoming freshmen in the department would be administered the test.
2. The tests are scored, and the results are filed.
3. When the students graduate, the GPA (grade point average) for each graduate is computed.
4. The correlation between the test score (predictor variable) and the GPA (dependent variable) is calculated.

5. The resultant correlation coefficient is the predictive validity between the test scores and the grade point averages.

Computing a test's predictive validity is a time-consuming and expensive process. The single greatest problem is selecting an appropriate criterion.

Concurrent Validity. Concurrent validity is concerned with determining how performance on some test relates to other measures of performance. To estimate concurrent validity, one needs to correlate the results from two measures. A common usage of concurrent validity is that which determines if a shorter version of some test is as valid as a longer version.

Concurrent validity coefficients are not useful for predicting behavior; that is not their intended purpose. Rather, they are best used for estimating some other concurrent criterion condition. Suppose, for example, the Oklahoma City Police Department's job performance test consists of 1000 items. Rather than administering the entire test to all officers, researchers might be called in to construct a shorter, valid test. In this instance, the researchers are concerned with the shorter test's concurrent validity.

Content Validity

Content validity measures how accurately an instrument estimates some concept; an intelligence test ought to measure the concept *intelligence,* for example. There are two types of content validity: face validity and sampling validity.

Face validity. Face validity assumes that an operational definition measures a specific concept. In other words, face validity does not involve empirical testing. (For this reason, some persons do not consider it a type of validity.) An illustration of an operational definition in criminal justice that has only face validity is Niederhoffer's (1967) police cynicism scale. Niederhoffer's scale was not empirically validated. Niederhoffer merely *assumed* validity, stating that "the items show a face . . . validity" (Niederhoffer, 1967, p. 200).

Sampling Validity. Sampling validity is a more sophisticated type of content validity. The purpose of *sampling validity* is to identify items which adequately represent a concept. Sampling validity assumes that every concept (e.g., *cynicism*) can be operationalized by a variety of variables (content population). An operational definition includes sampling validity to the degree it consists of a representative number of those variables. Herein lies the problem, specifying a concept's content population.

Because sampling validity requires items representative of the concept's content population, it is difficult to determine. Researchers ordinarily will never know if they have selected a sufficient number of items from *all* the items tapping the concept being measured. Not so surprisingly, then, determining content validity, like determining face validity, is highly judgmental and subjective.

Construct Validity

Constructs are abstract, rather than concrete, variables. Such variables are literally those which the researchers have constructed. For example, police cynicism is not an isolated, observable behavior, but rather it is a construct developed by researchers. Constructs are assumed to relate to some observable behavior. To determine their validity, hypotheses (consisting of constructs) are deduced from theoretical statements and tested. If the data support the hypotheses, the construct is assumed valid.

The uses of construct validity extend far beyond social or physical sciences. Consider the following application. Every year the National Football League holds its player draft. Each team selects, on the average, 17 college senior football players who, they think, can help the team in the coming years. In the early years of football, drafting was neither well financed nor well planned. Today most teams belong to one of three scouting syndicates. In addition each team has its personal scouts collecting data on approximately 1500 players from hundreds of schools. Every year each team spends hundreds of thousands of dollars scouting players before the draft. Players are rated on general characteristics, such as character, quickness, aggressiveness, and mental alertness, as well as on position-specific characteristics; a quarterback, for instance, will be rated on ability to throw short, ability to throw long, quickness to set up, and poise. The ratings of all these players are fed into computers, and when a team is about to draft a player, they obtain from the computer a printout on the type of players best fitting the team's need. Construct validity is important to professional football teams because the success of their draft largely determines the success of the team. Scouts are thus under heavy pressure to measure professional potential accurately.

Current practice is in sharp contrast to the earlier days of drafting, when one looked for promising prospects by scanning the college football preview magazines. Those days produced a flock of first-round choices who were white, well-known All-American players from major universities, many of whom soon failed miserably in professional football. Figure 4.3 schematically presents this picture.

Figure 4.3   Old Model for Drafting Football Players

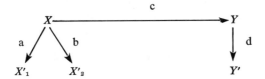

X = Player's professional football potential

X'_1 = Player's college football fame

X'_2 = Player's evaluation in sports journals

Y = Player's success in pro football

Y' = Player's outcome in pro football (first string, makes team, fails to make team)

a $= r_{XX'_1}$

b $= r_{XX'_2}$

c $= r_{XY}$

d $= r_{YY'}$

Note: r is a simple correlation coefficient which is a statistic that shows the degree to which two variables vary together. The coefficient ranges from $+1.00$ to -1.00. A relationship of 0.00 suggests that the two variables do not vary together.

The old model failed because its measures, X'_1 and X'_2, were not so closely related to the predictor variable X (professional potential) as they should have been. Under such conditions construct validity is relatively low, unless all the relationships (a, b, c, and d) are fairly strong. In the old model, of course, construct validity was low because a and b were low. This flaw in a drafting scheme can be corrected by selecting better predictor measures such as speed, height, weight, and IQ scores. Figure 4.4 illustrates such a model.

Of course, construct validity applies to a wide variety of practical and predictive problems besides recruiting football players. This model could just as easily be made to fit a favorite interest of experimental psychologists: X could be intelligence and Y could be scholastic performance. Then one would search for the most appropriate measures of X, whether they be math, verbal, or spatial scores. In any case, the objective is to maximize a, b, c, and d in order to increase construct validity. Though construct validity is not always a major concern, it does have considerable importance when the research problem focuses on prediction or decisionmaking. Generally, construct validity involves selecting measures which are strongly tied to one or more predictor (independent) variables, which in turn are important causes of the dependent variables.

Figure 4.4   The Dallas Cowboys Model for Drafting Football Players

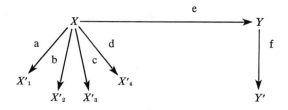

X = Player's pro football potential

X'_1 = Height, weight, strength

X'_2 = Speed

X'_3 = Intelligence test score

X'_4 = Motivation, toughness, character

Y = Player's pro success

Y' = Player's pro outcome

a • e • f = $r_{X'_1Y'}$

b • e • f = $r_{X'_2Y'}$

c • e • f = $r_{X'_3Y'}$

d • e • f = $r_{X'_4Y'}$

Ecological and Atomistic Fallacies

Another aspect of achieving validity involves a set of special problems affecting aggregate data users. Before units of analysis are selected, it must be determined what kinds of units to include and the boundaries of those units. These are fundamental considerations. If not handled properly they will make the rest of the research design confusing and unproductive.

In criminal justice research not all units of analysis are people. Sometimes the units are periods in time or they might be encounters between occupants of different positions, as in Reiss's (1971) research on police encounters with juveniles. Other possible units include criminal trials, government organizations, university departments, trucking companies, football teams, families, cliques, and countries. In short, many things besides individuals are units of analysis. Units other than individuals are usually collected by aggregates. There are two problems associated with analyzing aggregate data: the ecological fallacy (Robinson, 1950) and the atomistic fallacy (Riley, 1963). Both involve selecting units from one level and interpreting the findings as though the units were selected from another level.

The ecological fallacy refers to the practice of using *groups* as units, then providing theoretical *explanations* which assume that the findings are based on *individuals*. An example is Stark and Glock's (1970) work on religious commitment. While their work does not contain this fallacy, the type of data they used are the sort which might prompt lesser scholars to go astray. The units were religious denominations (e.g., Methodist and Presbyterian); the variables they used were the amount of church contributions donated and the members' annual income. Actually, the authors presented two tables. The first table showed that the percentage of large contributors is greater in conservative denominations (e.g., American Baptist, Missouri Synod Lutheran, and Southern Baptist) than it is in liberal denominations (e.g., Congregationalist, Methodist, and Episcopalian). The second table showed that members in liberal denominations tended to have higher incomes than did members of conservative denominations. Table 4.2 shows the relationship between income and contribution.

Table 4.2   Denominations by Church Contribution and Annual Income, Church Members in San Francisco Bay Area, 1963

(in percent)

Denominations

Average Weekly Contribution	Congregationalist	Methodist	Episcopalian	Disciples of Christ	Presbyterian	American Lutheran	American Baptist	Missouri Synod Lutheran	Southern Baptist
$7.50 or more	15	18	18	38	20	24	39	26	59
Income $10,000 or more	64	52	47	56	48	44	39	41	26

Source: Rodney Stark and Charles Glock, *American Piety*. Berkeley, California: University of California Press, 1968, p. 97.

By one method the degree of association is strongly negative; that is, as income increases, the amount contributed decreases — *for demoninations* (Stark and Glock, 1970). Less attentive researchers might have easily slipped into the ecological fallacy by implying that as a *person's* income goes up, *his or her* church contributions go down. However, since the units of analysis are denominations, it is not safe to draw conclusions about individuals.

Recasting the Stark-Glock data, Lotz (1974) found that when individuals are the units of analysis, the relationship is positive, not negative. In other words, the higher a person's income, the more that person contributes to the church. How can these findings be reconciled with those of Stark and Glock? It is known that members of the Congregationalists and other liberal denominations make more money and contribute less than do Southern Baptists and other conservative denominations, but people who make more money also *tend* to give more. *Both* can be true if affluent Congregationalists contribute more than do poorer Southern Baptists, and if affluent Baptists give more than poorer Congregationalists. When the units of analysis are *aggregates* (e.g., denominations and census tracts), researchers cannot automatically assume that the findings apply to *individuals.* Researchers commit the ecological fallacy when making such an assumption.

Another problem encountered with aggregate data analysis is the *atomistic fallacy,* the methodological sin of assuming that findings about individuals can be interpreted as though the units were aggregates. For instance, investigators would not wish to jump from the finding that as a person's income increases, his or her probability of voting Republican increases, to the *conclusion* that those states with high per capita income are more likely to elect Republicans than are states with low per capita income.

The following example also illustrates the atomistic fallacy. Among individuals (or families) the higher the income, the lower the infant mortality. For the United States the association is strongly negative (*The World Almanac*, 1981). If this is so among *individuals*, can researchers assume that it also holds among various *nations?*

Table 4.3 shows the per capita income and infant mortality rates for countries in North America, Northern Europe, and Western Europe. The association between income and mortality for these countries is negative and moderate ($-.42$). The point of this discussion is that researchers must always select units and make interpretations at the same level of analysis.

Another problem faced by researchers doing aggregate data analysis is the difficulty of setting up boundaries. This is a particularly vexing

Table 4.3   1977-1978 Infant Mortality Rate (X) and 1978 Per Capita Income (Y) in Countries of North America, Northern Europe, and Western Europe

	X	Y
Canada	12.4 (1977)	7572
United States	14.0 (1977)	8612
Belgium	11.9 (1978)	9025
France	11.4 (1977)	7908
Germany (Fed. Rep.)	15.5 (1978)	9278
Luxembourg	10.6 (1978)	10,040
Netherlands	9.5 (1978)	8509
Austria	14.9 (1978)	6739
Denmark	8.9 (1978)	9869
Finland	12.0 (1978)	6090
Iceland	10.8 (1978)	6392
Norway	9.2 (1977)	7949
Sweden	7.7 (1978)	9274
Switzerland	9.8 (1977)	12,408
United Kingdom	14.0 (1977)	4955

$$r = -0.42$$

Source: *The World Almanac and Book of Facts, 1981.* New York: Newspaper Enterprise Association, Inc., 1980, pp. 513-597.

problem, especially when studying organizational data. Where does one organization end and another begin? It also poses difficulties for studying population data; for example, how far should researchers go before they stop considering residents as part of a city's population? Different rules are used. Sometimes the city proper is used, and other times the Standard Metropolitan Statistical Area (SMSA) is used. Pittsburgh, for instance, has a population of 421,760, but the SMSA of Pittsburgh includes 2,277,326 people (*The World Almanac,* 1981).

Boundary difficulties also occur when assessing population *change.* Most cities find people emigrating to the suburbs, so the population of the city should be declining. However, cities frequently annex areas so that it *appears* that they are gaining population. During the 1960s Jacksonville, Florida, annexed territory. Instead of a 1970 population of 164,000 it showed a later population of 529,000!

The use of "family" as a unit of analysis provides another handy example. How is *family* defined? Where does it begin and end? Does it include everybody who lives together in a single household? What if some of these are not related by blood or marriage? Does it matter if one pays rent to another? What if more than two generations are represented? There are, in other words, many decisions to be made in setting the boundaries of units (unless a unit is a person). Usually the best hints are supplied by the research problem itself. If the problem is to isolate the causes of marital satisfaction and dissatisfaction, for instance, unmarrieds who live together should possibly be excluded. If two married couples live in the same household, each should be considered as one family.

Related to the question of boundaries is the question of how far to extend a unit of analysis. This is particularly important when testing other scholars' theories. If Cloward and Ohlin (1960) explicitly state that their opportunity theory applies only to delinquent gangs, then researchers can compare *delinquent gangs*. It would be inappropriate to test their theory by comparing delinquent with "nondelinquent" gangs. The point here is that the units *should not be more inclusive* than the research problem suggests.

Once the appropriate units are determined, the next step is to make sure that these units differ considerably on the crucial variable. If an implication model is being tested, the effect of the independent variable can be determined only if its values vary. If the independent variable is the amount of alcohol consumed and investigators wish to study the effects of differing amounts of alcohol consumption, they could not examine only those persons who drank *approximately the same amount,* say six ounces, of alcohol. However, if alcohol consumption ranged from zero ounces to ten or twelve ounces, the variation in amount of alcohol consumed is surely large enough for some effects to vary (such as staggering, slurred speech, and decreased tension).

When researchers are interested in what *causes* a change in the dependent variable (an accounting model), they must select units which do indeed show considerable difference in the dependent variable. The dependent variable might be body weight. In this case, the interest may be to find out why some people are emaciated while others are obese. It might be discovered that variation in obesity is related to such factors as genetic predisposition, excessive caloric intake, insufficient physical activity, or the increase in fat cells in infancy or youth. Researchers have an opportunity to uncover possible causes only when the dependent variable takes on widely differing values. Clearly, a very satisfactory picture of the *causes* of obesity cannot be obtained if all of the persons examined had approximately the same weight.

The important considerations which need to be addressed in insuring that the units of analysis fit the intent of the research problem include choosing the appropriate units of analysis and clearly delineating the boundaries of units.

Summary

Precise and accurate measurement is requisite for testing theoretical statements. Unfortunately, some error is always involved when measuring The error can be either systematic or random, or some combination of the two. Given the presence of error, two very important measurement-related concepts to consider are reliability and validity.

In addition to considering reliability and validity, researchers need to beware of the ecological fallacy (assuming that relationships among groups apply to individuals) and the atomistic fallacy (assuming that relationships among individuals apply to groups). Findings at one of these levels may differ drastically from findings at the other. It is unwise to design a study at one level when interpretations are to be developed at the other.

Review Questions

1. Explain the meaning and significance of the following terms and ideas:
   a. reliability
   b. validity
   c. coefficients of stability, equivalence, and internal consistency
   d. nominal and ordinal measures
   e. interval and ratio measures
2. Discuss (1) content validity; (2) criterion-related validity; and (3) construct validity.
3. Explain and give one example each of the ecological fallacy and the atomistic fallacy.

References

Allen, Mary and Yen, Wendy. *Introduction to Measurement Theory.* Monterey, CA: Brooks/Cole Publishing Company, 1979.

Babbie, Earl. *The Practice of Social Research.* Belmont, CA: Wadsworth Publishing Company, Inc., 1975.

Cloward, Richard and Ohlin, Lloyd. *Delinquency and Opportunity.* New York: The Free Press, 1960.

Lotz, Roy. "Problems with the Doctrine of Interchangeable Indices." *Sociological Quarterly* 15 (1974): 231-241.

Niederhoffer, Arthur. *Behind the Shield.* Garden City, NY: Doubleday & Co., Inc., 1967.

Nunnally, Jum. *Psychometric Theory*. New York: McGraw-Hill Book Co., 1967.

Penn, Roger. "Occupational Prestige in Hierarchies: A Great Empirical Invariant?" *Social Forces* 54 (1975): 355.

Reiss, Albert. *Police and the Public*. New Haven: Yale University Press, 1971.

Riley, Matilda. *Sociological Research I: A Case Approach*. New York: Harcourt, Brace and World, 1963.

Robinson, W. S. "Ecological Correlations and Behavior of Individuals." *American Sociological Review* 15 (1950): 351-357.

Stark, Rodney and Glock, Charles. *American Piety*. Berkeley, CA: University of California Press, 1968.

Thorndike, R. L. *Educational Measurement*. Washington, D.C.: American Council on Education, 1971.

The World Almanac and Book of Facts, 1981. New York: Newspaper Enterprise Association, Inc., 1980.

Chapter 5

Data Production:
Issues and Techniques

Learning Objectives

After reading this chapter, the reader should be able to:

1. Identify data production techniques
2. Differentiate among the types of field studies
3. Specify differences among laboratory experiments, field experiments, and experimental simulation
4. Identify the advantages and disadvantages of mail and telephone surveys
5. Explain the uses, advantages, and disadvantages of secondary data
6. Distinguish between obtrusive and unobtrusive measures

Introduction

Once the research problem has been determined, it is necessary to collect data. Data collection, often referred to as *data production*, occurs when observations about particular phenomena are recorded either by the researcher or by someone else. The choice of a data production technique depends on the type of information needed to address the research problem. Frequently, the use of more than one technique is encouraged because it increases the validity and the reliability of the findings. However, if there is reason to believe that one technique provides more valid and reliable data than do others, it should be given preference.

The principal task of data production is to gather and to record observations which allow for the testing of the research problem. The data which are produced can be either quantitative or categorical (Mayer and Greenwood, 1980, p. 201). *Quantitative data* are those that can be expressed as values on a ratio, interval, or ordinal measurement scale. *Categorical data* are those that can be expressed on a nominal scale. Data also can be either primary or secondary. *Primary data* are those collected first hand. *Secondary data* are those that have been collected previously for some other purpose but which are used to address the research problem (e.g., *Uniform Crime Report*). Secondary data frequently include the entire population rather than a sample of units. As the amount and the quality of information collected by criminal justice agencies have grown, secondary data are being used with increasing frequency.

This text emphasizes the active role researchers play when gathering data; hence, the term *data production* is used. Researchers must make things happen by asking questions, performing experiments, or gaining entry into positions where they can observe strategic interactions.

Data Production Techniques

Since there are many ways to produce data, the presentation here is not exhaustive. Instead, some of the most popular data production techniques are illustrated. To simplify the presentation, data production techniques are divided into three categories: (1) observational techniques, (2) survey techniques, and (3) secondary data techniques.

Observational Techniques

Observational techniques range from viewing subjects in their natural environment to viewing them in contrived settings. The four most frequently used observational techniques are: (1) field studies, (2) laboratory experiments, (3) field experiments, and (4) experimental simulations.

Field Studies. Of the various data production techniques, field studies most nearly approximate real-life situations. Field studies can be undertaken by using a variety of approaches such as intensive interviews and participant observations. Intensive interviews elicit large quantities of data on specific persons and/or subjects. They provide knowledge, insight, and understanding into some often "hidden" phenomenon.

Sutherland's (1937) account of the professional thief illustrates the intensive interviewing approach. He was able to develop a statement explaining a thief's life-style and work patterns. Sutherland's data were produced in two ways. First, he had the thief write out answers to a set of prepared questions, and second, Sutherland and the thief discussed the latter's responses (and related matters) for nearly seven hours per week for 12 weeks.

The most common way to produce data via field studies is through participant observation. Participant observation requires that researchers become fully involved in many aspects of their subjects' lives. One must be present to hear the informal discussions and to observe informal be-haviors. Thus, participant observation studies are a good way to learn about a single group. Like intensive interviews, participant observation is designed to gain knowledge of typical situations and/or interaction patterns.

Participant observation requires long periods of time. One classic participant observation study is Whyte's (1943) *Street Corner Society*. Whyte examined the behavioral and interactional patterns among a group of Italian slum residents. To acquire the necessary data, Whyte became thoroughly integrated into the slum's social network, a process which took him nearly three and one-half years.

Like any data production technique, field studies have limitations which revolve around the fact that field studies are based on small samples which frequently call into question their validity and reliability. In other words, although field studies are useful because they investigate subjects in their own settings, the studies are limited by the fact that their findings seldom can be generalized to a larger population.

Laboratory Experiments. Laboratory experiments permit most of the extraneous variables to be controlled for by manipulating the independent variable(s) while observing their effect(s) on the dependent variable(s). As the term suggests, laboratory experiments are undertaken in artificial settings.

Moriarity's (1974) study of the conditions under which an individual with a minority opinion feels deviant is a good illustration of how to produce data in the laboratory. Moriarity produced "deviance" by means of opinion divergence. The experiment's design was quite complex. Subjects discovered that their opinions on important social and political issues (e.g., the Vietnam war) were contrary to those expressed by other group members. From this starting point, Moriarity was able to manipulate the group's responses to the subject's opinions as well as to estimate the conditions under which opinion divergence occurs.

The most salient limitation of laboratory experiments is that they have negligible external validity; that is, the experiments generally relate poorly to real-life situations. In effect, critics argue that subjects are likely to perform one way in the laboratory and to act quite differently in their natural environment.

Field Experiments. Field experiments are designed to couple the strengths of laboratory experiments with field studies. Field experiments and field studies are similar in that the data are produced in the subject's natural setting. Moreover, field experiments, like laboratory experiments, permit the manipulation of the independent variable(s) while observing the effect(s) on the dependent variable(s). Although field experiments are similar to field studies and laboratory experiments, field experiments are not as controlled as are laboratory experiments, nor are they as comprehensive and detailed as field studies.

An example of a field experiment is the Steffensmeier and Terry (1975) study of shoplifting. Seeking to examine the relationship between observer and shoplifter characteristics (e.g., sex, personal appearance), they determined which customers were most willing to report a shoplifting incident to store personnel. The study, which was staged in three preselected stores in the Midwest, used a fictitious shoplifting incident (i.e., it had been prearranged between the researchers and store personnel). From data derived from the field experiment design, Steffensmeier and Terry concluded that customers were more likely to report an offender if he or she was perceived as a "hippie" rather than as "straight."

Experimental Simulations. Experimental simulations are techniques that artificially establish some set of circumstances to determine what would happen if certain changes occur. Such simulations are similar to laboratory experiments and field experiments in that experimental simulations allow one to manipulate independent variable(s) and observe their effect(s) on the dependent variable(s). Experimental simulations simulate data from which generalizations can be made.

An excellent illustration of a study using experimental simulation is the Haney, Banks, and Zimbardo (1973) research examining prison guard/inmate role structures. To assess the interpersonal dynamics of the prison environment, the researchers created a mock prison. Subjects were randomly assigned to play either the prison guard role or the inmate role. As the study progressed, rather obvious changes were noted in subjects playing the guard roles and the inmate roles alike. Prisoners experienced a loss of personal identity and arbitrary control over their behavior. Guards, on the other hand, experienced increased social power, status, and group identification. Then, too, a rather large percentage of the subjects assigned the guard role became increasingly aggressive and dehumanizing toward inmates.

Survey Techniques

Survey techniques are the most widely used of all data production techniques because they provide a way to collect large amounts of data inexpensively. Moreover, when survey units have been randomly sampled, the findings can be generalized to the population from which the sample was drawn. Thus, survey data are often used to explain, forecast, and predict some condition or behavior. Also, because survey techniques use systematic procedures, the data can be replicated (i.e., the study can be reproduced by others).

The three most frequently used survey techniques are: (1) assembled-group questionnaires, (2) mail questionnaires, and (3) telephone question-naires. Before these techniques can be presented individually, it is essential to discuss questionnaire construction itself, since it is the heart of survey research.

Questionnaire Construction. Constructing survey questionnaires is a serious matter. Questionnaires cannot be "thrown together." Instead, they must be systematically designed to elicit specific data. Before designing a questionnaire, one needs to know the type of information that is required. Generally, questionnaires generate information about attitudes, beliefs, be-haviors, and/or attributes.

Attitudes are not easily defined. Researchers have struggled with developing a precise meaning of that concept for many years. Since that discussion is beyond the scope of this text, it suffices to say that *attitudes are predispositions of an individual to evaluate something in a particular manner.* An example of an attitudinal question is, Should the police put homosexuals in jail?

While sometimes confused with attitudes, *beliefs are the acceptance of any statement as being true or false.* Questionnaires tapping beliefs are designed to determine a respondent's knowledge of specific facts. In other words, belief questions are designed to elicit people's perceptions of past, present, or future reality (Dillman, 1978, p. 81). An illustration of a ques-tion examining a belief is, Does being forcibly raped generate frigidity toward all future sexual partners? The distinguishing feature between beliefs and attitudes is that the "choices that are typically implied by belief questions include correct versus incorrect, accurate versus inaccurate, and what happened versus what did not happen" (Dillman, 1978, p. 81).

Behavior questions elicit a respondent's views about some behavior. Generally speaking, a behavior is the manner of acting in a given situation (Fairchild, 1970, p. 21). The distinction between a belief and a behavior is that a belief is experienced only cognitively while the latter is expe-rienced overtly. An illustration of a question tapping a behavior is, Have you ever forcibly raped another person?

Attributes refer to something people possess, not to something people do or feel. Commonly asked attribute questions examine sex, age, and education level. A question eliciting such information is, What is your age?

Question Format. Once the type of information is determined, the questions can be structured in several ways. They can be: (1) open-ended,

(2) close-ended with ordered choices, (3) rank-listed, or (4) partially close-ended. *Open-ended questions* do not provide respondents with a checklist of choices. An example of this type of question is, What is the most serious social problem facing United States citizens in the 1980s? Respondents can answer any way they choose.

Close-ended questions with ordered choices offer respondents a checklist ordered according to some greater-than or less-than continuum. The respondents select among the choices, such as in the question, How often have you reported a crime to the police? The ordered choices are: (1) never, (2) only once, (3) two or three times, (4) four or five times, and (5) six or more times.

Rank-listed questions permit respondents to evaluate priorities and alternatives. Respondents are asked to rank predetermined choices according to some criterion. Such a question might ask, What are the first, second, and third most serious social problems facing United States citizens in the 1980s? List them from the most severe to the least severe. The responses to be ranked might be: (1) crime, (2) poverty, (3) morals, (4) inflation, (5) energy, (6) defense, and (7) drugs. Rank-listed questions require considerably more from respondents than do the other types of questions since respondents must consider differences among choices and then rank the choices.

The *partially closed question,* which is actually a compromise between the open and closed formats, allows respondents to write responses beyond those provided, for example:

Homosexuals should:

1. Be fined $10,000 and released.
2. Serve at least 5 years in prison.
3. Serve a life-term prison sentence, with no parole option.
4. Receive the death penalty.
5. Other (please specify) _____

The precise question format selected is contingent upon the type of information sought, as different question formats elicit different kinds of information.

Question Wording. Backstrom and Hursh (1963, p. 84) have suggested that besides gathering data, a questionnaire should build and maintain rapport with respondents so that emotional issues can be broached without enmity. To do this, questions must be worded carefully so as not to elicit inaccurate information. When writing questions, researchers should:

    1. use common but precise language (questions should not be ambiguous and should be designed to avoid misinterpretation),

2. make sure respondents understand each question,
3. avoid arousing suspicion or resistance,
4. ascertain whether respondents have information to answer question,
5. pretest each question (practice interviewing with someone who understands the process), and
6. reduce any chronological confusion respondents may have.

To gain trust and rapport, the questions should:
1. try not to intimidate respondents,
2. make respondents feel comfortable,
3. give respondents recognition ("As you probably know . . ."),
4. encourage catharsis, and
5. be informal in tone.

Assembled-Group Questionnaires. Whenever people are surveyed in groups, data can be gathered by means of an assembled-group method. There are two generally recognized types of assembled-group techniques: one is the natural assembled-group method; the other is the artificial assembled-group method. Natural assembled-groups are those which are assembled regardless of whether researchers intervene. Students attending a class or police officers showing up at the shift roll call are examples. Artificial assembled-groups, on the other hand, are those which would not have been assembled had researchers not intervened. Fifteen police officers from each of eight precincts meeting at the request of researchers for a one-hour session at some designated location are an artificial assembled-group. In either case, once the group is assembled, each respondent is given a questionnaire and asked to complete it and return it before leaving the meeting.

Mail Questionnaires. Mail questionnaires are frequently used because they are relatively inexpensive. Unfortunately, designing and implementing a mail questionnaire is not so simple as it seems. After the questionnaire has been developed, it should be mailed in a packet to the respondents. The packet of information should include a personalized introductory letter, the questionnaire, and a self-addressed, stamped envelope.

The introductory letter introduces the study and its purpose, may explain why the study is being conducted and how the respondent has been selected, mentions the importance of each respondent's answer and the mechanics of returning the questionnaire, assures anonymity of the response, and states the auspices under which the study is being conducted. Sometimes the phone number or address of those sponsoring the study is included in the letter.

The following schedule of mailings is recommended: Survey packets are always sent first-class. Then, one week after the initial packet has been mailed, a postcard is sent to all the respondents. The postcard serves as a thank you for those who have already completed and returned their questionnaires and acts as a reminder for those who have not. Like the cover letter accompanying the initial survey packet, the postcard is personalized. Three weeks after the initial mailing, a second follow-up mailing is sent to all those persons who have not responded. This mailing packet includes a new cover letter which emphasizes even more the importance of the respondent's participation in the project; it includes also another questionnaire and a stamped, self-addressed envelope. A final mailing is sent seven weeks after the initial mailing. Like the other mailings, the final mailing contains a revised cover letter, a survey questionnaire, and a postage-paid return envelope. *The difference, though, is that the final survey packet is sent certified mail.* While this tactic increases the cost of the survey, it demonstrates to even the skeptical respondent the importance of his or her reply. It is money worth spending.

To increase returns, which generally are low for questionnaires, a questionnaire of reasonable length should be developed. The length depends on the type of persons being surveyed. Professional persons, for instance, will respond to a longer questionnaire than will the average citizen. Moreover, close-ended questionnaires should be used because they increase the return rate. For many mail surveys, an acceptable response rate is about 50 percent.

There are, according to Nachmias and Nachmias (1981, pp. 182-83), various limitations associated with a mail survey:

1. It can be used only when the questions are simple and straight-forward enough to be comprehended with the help of printed instructions.
2. The answers have to be accepted as final; there is no chance to probe, to clarify ambiguous answers, or to appraise nonverbal behavior.
3. The researcher cannot assure that the person addressed will complete the questionnaire.
4. The respondent can see all the questions before answering any one of them, so various answers cannot be regarded as independent.

Despite these limitations, the mail questionnaire is frequently used because it is inexpensive and easily administered.

Telephone Questionnaires. Telephone surveys are more than simple extensions of mail questionnaires. Both the design and the implementation are quite different. Telephone surveys rely heavily on the interviewer's verbal skills since the questions are verbally, rather than visually, communicated. An interviewer must read questions correctly, and the questions must be presented in such a way that subjects can respond coherently. Moreover, a telephone questionnaire should not take longer than 15 minutes to complete.

Telephone surveys are especially useful when time is of importance. Researchers staffed with adequate telephone lines can reach several hundred persons on any given day. In other words, telephone surveys are able to generate data very quickly. At one time it was felt that telephone surveys were biased toward particular economic classes. No doubt in an earlier time this claim was true. Today, nearly 94 percent of all United States residences have telephones (Dillman, 1978, p. 10).

The advantages and disadvantages of mail and telephone surveys are illustrated in Table 5.1. As with other data production techniques, the appropriateness of using either a telephone survey or a mail survey depends on the study's research problem and design.

Table 5.1   Relative Merits of Mail and Telephone Surveys

Advantages

Mail	Telephone
1. Respondents more honest on sensitive issues (e.g., sex)	1. Quick way to obtain data
2. No interviewer bias	2. Call-backs are simple and economical
3. Respondent can answer at his or her leisure	3. Permits question explanation
4. Certain segments of the population more easily approached	

Disadvantages

Mail	Telephone
1. Bias due to nonresponses sometimes difficult to determine	1. Often sufficient numbers of questions cannot be asked
2. No question interpretation permissible	2. Sensitive questions may affect future responses
3. Data collection can take a long time	3. Potential for interviewer bias
	4. People without telephones or ones with unlisted numbers are omitted
	5. Questions must be short and to the point

The most common method of selecting respondents for a telephone survey is to randomly select residential telephone numbers from a telephone directory. (This procedure is similar to the sampling procedures discussed in Chapter 6.) Another increasingly popular method of selecting telephone respondents is *random digit dialing*. When random digit dialing is used, the telephone numbers are generated by a computer, making it a purely random sample.

The major advantage of random digit dialing is that it includes those individuals who might otherwise be excluded from telephone directories: new listings, unlisted households, and normal printing errors. Random digit dialing also gives everyone with a telephone a chance of being included in the poll. Random digit dialing, however, does have one major disadvantage: not all numbers generated in this fashion are working numbers. Prior to actual interviewing, therefore, all of the numbers need to be dialed to eliminate as many of these non-working numbers as possible.

One other point regarding telephone surveys must be noted. Telephone interviews serve as an intermediary between the survey instrument and the subject. Telephone interviewers, in other words, are variables to be considered in the study. Among other things, factors like voice pitch and telephone mannerisms influence how a respondent answers the questions. Unfortunately, no one knows precisely how responses and response rates are affected by such factors. To the extent that these factors vary among interviewers, the results may become increasingly problematical.

Secondary Data Analysis

Many novice researchers are likely to assume that a research question can be answered only by using *primary data,* data gathered by researchers themselves. However, it is possible — and sometimes advisable — to rely upon *secondary data* which is originally gathered by someone else.

Why would researchers choose to use secondary data? The answer is twofold. First, using secondary data is more economical, and second, sometimes the research problem requires it. For example, if the research design calls for many variables and/or a large number of respondents, the cost of conducting the research might be prohibitive. Using secondary data is more economically feasible.

Besides the economic advantage associated with using secondary data, a second reason for using them is that often the research problem requires comparable data. Numerous studies of deterrence, for example, rely on data derived from the FBI's annual *Uniform Crime Report,* a secondary data source. Studies of prison tension and violence sometimes are based on data generated from a state's prison population statistics yearbook.

The point is clear: even though the primary advantage for using secondary data is an economic one, there are other reasons for using such data.

Unfortunately, there are disadvantages associated with using secondary data. Generally, when someone else's data are used, researchers are forced to use variables which were not initially intended to measure their key concepts or address the research problem.

Suppose the relationship between forcible rape and victim resistance is being examined. One of the issues raised in ercent years is whether women who resist or fight their assailant will be harmed more or less than women who do not resist. Using secondary data (perhaps from the files of metropolitan police departments) one could attempt to address this issue. Amir (1971, p. 171), for instance, points out that "the more severe the physical violence the victim was subjected to, the more intensive was her fighting." From this finding it might be presumed that women should not resist rapists since resistance from the victim tends to be accompanied by greater violence from the offender. However, the data do not specify *when* the victim resists — before or after the assault/rape. In general, if secondary data are used, one must be prepared to work with information which gets at his or her interest only indirectly, or one may even be forced to modify the research problem to accommodate the nature of the secondary data.

Another disadvantage of secondary data involves comparability of concepts for different times or places. When the data come from an official agency, such as the FBI, researchers must be attentive to problems of changing definitions or changing practices of measurement. The Philadelphia Police Department reported 28,560 index crimes in 1953; this figure represented an increase of 70 percent over the number of reported index crimes in 1951 (Gibbons, 1977, pp. 102-103). However, the difference reflected a change in recording practices and not an upsurge in crime. When different data are compared, it is essential to be aware of the possibility that the differences may be a matter of different data collection methods (e.g., the way questions are worded) and not different time periods.

Despite the disadvantages, secondary data provide relatively inexpensive data. One can usually rely on studies conducted by other researchers, research organizations, polling agencies, and data banks. Because there are so many sets of data available, resourceful persons can usually find available data which may be extremely useful to their particular research interests.

Obtrusive and Unobtrusive Techniques

Data are gathered either obtrusively or unobtrusively. *Obtrusive tech-*

niques are those which collect data when subjects know they are being observed. *Unobtrusive techniques* are those which gather data when subjects do not know they are being observed.

Observational and survey data gathering are examples of obtrusive techniques. In their book on unobtrusive measures, Webb and his associates (1966) discuss the use of such nonreactive data sources as physical traces, archives, and observation. *Physical traces* include erosion and accretion (growth) data. In museums, for instance, the relative popularity of exhibits can be measured by how often the tiles around each exhibit wear out and have to be replaced (an erosion measure). An example of an accretion measure is how many tons of confetti are picked up in New York City after a parade for a famous person. These presumably reflect popularity.

Archives provide actuarial records (e.g., records of births, deaths, and marriages), political and judicial records (e.g., the *Congressional Record*), and other government records, such as records of power failures, municipal water pressure, and parking meter collections.

Unobtrusive observations suggested by Webb and his associates include listening while hidden from view or while in a room or lobby crowded with strangers (as at a concert intermission). Of course, numerous possibilities present themselves with concealed equipment such as cameras and tape recorders, although serious ethical questions are involved in such situations.

One informal research project using such equipment is found in Chambliss (1975) study of organized crime. Concealing a tape recorder in a briefcase, Chambliss recorded conversations without the respondents' knowledge. Chambliss addressed the ethical problems by informing the respondents at the end of the conversation that it had been tape recorded. He then opened his briefcase, removed the tape from the recorder, and handed it to the respondents, explaining that the recording would be used only as part of his scientific research. If a respondent wished, he or she was free to take the tape and destroy it. (In only one instance did the respondent destroy the recording.)

The advantage of unobtrusive measures is that they capture the flavor of social behavior without interfering with it; they do not make respondents react. Surely these sorts of measures can be useful supplements to conventional research, but most unobtrusive measures contain serious flaws (poor sampling, unsystematic data), so they are rarely used. More often, the obtrusive features of the conventional data production techniques (surveys and experiments) are addressed and corrected. The works of Hyman (1954), Rosenthal (1976), and Edwards (1957) provide several guidelines for doing just that.

Data Distortion

Regardless of which data production technique is employed, care must be exerted to insure that data are not distorted. Data usually are distorted by unintended influences. First of all, a variety of distortions fall under the heading of *interviewer effects*. Interviewers may introduce distortions through faulty reading of questions or faulty recording of answers. They may, just by their presence, create a reactive effect upon the respondent. Reading errors and recording errors occur either from inadequately training the interviewer or from interviewer prejudgment about what a particular respondent really believes or feels.

While these errors are important, perhaps more important is another kind of interviewer effect, one in which the respondent reacts to some nonbehavioral characteristic of the interviewer such as race, sex, or social class. For example, in a study of interviewer effect, Schuman and Converse (1971) found that black respondents usually gave different answers to black interviewers than they did to white interviewers. Table 5.2 depicts their findings. The data were gathered from 1968 interviews with a cross-section of Detroit blacks months after a major riot and two weeks after the assassination of Martin Luther King. Thus, racial tensions were higher than usual.

Most of the 130 responses analyzed by Schuman and Converse (1971) were not affected by the race of the interviewers. Where noticeable differences did appear, the responses dealt with general attitudes about black militancy. Apparently the race of the interviewers affects militancy only when the items deal with relatively vague sympathies, not when they commit the person to strongly held views or actions (Schuman and Converse, 1971, p. 57).

Distortions also occur in laboratory settings, where they are called *experimenter effect* rather than interviewer effect. In some ways these effects are similar. Experimenters may introduce distortion by (1) faulty recording of data; (2) faulty perception of information (owing to the researcher's expectations or preconceptions); or (3) by injecting themselves too prominently into the subject's consciousness (even if only by having white or black skin). Studies of experimenter effect have focused primarily upon the *experimenter's expectations* about how subjects should respond to some stimulus or question. The experimenter somehow communicates this set of expectations to subjects, who in turn act in accord with them.

In a classic psychological study of experimenter effects with a nonhuman subject, Oskar Pfungst (1911) examined the behavior of a horse named Clever Hans who could by tapping his foot add, subtract, multiply, and divide (even with fractions), and read, spell, and identify musical tones. In 1904 a group of professionals certified that the owner was not giving any cues to Hans, intentionally or unintentionally. This prompted a more exhaustive examination of the phenomenon by Oskar Pfungst, a psychology student who found that Hans could answer not only his owner but most other questioners as well. But Hans's accuracy fell off considerably when (1) he wore blinders which prevented him from seeing the questioners, (2) the questioners were not physically close to him, or (3) the questioners did not know the answers to their own questions. In other words, Hans was clever only when he could readily see people who actually knew the answer.

Table 5.2   Effect of Interviewer's Race on Response of Black Respondents to Questions with Racial Content

(in percent)

Question	Answer Tested	Interviewer White	Black
1. Do you personally feel that you can trust most white people, some white people, or none at all?	Trust most whites	35	7
2. Would you say that because of the disturbance, Negroes in Detroit now feel *more* ready to stand up for their rights, *less* ready to stand up for their rights, or there hasn't been much change?	More ready	61	84
3. Some people feel that last summer's disturbance was a *step forward* for the cause of Negro rights. Others feel that it was a *step backward* for the cause of Negro rights. Which opinion comes closest to the way you feel?	Step forward	30	54
4. Do you think city officials in Detroit are *more* willing to listen to Negro demands since the disturbance, *less* willing to listen, or hasn't there been much change?	More willing	59	79

Source: Howard Schuman and Jean Converse, "The Effects of Black and White Interviewers on Response in 1968," *Public Opinion Quarterly* 35, (1971), pp. 54-55.

The importance of the Clever Hans study cannot be overstated. It demonstrates that one can convey cues through a subtle system of unintentional communication. If horses can pick up these cues, one might imagine that human subjects can do at least as well.

Evidently there are four dimensions which seem to exert an unintended influence on experimenter expectations (Rosenthal, 1976, p. 257):

1. *Professional status.* Experimenters who are more professional, businesslike, and consistent exert greater expectancy effects upon their subjects.

2. *Interpersonal style.* Experimenters who are more relaxed, interested, enthusiastic, and personal exert greater expectancy effects upon their subjects, but probably only as long as they maintain a professional manner.

3. *Kinesic communication.* Experimenters who employ subtle kinesic signals from the leg and head regions exert greater expectancy effects upon their subjects. However, if the kinesic signals become very obvious, they are likely to lead to a diminution of expectancy effects because they will detract from the professional demeanor of the experimenter.

4. *Paralinguistic communications.* Experimenters who speak slowly and in an expressive, nonmonotonous tone exert greater expectancy effects upon their subjects. The way in which experimenters deliver their programmed input probably serves to communicate their expectancy to their subject.

These comments indicate that researchers must consciously take steps to insure that the results of their experiments are not contaminated by experimenter and/or interviewer expectations.

Another form of distortion associated with obtrusive measures is the response set. Unlike interviewer and experimenter effects, *response sets* are part of the research instrument; they do not get transmitted by the interviewer or experimenter. There are two kinds which are of particular interest to criminal justice researchers: *acquiescence* and *social desirability.* Two important findings have been noted: (1) some *questions* seem to invite *positive responses* such as "yes," "true," or "agree," and (2) some *respondents* have a *tendency to agree* and others *to disagree* regardless of question content. The concern here is more with the kinds of questions that should be used. Psychologists indicate that the questions which people tend to agree with exceptionally often tend to be vague and ambiguous. One of the ways used to detect yeasaying or acquiescence is simply to compute what percentage of all responses are "yes," "true" or "agree."

Another way is to reverse wording of the question later in the questionnaire and compare the two responses.

Still another kind of response set is called *social desirability*. Edwards (1957) has shown that respondents often answer a question not so much in terms of what they really think but in terms of what they consider socially desirable. In one personality inventory, for instance, nearly everyone endorsed this item: "I like to be loyal to my friends." Hardly anyone endorsed the statement: "I like to avoid responsibilities and obligations." Similarly, many people refuse to acknowledge that they hold certain unpopular opinions. Because of this tendency to respond to questions according to an "irrelevant" dimension (social desirability) many answers to character judgment questions are not valid. One way to alleviate this problem is to allow, for any particular question, only those answers which have the *same level of social desirability*.

Summary

Data gathering is a serious research task. Researchers must know the type of information they need and then determine the best way (given existing constraints) to gather that information. While numerous data gathering techniques exist, no single data production technique is sufficient to answer every research question. The data gathering technique used depends entirely on the research problem. Using various data production techniques simultaneously is usually quite desirable. Since each technique furnishes different types of information, combining techniques probably will yield a more accurate picture of reality.

Regardless of the technique selected, researchers must be careful. They must be cognizant of their objectives and be able to relate the data technique adopted to those objectives. Otherwise, what is sought may not be delivered.

Review Questions

1. Explain the meaning and significance of the following terms and ideas:
   a. data production
   b. obtrusive and unobtrusive measures
   c. experimenter expectations
   d. response set
   e. systematic data production
   f. field studies
   g. laboratory experiments

     h. field experiments

     i. experimental simulations

     j. secondary and primary data

2. Explain the advantages and the disadvantages of producing data via the assembled-group method; the mail survey; and the telephone survey.

3. Give an illustration of a survey question examining each of the following: an attitude; a belief; a behavior; and an attribute.

4. Choose a criminal justice research topic and develop a two- or three-page questionnaire designed to elicit data on that topic.

5. For what reason(s) would investigators use secondary data instead of primary data?

6. In the library locate and identify studies using each of the following techniques:

     a. field study

     b. laboratory experiment

     c. field experiment

     d. experimental simulation

     e. assembled-group survey

     f. telephone survey

     g. mail survey

References

Amir, Menachem. *Patterns in Forcible Rape*. Chicago: The University of Chicago Press, 1971.

Backstrom, Charles, and Hursh, Gerald. *Survey Research*. Evanston, Ill.: Northwestern University Press, 1963.

Chambliss, William. "Paucity of Original Research on Organized Crime." *The American Sociologist* 10 (1975):36-39.

Dillman, Donald. *Mail and Telephone Surveys*. New York: John Wiley & Sons, Inc., 1978.

Edwards, Allen. *The Social Desirability Variable in Personality Research*. New York: Dryden Press, 1957.

Fairchild, Henry. *Dictionary of Sociology and Related Sciences*. Totowa, NJ: Littlefield, Adams, & Co., 1970.

Gibbons, Donald. *Society, Crime, and Criminal Careers*. 3rd ed. Englewood Cliffs, NJ: Prentice-Hall, Inc., 1977.

Haney, Craig et al. "Interpersonal Dynamics in a Simulated Prison." *International Journal of Criminology and Penology* 1 (1973): 69-97.

Hyman, Herbert. *Interviewing in Social Research.* Chicago: The University of Chicago Press, 1954.

McCall, George, and Simmons, J. L. *Issues in Participant Observation.* London: Addison-Wesley Publishing Co., Inc., 1969.

Mayer, Robert, and Greenwood, Ernest. *The Design of Social Policy Research.* Englewood Cliffs, NJ: Prentice-Hall, Inc., 1980.

Moriarity, Thomas. "Role of Stigma in Experience of Deviance." *Journal of Personality and Social Psychology* 29 (1974):849-855.

Nachmias, David, and Nachmias, Chava. *Research Methods in the Social Sciences.* New York: St. Martin's Press, 1981.

Pfungst, O. Max. *Clever Hans: The Contribution to Experimental, Animal, and Human Psychology.* Translated by C. L. Rahn. New York: Holt, 1911.

Rosenthal, Robert. *Experimenter Effects in Behavioral Research.* New York: Irvington Publishers, Inc., 1976.

Schuman, Howard, and Converse, Jean. "The Effects of Black and White Interviewers on Responses in 1968." *Public Opinion Quarterly* 35 (1971):44-68.

Steffensmeier, Darrell, and Terry, Robert. *Examining Deviance Experimentally.* Port Washington, NY: Alfred Publishing Co., 1975.

Sutherland, Edwin. *The Professional Thief.* Chicago: The University of Chicago Press, 1937.

Webb, Eugene et al. *Unobtrusive Measures: Nonreactive Research in the Social Sciences.* Chicago: Rand-McNally, 1966.

Whyte, William. *Street Corner Society: The Social Structure of an Italian Slum.* Chicago: The University of Chicago Press, 1943.

Chapter 6
Sampling

Learning Objectives

After completing this chapter, the reader should be able to:

1. Discuss the sampling process
2. Distinguish between probability and nonprobability samples
3. Comprehend the similarities and differences among various sampling methods
4. Know when it is appropriate to use one sampling method and not another
5. Explain the following kinds of samples: probability, simple random, systematic, stratified, nonprobability, quota, purposive, and convenience

Introduction

Once the research question has been stated and the research design formulated, researchers are concerned with making generalizations about some relationship or phenomenon. Time and money frequently prevent researchers from examining the entire population (Hy, 1977, p. 105), so they usually study a sample of the population. Then they infer from that sample to the population.

When a sample is drawn, a problem is faced: How does one know whether the sample represents the population from which the sample was drawn? Is it safe to generalize from the sample to the population? Systematic sampling procedures allow for the making of such generalizations.

A sample is comprised of units of analysis selected from the entire population. The term *population* (sometimes called the *universe*) refers to *all* units of analysis that might be studied. A *sample* is any combination of units of analysis that does not include the entire population. A *unit* is a single member of the population. For instance, if researchers are studying the effects of a police cadet training program in the city of Louisville, the population consists of each performance measure of each cadet enrolled in the training program. The sample is comprised of the subsets of performance measures that are being studied, and the units of analysis are the program measures.

Normal Distribution

The normal distribution generally is used to estimate sampling error and determine the size of the sample. *Sampling error* refers to the difference between the findings obtained by sampling and those which would have been obtained if the entire population had been analyzed (Smith et al., 1976, p. 147). Since the primary purpose of sampling is to make generalizations to a larger population, it is crucial that the amount of sampling error be known.

The normal distribution, which is a mathematical construct derived from probability theory, allows researchers to estimate sampling error. A *normal distribution* is a myriad of frequency distributions — one for each possible sample size — based not on empirical data but deduced from probability theory.

Such deductions are based on the statistical assumption that when a large number of samples is drawn randomly from the same population, the average of the sample statistics approximates the population statistics. Since the population statistics are ordinarily unknown, the statistics of several hundred samples are considered to be a close approximation of the population statistics. By drawing a large number of samples from the sample population, statisticians can approximate population statistics without knowing the actual population statistics. One can draw a sample, calculate sample statistics, and compare them to a normal distribution (an approximated sampling distribution) to determine how closely the sample statistics represent the population statistics.

The normal distribution is characterized by a bell curve because the distribution is unimodal, symmetrical, and asymptotic. The area under the curve equals 100 percent. *Unimodal* means that the median (middle point) and mode (datum value which occurs most frequently) coincide at the same value. *Symmetrical* means that 50 percent of the distribution exists on either side of the mean (arithmetic average). *Asymptotic* means that a distribution extends into infinity in both directions. Practically speaking, the distribution curve never touches the horizontal axis. Figure 6.1 shows a normal distribution curve.

Since the sampling distributions of many statistics approximate the normal distribution, it is ordinarily used to describe a sampling distribution.

Figure 6.1   A Normal Distribution Curve

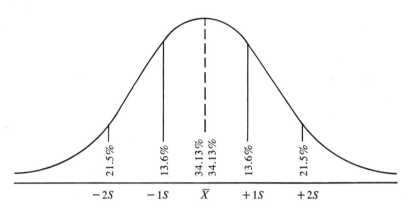

$\overline{X}$ = mean

S = approximated standard
deviation

To use the normal distribution, one must compute the *standard devi-ation* and the *standard error of the population*. While these can be cal-culated by hand, statisticians have computed a table, called the normal distribution table (Appendix B) which lists the proportion of units that lies between the mean of a normal distribution and the proportion of units that fall within a certain standard deviation above (or below) the mean. For instance, if one wants to know the proportion of units that lies between the mean and 1.82 standard error above the mean, one would proceed down the left-most column of the normal distribution table to the number 1.8 and read across that row until it intersects the column .02. The number at that intersection is .4656. That number is first multiplied by 2 (.4656 × 2 = .9312) and subtracted from 1.000 since the area under the normal distribution curve is 100 percent (1.0000 − .9312 ≅ .07). The level of sampling error is 7 percent; that it, there is a 7 percent chance of making an error when assuming that the statistics found in the sample are representative of the values in the population from which the sample was drawn. Convention suggests that a sampling error of 5 percent or less is acceptable.

Sample Size

The normal distribution is also used to determine the size of the sample. Generally, the greater the desired accuracy and the smaller the desired level of sampling error, the larger the sample size. While the size of the sample can be computed by hand, statisticians have developed tables indicating the sample size. Table 6.1 shows one of the many reference tables developed by statisticians to determine sample size.

Table 6.1   Sample Size for Various Levels of Error and Accuracy

Level of Desired Accuracy	Level of Error		
	.01	.05	.10
± 1%	16,587	9,604	6,765
± 2%	4,147	2,401	1,691
± 3%	1,843	1,067	752
± 4%	1,037	600	423
± 5%	663	384	271
± 6%	461	267	188
± 7%	339	196	138
± 8%	259	150	106
± 9%	205	119	84
± 10%	166	96	68
± 15%	74	43	30
± 20%	41	24	17

The *level of error* describes the chance of making an error when inferring from the sample to the population. The *level of desired accuracy* indicates the degree to which the findings could vary. For instance, if percentages were used, and if the level of desired accuracy were set at ± 4 (plus or minus 4 percent), and if it were found that 40 percent of the sampled persons favored gun control, then the actual percentage of persons who favored could range from 36 percent (40 − 4 = 36) to 44 percent (40 + 4 = 44). According to Table 6.1, researchers who want .05 level of error and ± 4 percent level of desired accuracy need a sample size of at least 600 units.

Note that the number of sampling units increases considerably as the level of accuracy increases. This table is appropriate only when the population is at least five times as large as the sample size. If cluster sampling is used, the sample size should be at least one and one-half times the number indicated in the table (Jones, 1971, p. 64).

When determining sample size, one should always oversample; that is, sample more than the minimum number of units. Not everybody will reply to a questionnaire, for example. If researchers are studying job stress among prison guards and they need 3,000 completed questionnaires, the initial sampling list should contain more than 3,000 names, since not all the sampled people will complete the survey instrument. Some people may be sick, others may be on vacation, and some will just refuse to complete the questionnaire. This problem can be overcome by estimating the probable nonresponse rate. This is easier said than done; no formula exists to compute this number. Instead, the response rates of others who have studied similar topics and/or subjects must be analyzed. This information will provide as accurate an estimate as possible. In the final analysis, one should always try to maximize the study's completion rate. This is the best single way to insure sample representativeness.

Sampling Objective

The objective of sampling is twofold. First, precise, prescribed, systematic procedures increase the reliability and the validity of the information generated from the sampled data. Second, sampling allows researchers to make inferences about the population based on a sample drawn from that population.

If sampling is conducted according to precise, prescribed, systematic procedures, confidence can be placed in the reliability and the validity of the findings of the sampled data. When a sample is drawn in accordance with systematic procedures, others can replicate the findings (reliability). Adherence to such procedures also insures that the sample is representative of the population (validity). Sampling procedures should allow for the selection of a sample that is so similar in characteristics to the population (customarily referred to as *representative*) that statistics of the sample can be safely assumed to be indicative of those of the population. Figure 6.2 illustrates three possible types of samples.

In the first case, the characteristics of the selected sample are identical to the characteristics of the population. Consequently, a statistic found in the sample can be imputed to the population with almost no risk of being wrong. In the second example, the sample, while not identical in characteristics to the population, is similar enough so that the statistic found in the sample can be inferred to be indicative of the population. While some risk would be taken in making such an inference, the risk would be small. In the last illustration, the sample is so dissimilar to the population that it would be quite risky to assume that the statistic found in the sample is representative of the values in the population.

Figure 6.2   Types of Samples

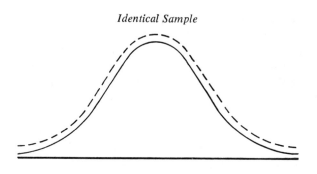

Identical Sample

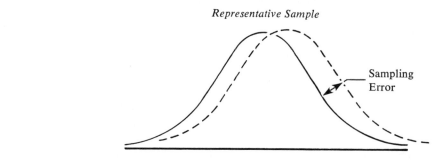

Representative Sample

Sampling Error

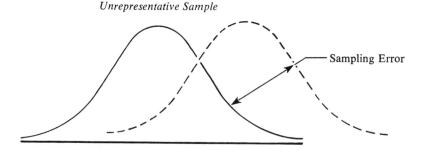

Unrepresentative Sample

Sampling Error

Nonprobability Sampling

There are two families of sampling designs: nonprobability designs and probability designs. The concept *representativeness* underlies this distinction. Nonprobability sampling occurs when the likelihood of any unit being selected is unknown. In other words, units are not randomly selected. The most salient difficulty with nonprobability samples is that it is not possible to calculate the sampling error. There is no way to determine how similar the sample is to the population from which it was drawn.

The primary disadvantage of nonprobability sampling is that it does not allow researchers to specify the amount of error involved when inferring that the characteristics found in the sample are indicative of those in the population. The advantage of nonprobability sampling is that it costs less in terms of money, time, and effort. Sometimes, this advantage outweighs the disadvantage, but nonprobability sampling does have its limitations, and these should be kept in mind. There are three commonly used types of nonprobability samples: quota, purposive, and convenience samples.

Quota Sampling

Quota sampling attempts to replicate the population's known characteristics in one or several categories. Suppose researchers want to know how Montana residents are likely to vote in an upcoming election. Known characteristics include the percentages of Montana residents that are (1) registered Democrats and registered Republicans, and (2) above and below the $20,000 income level. The following are hypothetical numbers for these categories:

I. Voter Registration
    A. Registered Democrat   60 percent
    B. Registered Republican   25 percent
    C. Other   15 percent
II. Income Level
    A. Above $20,000 Level   30 percent
    B. $20,000 or Below   70 percent

To draw a quota sample, a researcher selects units that fill specified categories. Any unit that fits the categories can be used, regardless of its other attributes. The primary focus of quota sampling is finding sufficient units to meet each category's allotted quota. In quota sampling, units are not randomly selected. Researchers merely go out and round up units possessing the necessary attributes to fill the category's quota. Usually, the most easily obtainable units are selected. Thus, not every unit has an equal chance of being selected.

Purposive Sampling

Purposive sampling selects the units of analysis based on the researcher's judgment that the selected units reflect the population's characteristics. When a sample is selected by means of a purposive sample, it is assumed to be representative of the population from which it is drawn. This assumption is problematical because the representativeness of the sample can never be determined, it can only be assumed.

Purposive samples are used primarily for exploratory research. A critical error, and one often made, is to generalize the results from a purposive sample to the larger population.

To illustrate the problem, imagine that investigators are studying through a survey questionnaire the job stress of police in the Boston Police Department. A purposive sample can be drawn by distributing a questionnaire to those officers whom the investigator *assumes* represent the Boston Police Department.

Convenience Sampling

A convenience sample is one in which the units of analysis are selected on the basis of immediate availability rather than on the degree of representativeness. For example, if a college professor draws a sample from all the students taking introductory criminal justice courses, that is a convenience sample.

The major problem with convenience sampling is that it is biased in an unascertainable way. There is no basis for generalizing to a larger population. However, convenience sampling does have its place. It is particularly useful for testing theoretical propositions. If a theoretical statement is correct, it will hold for any group of subjects. It does not matter if the subjects are randomly selected. Therefore, since convenience sampling is so easy, it is often used for theory testing and exploratory research.

Probability Sampling

A probability sample is one in which the probability of selection for each unit of the population is known. For instance, if a police department has 130 officers, 40 of whom are women, the probability (chance) of a woman's being selected is approximately 40 out of 130, or 31 percent.

The major advantage of probability sampling is that it is the only set of procedures that allows researchers to calculate the chance of making an error in generalizing from the sample to the population. The disadvantage, of course, is that such rigorous procedures are expensive and time-consuming. Ordinarily the advantage definitely outweighs the disadvantage.

There are four major types of probability samples: simple random, systematic, stratified, and cluster samples.

Simple Random Sampling

A simple random sample, which is the basis for all other probability sampling procedures, is one in which every unit in the population has an equal chance of being included in the sample. To insure that every unit has an equal chance of being selected, rigorous systematic procedures *must* be followed. In other words, not just *any* units can be included in the sample; such a selection process invariably supplies a faulty sample. For instance, suppose that an opinion poll about women's attitudes toward rape is being conducted. If one stands on a predetermined street corner in downtown Seattle at 2:00 P.M. on a Tuesday and surveys the first 40 women who pass, a faulty sample will be drawn because not every woman in the Seattle metropolitan area will have had an *equal* chance of being selected.

It should be apparent, then, that some prescribed, systematic procedures need to be followed which will guarantee that every unit has an equal chance of being selected. The operational procedure for drawing a simple random sample is quite easy. Figure 6.3 shows the basic steps used to draw a simple random sample.

Figure 6.3   Steps in Drawing a Simple Random Sample

1. Obtain a complete list of the population units.
2. Determine the number of units to be included in the sample.
3. Assign a number to each population unit.
4. Select a random number from a table of random numbers.
5. Select the unit with the number which corresponds to the number drawn from the table of random numbers.
6. Repeat the procedure outlined in step 5 until the desired number of sample units is selected.

The first step in drawing a simple random sample is to obtain a complete list of all units in a population. The next step is to determine the number of units to be included in the sample. The third step is to assign each population unit a distinct number, usually in ascending order.

Generally speaking, the larger the sample the smaller the sampling error, and the greater the probability that the statistics calculated from the sample are indicative of those in the population (Smith, 1976, p. 136). There is, however, a point beyond which increasing the sample size does not significantly reduce the sampling error. As a general rule of thumb, *researchers should select as large a sample as time and money permit.*

Once an accurate population list is obtained and an appropriate sample size is determined, a sample should be drawn in such a way as to insure that every unit has an equal chance of being selected. There are, to be sure, various ways this can be accomplished. The easiest and surest way is to use a table of random numbers, such as that given in Appendix A.

The following example illustrates the use of a table of random numbers. Suppose that the city of Omaha has 100 police cars, and a simple random sample of 30 cars is to be drawn. Each of the 100 automobiles is assigned a distinct number from 0 through 99. Since no unit in the population is numbered with more than two digits, the last two digits in the table of random numbers are used. Then any number within the table of random numbers is selected. The table of random numbers can be read in any order (up, down, sideways — the direction does not matter as long as it is consistent).

Assume one starts on the first page of the table of random numbers in Appendix A and selects the number 49. This means that the 49th police car on the list should be selected as part of the sample. Proceeding down the same column, the next number is 81. If a number already has been used, the next number listed in the table of random numbers should be selected. This process continues until 30 automobiles from the population are identified for the sample.

Systematic Sampling

A systematic sample is one in which an appropriate interval is used to select units. A systematic sample often is confused with a simple random sample, probably because the sampling procedures for each are so similar. In fact, a systematic sampling follows rigorous procedures which are similar, though not identical, to those used to draw a simple random sample. In the first phase, the population list is obtained and then each unit of the population is assigned a distinct number, usually in ascending order. After the sample size has been ascertained, the next step is to determine an *appropriate interval* by dividing the number of population units by the desired number of sample units. For instance, if the population consists of 100 police cars and a sample of 20 units is to be drawn, the appropriate interval is every five units ($100 \div 20 = 5$).

In the second phase, a number less than or equal to the interval size is drawn from the table of random numbers and the numbered unit corresponding to the number just drawn from the table of random numbers is selected. After the first unit is selected, every unit conforming to the appropriate interval is then chosen. Suppose that the appropriate interval is five units and the first unit selected is unit 2. The sample then would consist of cars numbered 2, 7, 12, 17, and so forth.

Systematic sampling is easier and faster than simple random sampling. However, in some instances, systematic sampling may not produce a sample as representative of the population as would simple random sampling, principally because a systematic pattern may occur in the ordering of the population units; that is, units may be listed according to some periodic or cyclical characteristics (e.g., listing crime rates by months or listing officers by seniority or rank). Such an ordering may produce a distorted sample. The best and easiest way to neutralize the possibility of such a distortion is to "shuffle" the list in a manner that will insure random ordering. Even with this shortcoming, however, systematic sampling is not terribly risky.

Stratified Sampling

Stratified sampling is a procedure in which the population is separated into categories or strata and then the units within each strata are randomly selected. Stratified sampling insures that a sufficient number of units is selected from each population strata and thereby assures greater representativeness than either simple random sampling or systematic sampling. Stratified sampling, in other words, reduces the likelihood of drawing an atypical sample.

Imagine that a research project is designed to assess criminal victimization rates in Muncie, Indiana. There are several ways to sample Muncie's residents. One is to use stratified sampling which integrates existing information about the population into the sample selection process. Suppose that previous research has shown that Muncie's victimization rate varies according to the section of the city. The victimization rate in Muncie's southeast side is 50 percent of the total population, in the southwest section, 35 percent, in the northeast part, 10 percent, and in the northwest section, 5 percent. If the sample size is 500 residents, then 250 would be randomly selected from the southeast side, 175 from the southwest section, 50 from the northeast part, and 25 from the northwest section.

Given the known information, the logical stratification trait is "city quadrant." This is a relatively sound way to stratify because residents must live in only one quadrant, and place of residence is related to victimization rate. The attitude of Muncie residents toward the 55 miles per hour speed limit is not a good stratification trait because it in no way is related to the research problem. It is critical that the stratification trait be easily measured and that it is related in some way to the problem.

Some often-used stratification traits include, but are not limited to, age, sex, race, and income. Once the strata are determined, the sampling units are selected in the same way as are random or systematic samples.

Cluster Sampling

Cluster sampling selects groups of units rather than individual units. Suppose that a survey of New York City police officers is being made to determine their general level of work alienation. Like many other large urban police departments, New York City's is decentralized. Assume there are 51 separate precincts and each precinct is staffed by 500 police officers. The initial task is to determine how many respondents are needed for the research. It is decided that 2,500 police officers need to be sampled. The next task is to select the sample. To draw a cluster sample, five of the 51 precincts would be randomly sampled (since each precinct has 500 police officers). Officers in the remaining precincts would be ignored for the remainder of the research.

Some may doubt that a cluster sample is a probability sample. It is, though, because each precinct had an equal chance of being selected; hence each officer had an equal chance of being selected. For cluster samples, the sampling unit is some grouped phenomenon, like police precincts. No doubt, a different set of responses would have been received had the 2,500 police officers sampled been from other police precincts, or had the sample been drawn by means of a simple random, systematic, or stratified sample. However, it is quicker and less expensive to sample grouped individuals.

Cluster sampling provides an alternative to the three previously mentioned probability sampling designs. However, there are risks taken when using cluster samples instead of the other types of probability samples. Cluster samples do not generate as varied a number of respondents as do other probability samples. It also is difficult to estimate the sampling error (Cochran et al., 1954, p. 168). Whether or not a cluster sample is used depends upon specific constraints. When other probability sampling designs cannot be used, cluster sampling is permissible.

Summary

Sampling designs enable researchers to select their units for analysis. The way in which units are selected is based on either probability theory or nonprobability theory. Samples derived from probability theory are simple random sampling, systematic sampling, stratified sampling, and cluster sampling. For probability sampling, the likelihood of any single unit being selected is known. This is important since it allows one to use inferential statistics to generalize the findings. Samples not based on probability theory are quota sampling, purposive sampling, and convenience sampling. For nonrandom samples the likelihood of any single unit being selected is unknown. Thus, data from these samples cannot be used to make generalizations.

Review Questions

1. Explain the meaning and the significance of the following terms and ideas:
   a. population
   b. identical, representative, and unrepresentative samples
   c. sampling error
   d. units of analysis
2. Explain fully the primary strengths and weaknesses of these samples:
   a. simple random
   b. systematic
   c. stratified
   d. cluster
   e. quota
   f. purposive
   g. convenience
3. Compare and contrast (1) a probability and nonprobability sample; (2) a population and a sample; and (3) a population and sampling distribution.
4. Explain the objectives of probability sampling.

References

Cochran, William et al. "Principles of Sampling," *Journal of the American Statistical Association* 49 (1954): 13-15.

Hy, Ronald. *Using the Computer in the Social Sciences: A Nontechnical Approach.* New York: Elsevier North-Holland, 1977.

Jones, E. Terrence. *Conducting Political Research.* New York: Harper & Row Publishers, Inc., 1971.

Smith, Barbara et al. *Political Research Methods: Foundations and Techniques.* Boston: Houghton-Mifflin Co., 1976.

Chapter 7
Univariate Analysis

Learning Objectives

After completing this chapter the reader should be able to:

1. Identify three methods of analysis
2. Construct tables (frequency distributions)
3. Compute percentages and cumulative percentages
4. Construct bar graphs and pie charts and know when to use each
5. Compute appropriate measures of central tendency: the mode, the median, and the mean
6. Compute measures of dispersion: the range, the interquartile range, and the standard deviation
7. Compute a measure of skewness
8. Explain how univariate analysis might be used to address problems of interest to criminologists

Introduction

After the research hypothesis is stated, the units selected, and the data produced, the data must be analyzed. There are several commonly used methods of data analysis, including (1) the construction of tables; (2) the preparation of graphs and charts; and (3) the calculation and interpretation of statistics. Typically, data analysis begins by examining each of the variables individually. This type of data analysis is called *univariate* analysis since it involves dealing with each variable *separately* rather than in relationship with other variable(s). It is only after this first step is completed that analysts study relationships among the variables. This chapter deals with univariate analysis. It demonstrates and explains the use of the three aforementioned methods of data analysis as they are applied to the variables individually.

Tables

Data analysis begins with the construction of separate tables for each of the study's variables. These tables are commonly called *frequency distributions*. For example, Table 7.1 shows frequency distribution for one variable, sentence.

Table 7.1   Number of Convicted Felons Given Various Sentences in King County Court, Washington, 1973

Sentence	Frequency	Percent
Suspended	310	62.0%
Jailed	110	22.0
Imprisoned	80	16.0
Total	500	100.0%

Source: Modification of data in Roy Lotz and John Hewitt, "The Influence of Legally Irrelevant Factors on Felony Sentencing," *Sociological Inquiry* 47, No. 1, pp. 39-48.

As Table 7.1 shows, a frequency distribution is a set of categories for a variable together with the number of units falling into each category. For example, there are three categories for the variable of sentence: a suspended sentence, a jail sentence, and a prison sentence. Each of the 500 convicted felons in Table 7.1 received one of these three sentences: 310 received suspended sentences; 110 received jail sentences; and 80 received prison sentences.

Although tables seem easy enough to construct, there are a few rules researchers should follow when setting them up. First, every table needs a title to identify the material in the table. The title must indicate the variable it displays (e.g., sentence). Sometimes, it is a good idea to mention where the data are from (e.g., King County Court, Washington) and the time period involved (e.g., 1973). In addition, analysts should also include in the title any other information which is needed for properly interpreting the table. Thus, in Table 7.1, the title indicates that the units are convicted *felons* rather than misdemeanants. Second, if the data come from some other study, this should be acknowledged. In Table 7.1 the source of the data is indicated at the foot of the table. This is required in order to give proper credit to the work of others. The third rule requires that the variable and its categories both be named (e.g., the categories of sentence are suspended, jailed, and imprisoned). This facilitates reading the table correctly.

Percentages

Tables are constructed to serve a simple purpose, namely to show how many units fall into each of a variable's categories. When tables are read, one is interested mainly in comparing the number of units in each of the given categories. For example, from Table 7.1 it is clear that in King County Court, most convicted felons were given suspended sentences (310 out of 500). On the other hand, only a relatively small number were sentenced to prison (80 out of 500). Sometimes, it is easier to see how the units are distributed among the categories if the frequencies are converted into percentages. This is done by dividing each frequency by the total number of units and then multiplying the resulting quotient by 100. Both frequencies and percentages are shown in Table 7.1.

Since percentages are computed from frequencies, they cannot contain any more information than do the frequencies themselves, but they do communicate information in a more standardized form. For example, according to Table 7.1, 62 percent of the convicted felons are given suspended sentences. The earlier observation that 310 of the 500 convicted felons received suspended sentences conveys the same information but in a less readily understood form. Thus, percentages are computed primarily because they communicate findings more quickly and more readily than do frequencies.

Researchers use tables to summarize and communicate quickly certain kinds of information to readers. This way readers can easily grasp what the researchers' body of data is like in terms of the variables being studied. Consider Tables 7.1, 7.2, 7.3, and 7.4.

Table 7.2   Number of White and Nonwhite Convicted Felons in King County Court, Washington, 1973

Race	Frequency	Percent
White	340	68.0%
Nonwhite	160	32.0
Total	500	100.0%

Source: Modification of data in Roy Lotz and John Hewitt, "The Influence of Legally Irrelevant Factors on Felony Sentencing," *Sociological Inquiry* 47, No. 1, pp. 39-48.

By examining these four tables it is possible to get a clear picture of the 500 convicted felons being studied. Table 7.2 reveals that a majority are white (68 percent); and Table 7.4 reveals that most of the convicted felons have from 9 to 12 years of education (71 percent). As was noted earlier from Table 7.1, almost two-thirds of the convicted felons received suspended sentences (62 percent). Hence, the typical convicted felon in King County Court in 1973 was white, a male, had a modest level of education, and received a suspended sentence.

Table 7.3   **Number of Male and Female Convicted Felons in King County Court, Washington, 1973**

Sex	Frequency	Percent
Male	400	80.0%
Female	100	20.0
Total	500	100.0%

Source: Modification of data in Roy Lotz and John Hewitt, "The Influence of Legally Irrelevant Factors on Felony Sentencing," *Sociological Inquiry* 47, No. 1, pp. 39-48.

Table 7.4   **Education of Convicted Felons in King County Court, Washington, 1973**

Years of Education	Frequency	Percent	Cumulative Percent
Less than 8	45	9.0%	9.0%
9 through 11	175	35.0	44.0
12	180	36.0	80.0
13 or More	100	20.0	100.0
Total	500	100.0%	

Source: Modification of data in Roy Lotz and John Hewitt, "The Influence of Legally Irrelevant Factors on Felony Sentencing," *Sociological Inquiry* 47, No. 1, pp. 39-48.

Cumulative Percentages

Sometimes researchers are not interested in knowing the number or percentage of units falling in each category of a table. More specifically, when the variable in the table is measured ordinally or intervally, researchers are often interested in cumulative percentages. *A cumulative percentage is the percentage of units which fall in a given category or any lower category.* Thus, criminologists interested in knowing the percentage of convicted felons with less than a high school education could consult Table 7.4. The cumulative percentage for category "9 through 11" provides the desired information. According to Table 7.4, 44.0 percent of all convicted felons have 9 through 11 or fewer years of education. Similarly, Table 7.4 shows that 80.0 percent of these felons have 12 or fewer years of education.

Other questions of interest to researchers might be addressed using cumulative percentages. For example, a researcher studying sentence severity might want to know the percent of all convicted felons given sentences less severe than imprisonment. According to Table 7.1, in King County, 84.0 percent of all felons studied were given either a jail sentence or a sentence less severe than jail. Similarly, researchers might want to know the percentages of all meals served in a state penitentiary which fall below minimum state quality standards. Cumulative percentages could be used to answer this question.

Fortunately, cumulative percentages are very easy to compute. Cumulative percentages are calculated by merely adding one or more ordinary percentages together. In particular, a given category's cumulative percentage is the sum of the regular percentages associated with that category and all lower categories. Thus, according to Table 7.4, the cumulative percentage for 12 years of education (80.0 percent) is the sum of the percentages of felons with less than 8 years of education (9.0 percent), 9 through 11 years of education (35.0 percent), and 12 years of education (36.0 percent). Hence, once the percentages in a table have been computed, the cumulative percentages can be calculated by just adding the right percentages together.

Notice that cumulative percentages are not presented in Tables 7.2 and 7.3. This is because these two tables involve nominal variables (race and sex, respectively). Since the categories of a nominal variable usually have no inherent order, the percentages associated with those categories should not be summed to form cumulative percentages. Cumulative percentages only make sense for ordinal and interval variables.

Grouped Data

Imagine that the investigators who collected the data in Table 7.1 are especially interested in the 190 convicted felons sentenced to jail or prison. In particular, suppose that they are interested in the ages of these convicted felons. They begin their analysis by constructing Table 7.5 — a frequency distribution of age.

Table 7.5   Ages of Convicted Felons Given Jail or Prison Sentences

Age	Frequency	Percent	Cumulative Percent
17	2	1.05%	1.05%
18	7	3.68	4.73
19	8	4.21	8.94
20	11	5.79	14.73
21	16	8.42	23.15
22	12	6.32	29.47
23	19	10.00	39.47
24	17	8.95	48.42
25	16	8.42	56.84
26	8	4.21	61.05
27	13	6.84	67.89
28	9	4.74	72.63
29	7	3.68	76.31
30	6	3.16	79.47
31	9	4.74	84.21
32	6	3.16	87.37
33	3	1.58	88.95
34	7	3.68	92.63
35	4	2.10	94.73
36	3	1.58	96.31
37	2	1.05	97.36
38	3	1.58	98.94
39	1	.53	99.47
40	0	.00	99.47
41	1	.53	100.00%
Total	190	100.00%	

With 25 categories, Table 7.5 is considerably more ungainly than the tables discussed above. As a result, it is difficult to take in this table merely by examining its frequencies, percentages, and cumulative percentages. There are two ways to overcome this difficulty. First, the data in tables like Table 7.5 can be summarized with statistics. Such summary statistics are the subjects of the following section. Second, researchers can simplify such tables by grouping their categories together into broader categories. For example, the 25 age categories in Table 7.5 could be grouped to form Table 7.6.

Table 7.6   Ages of Convicted Felons Given Jail or Prison Sentences
(Grouped Data)

Age	Frequency	Percent	Cumulative Percent
17 - 19	17	8.95%	8.95%
20 - 24	75	39.47	48.42
25 - 29	53	27.89	76.31
30 - 34	31	16.32	92.63
35 - 39	13	6.84	99.47
40 - 41	1	.53	100.00%
Total	190	100.00%	

Table 7.6 is much easier to understand than Table 7.5. At a glance, Table 7.6 shows that most of these convicted felons are in their twenties and that nearly one-half are less than 25 years old. Grouped data are almost always easier to grasp than ungrouped data.

However, there are some guidelines to follow when grouping data. First, the categories which are to be grouped together must have something in common. With interval variables, such as age in Table 7.5, this poses no problem. By grouping *adjacent* categories, the broader categories which result contain units with similar scores on the interval variable. The same recommendation applies when an ordinal variable is grouped: if adjacent categories are grouped, units which fall into the same broad category will have similar ordinal scores.

The solution is not so simple when a nominal variable is involved since with a nominal variable it makes no sense to talk of *adjacent* categories. Instead, when grouping a nominal variable researchers must decide for themselves which categories they think belong together. For example, Table 7.2 lists only two "races": white and nonwhite. Since the 500 convicted felons studied probably include persons of several races, the data in Table 7.2 are, in fact, grouped data. Thus, the researchers who constructed Table 7.2 must have felt that, among convicted felons in King County, the only significant distinction that needs to be made on the basis of race is between whites and nonwhites. Perhaps they were wrong. In either event, the important point is this: when grouping a nominal variable, researchers must make some assumptions concerning which of the original categories properly belong together.

The second guideline to follow when grouping data only applies to interval variables. When an interval variable is grouped, the broader categories which result are literally "intervals." It is common practice to make these intervals of equal width. Thus, in Table 7.6 the intervals are five years in width (with two exceptions: the first interval is only three years wide and the last is only two years wide). This practice of using intervals of equal width is done so as to avoid inadvertently distorting the data when grouping them. But, there are occasions when this common practice is abandoned. For example, consider Table 7.4. Clearly, this is grouped interval data; yet, the intervals are *not* of equal width. Still, anyone familiar with the system of education in the United States knows why the data in Table 7.4 are grouped this way. These categories correspond to important milestones in educational accomplishment: no high school, some high school, high school graduation, and schooling beyond high school graduation. Whenever there are good, substantive reasons for departing from the practice of equal width intervals, researchers should feel free to group the data in whichever way makes the most sense.

Summary

Since tables are so easy to construct and percentages and cumulative percentages are so easy to compute, it is truly regrettable that researchers make relatively little effective use of them. Instead, researchers tend to present their data in tables, compute some percentages, and then turn to more sophisticated methods of data analysis. Clearly, these more sophisticated methods of analysis have their place. But, so do simple tables and percentages. A series of well constructed tables quickly communicates the number of units which are found in the categories of the variables involved. Percentages identify the relative numbers of units found in the categories. Cumulative percentages indicate the percentages of units falling in, or below, given categories of interval and ordinal variables. Many questions of interest to criminologists can be addressed using such tables and percentages. What percentage of all felonies is reported to the police? Of those reported, what percentage culminates in an arrest? What percentage culminates in an arrest within 24 hours, or one week, or three months? These are important questions and they can be answered without making use of the chi-square test, analysis of variance, or regression analysis. Tables and percentages are often perfectly adequate for the task researchers have in mind. When this is the case, they should be used with confidence.

Bars and Charts

As they examine variables, researchers often find it helpful to make use of graphs and charts. Graphs and charts are based on frequency distributions. The advantage of using graphs and charts is that they display information *visually* and usually visual displays are more easily grasped than are numerical displays, such as tables. Two types of visual displays commonly used are bar graphs and pie charts.

Bar Graphs

A bar graph represents the number of units in a category by the length of a bar. A collection of such bars, each of an appropriate length, constitutes a bar graph. Figure 7.1 is a bar graph for the variable sentence based on Table 7.1.

Figure 7.1   Bar Graph of the Sentences Given Convicted Felons in King County Court, Washington, 1973

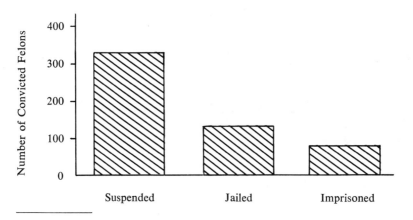

Source: Based on modified data from Roy Lotz and John Hewitt, "The Influence of Legally Irrelevant Factors on Felony Sentencing," *Sociological Inquiry* 47, No. 1, pp. 39-48.

Several things should be noted about this bar graph. First, the number of convicted felons is indicated on the vertical line running along the left side of the bar graph. Second, the bars representing the three categories are all of equal width. Third, the three categories of sentence are arrayed from left to right in the correct order (in a way, sentence is an ordinal variable, with a suspended sentence being the least severe and a prison sentence being the most severe). Fourth, in this bar graph the three bars do not touch each other; they are separated by small spaces. This is done in order to show that the three categories of sentence are also discrete types of sentence and not only different levels of sentence severity. In general, when the variable being graphed is measured at the nominal level, the bars are separated by small spaces to ensure that the categories are perceived as discrete. The bar graph for race, a nominal variable, is shown in Figure 7.2.

Figure 7.2   Bar Graph of the Race of Convicted Felons in King County Court, Washington, 1973

Source: Based on modified data from Roy Lotz and John Hewitt, "The Influence of Legally Irrelevant Factors on Felony Sentencing," *Sociological Inquiry* 47, No. 1, pp. 39-48.

On the other hand, when the variable being graphed is ordinal and researchers want to call attention to the fact that the categories are all ordered along a single continuum, the bars are not separate but abut each other.

When the variable being graphed is measured at the interval level, bar graphs are constructed somewhat differently than described above because the categories of an interval variable are actually intervals. Thus, in Table 7.4 above the first category of education is the interval from zero through eight years; the second category is the interval from nine through 11 years; the third category is 12 years; and the fourth category is the interval of 13 or more years. This affects the construction of bar graphs in two ways as shown in Figure 7.3, a bar graph of Table 7.4.

Figure 7.3   Bar Graph of the Years of Education of Convicted Felons in King County Court, Washington, 1973

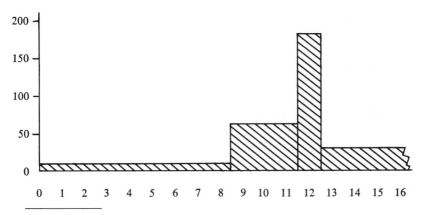

Source: Based on modified data from Roy Lotz and John Hewitt, "The Influence of Legally Irrelevant Factors on Felony Sentencing," *Sociological Inquiry* 47, No. 1, pp. 39-48.

First, the bars are not of equal width; instead, the width of each category's bar is equal to the width of its interval. In this instance, the bar for the first category (which spans nine years) is three times as wide as the bar for the second category (which spans three years) and nine times as wide as the bar for the third category (which spans just one year). Categories of indeterminate width, such as the fourth category, create a problem. A common solution is to draw the bar for this type of category so that readers are alerted to its indeterminate width. In Figure 7.3 this is done by giving the bar an uneven end line to suggest that the bar does not actually end there.

Second, the lengths of the bars are not equal to the number of units in the categories. Instead, the *areas* of bars are equal to the numbers of units in the categories. These bars are actually rectangles and the area of a rectangle is the product of its length and its width ($A = L \cdot W$). Hence, its length is its area divided by its width ($L = A \div W$). Therefore, since the area of each bar is equal to the number of units in its category, the length of each bar is equal to the number of units in its category divided by its width. For example, in Table 7.4 the second and third categories have about the same number of units (175 and 180). However, the second category encompasses three years while the third includes only one year. Thus, in Figure 7.3 the second bar is only about one third as long as the third bar.

Categories of indeterminate width also create a problem. Researchers usually deal with this problem by first estimating the effective width of such an interval and then proceeding as described above. Table 7.4 reveals that 100 convicted felons have 13 or more years of education. In Figure 7.3 the effective width of this fourth category is estimated to be four years (13 through 16 years of education). Therefore, the length of the fourth bar is 100 divided by 4, or 25.

When constructing bar graphs for interval variables, it is essential that researchers adhere to both of these special rules. In particular, if the first rule is followed but the second is not, the resulting bar graph is misleading. This is illustrated in Figure 7.4 which is an *improperly* constructed bar graph for the data in Table 7.4.

Figure 7.4   **Faulty Bar Graph of the Years of Education of Convicted Felons in King County Court, Washington, 1973**

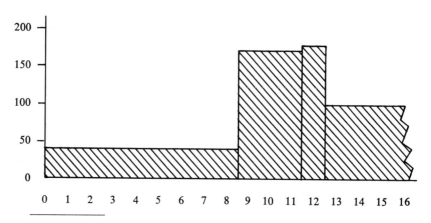

Source: Based on modified data from Roy Lotz and John Hewitt, "The Influence of Legally Irrelevant Factors on Felony Sentencing," *Sociological Inquiry* 47, No. 1, pp. 39-48.

Here the widths of the bars are correct, but the lengths are wrong because they are equal to the numbers of units in the categories. Most people examining Figure 7.4 would probably conclude that there are many felons in the first, the second, and the fourth categories but only a few in the third category. Actually, the exact opposite is nearer to the truth!

Pie Charts

A pie chart looks like a circle divided up into wedge-like segments. The number of segments is equal to the number of categories and the area of each segment is based on the percentage of all units which fall in its category. For example, Figure 7.5 is a pie chart for the variable of race based on Table 7.2.

Figure 7.5   Pie Chart of the Race of Convicted Felons in King County Court, Washington, 1973

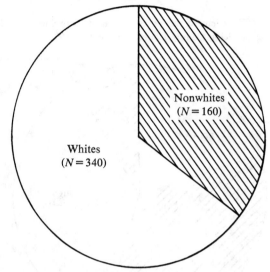

Source: Based on modified data from Roy Lotz and John Hewitt, "The Influence of Legally Irrelevant Factors on Felony Sentencing," *Sociological Inquiry* 47, No. 1, pp. 39-48.

According to Table 7.2, 68 percent of the convicted felons were whites and 32 percent of them were nonwhites. Analogously, the circle in Figure 7.5 is divided so that 68 percent of its area is labeled "whites" and 32 percent of its area is labeled "nonwhites." Thus, the basic idea behind a pie chart is very simple.

When constructing pie charts, researchers have the option of using either percentages or frequencies or both. Thus, rather than listing the frequencies of whites and nonwhites, as in Figure 5.5, it is quite acceptable to list the percentages of whites and nonwhites instead.

Pie charts have one major strength and one major weakness. Their strength is that they make it easy to see how the several categories add up to a single whole. This is because a pie chart begins as a whole (a circle) which is then divided into parts which, when combined, once again form a circle. A bar graph does not illustrate this wholeness. Figure 7.5 shows how the 160 nonwhites and 340 whites, when added together, constitute the total of 500 convicted felons. The analogous bar graph, Figure 7.2, does not illustrate this point as well.

The major weakness of pie charts is that they do not convey any sense of dimensionality among the categories. When investigators want to convey the sense that the several categories are ordered along a single dimension, they use a bar graph (with bars abutting each other as in Figure 7.3). Figure 7.6 is a pie chart for the variable of education based on Table 7.4.

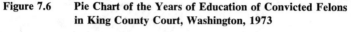

Figure 7.6   Pie Chart of the Years of Education of Convicted Felons in King County Court, Washington, 1973

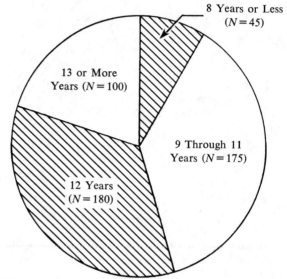

Source: Based on modified data from Roy Lotz and John Hewitt, "The Influence of Legally Irrelevant Factors on Felony Sentencing," *Sociological Inquiry* 47, No. 1, pp. 39-48.

Notice that Figure 7.6 does not clearly imply that the first category (eight years or less) precedes the second category (nine through 11 years) which precedes the third category (12 years) and so on. The bar graph does illustrate this continuum.

Properly constructed bar graphs and pie charts frequently communicate findings more readily than do either lengthy explanations or tables. Today, with the availability of computers, researchers are tempted to rely on tables and, especially, statistics. Although it is hard to imagine what criminology would be like without data tables and statistics, it is important that researchers not overlook these ways to visually summarize data.

Statistics

Just as bar graphs and pie charts are visual summaries of a data set, so are statistics numerical summaries of a data set. What visual displays do with graphics, statistics do with numbers. Ordinarily, when researchers perform univariate analysis (i.e., examine their variables one at a time), they compute three types of statistics for each variable: (1) measures of central tendency, (2) measures of dispersion, and (3) measures of skewness. In the remainder of this chapter, these three types of summary statistics are discussed.

Measures of Central Tendency

Researchers often want to know the single value, or category, which best represents the entire frequency distribution; that is, they want to know the single value which is most common, or is in the middle of the frequency distribution. There are three commonly used methods for identifying, or measuring, this representative value. These three methods are called measures of central tendency.

The Mode. The mode (denoted Mo) is the most frequently occurring category in a distribution. Researchers identify the mode by simply scanning a frequency distribution to find the category or interval with the most units in it. In Table 7.5 the modal age is 23 since 19 of the convicted felons are 23 years old.

As a measure of central tendency, the mode has a number of advantages and disadvantages. The first advantage is that the mode is very easy to determine. A second advantage is that the mode can be determined for any type of variable: nominal and ordinal, as well as interval. The mode of race in Table 7.2 (a nominal variable) is "white" since 340 is greater than 160. The mode of sentence severity in Table 7.1 (an ordinal variable) is "suspended" since 310 is greater than both 110 and 80.

The major disadvantage of the mode as a measure of central tendency is that it is not necessarily representative of the rest of the frequency distribution. In Table 7.5 the modal category (23) contains only 10 percent of the units (19 out of 190). In general, if a variable has many different categories, it is possible for the modal category to contain only a small percentage of the total number of units while the rest of the units are scattered among the remaining categories. The only solution to this problem is to group the categories into a smaller number of broader categories as discussed above. For example, in Table 7.6 the modal age category is "20-24," with 75 of the 190 units in it. This amounts to nearly 40 percent of the units which is much better than the 10 percent in the original modal category.

Unfortunately, there are two problems with this solution. First, there are always several ways that a given set of categories can be collapsed. For example, the 25 age categories in Table 7.5 could be collapsed into just four categories: (1) 17-19, (2) 20-29, (3) 30-39, and (4) 40-41. These categories make as much sense as those found in Table 7.6.

The way the categories are grouped clearly affects the mode. A reported mode depends in part on decisions about grouping made by researchers. Second, grouping categories produces broader categories, including the modal category. A broad modal category is necessarily less informative than a narrower modal category. For example, a modal category of 23 years is more precise than a modal category of 20 through 24 years. When categories are grouped, information is lost. This is inevitable. Thus, some research might require using the ungrouped data in Table 7.5.

The Median. The median (denoted Md) is the value which divides the upper one half of a frequency distribution from the lower one half. It is the middle value. Thus, the median assumes that it is possible to rank the units from highest to lowest. This means that the data must be measured at least at the ordinal level of measurement.

In principle, the median is easy to compute. First, the units are ranked from highest to lowest. After this is done, the value in the middle of this ranked list is found. This value is the median. In practice, computing the median this way gets a bit tedious. When there are many units, ranking them all from highest to lowest takes a great deal of time. But, when the data are arranged in a frequency distribution, then the median is simple to compute.

The median is the middle value, the value which divides the frequency distribution into two exact halves. Fifty percent of the units have lower values than the median and 50 percent have higher values than the median. Thus, the median value in a frequency distribution is the value whose cumulative percentage is 50. For example, according to Table 7.5 the group of felons who are 24 or younger constitutes 48.42 percent of the 190 felons studied. The median age, then, must be greater than 24. However, if all 16 felons age 25 are included, the resulting group would constitute 56.84 percent of the total. Therefore, it is one of these 25 year old felons which divides the frequency distribution into two exact halves. Hence, the median is 25 years. This is illustrated in Figure 7.7.

Figure 7.7   Computing the Median for the Age of Convicted Felons: An Illustration

		The Median — 50.00%		
Cumulative Percentage	39.47%	48.42%	56.84%	
Frequency	19 Felons	17 Felons	16 Felons	8 Felons
Age	23	24	25	26

Md = 25 Years of Age

In a similar way, the median educational level of the convicted felons shown in Table 7.4 is computed in Figure 7.8.

Figure 7.8   Computing the Median for the Years of Education of Convicted Felons: An Illustration

	The Median — 50.0%		
Cumulative Percentage	9.0%	44.0%	80.0%
Frequency	45 Felons	175 Felons	180 Felons	100 Felons
Years of Education	8 or Less	9 Through 11	12	13 or More

Md = 12 Years of Education

Here the median educational level is 12 years. Of course, it is not necessary to construct diagrams like Figures 7.7 and 7.8 in order to identify the median. It can be identified by just looking at the column of cumulative percentages in Table 7.4. The median is the lowest value or category whose cumulative percentage equals or exceeds 50 percent.

The Mean. The most commonly used measure of central tendency is the mean. It is the sum of all the values divided by the number of units. The formula for the mean (designated $\overline{X}$) is:

$$\overline{X} = \frac{\Sigma X}{N}$$

where: $\overline{X}$ = the mean
  N = the number of units
  X = the value of any unit
  ΣX = the sum of the values of the units

When the data are presented in a frequency distribution, a different formula is used to compute the mean:

$$\overline{X} = \frac{\Sigma(f \cdot X)}{N}$$

where: X = the value of any given category
  f = the number of units in any given category

The first formula calls for adding up all of the values. For the data in Table 7.5 this entails adding two 17s, seven 18s, eight 19s, and so on. The second formula produces the same results by multiplying 2 times 17, adding the result to the product of 7 and 18, adding this result to the product of 8 and 19, and so on. The final results are identical. The mean age of the convicted felons is 25.76. This is computed in Figure 7.9.

Since computing the mean involves adding up the values, these values must be numbers. Hence, the data must be at the interval level in order for the mean to be used. Looking at Table 7.1 it would be absurd to try to add suspended sentences to jail sentences to prison sentences so that the mean severity of sentence could be calculated.

Figure 7.9   Computing the Mean Age of Convicted Felons

$$X = \text{Age} \qquad f = \text{Frequency}$$

Step 1: Prepare the data

X	f	$f \cdot X$
17	2	34
18	7	126
19	8	152
20	11	220
21	16	336
22	12	264
23	19	437
24	17	408
25	16	400
26	8	208
27	13	351
28	9	252
29	7	203
30	6	180
31	9	279
32	6	192
33	3	99
34	7	238
35	4	140
36	3	108
37	2	74
38	3	114
39	1	39
41	1	41
	$N = 190$	$\Sigma\,(f \cdot X) = 4895$

Step 2: Compute the mean

The computational formula:

$$\overline{X} = \frac{\Sigma\,(f \cdot X)}{N}$$

By substitution:

$$\overline{X} = \frac{4895}{190}$$
$$= 25.76$$

When the data in a table are visually displayed in a bar graph, the mode, the median and the mean have geometric interpretations. Many researchers find that these geometric interpretations make it easier to understand the particular strengths and weaknesses of the three measures of central tendency.

Geometric Interpretations for the Mode, the Median, and the Mean. Figure 7.10 is a bar graph of the age of convicted felons as found in Table 7.5.

The mode, the median, and the mean have unique geometric interpretations when the data are displayed in a bar graph such as Figure 7.10. The mode is the category, or value, with the longest bar.[1] In Figure 7.10 the mode is easily identified as 23 years since the bar directly above 23 is taller (longer) than any other in the bar graph.

The median is the value which divides the entire area under the bar graph into two equal halves. Figure 7.10 illustrates that the median is not sensitive to the shape of the bar graph or frequency distribution. The median simply divides the older half of the group of felons from the younger half. But, the median does not depend upon the actual ages of either half.[2] For example, according to Table 7.5, there are two 17 year old felons and seven 18 year old felons. If all nine of these felons were, instead, 17 years old, the median would still be 25 years. The fact that the median does not depend upon the actual values in a frequency distribution, but only upon their rank, is a strength in some circumstances and a weakness in others. (This issue is discussed later in this chapter.)

The mean has a geometric interpretation, too. Suppose that someone made a model of the bar graph in Figure 7.10 by cutting a flat piece of wood in just the right shape. If criminologists take this wooden bar graph and balance it along its base (the straight side), they will find that the balance point is at 25.76 years — the mean. If they try to balance the model at some point below the mean, say 25, the right side of the model will outweigh the left side and the model will not balance properly. In a sense, the mean is the balance point, or center of gravity, of a frequency distribution. Clearly, then, the mean does depend upon the actual values of the units. For example, if the seven 18 year old felons in Table 7.5 were actually 17, the mean would not be 25.76 years. Therefore, the mean differs from the median in this respect. The mean does depend upon the actual values in a frequency distribution and not on only their rank.

Measures of Dispersion

Suppose that researchers are studying changes in the incidence of index crimes in two cities. They are doing an aggregate data study with

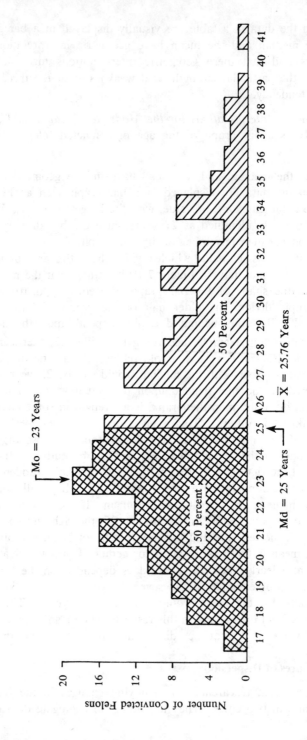

Figure 7.10   Geometric Interpretations of the Mode, the Median, and the Mean

police precincts as the units of analysis. For each precinct, they determine the percentage increase in the number of index crimes over a one year period. Table 7.7 contains the frequency distributions of the increase in index crimes for both of the cities studied.

Table 7.7   Percentage Increase of Index Crime in Two Cities

Percentage Increase	City A		City B	
	Frequency	Percentage	Frequency	Percentage
−2	0	0.00%	1	2.22%
−1	0	0.00	0	0.00
0	0	0.00	1	2.22
1	0	0.00	1	2.22
2	0	0.00	2	4.44
3	0	0.00	1	2.22
4	0	0.00	0	0.00
5	0	0.00	1	2.22
6	1	4.34	4	8.90
7	0	0.00	2	4.44
8	2	8.70	4	8.90
9	7	30.44	3	6.67
10	7	30.44	3	6.67
11	2	8.70	5	11.10
12	1	4.34	2	4.44
13	1	4.34	1	2.22
14	2	8.70	3	6.67
15	0	0.00	4	8.90
16	0	0.00	3	6.67
17	0	0.00	1	2.22
18	0	0.00	2	4.44
19	0	0.00	0	0.00
20	0	0.00	1	2.22
Total	23	100.00%	45	100.00%

The mean increase for both cities is 10 percent, so the two cities appear to be similar in terms of the increase in index crimes. However, a closer look at Table 7.7 shows that the cities differ significantly, too. In City A, most precincts (19 out of 23) experienced an 8 to 12 percent increase in the number of index crimes. In City B the precincts varied widely in the percentage increase in the number of index crimes. In effect, City A is internally rather homogeneous in this respect while City B is internally heterogeneous. Some statistic is needed which measures this variation or dispersion. Three measures of dispersion are discussed here: the range, the interquartile range, and the standard deviation.

The Range. The range is simply the highest score minus the lowest score. Thus, in City A the range, (denoted Rg) is:

$$Rg = 14 - 6$$
$$= 8$$

In City B, the range is:

$$Rg = 20 - (-2)$$
$$= 22$$

The range shows that the percentage increases in the number of index crimes are more widely dispersed in City B than in City A.

Although the range is easy to compute, it suffers from one major drawback: it is very sensitive to just a few extreme scores. Suppose that City A has 24 precincts rather than 23 and that the increase in index crimes for this additional precinct is 28 percent. The range for City A, then, is also 22 ($28 - 6 = 22$), even though just one additional value is added to the frequency distribution. The interquartile range is designed to deal with this shortcoming.

The Interquartile Range. The interquartile range (denoted IQR) is the range of the middle 50 percent of the values in a frequency distribution. It is computed in this way. First, the value which divides the highest 25 percent of the values from the lowest 75 percent is identified. This value is called the third quartile (denoted Q_3). Then the value which divides the highest 75 percent of the values from the lowest 25 percent is identified. It is called the first quartile (denoted Q_1). The interquartile range is the difference between the third quartile and the first quartile.

$$IQR = Q_3 - Q_1$$

This is illustrated in Figure 7.11.

Figure 7.11   Rationale for the Interquartile Range

Interquartile Range (IQR) = Range of the Middle 50 Percent = $Q_3 - Q_1$

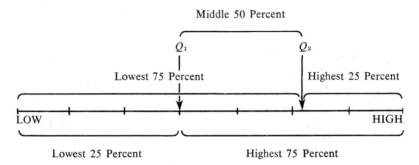

The third and first quartiles are easily identified in a table of cumulative percentages. The third quartile is the lowest value whose cumulative percentage equals or exceeds 75 percent. The first quartile is the lowest value whose cumulative percentage equals or exceeds 25 percent. The cumulative percentages for City A and City B, based on Table 7.7, are found in Table 7.8.

Looking first at the figures for City A, according to Table 7.8 the first quartile, or Q_1, is 9. Among the precincts, 13.04 percent have an increase of 8 percent or less while 43.48 percent of the precincts have an increase of 9 percent or less. One of the precincts having a 9 percent increase divides the lowest 25 percent of the precincts from the highest 75 percent. The third quartile (Q_3) for City A is 11. Thus the interquartile range for City A is:

$$IQR = 11 - 9$$
$$= 2$$

The first and third quartiles for City B are: $Q_1 = 7$ and $Q_3 = 14$. Hence the interquartile range for City B is:

$$IQR = 14 - 7$$
$$= 7$$

According to the interquartile range, the dispersion among precinct percentage increases in index crimes for City B is three and one-half times as large as that for City A.

The interquartile range is not affected by a few extreme values. This is because it measures the range of the middle 50 percent of the values

Table 7.8   Cumulative Percentages of the Percentage Increase of Index
             Crime in Two Cities

Percentage Increase	City A	City B
−2	0.00%	2.22%
−1	0.00	2.22
0	0.00	4.44
1	0.00	6.66
2	0.00	11.10
3	0.00	13.32
4	0.00	13.32
5	0.00	15.54
6	4.34	24.44
7	4.34	28.88
8	13.04	37.78
9	43.48	44.45
10	73.92	51.12
11	82.62	62.22
12	86.96	66.66
13	91.30	68.88
14	100.00	75.55
15	100.00	84.45
16	100.00	91.12
17	100.00	93.34
18	100.00	97.78
19	100.00	97.78
20	100.00	100.00

in frequency distribution. The actual values of those units which are not
in the middle 50 percent make absolutely no difference. For example, if
one of the two precincts in City A which experienced a 14 percent increase
in the number of index crimes actually experienced a 100 percent increase instead, the interquartile range would still be 2 because the first and
third quartiles would stay the same.

Some researchers believe that the interquartile range is too narrow
a measure, looking only at the middle half of the frequency distribution.

But there is nothing sacred about 50 percent. If researchers think that looking at just the middle 50 percent is too narrow, they can compute the range of the middle 60 percent of the values in a frequency distribution or they can compute the range of the middle 70 percent or 80 percent of the values. As the size of the "middle" of the frequency distribution increases from 50 to 60 to 70 to 80 percent, the chance increases that the value of the range which results is influenced by a small number of extreme values.

The Standard Deviation. Since the range and the interquartile range both involve the operation of subtraction, they can be computed only for interval variables, such as the variable of age in Table 7.5. For interval variables it is also possible to compute a much more widely used measure of dispersion: the standard deviation.

With an interval variable (X), it is possible to compute the difference between each value in a frequency distribution and the mean of the distribution: $X - \overline{X}$. This is done for the data given in Table 7.7 for City A only, and shown in Figure 7.12, step 1, column 2.

These differences are the basis for computing the standard deviation.

Since the goal is to determine how dispersed, or spread out, the values in a frequency distribution are, some students might think that the solution is to simply average these differences. Intuitively, this certainly makes sense. If the average difference is small, most of the values in the frequency distribution must be close to the mean. If the average difference is large, at least some of the values must be a good distance from the mean. Common sense and intuition both seem to commend the average difference as a measure of dispersion.

Unfortunately, the average difference is useless for this purpose because the average of the differences between the values in a frequency distribution and the mean is always zero. Here is how this works. Regardless of whether most values in a frequency distribution are close to the mean (as in City A) or many values are distant from the mean (as in City B), some of the differences are negative and some are positive. When added together, these negative and positive differences cancel each other out. Their sum is zero. If most of the values are close to the mean, both negative and positive differences are small in magnitude. Still, they add to zero. Similarly, if many of the values are distant from the mean, many negative and positive differences are large in magnitude but they add to zero, too. Because the mean is the balance point of a frequency distribution, it always turns out that the sum of the differences between the values and the mean is zero. Hence, the average difference is always exactly equal to zero.

Figure 7.12   Computing the Mean Deviation and the Standard Deviation

Step 1: Prepare the data

X = percentage increase in index crime in the 23 precincts of City A
$\overline{X}$ = 10 percent

X	$X - \overline{X}$	$|X - \overline{X}|$	$(X - \overline{X})^2$
6	−4	4	16
8	−2	2	4
8	−2	2	4
9	−1	1	1
9	−1	1	1
9	−1	1	1
9	−1	1	1
9	−1	1	1
9	−1	1	1
9	−1	1	1
10	0	0	0
10	0	0	0
10	0	0	0
10	0	0	0
10	0	0	0
10	0	0	0
10	0	0	0
11	1	1	1
11	1	1	1
12	2	2	4
13	3	3	9
14	4	4	16
14	4	4	16
$\Sigma = 230$	0	30	78

Step 2: Compute MD

The computational formula: By substitution:

$$MD = \frac{\Sigma |X - \overline{X}|}{N}$$ $$MD = \frac{30}{23}$$

$$= 1.30$$

Figure 7.12   (Continued)

Step 3: Compute SD

The computational formula:

$$SD = \sqrt{\Sigma (X - \overline{X})^2 / N}$$

By substitution:

$$SD = \sqrt{78/23} \cong \sqrt{3.39}$$
$$\cong 1.84$$

If the trouble with the average difference is that the negative and positive differences cancel out, one solution is to take these differences, ignore their signs, and average their magnitudes. This new statistic is called the mean deviation (denoted MD). The formula for MD is:

$$MD = \frac{\Sigma |X - \overline{X}|}{N}$$

The vertical lines denote the absolute value operator, and they indicate that the signs of the differences $(X - \overline{X})$ are to be ignored. The mean deviation for City A is computed in Figure 7.12, steps 1 and 2. In City A, MD = 1.30. The average percentage increase in index crimes in the 23 precincts of City A is 10 percent and the average dispersion around the mean of 10 percent is 1.30 percent. Clearly, the percentage increase in index crime in most of the precincts is close to the mean increase of 10 percent.

The mean deviation has much to commend it as a measure of dispersion. First, it is easy to compute. Only three operations are required: subtraction, addition, and division. Second, it has an easy-to-understand interpretation. The mean deviation is the average of the deviations from the mean. It is literally the average deviation. Yet even with these strengths, the mean deviation is almost never used as a measure of dispersion. Instead, the standard deviation (denoted SD) is used even though it is not as easy to compute or interpret as the mean deviation. In a way, learning to understand the standard deviation is like making an investment. Any hardship encountered in the short run is more than made up by payoffs accruing in the long run.

Computing the Standard Deviation. The average difference is useless as a measure of dispersion because the negative differences from the mean exactly balance the positive differences so that their sum is always zero. The mean deviation (MD) deals with this problem by ignoring the minus signs and averaging the resulting deviations from the mean. The standard deviation sidesteps the minus signs by squaring all of the differences (e.g., Figure 7.12, step 1, column 4). The mean of these squared deviations is called the variance (denoted SD^2):

$$SD^2 = \frac{\Sigma (X - \overline{X})^2}{N}$$

The square root of the variance is the standard deviation (SD):

$$SD = \sqrt{\Sigma(X - \overline{X})^2/N}$$

Notice that the standard deviation is not that difficult to compute. It requires the following operations: subtracting, squaring, adding, dividing, and taking the square root. First, the mean is subtracted from each of the values (Figure 7.12, step 1, column 2). Then, these differences are squared and the squares added up (column 4). This sum is then divided by the number of values (N) to produce the variance (step 3). Finally, the standard deviation is computed by taking the square root of the variance (step 3).

When the data are given in a frequency distribution, the standard deviation is computed differently. Figure 7.13 shows how the standard deviation for City A is computed using this different formula.

Figure 7.13   Computing the Standard Deviation from a Frequency Distribution

Step 1: Prepare the data

X = percentage increases in index crime in the 23 precincts in City A
$\overline{X}$ = 10 percent

Percentage Increase (X)	Frequency (f)	$X - \overline{X}$	$(X - \overline{X})^2$	$f(X - \overline{X})^2$
6	1	-4	16	16
8	2	-2	4	8
9	7	-1	1	7
10	7	0	0	0
11	2	1	1	2
12	1	2	4	4
13	1	3	9	9
14	2	4	16	32
	$\Sigma = 23$			$\Sigma = 78$

Step 2: Compute SD

The computational formula:

$$SD = \sqrt{\Sigma f(X - \overline{X})^2/N}$$

By substitution:

$$SD = \sqrt{78/23} \cong \sqrt{3.39}$$
$$\cong 1.84$$

Comparing Figure 7.13 with Figure 7.12 demonstrates that the two formulas always produce the same result. For example, consider the seven precincts which experienced a nine percent increase in index crime. In Figure 7.12, the squared deviation of each such precinct is calculated separately, although the same result is arrived at each time! These seven results are then added together with the squared deviations of the other 16 precincts. In Figure 7.13, the squared deviation for the seven precincts is only calculated once and is then multiplied by seven before it is added to the squared deviation of the other 16 precincts. The two results must be the same.

Interpreting the Standard Deviation. The standard deviation is often interpreted as if it were the mean deviation; that is, the standard deviation frequently is interpreted as the average deviation from the mean. Based on Figure 7.13 it might be asserted that among the 23 precincts in City A the average percentage increase in index crime is 10 percent and the average deviation from this mean is 1.84 percent. Although this interpretation of the standard deviation is not literally correct, it is quite common. As long as researchers are aware that this usage is only approximately correct, little harm is done. Interpreting the standard deviation for what it actually is — the square root of the average squared deviation from the mean — is far too awkward.

When two frequency distributions are being examined, the standard deviation is used to compare the dispersion among the values in the two distributions. For example, the standard deviation for the increase in index crime in City A is 1.84. According to Figure 7.13, the standard deviation for the same variable in City B is 5.13. Clearly, then, there is much more variation among the precincts in City B in terms of the increase in index crime than is the case in City A. Most precincts in City A have a percentage increase close to the mean, 10 percent, but in City B a good many precincts have increases either less than the mean or more than the mean. This is the sort of finding that interests researchers.

Review. Look at Figure 7.14, which contains the range, the interquartile range, and the standard deviation of the percentage increases in index crime in City A and City B.

Figure 7.14   The Range, Interquartile Range, and Standard Deviation for City A and City B

	Range	Interquartile Range	Standard Deviation
City A	8	2	1.84
City B	22	7	5.13

All three statistics tell much the same story: the dispersion in City B is about three times as great as that in City A. The greater dispersion in City B is easily seen by examining bar graphs for both cities, as shown in Figure 7.15.

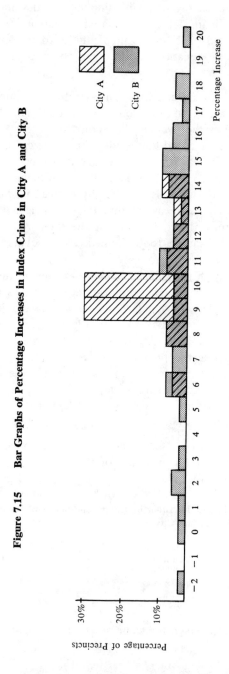

Figure 7.15   Bar Graphs of Percentage Increases in Index Crime in City A and City B

The bar graph for City A (lined in) shows that the percentage increases for most precincts are tightly clustered around 10 percent. The bar graph for City B (shaded in) is much wider and flatter, showing that in City B the percentage increases in index crime are much more widely dispersed.

All three of the measures of dispersion discussed in this chapter can be used only with interval variables. This is because there exist no generally accepted measures of dispersion for either nominal or ordinal variables. All too often, the most sophisticated statistical methods are based on demanding assumptions, one of which is that all variables be intervally measured.

Measures of Skewness

With interval variables, univariate statistical analysis goes beyond measures of central tendency and dispersion. Specifically, with an interval variable, investigators can measure how skewed the frequency distribution is. A skewed frequency distribution is one where there are many more extreme values in one direction than the other. A frequency distribution is said to be positively skewed if there are many more very large values than very small values. Figure 7.16 is a bar graph of a positively skewed frequency distribution.

Notice that most values are between 18 and 32, but outside this interval there are many more relatively high values (over 32) than there are relatively low values (under 18). That is why the frequency distribution upon which Figure 7.16 is based is called positively skewed. On the other hand, a frequency distribution is called negatively skewed if there are many more very small values than very large values.

The measure of skewness discussed here is based on the above mentioned fact that the mean of a frequency distribution depends upon the actual values in the distribution whereas the median depends only upon their rank order. If the large values in a frequency distribution are extremely large, the mean (being affected by these extremely large values) will be relatively large, but the median will not. On the other hand, if the small values in a distribution are extremely small, the mean will be relatively small while the median will not be affected. Therefore, with a positively skewed frequency distribution the mean is larger than the median, as in Figure 7.16. In a negatively skewed distribution, the mean is smaller than the median.

Based on this rationale, the skewness of a frequency distribution (denoted SK) is measured as follows:

$$SK = \frac{3(\overline{X} - Md)}{SD}$$

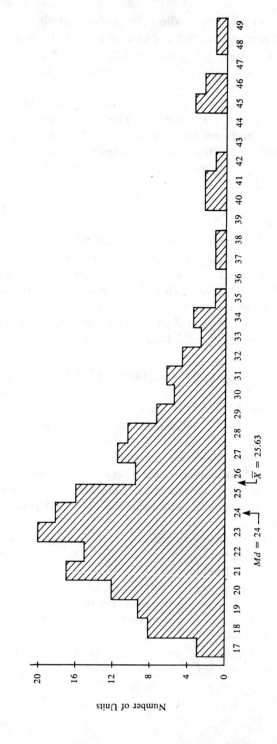

Figure 7.16   Bar Graph of a Positively Skewed Frequency Distribution

When a frequency distribution is positively skewed, the mean exceeds the median and SK is a positive number. For example, the mean, the median, and the standard deviation of the frequency distribution upon which Figure 7.16 is based are:

$$\overline{X} = 25.63$$
$$Md = 24$$
$$SD = 6.36$$

hence,

$$SK = \frac{3(25.63 - 24)}{6.36} = \frac{4.89}{6.36} = .77$$

When a distribution is negatively skewed, the median exceeds the mean and SK is a negative number. The sign of the skewness measure (SK) indicates if the frequency distribution is negatively or positively skewed while the magnitude of the skewness measure indicates the amount of skewness present.

A Note on the Median and the Mean. The fact that the mean and the median are quite different from one another when the frequency distribution is skewed is a very important point. When a frequency distribution is skewed, researchers often prefer to use the median, rather than the mean, as a measure of central tendency. This is because the value of the mean is greatly affected by the presence of a few scores in the distribution. Under these circumstances, the median is a more representative value. This is the exceptional case. Ordinarily, the mean is preferred to the median as a measure of central tendency. The mean of a frequency distribution depends on the actual values in the distribution. In other words, the mean is based on all the information that researchers have concerning the frequency distribution. The median depends only upon the rank order of the values, not upon the actual numerical values themselves. In effect, the median ignores the actual values and takes notice only of their rank order. As a general rule, researchers prefer to use statistics which take full advantage of the data that they have collected.

Summary

In this chapter little mention is made of the source of the data being analyzed. This is perfectly appropriate. The methods of analysis discussed in this chapter can be applied to various kinds of data. Frequently, the data criminologists examine are samples from some larger population. This does not affect the methods of analysis discussed here. One can still construct tables, draw graphs, and compute and interpret statistics. But when interest centers not on the sample but on the population, sample percentages and means are of little intrinsic interest. It is the population percentages and means about which one wants to learn something. In the next two chapters, methods will be presented for dealing with these topics.

Notes

[1]When each bar corresponds to an interval rather than a discrete category, the modal category is the bar with the greatest *area*. For an example of this type of bar graph, see Figure 7.5.

[2]Actually, the median does depend on some of the ages — but only to a very limited degree. When there is an even number of units as in this example (N = 190), the median is the average of the scores (in this case, ages) of the two middle units. Thus, its value clearly depends on the scores of those two units. When there is an odd number of units, the median is the score of the middle unit and, thus, depends upon the actual score of that unit.

Review Questions

1. Explain the meaning and significance of the following terms and ideas:
   a. Frequency distribution
   b. Bar graph
   c. Pie chart
   d. Measures of central tendency: mode, median, and mean
   e. Measures of dispersion: range, interquartile range, and standard deviation
   f. Measures of skewness
2. Suppose criminologists gather sample data on the disposition times (in days) of 50 court cases, as follows: 64, 56, 17, 38, 125, 94, 78, 101, 71, 63, 65, 58, 49, 111, 88, 70, 51, 61, 80, 67, 53, 74, 73, 29, 64, 48, 117, 98, 78, 67, 65, 76, 59, 50, 65, 89, 43, 58, 74, 68, 65, 98, 91, 66, 103, 64, 69, 86, 63, 74.
   a. Construct a frequency distribution using intervals of a width you deem appropriate.
   b. Draw a bar graph or pie chart of the frequency distribution.
   c. Compute the mode, median, mean, range, interquartile range, and standard deviation.
   d. In your own words, describe this data set using your answers to parts a, b, and c to support your description.

3. Why is the median sometimes preferred to the mean even though the data involved are intervally measured?

4. Since graphs, charts, and univariate statistics are all based on frequency distributions, why not just rely on the latter? What is to be gained by using graphs, charts, and univariate statistics to describe a data set?

Chapter 8
One-Sample Tests

Learning Objectives

After completing this chapter, the reader should be able to:

1. State the purpose for which one-sample tests are used
2. Determine which one-sample test to use
3. Set up the nondirectional and the directional hypotheses employed in one-sample tests
4. Conduct one-sample mean tests: z tests and t tests
5. Conduct a one-sample median test

Introduction

Investigators frequently want to know if the performance of those in some group exceeds or falls short of a given standard. For example, a sheriff may want to know if the meals offered in the county jail meet state quality standards, or a judge's clerk might wonder how the case disposition times in one courtroom compare to the average for all courtrooms in the same county. Perhaps a county prosecutor might want to know whether his conviction rate is less than, equal to, or greater than the average for all the county's prosecutors. All of these criminal justice actors confront the same problem. In each instance, they want to know how some group "measures up" when compared to an externally established standard. All three questions can be answered by using the same statistical methods: one-sample tests of significance.

One-sample tests are used to compare some population statistic (say, a mean) with a hypothesized value. For instance, the quality of meals served at the county jail can be compared with a certain state quality standard; the mean disposition time for cases in one courtroom can be compared to the mean disposition time for the entire jurisdiction; or one prosecutor's conviction rate can be compared to the county-wide average.

When it is possible to collect the necessary information for the entire population (i.e., *all* meals or *all* cases), then the statistic can be computed and the comparison made. However, this is rarely possible. When it is not possible, or advisable, to gather information for the entire population, it is necessary to draw a sample, compute a *sample* statistic, and then make the comparison. This is where one-sample tests can be used.

Because of chance, no *sample* statistic can be an exact estimate of its corresponding *population* statistic. Even if the population statistic is equal to the hypothesized value, mere computation of a *sample* statistic cannot be expected to demonstrate this. However, the greater the difference between a statistic based on a simple random sample and this hypothesized value, the more suspicious one becomes about that hypothesized value. For example, a court clerk might hypothesize that the mean disposition time for cases from the courtroom is 61.5 days, the county average. If a simple random sample of 50 cases is drawn from the courtroom docket and a mean disposition time of 67.3 days is found, the clerk might well be content. However, if the sample mean is 88.4 days, the clerk will most likely reject the original hypothesis. Similarly, a sheriff might initially think (hypothesize) that the diet served inmates at the county jail meets the state requirement of a daily intake of 3000 calories. If daily diets for a sample of 35 days show an average intake of 1900 calories, the sheriff might reconsider. The two factors which produce conclusions like those finally reached by the clerk and the sheriff are: (1) the disparity between the hypothesized value of the population statistic and the observed value of the sample statistic, and (2) a judgment that this disparity is too great to be due to chance.[1] One-sample tests enable investigators to reach such conclusions scientifically.

One-Sample Mean Test

The most commonly used one-sample test is the *mean test*. This test concerns a single population. It tests the hypothesis that the population mean equals a given value by comparing this hypothesized value to the mean of a random sample drawn from that population. Since this test requires the calculation of a sample mean, the data must be measured at the interval or ratio level.

A Nondirectional Test

The one-sample mean test can be conducted as a nondirectional test or a directional test. If a nondirectional test is conducted, the null hypothesis *always* asserts that the population mean is equal to some particular value, say, *v* (for *v*alue). The research hypothesis always asserts the opposite — that the population mean is *not* equal to *v*. Statistically, this is written:

$$H_o: \mu = v$$
$$H_a: \mu \neq v$$

Where: μ = the actual population mean

v = the hypothesized value of the population mean

It is very important to realize that *v* is *not* computed as part of the one-sample mean test. It is given, or assumed, from the beginning.

Recall the illustration of the court clerk. Imagine that the annual report of the county court administrator shows an average case disposition time of 61.5 days for all courtrooms in that jurisdiction. If the court clerk is merely curious about how well the case docket is being managed in the courtroom, a nondirectional one-sample mean test might be conducted. Such a test would be set up as follows:

$$H_o: \mu = 61.5$$
$$H_a: \mu \neq 61.5$$

Where: μ = the mean case disposition time for *all* cases docketed in the clerk's courtroom.

In this example, if the mean case disposition time for a *sample* of cases from the clerk's courtroom docket greatly exceeds *or* falls short of 61.5, the null hypothesis is rejected in favor of the research hypothesis. If the sample mean is greatly different from 61.5, it is likely that the population mean is not equal to 61.5. Hence, with a nondirectional one-sample mean test the critical region is divided equally between the two tails of the sampling distribution as shown in Figure 8.1.

Figure 8.1   Court Clerk's Sampling Distribution when Conducting a Nondirectional Test

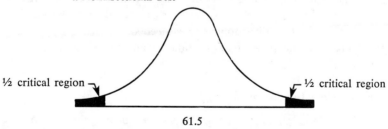

½ critical region

½ critical region

61.5

For this reason, nondirectional tests are sometimes called *two-tailed tests*.

A Directional Test

On the other hand, the court clerk might be solely interested in demonstrating that the mean case disposition time in the courtroom does not *exceed* the overall average (61.5 days). In this instance, a directional test is used. Such a test would be set up as follows:

$$H_o: \mu \leq 61.5$$

$$H_a: \mu > 61.5$$

If the sample mean case disposition time greatly exceeds 61.5, the null hypothesis is rejected in favor of the directional alternative hypothesis. A sample mean much larger than 61.5 suggests that the population mean is also larger than 61.5. If the sample mean falls short of 61.5 by a substantial amount, the null hypothesis is left undisturbed. This is because a sample mean smaller than 61.5 is not at all inconsistent with *this* null hypothesis. Thus, the critical region is concentrated in just the positive tail of the sampling distribution as shown in Figure 8.2. Directional tests are sometimes called *one-tailed tests*.

Figure 8.2   Court Clerk's Sampling Distribution when Conducting a Directional Test

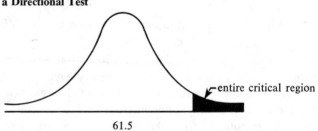

entire critical region

61.5

In general, the choice between whether to conduct a nondirectional or a directional test depends almost totally upon what one wants to know. If one wants to know whether a group's performance record differs from some established standard, a nondirectional test is called for. If one wants to know whether a group's record either exceeds the standard or falls short of it *but not both,* a directional test is needed. This decision is important. It affects both the type of one-sample mean test selected and the results arrived at.

Applying the One-Sample Mean Test

Because of chance, a sample mean cannot be expected to be exactly equal to the hypothesized value. Therefore, one must do more than merely compare the sample mean to the value of the population mean indicated in the null hypothesis. Instead, one must determine whether the difference between the sample mean and the hypothesized value seems too large to be due to chance. This is precisely what the one-sample mean test helps one do. It is a relatively easy test to conduct as long as the essential steps are followed in sequence. Figure 8.3 lists these steps.

Figure 8.3   Steps to Follow when Using One-Sample Mean Tests

1. Decide which one-sample mean test to use.
2. Set the permissible level of error.
3. Compute the test statistic.
4. Compare the test statistic to the appropriate sampling distribution table.

Deciding Which One-Sample Mean Test to Use

There are two types of one-sample mean tests: the z test for large samples and the t test for small samples. While both types of tests are carried out similarly, it is essential to understand the circumstances appropriate for each type.

The z Test. The z test is normally selected when the random sample drawn by researchers consists of 100 or more units (i.e., cases or diet-days). No assumptions need be made about the shape of the population distribution. In particular, the population does not have to be normally distributed. For example, the court clerk can use the z test if the sample includes at least 100 cases even if the clerk strongly suspects that the population of case disposition times from her courtroom docket is not normally distributed. The absence of this restrictive assumption is extremely fortunate. Since the researchers do not know the population mean (the reason the test is being conducted), it is unlikely that they will possess any information concerning the shape of the population distribution.

The t Test. The t test is normally selected when the sample consists of less than 100 units. However, the t test also requires that the population from which the sample is drawn be normally distributed. This appears to limit the applicability of the t test since researchers seldom know much about the distribution of the population. Fortunately, the t test's normality assumption can be relaxed, especially for larger sample sizes. For samples of less than approximately 30 units, the requirement that the sample be drawn from a normally distributed population must be taken more seriously.

In practice, the following rules of thumb should be followed:

1. With samples of more than 100 units, the z test should be used; no assumptions need be made about the shape of the population distribution.

2. With samples of between 30 and 100 units, the *t* test can be used without any need to assume that the population is normally distributed.

3. With samples of fewer than 30 units, the *t* test should be used only when it is reasonable to assume that the population is normally distributed.

Setting the Level of Error

It must be remembered that as long as information from a sample is used to reach conclusions about the population, there is always a chance that a mistake will be made. No test of significance totally eliminates this risk. Rather, the risk is inherent in trying to learn about a population while studying only a sample. Thus, the sheriff wants to know about the quality of all the food served in county jail but studies only the food served on 35 randomly selected days. The court clerk wants to learn something about the mean disposition time for all cases in the courtroom but investigates only disposition times for 50 randomly selected cases. However, by *randomly* selecting the sample, researchers take a great step in the right direction. (See Chapter 6.) This is because having a random sample makes it possible to use tests of significance such as the one-sample tests discussed in this chapter.

As was explained in some detail in Chapter 2, when researchers engage in hypothesis testing there are really only two basic types of error they can make. They can mistakenly reject a true null hypothesis and thereby make a Type I error; or they can mistakenly *fail* to reject a false null hypothesis and thereby make a Type II error. Of course, researchers want to avoid both types of error if at all possible, but ordinarily this is *not* possible. As was shown in Chapter 2, taking steps to *reduce* the chance of making a Type I error *increases* the chance of making a Type II error, and vice versa. The solution to this dilemma is to:

1. Decide how great a risk of making a Type I error one can tolerate; that is, determine an acceptable level of Type I error; and then

2. Use a hypothesis test which minimizes the chance of making a Type II error.

All of the hypothesis tests discussed in this text meet this last requirement — they minimize the chance of making a Type II error given that an acceptable level of Type I error has been set. Therefore, all that one needs to do is to determine just how great a risk of making a Type I error one can accept. The grounds for making such a determination were discussed in Chapter 2.

Computing the Test Statistic

The easiest way to explain how the test statistics for the one-sample mean tests are computed is through an example.

The z Test. Imagine the court clerk who wants to know how case disposition times in one courtroom compare to those in other courtrooms in the county court. A random sample of 160 cases disposed of during the previous year is drawn. From the county court administrator's report the clerk knows that the county-wide mean case disposition time was 61.5 days over the past year. The clerk wonders, "Was the mean case disposition time in my courtroom different from the county-wide average?" Clearly, this calls for a nondirectional test where the research and alternative hypotheses look like this:

H_o: $\mu = 61.5$

H_a: $\mu \neq 61.5$

Where: μ = the mean case disposition time for the population of all cases disposed of in the clerk's courtroom last year.

61.5 = the county-wide average = the hypothesized mean of the clerk's courtroom

Figure 8.4 illustrates the steps involved in calculating the z statistic.

Figure 8.4   Computing the z Statistic

Step 1: Prepare the Data

Case	Case Disposition Time (X)	X^2
1	70	4900
2	35	1225
3	86	7396
4	81	6561
5	63	3969
⋮	⋮	⋮
156	71	5041
157	58	3364
158	53	2809
159	99	9801
160	85	7225
$N = 160$	$\Sigma X = 10{,}254$	$\Sigma X^2 = 695{,}089$

Figure 8.4   (Continued)

Step 2: Compute the Mean

The computational formula:

$$\overline{X} = \frac{\Sigma X}{N}$$

By substitution:

$$\overline{X} = \frac{10,254}{160} = 64.088$$

Step 3: Compute the Standard Deviation

The computational formula:

$$SD = \sqrt{\Sigma X^2/N - \overline{X}^2}$$

By substitution:

$$\begin{aligned} SD &= \sqrt{695,089/160 - 64.088^2} \\ &= \sqrt{4344.306 - 4107.272} \\ &= \sqrt{237.034} \\ &= 15.396 \end{aligned}$$

Step 4: Compute the Standard Error of the Mean

The computational formula:

$$SE = SD/\sqrt{N-1}$$

By substitution:

$$\begin{aligned} SE &= 15.396/\sqrt{160-1} \\ &= 15.396/\sqrt{159} \\ &= 15.396/12.610 \\ &= 1.221 \end{aligned}$$

Step 5: Compute the z Statistic

The computational formula:

$$z = \frac{\overline{X} - \mu}{SE}$$

By substitution:

$$\begin{aligned} z &= \frac{64.088 - 61.500}{1.221} \\ &= \frac{2.588}{1.221} \\ &= 2.120 \end{aligned}$$

On the other hand, if the court clerk is worried only that the mean case disposition time for the courtroom might *exceed* the county-wide average, a directional test is needed. In this case, the two hypotheses would be:

$$H_o: \mu \leq 61.5$$
$$H_a: \mu > 61.5$$

Here, a one-tailed test is called for. As it turns out, the z statistic for a one-tailed test is computed in precisely the same way as the z statistic for a two-tailed test. Therefore, Figure 8.4 provides the necessary information for a directional (one-tailed) test as well as for a nondirectional (two-tailed) test. However, with a one-tailed test the critical region is located in just one tail of the sampling distribution.

The t Test. Now imagine that the court clerk is able to draw only a random sample of 20 cases rather than 160. The null, and alternative, hypotheses remain the same and a two-tailed test must be used. Thus:

$$H_o: \mu = 61.5$$
$$H_a: \mu \neq 61.5$$

With just 20 cases, the clerk can conduct only a t test — and then only if the population distribution is assumed normal. The distribution of case disposition times for the 20 cases in the *sample* gives a clue to the shape of the *population* distribution. This sample distribution is found in Figure 8.5.

Figure 8.5   Distribution of Case Disposition Times for Twenty-Case Sample

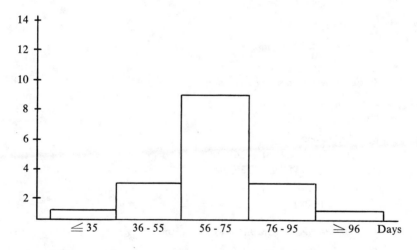

From this figure it can be seen that the distribution of the clerk's sample is symmetric and unimodal and, hence, approximately normal. Therefore, the t test can be used. Figure 8.6 illustrates the steps involved in calculating the t statistic.

Figure 8.6   Computing the t Statistic

Step 1: Prepare the Data

Case	Case Disposition Time (X)	X^2
1	32	1024
2	76	5776
3	73	5329
4	46	2116
5	89	7921
⋮	⋮	⋮
16	52	2704
17	72	5184
18	109	11881
19	78	6084
20	76	5776
$N = 20$	$\Sigma X = 1,328$	$\Sigma X^2 = 93,352$

Step 2: Compute the Mean

The computational formula:

$$\overline{X} = \frac{\Sigma X}{N}$$

By substitution:

$$\overline{X} = \frac{1,328}{20} = 66.400$$

Step 3: Compute the Standard Deviation

The computational formula:

$$SD = \sqrt{\Sigma X^2/N - \overline{X}^2}$$

By substitution:

$$SD = \sqrt{93,352/20 - 66.400^2}$$
$$= \sqrt{4667.600 - 4408.960}$$
$$= \sqrt{258.640}$$
$$= 16.082$$

Step 4: Compute the Standard Error of the Mean

The computational formula:

$$SE = SD/\sqrt{N-1}$$

By substitution:

$$SE = 16.082/\sqrt{20-1}$$
$$= 16.082/\sqrt{19}$$
$$= 16.082/4.359$$
$$= 3.689$$

Figure 8.6   (Continued)

Step 5: Compute the t Statistic

The computational formula:

$$t = \frac{\overline{X} - \mu}{SE}$$

By substitution:

$$t = \frac{66.400 - 61.500}{3.689}$$

$$= \frac{4.900}{3.689}$$

$$= 1.328$$

Step 6: Compute the Degrees of Freedom

The computational formula:

$$df = N - 1$$

By substitution:

$$df = 20 - 1$$

$$= 19$$

As with the z test, so also with the t test! If the court clerk is worried only that the mean case disposition time might be *higher* than the countywide average, then, as before with the z test, a directional test should be conducted. Thus:

$$H_o: \mu \leq 61.5$$

$$H_a: \mu > 61.5$$

The t statistic for a one-tailed test is calculated the same way as the t statistic for a two-tailed test. In this case, Figure 8.6 provides the necessary information for the clerk regardless of which type of t test is conducted.

Comparing the Test Statistic to the Appropriate Sampling Distribution

Researchers are now ready to conclude their one-sample mean test. The null hypothesis will be rejected if the sample mean differs by an amount too large to be due to chance from the value of the population mean assumed in that hypothesis. Their readiness to reject the null hypothesis is nicely summed up by the permissible level of error they have set. This level of error indicates how great a risk of falsely rejecting a true null hypothesis researchers are willing to run. *If the calculated level of error is less than or equal to the level of error set by researchers, the null hypothesis will be rejected. If the calculated level of error exceeds the level of error, the null hypothesis will not be rejected.* The rationale for this decision rule is simple. The calculated level of error estimates how likely it would be for researchers to get a sample mean as extreme as the one they got *if* the null hypothesis is true. Thus, it tells researchers how great a risk they run of falsely rejecting a true null hypothesis should they reject the present null hypothesis. Clearly, if this risk (estimated by the calculated level of error) is *less* than the maximum risk researchers have agreed to run (the permissible level of error), they should run that risk and reject the null hypothesis. If this risk is *greater* than the maximum risk researchers have agreed to run, then they should refuse to run that excessive risk and not reject the null hypothesis. The null hypothesis should be rejected if and only if the calculated level of error is less than or equal to the permissible level of error. This can easily be determined with the aid of an appropriate sampling distribution table. Just how this is done with one-sample mean tests is explained in the following sections.

The z Test. When the hypotheses are nondirectional, a two-tailed *z* test is used and the critical region is evenly divided between the two tails of the sampling distribution (Figure 8.1). Clearly, the calculated level of error will be less than or equal to the permissible level of error if and only if the *z* statistic falls within the critical region. Thus, *the* question is really *two* questions:

1. How large must a positive *z* statistic be in order to fall into the one half of the critical region located in the positive tail of the sampling distribution?
2. How small must a negative *z* statistic be in order to fall into the one half of the critical region located in the negative tail of the sampling distribution?

The answers to both questions clearly depend upon the permissible level of error, since it determines the size of the critical region. These answers are presented in Figure 8.7 and illustrated in Figure 8.8.

As can be seen in Figure 8.4, for the court clerk the value of the *z* statistic is 2.12. If the clerk uses .05 as the permissible level of error, the null hypothesis (H_o: $\mu = 61.5$) is rejected in favor of the research hypothesis (H_a: $\mu \neq 61.5$) since 2.12 is greater than 1.96 (Figure 8.8). If the clerk uses .01 as the permissible level of error, the null hypothesis is not rejected since 2.12 is less than 2.58. On the other hand, if the clerk's *z* statistic is equal to 1.12 rather than 2.12, she will not reject the null hypothesis *regardless* of which permissible level of error is used. Clearly, then, once researchers have decided to use a two-tailed *z* test, their decision to reject or not to reject the null hypothesis depends solely upon the value of their *z* statistic and the permissible level of error.

Identifying the Boundaries of the Critical Region. The numbers found in Figure 8.7 (± 1.96 and ± 2.58) are taken from a sampling distribution of the *z* statistic (Appendix B). *The sampling distribution for the z statistic is based on the assumption that the null hypothesis is true.* If the null hypothesis is true, and if many simple random samples are drawn from the population, and if a z statistic is computed for each such sample, then a distribution of these z statistics will be *normal* with a mean of zero (0) and a standard deviation of one (1). This distribution is called a sampling distribution and looks like the curves in Figure 8.8. Appendix B is a numerical description of this sampling distribution just as these curves are visual descriptions. The entries in Appendix B report the proportion of all z statistics making up the sampling distribution which fall between 0 (the mean) and a given z statistic. This is depicted in Figure 8.9.

Figure 8.7   Boundaries for the Critical Region in Two-Tailed z Tests

Permissible Level of Error	Negative Half of Critical Region	Positive Half of Critical Region
.05	$z \leq -1.96$	$z \geq 1.96$
.01	$z \leq -2.58$	$z \geq 2.58$

Figure 8.8   Critical Regions for Two-Tailed z Tests

.05 Permissible Level of Error

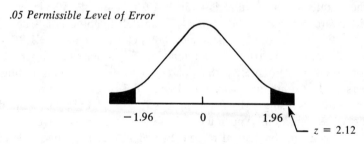

.01 Permissible Level of Error

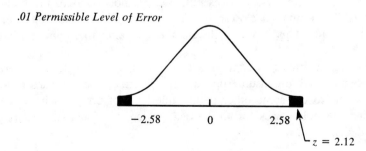

Figure 8.9   The Sampling Distribution of the z Statistic, Using Appendix B

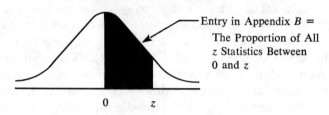

Entry in Appendix B =
The Proportion of All
z Statistics Between
0 and z

For example, researchers might be interested in knowing the proportion of z statistics falling between 0 and, say, 1.75. To find out, they read down the left margin of Appendix B until they find the row headed by 1.7. Then they find the column headed by .05. At the intersection of this row and column they find the proportion they are looking for (.4599). Thus, 45.99 percent of all z statistics are between 0 and 1.75 — if the null hypothesis is true.

Researchers using .05 as the permissible level of error want to know the z statistic whose entry is 4750 because of a very simple fact: if 47.50 percent of all z statistics are between 0 and a given value, then 2.50 percent of all z statistics *exceed* that value. The same argument applies to the negative half of the sampling distribution. These two extreme portions of the sampling distribution, each containing 2.50 percent of all z statistics, constitute the critical region for researchers using the .05 permissible level of error. By looking in the body of Appendix B for 4750, one can see that the z statistic whose entry is 4750 is 1.96. Thus, 47.50 percent of all z statistics are between 0 and 1.96 — if the null hypothesis is true. Similarly, 47.50 percent of all z statistics are between 0 and -1.96 — if the null hypothesis is true. The remaining 5 percent are either greater than or equal to 1.96 or less than or equal to -1.96. This is how the numbers ± 1.96 find their way into Figure 8.7.

Researchers using .01 as the permissible level of error want the z statistic whose entry in Appendix B is 4950. This will leave 1 percent of all z statistics in the critical region divided between the two tails of the sampling distribution. As it turns out, 4950 is not found in the body of Appendix B; the number closest to it is 4951. The z statistic whose entry is 4951 is 2.58. This is where the numbers ± 2.58 in Figure 8.7 come from.

As long as one uses either .05 or .01 as permissible levels of error, one does not need to consult Appendix B. Figure 8.7 can be used instead. If one wants to use some other permissible level of error, such as .10 or .02, then the boundaries for the critical region are found by examining Appendix B.

A Directional z Test. When the null and research hypotheses are directional, a one-tailed z test is used and the critical region is confined to one tail of the sampling distribution (Figure 8.2). Here, too, it is clear that the calculated level of error will be less than or equal to the permissible level of error if and only if the z statistic falls within the critical region. The conditions under which the calculated level of error will be less than the permissible level of error with a one-tailed test are given in Figure 8.10 and illustrated in Figures 8.11 and 8.12.

Figure 8.10   Boundaries for the Critical Region in One-Tailed z Tests

Permissible Level of Error	Test on Negative Tail	Test on Positive Tail
.05	$z \leqq -1.65$	$z \geqq 1.65$
.01	$z \leqq -2.33$	$z \geqq 2.33$

Figure 8.11   Critical Regions for One-Tailed z Tests at the .05 Permissible Level of Error

Test on the Positive Tail

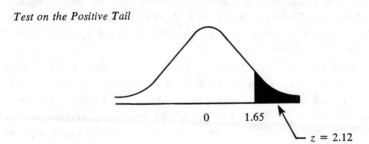

0   1.65

$z = 2.12$

Test on the Negative Tail

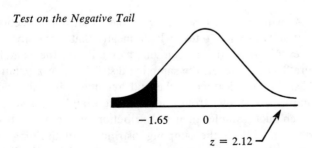

-1.65 0

$z = 2.12$

Figure 8.12   Critical Regions for One-Tailed _z_ Tests at the .01 Permissible Level of Error

Test on the Positive Tail

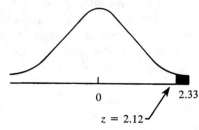

Test on the Negative Tail

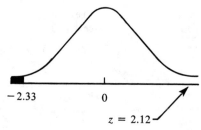

Assuming that the court clerk uses the .05 level of error and is testing on the positive tail of the sampling distribution, the null hypothesis is rejected since 2.12 is greater than 1.65 (Figure 8.11). However, if she uses the .01 level of error, the null hypothesis is not rejected since 2.12 is less than 2.33 (Figure 8.12).

The numbers found in Figure 8.10 (± 1.65 and ± 2.33) are also taken from Appendix B. For example, if researchers use the .05 level of error, they want the z statistic whose entry in Appendix B is 4500, because if 45.00 percent of all z statistics are found between 0 and a given value, then 5.00 percent exceed that value. When a one-tailed test is conducted, this 5 percent constitutes the entire critical region.

The t *Test.* As with the z test, so also with the t test! Nondirectional hypotheses call for a two-tailed t test which means that here, too, the critical region is evenly divided between the two tails of the sampling distribution (Figure 8.1). However, the sampling distribution of a t statistic is *not* a normal distribution. Rather, if the null hypothesis is true, and if many random samples are drawn from the population, and if a t statistic is computed for each such sample, then a distribution of these t statistics is called a t distribution. This is the sampling distribution of the t statistic. It looks very much like a normal distribution (Figure 8.8), but it is slightly different. A different sampling distribution table must be used for a t test than is used with a z test.

As always, the null hypothesis is rejected if and only if the t statistic falls within the critical region. The value which the t statistic must equal or exceed in order to fall into the positive one half of the critical region is found in Appendix C. In order for investigators to identify the particular value of interest to them, they need to know two things: (1) the permissible level of error, and (2) the degrees of freedom. The level of permissible error is easily determined since it is set by the investigators themselves. As is indicated in Figure 8.6, for one-sample t tests, the number of *degrees of freedom* are always equal to one less than the number of observations. That is:

$$df = N - 1$$

For the court clerk with a sample of 20 cases, the number of degrees of freedom are 19 ($20 - 1 = 19$). If the clerk is conducting a two-tailed test and is using .05 as the permissible level of error, the t statistic must equal or exceed 2.093 if it is to fall into the positive one half of the critical region (Appendix C).

The boundary of the half of the critical region in the negative tail of the sampling distribution is merely -1 times the boundary of the first half of the critical region. Thus, the court clerk's t statistic must be less than or equal to -1 times 2.093 (i.e., -2.093) to be in the negative one half of the critical region. Therefore, if the clerk's t statistic is either (1) greater than or equal to 2.093, or (2) less than or equal to -2.093, then the null hypothesis will be rejected and the research hypothesis accepted. Otherwise it will not be rejected.

According to Figure 8.6 the clerk's t statistic is equal to 1.328. Thus, the clerk does not reject the null hypothesis.

On the other hand, if the court clerk uses the .01 level of error to conduct the two-tailed t test, then according to Appendix C, it can be seen that the null hypothesis is rejected when the t statistic is either (1) greater than or equal to 2.861, or (2) less than or equal to -2.861.

The decision whether or not to reject the null hypothesis is made with the two-tailed t test in very much the same way as it is made with the two-tailed z test. The only real difference is that for the t test the degrees of freedom must be computed in order to identify the value with which the test statistic is to be compared. For a two-tailed z test this value depends only upon the permissible level of error: at the .05 level of error it is ± 1.96, while at the .01 level it is ± 2.58. For a two-tailed t test, this value depends upon the degrees of freedom as well. This can easily be seen by scanning down any column of Appendix C. Notice that as the degrees of freedom *increase,* the values in Appendix C *decrease* until they are identical to those for a two-tailed z test! Hence, the two tests yield the same results when used with large samples.

The parallel between z tests and t tests is also found with one-tailed tests where the hypotheses are directional. In this situation, the entire critical region is located either in the positive tail or in the negative tail of the sampling distribution — depending upon the null and research hypotheses (Figure 8.2). The value which the t statistic must equal or exceed in order to fall within the critical region in the positive tail is found in Appendix C and depends only upon the permissible level of error and the degrees of freedom. If the court clerk continues to use the .05 level of error, then with nineteen degrees of freedom, the value the t statistic will have to equal or exceed in order to reject the null hypothesis is 1.729. If the .01 level of error is used, the value is 2.539.

Finally, the value which the t statistic must be less than or equal to in order to fall into the critical region in the negative tail is just -1 times the corresponding value for the positive tail. If the clerk conducts a one-tailed t test on the negative tail of the sampling distribution and uses the .05 level of error, the null hypothesis will be rejected if and only if the t statistic is less than or equal to -1 times 1.729 (i.e., -1.729). If the .01 level of error is used, the null hypothesis will be rejected if and only if the t statistic is less than or equal to -2.539.

Looking at Appendix C, notice that with one-tailed t tests (as well as two-tailed t tests), as the degrees of freedom *increase,* the values in Appendix C *decrease* until, eventually, they equal those for the z test: ± 1.65 at the .05 level of error, and ± 2.33 at the .01 level.

These z test and t test examples illustrate two very important points. First, with both z and t tests, it is quite possible that using a two-tailed test might lead to a decision to *not reject* the null hypothesis while using a one-tailed test might lead to a decision to *reject!* This can be seen by comparing Figures 8.7 and 8.10. Invariably, the boundary values for the two-tailed test are more extreme than those for the one-tailed test. Hence, it is quite possible that one's z statistic will be large (or small) enough to reject the null hypothesis when a one-tailed test is used, but not large (or small) enough when a two-tailed test is used. Thus, the choice between conducting a nondirectional, two-tailed test and conducting a directional, one-tailed test is an extremely important one and must be carefully thought through.

Second, the calculated level of error depends not only on the size of the difference between the sample mean and the hypothesized value of the population mean but also on the sample size. For example, compare the results of the court clerk's two-tailed z test (Figure 8.4) with those of the two-tailed t test (Figure 8.6). For the z test, the difference between the sample mean and the hypothesized value of the population mean is

64.087 − 61.500 = 2.587. For the *t* test this difference is 66.400 − 61.500 = 4.900. Since 2.587 is less than 4.900, it would seem only logical that if the null hypothesis is rejected using the *z* test, it will also be rejected using the *t* test. However, as has just been shown, this is *not* true. The reason for this seemingly surprising result is really quite simple. With the *z* test, the difference, though rather small, is based on a large sample ($N = 160$). The court clerk can be quite confident that this difference is genuine and not caused merely by chance. On the other hand, with the *t* test, the difference, though larger, is based on a small sample ($N = 20$). Consequently, the clerk cannot be so confident that this difference is not just due to chance. The larger the sample size, the more confident investigators can be that a difference of a given size between the sample mean and the hypothesized value of the population mean is genuine and not due to chance.

Figure 8.13 reviews the four steps involved in one-sample mean tests and summarizes the options open to investigators at each step along the way.

Figure 8.13   The Four Steps Involved in Using One-Sample Mean Tests

1. Decide which one-sample mean test to use. This decision is based upon two factors: (1) the null and research hypotheses, and (2) the size of the sample.
2. Set the permissible level of error. This decision is based upon one's willingness to risk falsely rejecting a true null hypothesis.
3. Compute the test statistic. This computation depends solely upon whether a *z* test or a *t* test is conducted — not on whether the test is nondirectional or directional.
4. Compare the test statistic to the appropriate sampling distribution table. This comparison is based on four choices: (1) whether a *z* test or *t* test is conducted; (2) whether a one-tailed or two-tailed test is conducted; (3) the permissible level of error; and (4) for *t* tests only, the degrees of freedom.

One-Sample Median Test

On some occasions, it may be unwise to use a one-sample mean test. Researchers might have a small sample and suspect that the distribution of their population is not normal. When this is the case, neither of the one-sample mean tests is appropriate. Researchers also might hesitate to use any test whose test statistic is based on the sample mean since the sample mean can be so easily influenced by just a few extreme scores. (See Chapter 7.) The court clerk, for example, might have good reason to think that the distribution of case disposition times for her courtroom is positively skewed with a small number of cases taking an inordinately long time to dispose of. If the sample is small, a *t* test cannot be used since a population distribution which is positively skewed is, by definition, *not normal.* In addition, when the random sample includes a few cases with very long disposition times, their inclusion will produce a sample mean which overestimates the disposition time of a "typical" case. These problems are solved by using a significance test which (1) does not depend in any way upon the shape of the population distribution and (2) employs a test statistic which is insensitive to extreme scores. The one-sample median test is such a test.

Rationale for the One-Sample Median Test

The one-sample median test is based on the fact that the median is a locational measure. It divides a distribution into two equal-sized parts: those scores above the median and those scores below the median. Thus, the median of the population in which researchers are interested evenly divides that population into two parts. Assume that they draw a random sample from that population. Because of chance, the sample median will not be exactly equal to the population median. Hence, *the population median will not evenly divide the sample into two parts.*

A Nondirectional Test

Suppose investigators want to know if the performance of those in some group exceeds or falls short of a given standard of performance. Consider again the court clerk who wonders how the case disposition times in one courtroom compare to those for all courtrooms in the same county. Earlier in this chapter, the investigators' "given standard of performance" was stated as a *mean,* but here it is considered as a *median.* The court clerk now wants to know how the case disposition times in one courtroom compare to the *median* case disposition time for the entire county court. If the report of the county court administrator identifies the median case disposition time as 58 days, the clerk's null and research hypotheses are as follows:

$$H_o: Md = 58$$
$$H_a: Md \neq 58$$

The clerk knows that if a sample of 25 cases is drawn from the docket, then because of chance the median disposition time for the sample may well differ from 58 days even if the median disposition time for all cases on the docket *is* 58 days. Hence, 58 cannot be expected to evenly divide the sample of 25 disposition times into two equal-sized parts. Instead, there will be *either* more cases with disposition times above 58 days than below 58 days *or* more cases below than above. The greater the imbalance, the more tempted the clerk will be to reject the null hypothesis in favor of the alternative hypothesis.

A Directional Test

On the other hand, the court clerk might be interested solely in show-ing that the median disposition time in one courtroom does not *exceed* the overall, county-wide median of 58 days. In this instance, a directional test is set up as follows:

$$H_o: Md \leq 58$$
$$H_a: Md > 58$$

If, in the sample, there are many more disposition times *above* 58 days than below, then the null hypothesis would be rejected in favor of the research hypothesis. If many more disposition times are above 58 days than below, then the population median is probably higher than 58. If there are many more disposition times *below* 58 days than above, then the null hypothesis would not be rejected.

As with the one-sample mean tests, only investigators can decide whether to employ a nondirectional or a directional test. The choice depends solely upon what it is that they want to know. If they merely want to know if a group's performance record differs from an established standard, then a nondirectional test is used. If they want to know if this record *either* exceeds the standard *or* falls short of it, then a directional test is needed.

Applying the One-Sample Median Test

As previously noted, because of chance, the population median can-not be expected to divide evenly any given sample. Researchers must do more than merely find out if the sample is evenly divided by the value of the population median assumed in the null hypothesis. Instead, they must determine whether or not the *imbalance* in the sample created by dividing it at the assumed population median is too great to be due to chance. The one-sample median test helps researchers make this determination. The essential steps involved in the one-sample median test are given in Figure 8.14.

Figure 8.14   Steps to Follow When Using the One-Sample Median Test

1. Set the permissible level of error.
2. Compute the test statistic.
3. Compare the test statistic to the appropriate sampling distribution table.

These steps parallel those for the one-sample *mean* tests (Figure 8.3) with one exception: since there is only a single one-sample median test, there is no need to decide which one to use.

Setting the Level of Error

As was mentioned earlier, the permissible level of error selected by researchers reflects their willingness to risk falsely rejecting a true null hypothesis. The *lower* the level of error, the less willing researchers are to run this risk. However, setting an extremely low level of error is not without its costs. Specifically, conducting the one-sample median test, or any hypothesis test, at an extremely low permissible level of error increases the likelihood that researchers will mistakenly *not* reject a false null hypothesis and make a Type II error. There is a trade-off between the risk of making a Type I error and the risk of making a Type II error (see Chapter 2). The solution to this dilemma is to select a reasonable permissible level of error as discussed earlier in this chapter.

Computing the Test Statistic

The easiest way to explain how the test statistic for the one-sample median test is computed is by way of an example. An example will also clarify the *rationale* for the one-sample median test which, in a way, is quite different from the rationale for the one-sample mean tests.

A Nondirectional Test. Recall the court clerk who wants to know how case disposition times in one courtroom compare to those in other courtrooms in county court. To investigate this, a random sample of 25 cases disposed of during the previous year is drawn. The clerk knows that throughout the county, the median case disposition time was 58 days over the past year. She wonders, "Was the median case disposition time in my courtroom different from the county-wide median?" Clearly, this calls for a nondirectional test which is set up as follows:

H_o: Md = 58

H_a: Md $\neq$ 58

Figure 8.15 illustrates the steps involved in calculating the χ^2 (Chi square) statistic.

Figure 8.15   Calculating the χ^2 (Chi Square) Statistic

Step 1: Prepare the Data Comparison Table

	$\leq$ Md	$>$ Md	Total
Expected Frequencies (E)	N/2	N/2	N
Observed Frequencies (O)	f_1	f_2	N

where: f_1 = the number of cases in the clerk's sample with disposition times less than or equal to 58 days (the assumed value of the population median)

f_2 = the number of cases in the clerk's sample with disposition times greater than or equal to 58 days (note: $f_1 + f_2 = N$)

Figure 8.15   **(Continued)**

By substitution:

	≤ 58	> 58	Total
Expected Frequencies (E)	12.5	12.5	25
Observed Frequencies (O)	7	18	25

Step 2: Compute the χ^2 Statistic

The computational formula:

$$\chi^2 = \Sigma \frac{(O - E)^2}{E}$$

By substitution:

$$\chi^2 = \frac{(7 - 12.5)^2}{12.5} + \frac{(18 - 12.5)^2}{12.5}$$

$$= \frac{-5.5^2 + 5.5^2}{12.5} = \frac{60.50}{12.5}$$

$$= 4.84$$

A brief explanation of the rationale for the one-sample median test is in order. If the null hypothesis is correct and if the sample drawn is truly random, the value of the population median assumed in the null hypothesis should come close to evenly dividing the sample into two equal-sized parts. If the null hypothesis is correct, about one half of the sample case disposition times will be less than the assumed population median and about one half of them will be greater than this value. This is why both expected frequencies are equal to $N/2$. Ordinarily the observed frequencies (f_1 and f_2) will differ from $N/2$; that is, the assumed value of the population median will *not* divide the sample into two equal-sized parts. The χ^2 statistic measures just how different the observed frequencies (f_1 and f_2) are from the expected frequencies ($N/2$ and $N/2$). Generally, the greater the difference between the expected frequencies and the observed frequencies, the greater will be the value of the χ^2 statistic.

A Directional Test. If the court clerk is worried that the median case disposition time for one courtroom might exceed the county-wide median, a directional test should be used. Here, the two hypotheses are:

H_o: Md ≤ 58

H_a: Md > 58

With a directional hypotheses, a one-tailed test is called for; that is, only when the clerk finds too many cases with *long* disposition times will she reject the null hypothesis in favor of the research hypothesis. If a large number of cases with *short* disposition times is found, the null hypothesis will not be rejected. As it turns out, whether the clerk conducts a directional test or a nondirectional test, the χ^2 test statistic is computed in precisely the same way (Figure 8.15).

Comparing the Test Statistic to the Appropriate Sampling Distribution

The one-sample median test is now ready to be completed. The null hypothesis will be rejected if the sample is so unevenly divided by the assumed population median that the imbalance cannot be reasonably attributed to chance. There are two possibilities:

1. If the χ^2 statistic equals or exceeds the boundary value of the critical region of the sampling distribution, the null hypothesis is rejected.

2. If the χ^2 statistic is less than the boundary value of the critical region, the null hypothesis is not rejected.

This is illustrated in Figure 8.16.

Figure 8.16   **Sampling Distribution of the χ^2 Statistic with One Degree of Freedom**

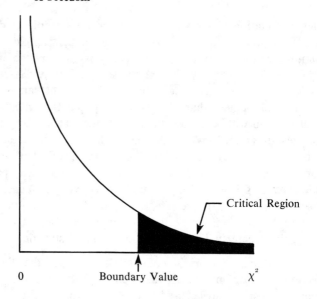

Notice that the sampling distribution of the χ^2 statistic is very different from the sampling distribution of the z and t statistics. This difference is easy to understand when one recalls the definition of a sampling distribution: If the null hypothesis is true (H_o: $Md = 58$), and if many random samples are drawn from the population, and if a χ^2 statistic is computed for each of these samples, then a distribution of these χ^2 statistics forms a χ^2 sampling distribution. From Figure 8.15 it is clear that a χ^2 statistic cannot be negative. If the null hypothesis is true, most samples will be *almost* evenly divided by the hypothesized population median and, therefore, most χ^2 statistics will be small, positive numbers. Only a few samples will be very unevenly divided by the supposed population median and, for this reason, produce large, positive χ^2 statistics — if the null hypothesis is true. Thus, the shape of the χ^2 sampling distribution will be as follows: many small positive values, fewer larger values, and very few extremely large values. This is just the shape shown in Figure 8.16.

To conclude the one-sample median test, researchers need only to determine if the calculated χ^2 statistic equals or exceeds the boundary value shown in Figure 8.16. If it does, the null hypothesis is rejected. If it does not, the null hypothesis is not rejected. This boundary value depends upon two things: the permissible level of error and the type of test being conducted, i.e., nondirectional or directional. These boundary values are presented in Figure 8.17.

Figure 8.17   Boundary Values for the One-Sample Median Test

	.05 Level of Error	.01 Level of Error
Directional Test	2.706	5.412
Nondirectional Test	3.841	6.635

Since the χ^2 statistic's sampling distribution has only one tail, both nondirectional and directional tests are conducted on this single tail. This can make things confusing. In fact, at first glance, it looks as if the critical region for a directional test is larger than the critical region for a nondirectional test — but appearances are deceiving. Researchers must remember that when conducting a directional median test, *only when the imbalance in the sample is in the correct direction* does a large enough χ^2 statistic lead to a rejection of the null hypothesis. When this imbalance is in the *wrong direction,* an otherwise large enough χ^2 statistic does not result in a rejection of the null hypothesis. For example, when the court clerk is worried that the median case disposition time for one courtroom might exceed the county-wide median, the null and research hypotheses are as follows:

$$H_o: Md \leq 58$$
$$H_a: Md > 58$$

A sample of 25 cases is drawn and their case disposition times are ascertained. Imagine that 18 of the 25 sample cases have disposition times *less than or equal to* 58 days while only seven have disposition times *in excess* of 58 days. In such a situation, the clerk does not even need to compute the χ^2 statistic. No matter how large it might be, the clerk cannot reject the null hypothesis in favor of the research hypothesis because the imbalance in the sample created by dividing it at 58 days is in the wrong direction (i.e., the direction *opposite* to that called for by the research hypothesis).

Figure 8.18 briefly reviews and summarizes the three steps researchers must take to carry out the one-sample median test.

Figure 8.18   Steps Involved in Using the One-Sample Median Test

1. Set the permissible level of error. This decision is based upon one's willingness to risk falsely rejecting a true null hypothesis.
2. Compute the test statistic. This computation is carried out in precisely the same way regardless of whether a nondirectional or directional test is conducted.
3. Compare the test statistic to the appropriate sampling distribution table. This comparison is based on two choices: (1) whether a nondirectional or directional test is being conducted and (2) the permissible level of error.

Summary

This chapter focused on one-sample tests of significance. All of the tests examined in this chapter have one common feature: they assist researchers in determining whether or not a group's performance falls short of, meets, or exceeds a given standard of performance. The one-sample mean tests and the one-sample median test are applied in *different circumstances,* but both help researchers address this *same central question.* Furthermore, it is easy to see how the researchers might be interested in similar, yet different, questions. For example, a court administrator might want to know if the case disposition times in one courtroom differ from those in another courtroom. A state prison official might wonder if the quality of the food served in one state prison differs from the quality of the food served in another state prison. A police administrator might want to know if one fleet of police cars is more economical to operate than another fleet of police cars. In all three cases, one wants to know if two groups are the same or different with regard to some factor, such as disposition time, diet, quality, or economy of operation.

Notes

[1]The judgment that this disparity is "too great to be due to chance" is based on several considerations — not just the size of the disparity, but also the standard deviation of the population and the size of the sample.

Review Questions

1. Explain the meaning and significance of the following terms and ideas:
   a. one-sample tests
   b. one-sample z test
   c. one-sample t test
   d. one-sample median test
   e. sampling distribution
   f. critical region
   g. boundary value of the critical region
   h. calculated level of error

2. Using the data from question 2 at the end of Chapter 7, conduct a one-sample mean test on the following null and research hypotheses:

   $$H_o: \mu \leq 63$$
   $$H_a: \mu > 63$$

   Use whichever permissible level of error you choose. Illustrate the sampling distribution for this problem, indicating the critical region, boundary value, and value of the test statistic.

3. Using the same data as in question 2, conduct a one-sample median test on the following null and research hypotheses:

   $$H_o: Md = 60$$
   $$H_a: Md \neq 60$$

   Select the permissible level of error you want. How does your conclusion here compare with your conclusion to question 2?

Chapter 9
Two-Sample Tests

Learning Objectives

After completing this chapter, the reader should be able to:

1. State the purposes for which two-sample tests are used
2. Distinguish between independent samples and matched samples and the two-sample tests used with each
3. Understand when to use two-sample mean tests, a Mann-Whitney test, and a sign test
4. Set up the nondirectional and the directional hypotheses employed in two-sample tests
5. Conduct two-sample mean tests with both independent samples and matched samples: z tests and t tests
6. Conduct a Mann-Whitney test
7. Conduct a sign test

Introduction

Investigators are often interested in finding out if two groups differ in terms of some variable. They might want to know if the homicide rate in states with the death penalty is different from the homicide rate in states without the death penalty. In this example, the states with and without the death penalty are the two groups and the homicide rate is the variable in terms of which they are compared. Perhaps a municipality might want to know if two groups of police officers, one of which has participated in a program to improve driving habits, differ in terms of the mileage of the patrol cars they drive. Here, the two groups of police officers are the two groups and the mileage of the patrol cars they drive is the variable in terms of which they are compared. These examples both involve the same question, How can investigators determine if two groups are the same or different with regard to some variable? This question can be answered by using two-sample tests.

Two-sample tests compare two groups in terms of some population statistic, typically a mean. For instance, the *mean* mileage of police officers who participated in the driving improvement program can be compared to the *mean* mileage of officers who did not participate. As with one-sample tests, when it is possible to collect the needed information for both populations (i.e., *all* those who participated in the program and *all* those who did not), then the two population statistics (i.e., means) can be computed and compared. This, however, is rarely possible, and when it is not possible to do so, it is necessary to draw two samples, compute two *sample* statistics, and then make the comparison. Two-sample tests are used in this context.

Unfortunately, because of chance, the two sample statistics are not exact estimates of the two population statistics which investigators wish to compare. Even when the two population statistics are identical, the two sample statistics will differ. The two-sample mean test determines the ratio between the observed difference between two sample means and the difference that would have occurred if chance alone were operating. The greater the observed difference between the two sample statistics, the more one suspects that this difference is *not* due to chance but that, instead, it reflects genuine differences between the two population statistics.[1] Two-sample tests are used by investigators to help make these kinds of judgments.

Two-Sample Mean Test

By far the most commonly used two-sample test is the two-sample mean test. It tests the hypothesis that the two population means are equal by comparing two sample means based on random samples drawn from these populations. Because sample means are computed when using the two-sample mean test, only interval or ratio level data can be used. The two-sample mean test is very similar to the one-sample mean test, so this discussion will parallel the discussion of the one-sample mean test found in Chapter 8.

A Nondirectional Test

The two-sample mean test can be conducted as a nondirectional test or a directional test. When a nondirectional test is used, the null hypothesis always states that the two population means are equal while the research hypothesis claims they are not:

H_o: $\mu_1 = \mu_2$

H_a: $\mu_1 \neq \mu_2$

where: μ_1 = the mean of the first population

μ_2 = the mean of the second population

An example illustrates how this nondirectional test is conducted.

Recall the driving improvement example. Suppose that a police administrator has information on the mileage of patrol cars driven by two samples of police officers: those who did *not* participate in the special driving improvement program (group 1) and those who did participate (group 2). If the police administrator wants to know merely if these two groups differ, a nondirectional test is called for. Such a test is set up this way:

H_o: $\mu_1 = \mu_2$

H_a: $\mu_1 \neq \mu_2$

where: μ_1 = the mean mileage of *all* officers who did not participate in the driving improvement program

μ_2 = the mean mileage of *all* officers who did participate in the driving improvement program

Here, if the two *sample* means differ greatly from one another, the null hypothesis is rejected in favor of the research hypothesis. This is the case regardless of whether the mean for group 1 ($\overline{X}_1$) greatly exceeds the mean for group 2 ($\overline{X}_2$), or vice versa. Therefore, with a nondirectional two-sample mean test the critical region is evenly distributed between the two tails of the sampling distribution, as shown in Figure 9.1.

Figure 9.1   Police Administrator's Sampling Distribution when Conducting a Nondirectional Test

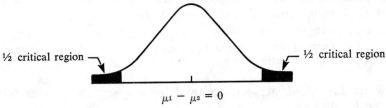

½ critical region ⌐

½ critical region ⌐

$\mu_1 - \mu_2 = 0$

A Directional Test

It may be that the police administrator is interested only in finding out if the mean mileage of officers who participated in the driving improvement program exceeds the mean mileage of officers who did not participate. If this is the case, a directional test is called for, as follows:

$$H_o: \mu_1 \geq \mu_2$$
$$H_a: \mu_1 < \mu_2$$

Here, if $\overline{X}_2$ is significantly larger than $\overline{X}_1$, the null hypothesis is rejected in favor of the research hypothesis. If $\overline{X}_2$ is much larger than $\overline{X}_1$, then it is likely that μ_2 is greater than μ_1 — and this is precisely what the research hypothesis asserts. If $\overline{X}_1$ greatly exceeds $\overline{X}_2$, the null hypothesis is *not* rejected since such a result is perfectly consistent with the claim made in this hypothesis. Thus, with a directional two-sample mean test the critical region is concentrated in just one tail of the sampling distribution. In this example, the critical region is in the positive tail as shown in Figure 9.2.

Figure 9.2   Police Administrator's Sampling Distribution when Conducting a Directional Test

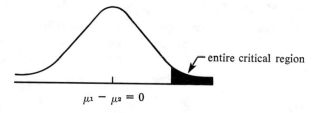

$$\mu_1 - \mu_2 = 0$$

Applying the Two-Sample Mean Test

The four steps one must follow when using the two-sample mean test are very similar to those for the one-sample mean test and are listed in Figure 9.3.

Figure 9.3   Steps to Follow when Using Two-Sample Mean Tests

1. Decide which two-sample mean test to use.
2. Set the permissible level of error.
3. Compute the test statistic.
4. Compare the test statistic to the appropriate sampling distribution table.

When these four steps are followed in sequence, the two-sample mean test is relatively easy to conduct.

Deciding Which Two-Sample Mean Test to Use

There are two ways to characterize the various types of two-sample mean tests. First, one can distinguish between z tests (for large samples) and t tests (for small samples). These two types of two-sample mean tests are used in precisely the same circumstances as their one-sample mean test counterparts are used (see Chapter 8). The following rules of thumb should be followed:

1. When the two samples add to over 100 units, z tests should be used; no assumptions need be made about the shapes of the population distributions.

2. When the two samples add to between 30 and 100 units, t tests can be used without any need to assume that the two populations are normally distributed.

3. When the two samples add to fewer than 30 units, t tests should be used only when it is reasonable to assume that both populations are normally distributed.

Two-sample mean tests can also be distinguished by the types of samples involved: independent samples and matched samples. Basically, researchers are dealing with independent samples when their two samples consist of two distinct sets of units. The most common situation in which researchers deal with matched samples is when their two samples consist of the *same* units measured twice.

Independent Samples and Matched Samples. The independent samples to which two-sample mean tests are applied can be drawn by researchers in two different ways. First, they can separately sample each of two populations. For example, separate samples of police officers can be drawn from lists of those who have, or have not, participated in the driving improvement program. Independent samples need not be drawn in this way. Another way to select independent samples is to draw a single sample from the population and then divide this sample into two groups. Researchers can draw a single sample of police officers and then divide this sample into two groups: (1) those who have not participated in the driving improvement program, and (2) those who have participated in the driving improvement program. Both of these methods of sampling produce independent samples.

Matched samples are ordinarily produced when researchers draw a single sample of units and then observe them at two points in time, thereby producing two groups of scores to which two-sample mean tests can be applied. However, this is not the only way to draw matched samples. *Anything* which links the observations in one group with companion observations in the other group produces matched samples. Thus, the observations in the two groups do not actually have to be on the *same* units.

Altogether there are four types of two-sample mean tests, depending upon the total number of units in the two samples and the type of samples drawn. They are shown in Figure 9.4.

Figure 9.4   Types of Two-Sample Mean Tests

	Total Sample Size < 100	Total Sample Size ≥ 100
Independent Samples	t test	z test
Matched Samples	t test for matched samples	z test for matched samples

Setting the Level of Error

The permissible level of error is set by researchers with the same considerations in mind regardless of the type of hypothesis test being conducted. These considerations are discussed in detail in Chapters 2 and 8.

Computing the Test Statistic

The best way to explain how the test statistics are computed for two-sample mean tests is through examples. These test statistics are computed differently, depending upon whether independent or matched samples are used.

Independent Samples: The z Test. Suppose a police administrator wants to know if a driving improvement program has any effect on the mileage of patrol cars. To investigate this possibility, two samples are drawn. First, a sample of 100 police officers who have not participated in the program is drawn. Then, a sample of 50 officers who have participated in the program is drawn. The question is, does the mean mileage of patrol cars driven by officers who participated in the driving improvement program differ from the mean mileage of cars driven by officers who did not participate? This calls for a nondirectional test with the usual null and research hypotheses:

$$H_o: \mu_1 = \mu_2$$
$$H_a: \mu_1 \neq \mu_2$$

Figure 9.5 illustrates how the z statistic is computed for this problem.

Figure 9.5   Computing the z Statistic for Independent Samples

Step 1: Prepare the Data

Compute the mean, standard deviation, and sample size for both samples.

$\overline{X}_1 = 17.58$	$\overline{X}_2 = 19.00$
$SD_1 = 1.93$	$SD_2 = 2.01$
$N_1 = 100$	$N_2 = 50$

Figure 9.5   (Continued)

Step 2: Compute the Pooled Estimate of the Standard Deviation

Computational formula:

$$SD = \sqrt{(N_1 \cdot SD_1^2 + N_2 \cdot SD_2^2)/(N_1 + N_2)}$$

By substitution:

$$SD = \sqrt{[100(1.93)^2 + 50(2.01)^2]/(100 + 50)}$$
$$= \sqrt{(372.49 + 202.01)/150}$$
$$= \sqrt{3.83}$$
$$= 1.96$$

Step 3: Compute the Standard Error

Computational formula:

$$SE = SD \cdot \sqrt{1/(N_1 - 1) + 1/(N_2 - 1)}$$

By substitution:

$$SE = 1.96\sqrt{1/99 + 1/49} = 1.96\sqrt{.0305}$$
$$= 1.96(.1747)$$
$$= .34$$

Step 4: Compute the z Statistic

Computational formula:

$$z = \frac{\overline{X}_1 - \overline{X}_2}{SE}$$

By substitution:

$$z = \frac{17.58 - 19.00}{.34} = \frac{-1.42}{.34}$$
$$= -4.14$$

As Figure 9.5 makes clear, the z statistic for the two-samples mean test with independent samples is quite easy to compute. Once the two means, standard deviations, and sample sizes have been computed, it is just a matter of inserting these expressions into the various computational formulas.

If the police administrator is interested only in finding out if the driving improvement program *increases* mileage, a directional test is called for. In this case, the null and research hypotheses are the ones typically used in directional two-sample mean tests:

$$H_o: \mu_1 \geq \mu_2$$
$$H_a: \mu_1 < \mu_2$$

With a directional test, the z statistic is computed just as it is with a nondirectional test. Figure 9.5 shows the necessary calculations and results.

The t *Test.* Suppose that the police administrator does not have the resources to draw samples with a total of 150 units. Instead, imagine that a sample of only 30 police officers who have not participated in the program is drawn and a sample of just 20 officers who have participated is drawn. Whether the administrator is interested in a nondirectional test or a directional test, the null and research hypotheses are identical to those used for the z test, discussed above. Since the total sample size is just 50 units, a t test will have to be used. Figure 9.6 illustrates the steps involved in calculating the t statistic.

Figure 9.6   Computing the t Statistic for Independent Samples

Step 1: Prepare the Data

Compute the mean, standard deviation, and sample size for both samples:

$$\overline{X}_1 = 17.52 \qquad\qquad \overline{X}_2 = 19.37$$
$$SD_1 = 2.26 \qquad\qquad SD_2 = 1.86$$
$$N_1 = 30 \qquad\qquad N_2 = 20$$

Step 2: Compute the Pooled Estimate of the Standard Deviation

Computational formula:
$$SD = \sqrt{(N_1 \cdot SD_1{}^2 + N_2 \cdot SD_2{}^2)/(N_1 + N_2)}$$
By substitution:
$$SD = \sqrt{[30(2.26)^2 + 20(1.86)^2]/(30 + 20)}$$
$$= \sqrt{(153.41 + 69.31)/50}$$
$$= \sqrt{4.45}$$
$$= 2.11$$

Step 3: Compute the Standard Error

Computational formula:
$$SE = SD \cdot \sqrt{1/(N_1-1) + 1/(N_2-1)}$$
By substitution:
$$SE = 2.11\sqrt{1/29 + 1/19} = 2.11\sqrt{.0871}$$
$$= 2.11(.2952)$$
$$= .62$$

Step 4: Compute the t Statistic

Computational formula:
$$t = \frac{\overline{X}_1 - \overline{X}_2}{SE}$$
By substitution:
$$t = \frac{17.52 - 19.37}{.62} = \frac{-1.85}{.62}$$
$$= -2.97$$

Step 5: Compute the Degree of Freedom

Computational formula:
$$df = N_1 + N_2 - 2$$
By substitution:
$$df = 30 + 20 - 2$$
$$= 48$$

Like those in Figure 9.5, the calculations in Figure 9.6 are quite simple. Once both means, standard deviations, and sample sizes have been computed, the rest is easy.

Matched Samples. Researchers are dealing with matched samples whenever they have two sets of scores on the same units rather than single scores on two distinct sets of units. Typically, one set of scores is taken before some event or "treatment" occurs, while the second set of scores is taken afterwards. For example, the effects of a driving improvement program might be examined this way. First, a single sample of, say, 40 police officers is selected for study. Second, the mileages attained by these officers are determined. These mileages constitute the "before" scores. Third, the same 40 police officers are enrolled in the driving improvement program. Finally, once they have completed the program, their mileages are ascertained again. These mileages constitute the "after" scores. These "before" and "after" scores are listed in Table 9.1.

Table 9.1   Before, After, and Change Scores for 40 Police Officers

Unit	X_B	X_A	X_C
1	16.5	16.4	−.03
2	17.5	17.1	−.46
3	18.4	23.2	4.78
4	17.5	16.6	−.83
5	16.9	17.9	.96
6	20.6	25.0	4.34
7	19.2	20.0	.82
8	20.2	23.9	3.64
9	18.6	17.6	−.93
10	20.3	18.5	−1.79
11	14.3	17.4	3.11
12	18.3	15.7	−2.60
13	14.6	14.5	−.02
14	14.5	16.6	2.07
15	15.3	16.6	1.25
16	15.7	12.5	−3.15
17	16.0	17.4	1.39
18	16.4	14.8	−1.60
19	18.7	19.4	.69

Table 9.1 (Continued)

20	17.6	17.2	−.44
21	15.6	16.8	1.16
22	16.3	14.5	−1.76
23	18.6	17.8	−.79
24	18.9	22.4	3.41
25	21.8	23.0	1.20
26	19.6	20.0	.41
27	17.2	16.9	−.35
28	21.0	22.2	1.25
29	21.0	21.9	.89
30	16.0	18.8	2.81
31	18.4	20.2	1.80
32	22.5	26.6	4.08
33	18.3	16.3	−1.97
34	21.5	22.4	.96
35	16.7	16.4	−.31
36	17.0	18.3	1.25
37	14.4	17.0	2.56
38	16.2	16.7	.54
39	17.3	17.2	−.12
40	19.5	17.4	−2.11

The two-sample mean test is then applied to the two sets of scores.

With matched samples, researchers face a decidedly different problem than with independent samples. In a way, it is *easier* to deal with matched samples. When matched samples are used, each before-score is matched with a particular after-score — because they are both measurements on the same unit. For example, each before-mileage score is matched with the after-mileage score of the same police officer. Since each before-score is matched with an after-score, it is possible to compute a change score, namely, the after-score minus the before-score. For the 40 police officers in the example, these change scores are found in Table 9.1. Column X_C is merely equal to column X_A minus column X_B (there are some minor discrepancies because of rounding). *The first step in computing a test statistic for a two-sample mean test with matched samples is to convert the before- and after-scores into a single set of change scores.* The test statistic is then computed on the change scores alone.

If the police administrator wants to know merely whether the before-
and the after-scores differ from one another, the null and the research
hypotheses could be set up as follows:

H_o: $\mu_B = \mu_A$

H_a: $\mu_B \neq \mu_A$

where: μ_B = the population mean mileage of all officers before the
driving improvement program

μ_A = the hypothetical population mean mileage of all officers
after the driving improvement program

Since with matched samples it is possible to compute change scores, this
test can be set up another way as well:

H_o: $\mu_C = 0$

H_a: $\mu_C \neq 0$

where: μ_C = the population mean mileage change for all police
officers

This formulation of the administrator's test should look familiar. It is
nothing more than a nondirectional one-sample mean test with $v = 0$ (see
Chapter 8). *A two-sample mean test is conducted on the first pair of hypotheses by conducting a one-sample mean test using the change scores
with the second pair of hypotheses.* Therefore, a two-sample mean test
with matched samples is conducted in two steps:

1. First, change scores are computed by subtracting the before scores
    from the after scores.
2. Second, the appropriate one-sample mean test is conducted on
    the change scores.

This is illustrated for both nondirectional and directional tests using the
previously introduced example.

A Nondirectional Test. When the police administrator wants to know
only if the driving improvement program has any effect on mileage, a nondirectional test is called for. After change scores are computed, the null
and research hypotheses are as follows:

H_o: $\mu_C = 0$

H_a: $\mu_C \neq 0$

Since the sample size ($N = 40$) is between 30 and 100, a t test is used.
The test statistic is computed using the change scores exactly as it was in
Chapter 8. This is demonstrated in Figure 9.7; the corresponding figure
in Chapter 8 is Figure 8.6.

Figure 9.7   Computing the *t* Statistic with Matched Samples

Step 1: Prepare the Data

Unit	Change Score (X_C)	X_C^2
1	$-.03$	.0009
2	$-.46$	.2116
3	4.78	22.8484
4	$-.83$	.6889
5	.96	.9216
⋮	⋮	⋮
36	1.25	1.5625
37	2.56	6.5536
38	.54	.2916
39	$-.12$	.0144
40	-2.11	4.4521
$N = 40$	$\Sigma X_C = 26.15$	$\Sigma X_C^2 = 165.3967$

Step 2: Compute the Mean

The computational formula:

$$\overline{X}_C = \frac{\Sigma X_C}{N}$$

By substitution:

$$\overline{X}_C = \frac{26.15}{40}$$
$$= .654$$

Step 3: Compute the Standard Deviation

The computational formula:

$$SD = \sqrt{\Sigma X_C^2 / N - \overline{X}_C^2}$$

By substitution:

$$SD = \sqrt{165.3967/40 - .654^2} = \sqrt{4.1349 - .4275}$$
$$= \sqrt{3.7074} = 1.926$$

Step 4: Compute the Standard Error

The computational formula:

$$SE = SD/\sqrt{N-1}$$

By substitution:

$$SE = 1.926/\sqrt{40-1}$$
$$= 1.926/\sqrt{39}$$
$$= 1.926/6.245$$
$$= .308$$

Figure 9.7   (Continued)

Step 5: Compute the t Statistic

The computational formula:

$$t = \frac{\overline{X}_c}{SE}$$

By substitution:

$$t = \frac{.654}{.308}$$

$$= 2.121$$

Step 6: Compute the Degrees of Freedom

The computational formula:

$$df = N - 1$$

By substitution:

$$df = 40 - 1$$

$$= 39$$

The six steps in these two figures directly parallel one another. Once the change scores are computed, one can proceed as if all that is involved is a one-sample mean test.

When the sample size exceeds 100, a z test is conducted. The test statistic is still computed using the change scores just as if a one-sample mean test is being conducted. Figure 8.4 shows the necessary steps in computing the z statistic. Since the parallel is so close, no new example illustrating these calculations is given here.

A Directional Test. When the police administrator wants to know if the driving improvement program increases mileage, a directional test is needed. The null and research hypotheses are just what one would expect:

$$H_o: \mu_C \leq 0$$
$$H_a: \mu_C > 0$$

Since the sample size is 40, a t test is used again. The t statistic is computed for this directional test in just the same way as for the earlier non-directional test (Figure 9.7). Of course, if the sample size exceeds 100, a z test is used. The procedure is identical to that discussed in Chapter 8, especially in Figure 8.4.

In conclusion, it is worth observing again that computing the test statistic for two-sample mean tests with matched samples is very straightforward. All one has to do is (1) compute change scores and (2) return to Chapter 8 and use the appropriate one-sample mean test formulas to compute the test statistic from those change scores.

Comparing the Test Statistic to the Appropriate Sampling Distribution

Discussion of the two-sample mean tests can now be quickly concluded. The procedure corresponds precisely to that used with one-sample mean tests. The process is easy — almost automatic. The basic question is, Does the test statistic fall within the critical region of the sampling distribution? If it does, the null hypothesis is rejected. If it does not, the null hypothesis is not rejected.

The z Test. With a nondirectional z test, the critical region is evenly divided between the two tails of the sampling distribution. The boundary values for the two halves of the critical region are the same here as they were for one-sample mean tests and are given again in Figure 9.8.

Figure 9.8   **Boundaries for the Critical Region in Two-Tailed z Tests**

Permissible Level of Error	Negative Half of Critical Region	Positive Half of Critical Region
.05	$z \leq -1.96$	$z \geq 1.96$
.01	$z \leq -2.58$	$z \geq 1.96$

Since the z statistic for the police administrator's nondirectional z test is -4.14 (Figure 9.5) and since -4.14 is less than -1.96 and -2.58, the null hypothesis is rejected regardless of which permissible level of error is used (.05 or .01, respectively). Thus, it is concluded that the driving improvement program does affect mileage.

The critical region is concentrated in just one tail of the sampling distribution when a directional z test is used. The boundary values for the critical region are found in Figure 9.9 and are identical to those used in one-sample mean tests.

Figure 9.9   **Boundaries for the Critical Region in One-Tailed z Tests**

Permissible Level of Error	Test on Negative Tail	Test on Positive Tail
.05	$z \leq -1.65$	$z \geq 1.65$
.01	$z \leq -2.33$	$z \geq 2.33$

Thus, the null hypothesis is rejected no matter which permissible level of error is chosen, since -4.14 is less than both -1.65 and -2.33. According to the directional test, the driving improvement program does improve mileage.

The t Test. As was the case with the one-sample mean tests, the boundaries of the critical regions of the two-sample mean tests depend upon the degrees of freedom as well as the permissible level of error. These boundary values are found in Appendix C. Fortunately, Appendix C is read for these two-sample mean tests just as it was for the one-sample mean tests discussed in Chapter 8.

When a nondirectional test is used, the critical region is, as usual, divided between the two tails of the sampling distribution. The question, then, is, Is the t statistic either greater than or equal to the appropriate boundary value found in Appendix C *or* less than or equal to -1 times that value? If it is, the null hypothesis is rejected. If it is not, the null hypothesis is not rejected. For example, according to Figure 9.6, the police administrator's t statistic, when using independent samples, is -2.97 and the degrees of freedom $= 48$. When we check the row marked by 40 in Appendix C (there is no row marked by 48), the boundary values are found to be 2.021 and 2.704 for the .05 and .01 permissible levels of error, respectively. Since -2.97 is less than both -2.021 and -2.704, the null hypothesis is rejected regardless of which level of error is used.

In the example using matched samples, according to Figure 9.7, the t statistic and degrees of freedom are 2.12 and 39, respectively. The boundary values for the .05 and .01 permissible levels of error are found in row 30 of Appendix C (there is no row 39). They are 2.042 and 2.750, respectively. Since 2.12 is greater than 2.042, the administrator's nondirectional null hypothesis is rejected at the .05 level. Since 2.12 is less than 2.750, it is not rejected at the .01 level. Thus, the decision made concerning the null hypothesis depends upon the permissible level of error used.

When a directional test is conducted, the process is much the same except that the critical region is located in just one tail of the sampling distribution. The boundary value for the critical region is found in Appendix C. In the first example (Figure 9.6), $t = -2.97$ and $df = 48$. According to Appendix C, the boundary values for the .05 and .01 levels of error are 1.684 and 2.423, respectively. Thus, the null hypothesis is rejected in both cases. With the matched samples, $t = 2.12$ and $df = 39$ (Figure 9.7). The boundary values for the .05 and .01 levels of error are 1.697 and 2.457, respectively. Here, the null hypothesis is rejected at the .05 level of error but not at the .01 level.

Summary of Two-Sample Mean Tests

The two-sample mean tests discussed in this chapter address different questions than the one-sample mean tests introduced in Chapter 8. The one-sample mean tests deal with the question, Do the scores of some group, on the average, differ from an externally established standard? The two-sample mean tests deal with the question, Do the scores of two groups, on the average, differ from one another? Yet, both types of hypothesis tests are applied in very much the same way. This can be seen in the fact that this chapter parallels Chapter 8 in many ways. It is also reflected in the fact that Figure 9.10, which reviews the basic steps involved in using two-sample mean tests, closely resembles Figure 8.13, which reviews the steps involved in using one-sample mean tests.

Figure 9.10   The Four Steps Involved in Using Two-Sample Mean Tests

1. Decide which two-sample mean test to use. This decision is based upon three factors: (1) the null and research hypotheses, (2) the size of the samples, and (3) whether independent samples or matched samples are drawn.
2. Set the permissible level of error. This decision is based upon one's willingness to risk falsely rejecting a true null hypothesis.
3. Compute the test statistic. This computation is based upon two factors: (1) whether a z test or a t test is conducted, and (2) whether independent samples or matched samples are drawn. It does not depend upon whether the test is nondirectional or directional.
4. Compare the test statistic to the appropriate sampling distribution table. This comparison is based upon four choices: (1) whether a z test or a t test is conducted, (2) whether a one-tailed or two-tailed test is being conducted, (3) the permissible level of error, and (4) for t tests only, the degrees of freedom.

The only substantial difference is in the ways the test statistics are computed. Even here, when a two-sample mean test with matched samples is conducted, the difference is a very minor one.

Of course, there are some occasions when it is best not to use any of these two-sample mean tests. These reasons parallel those discussed in Chapter 8 for not using one-sample mean tests. Basically, there are two major reasons for avoiding these hypothesis tests:

1. If the samples are small (under 30) and the two populations cannot be assumed to be normal, none of the z and t tests discussed in this chapter should be used.
2. If the scores are not measured at the interval level, these hypothesis tests cannot be used.

Fortunately there are other hypothesis tests which can be used when one or both of these circumstances prevail. Two such tests will be discussed in the remainder of this chapter: (1) the Mann-Whitney test, a replacement for z and t tests with independent samples; and (2) the sign test, a replacement for z and t tests with matched samples.

The Mann-Whitney Test

The Mann-Whitney test is used when the two samples are small and/or the scores are measured only at the ordinal level. It can be conducted either as a nondirectional test or as a directional test. When a nondirectional test is used, the null hypothesis asserts that the two populations from which the samples were drawn are equal (as far as the ordinal level variable is concerned), while the research hypothesis asserts that they are not. This is written:

$$H_o: S_1 = S_2$$
$$H_a: S_1 \neq S_2$$

where: S_1 = the ordinal level scores of all the units in the first population

S_2 = the ordinal level scores of all the units in the second population

When a directional test is used, the null hypothesis claims that one population (say, the first) does *not* have higher scores on the ordinal variable than does the other population (the second), while the research hypothesis claims that it does; that is:

$$H_o: S_1 \leq S_2$$
$$H_a: S_1 > S_2$$

Only the *directional* Mann-Whitney test is discussed in this text. An example is used to illustrate this important test.

Suppose that researchers are evaluating a new pedagogical program designed to teach police officers first-aid techniques. The first sample consists of five officers who have been exposed only to the *new* pedagogical program. The second sample is comprised of four officers who have been exposed only to the *old* pedagogical program and not to the new one. A test measuring the officers' retention of first-aid knowledge is administered to both groups of officers after they participate in their respective programs.

The research hypothesis is: Those police officers who are exposed to the new pedagogical program score higher on the first-aid knowledge test. The null hypothesis is: Those officers who are exposed to the new pedagogical program do not score higher on the first-aid knowledge test. Statistically, the two hypotheses are:

$$H_o: S_1 \leq S_2$$
$$H_a: S_1 > S_2$$

where: S_1 = the scores of the police officers exposed to the new pedagogical program

S_2 = the scores of the police officers exposed to the old pedagogical program

The scores of the nine police officers are now ranked and compared to each other as shown in Figure 9.11.

Figure 9.11   Conducting the Mann-Whitney Test

Rank	Sample	S_1 Precedes S_2	S_2 Precedes S_1
1	S_1	0	0
2	S_1	0	0
3	S_1	0	0
4	S_1	0	0
5	S_2	4	0
6	S_1	0	1
7	S_2	5	0
8	S_2	5	0
9	S_2	5	0
		$U_1 = 19$	$U_2 = 1$

Here all nine scores (from both samples) are jointly ranked from first to ninth. A low rank number corresponds to a high score on the first-aid knowledge test. In the third column, for each officer in the second sample, the number of officers in the first sample with lower ranks is given. For example, the officer in the second sample with the lowest rank is ranked fifth. The number of officers in the first sample with lower ranks is clearly four since the first four ranks all went to officers in the first sample. The next lowest ranking officer in the second sample is ranked seventh. All five officers in the first sample have lower ranks. This third column sums to 19 ($U_1 = 19$).

In the fourth column, for each officer in the first sample, the number of officers in the second sample with lower ranks is given. Only the officer from the first sample who is ranked sixth has an officer from the second sample with a lower rank. Therefore, the fourth column sums to one ($U_2 = 1$).

Now, if the null hypothesis is true (H_o: $S_1 \leqslant S_2$), one of two things *must* also be true: (1) S_1 is less than S_2, or (2) S_1 equals S_2. If the first of these is true, then officers in the second sample should *frequently* precede officers in the first sample and officers in the first sample should *infrequently* precede officers in the second sample; that is, U_2 should be large and U_1 should be small. According to Figure 9.11, this is certainly not true.

If the second of these two possibilities is true, then officers in the first sample should precede officers in the second sample about as frequently as they are themselves preceded by officers in the second sample; that is, U_1 and U_2 should be approximately equal. According to Figure 9.11, U_1

is 19 and U_2 is one. Thus, this second possibility seems to be false as well. *Intuitively*, then, the research hypothesis $(H_a: S_1 > S_2)$ appears to be correct. If it is true, then officers in the first sample should frequently precede officers in the second sample and officers in the second sample should infrequently precede officers in the first sample. In other words, U_1 should be large and U_2 should be small. This is just what Figure 9.11 shows. However, intuition is unreliable. After all, these findings could be due to chance. The Mann-Whitney test poses the question this way: Given that the sample size is 9, if the null hypothesis is true, what is the probability that units from the first sample will outrank units from the second sample 19 times and be outranked in return only once? This probability is the researchers' calculated level of error. If it is less than the permissible level of error, the null hypothesis is rejected. Otherwise, it is not rejected.

The calculated level of error for the Mann-Whitney test is determined using the set of tables in Appendix G. In these tables, N_2 stands for the size of the *largest* sample and N_1 for the size of the remaining sample. In the example, N_2 is equal to five — the size of the first, and largest, sample. To locate the calculated level of error, one finds the table in Appendix G corresponding to the appropriate value of N_2. Then in that table, one goes to the column headed by N_1 and the row headed by U_1 or U_2, whichever is smaller. The calculated level of error is found at the intersection of this column and row in the correct table.

Now, in this example:

$$N_2 = 5$$
$$N_1 = 4$$
$$U_1 = 19$$
$$U_2 = 1$$

Thus, to determine their calculated level of error the researchers must first locate the table in Appendix G identified by $N_2 = 5$. Then they go to the fourth column and the row headed by 1 (since U_2 is less than U_1). The calculated level of error is .016. Therefore, if the researchers use the .05 permissible level of error, the null hypothesis is rejected. If the .01 level of error is used, the null hypothesis is not rejected.

Final Comments on the Mann-Whitney Test

The example used here involves a directional test and the tables in Appendix G assume a directional test. Specifically, the calculated levels of error found in these tables are based only on one tail of the sampling distribution. If a nondirectional Mann-Whitney test is used, the figures in these tables must be *doubled* to yield the correct calculated levels of error.

Finally, it should be noted that the tables in Appendix G can be used only with very small samples. The same Mann-Whitney test can be used with larger samples but additional, somewhat different, tables are needed. Those interested in using the Mann-Whitney test with larger samples should consult Siegel (1956).

The Sign Test

The sign test is a two-sample test used with matched samples. It can be conducted as either a nondirectional test or a directional test. Basically, the sign test employs the same null and research hypotheses as does the Mann-Whitney test. If a nondirectional test is used, the two hypotheses are:

$$H_o: S_B = S_A$$
$$H_a: S_B \neq S_A$$

where: S_B = the ordinal scores for the population from which the first sample is drawn

S_A = the ordinal scores for the population from which the second, matched sample is drawn

Typically, of course, S_B and S_A are scores on the same sample at two different points in time. If a directional test is used, the two hypotheses are:

$$H_o: S_B \geq S_A$$
$$H_a: S_B < S_A$$

Only a directional test is discussed here.

The rationale for a directional sign test is fairly straightforward. It is based upon the change scores discussed earlier when the two-sample mean test for matched samples was introduced. Since the scores for the matched samples are measured ordinally, it is impossible to assign *numerical* values to these change scores, but their *signs* can be ascertained. Thus, for some units S_A is greater than S_B; the change scores of these units have a positive sign $(+)$. For other units, S_B is greater than S_A; their change scores get a negative sign $(-)$. Some units may have two equal scores; here the change score is zero (0).

If the null hypothesis is true, most of the signs should be negative or zero. On the other hand, if the research hypothesis is true, there should be quite a few positive signs. The sign test poses this question: Given the sample size, if the null hypothesis is true, what is the probability of receiving the number of positive signs that were actually received? This probability is the calculated level of error and is found in Appendix F. If it is less than or equal to the permissible level of error, the null hypothesis is rejected. If it is greater than the permissible level of error, the null hypothesis is not rejected. This is easily illustrated with an example.

Suppose police administrators are interested in the attitudes of police-*men* concerning the use of police*women* on night patrol. Investigators conduct the following study to determine the effects of an educational program designed to encourage increased tolerance on the part of police-men toward this use of policewomen. A sample of ten policemen is drawn. Their attitudes toward the use of policewomen on night patrol are mea-sured on an ordinal scale. Then they are enrolled in the educational pro-gram. After completing the program, their attitudes are measured a second time. The question is, Does the educational program increase tolerance of the use of policewomen on night patrol? The null and research hy-potheses are as follows:

$$H_o: S_B \geq S_A$$
$$H_a: S_B < S_A$$

where: S_B = the ordinal tolerance scores of all policemen before the educational program

S_A = the ordinal tolerance scores of all policemen after the educational program

Suppose the investigators' results are those found in Figure 9.12.

Figure 9.12   Conducting the Sign Test for Matched Samples

Unit	S_B	S_A	Sign
1	16	18	+
2	19	19	0
3	16	17	+
4	18	22	+
5	17	15	−
6	15	16	+
7	14	18	+
8	12	19	+
9	10	13	+
10	17	20	+

Number of positive signs = 8
Number of negative signs = 1
Number of zeros = 1

Since there are so many positive signs, it appears that the research hypoth-esis is more nearly correct than the null hypothesis. Again, this result might be due to chance. The question is, Given that the sample size is ten, if the null hypothesis is true, what is the probability that eight of the change scores will be positive? This probability (the calculated level of error) is found in Appendix F. To locate it in Appendix F, two numbers are needed: (1) N, the sample size, and (2) x, the number of positive signs or negative signs, whichever is *smaller*. The calculated level of error is located at the intersection of the row headed by N and the column headed by x. Here, N is 10 and x is 1. Hence, the calculated level of error is .011. Therefore, the null hypothesis is rejected if the .05 permissible level of error is used, but not rejected if the .01 level is used. If the investigators use the .05 level, their conclusion is that the educational program does increase the tolerance of policemen toward the use of policewomen on night patrol.

Like the Mann-Whitney test for independent samples, the sign test for matched samples can also be conducted as a nondirectional test. If it is used in this fashion, the figures in Appendix F must be doubled in order to yield the correct calculated level of error.

Review of the Distribution-Free Tests

Because the Mann-Whitney and sign tests do not require that researchers make any assumptions concerning the shapes of the populations from which their samples are drawn, they are sometimes called distribution-free tests. They can be used with very small samples. Furthermore, both tests also have the advantage of requiring only ordinal level measurement of the scores to which they are applied. These two tests share one additional advantage — they are very easy to carry out. Once the null and the research hypotheses are set up, only two operations are required:

1. One must be able to determine which of two scores is greater than the other (i.e., rank them or assign a sign value).
2. One must be able to count.

For all of these reasons, the Mann-Whitney test and the sign test are very popular. One is well-advised to master these two simple and versatile hypothesis tests.

Figure 9.13 is a guide for deciding which two-sample test to use.

Summary

In many ways, this chapter parallels Chapter 8. Of course, Chapter 8 deals with whether a single group falls short of, equals, or exceeds a given external standard, while this chapter deals with whether two groups differ from each other. Both chapters focus heavily on hypothesis tests which use the mean: a z test for large samples and a t test for small samples.

Both chapters also introduce alternative, distribution-free tests which are used when the samples are very small and/or when only ordinal level measurement is available. More importantly, both chapters repeatedly illustrate the fundamental process of hypothesis testing which is introduced in Chapter 2. By showing how particular hypothesis tests are actually conducted, light is shed on the fundamental process of hypothesis testing that is involved. This is an appropriate place to review this process. Figure 9.14 reviews the basic steps involved in hypothesis testing first listed in Figure 2.1, but some additional details are added which reflect the particular hypothesis tests discussed in Chapter 8 and this chapter.

Figure 9.13   Deciding Which Two-Sample Test to Use

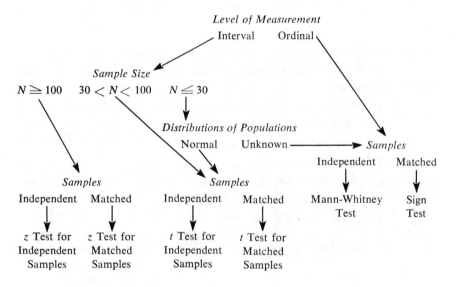

Figure 9.14   Steps for Hypothesis Testing

1. Select the sample(s):
   — one sample or two samples
   — independent samples or matched samples.
2. Formulate a hypothesis:
   — the null hypothesis
   — the research hypothesis.
3. Set the level of error.
4. Test the hypothesis:
   — compute the test statistic
   — compare the test statistic with the appropriate sampling distribution table.

In the chapters which follow, still other hypothesis tests are introduced. In many ways, these tests may well appear quite different from the tests discussed so far. However, with all of these tests, the fundamental process remains the same. As these chapters are read, one should attempt to continually relate the individual hypothesis tests discussed to the fundamental process of hypothesis testing introduced in Chapter 2.

Notes

[1]The size of the observed difference is not the only factor which leads one to suspect that the difference is not due to chance. Other factors include the size of the samples and the standard deviations of the two populations.

Review Questions

1. Explain the meaning and significance of the following terms and ideas:
   a. independent samples
   b. matched samples
   c. z test for independent samples
   d. z test for matched samples
   e. t test for independent samples
   f. t test for matched samples
   g. distribution-free tests
   h. Mann-Whitney test for independent samples
   i. sign test for matched samples
2. Using the following data, conduct a directional t test using the following research hypothesis: $\mu_1 < \mu_2$. Assume independent samples (for obvious reasons) and use the .05 permissible level of error.

	Sample 1	Sample 2	Combined Samples
$N =$	25	18	43
$\overline{X} =$	32.4	34.6	33.3
$SD =$	5.9	7.2	—

3. A sample of various precincts in a small Standard Metropolitan Statistical Area (SMSA) indicates that in 1977 there was an average of 110 robberies in these precincts. After a robbery reduction program was implemented in 1978, the average num-

ber of robberies in the same precincts was 98. If researchers were to conduct a two-samples test on this sort of data, what would the null and research hypotheses be? Which one-sample test would they use to determine whether the null hypothesis should be rejected in favor of the research hypothesis?

References

Siegel, Sidney. *Nonparametric Statistics for the Behavioral Sciences.* New York: McGraw-Hill Book Co., 1956.

Figure 7.12 Comparing the Mean Deviation and the Standard Deviation

Chapter 10

Contingency Table Analysis

Learning Objectives

After completing this chapter, the reader should be able to:

1. Construct contingency tables
2. Compute column, row, and corner percentages and appreciate the special importance of column percentages in establishing causal relationships
3. Define spuriousness, interaction, and suppression; explain the importance of each
4. Understand and carry out the χ^2 hypothesis test for contingency tables
5. Measure the strength of a relationship using: Cramer's V when at least one variable is measured nominally; γ and τ_C when both variables are measured ordinally
6. Explain how contingency table analysis might be used to address problems of interest to researchers

Introduction

Often the research hypotheses cannot be properly tested with either one-sample or two-sample tests. When a research hypothesis asserts that X (the independent variable) is related to Y (the dependent variable), a two-sample test can be used only if two conditions are met: (1) X is dichotomous and (2) Y is measured at the interval level. Even if just one of these conditions is not met, none of the two-sample tests introduced in Chapter 9 can be used. What, then, are researchers to do? The answer depends on which condition is not met. If the first condition is not met but the second one is, then either analysis of variance or regression analysis may be appropriate. These techniques are discussed in Chapters 11 and 12, respectively. On the other hand, if the second condition is not met, then regardless of whether the first one is, contingency table analysis may be called for. *Contingency table analysis is a way of investigating relationships among two or more categorical variables arrayed in a table.*

Although contingency table analysis is used frequently, many criminal justice students do not seem to fully appreciate its value. Contingency table analysis is both *powerful* and *easy to do*. This is a rare combination.

Contingency Tables

A contingency table is nothing more than a joint frequency distribution. When frequency distributions were introduced in Chapter 7, a frequency distribution was defined as the set of categories for one variable together with the number of units falling into each category. A *joint* frequency distribution is a frequency distribution for two or more variables. Table 10.1 shows a joint frequency distribution, or contingency table, for two variables, sex and sentence.

Table 10.1   Number of Male and Female Convicted Felons Given Various Sentences in King County Court, Washington, 1973

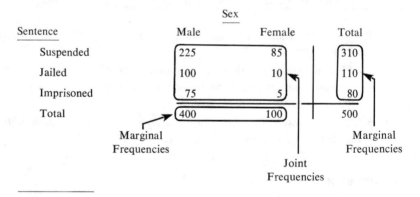

Source: Modification of Table 7 in Roy Lotz and John Hewitt, "The Influence of Legally Irrelevant Factors on Felony Sentencing," *Sociological Inquiry* 47, No. 1, pp. 39-48.

There are two types of frequencies in a contingency table such as Table 10.1: (1) marginal frequencies and (2) joint frequencies. *Marginal frequencies are the numbers on the edges, or margins, of a contingency table* (as opposed to those inside). In Table 10.1, the numbers 310, 110, and 80 are marginal frequencies. They stand for the number of convicted felons whose sentences were suspended or those who were jailed or who were imprisoned, respectively. Table 10.1 also has two other marginal frequencies, 400 and 100. They stand for the number of convicted felons who are men or women, respectively. These two sets of marginal frequencies are called *marginal distributions,* since each set is a frequency distribution for one of the two variables composing the contingency table. Hence, Table 10.1 includes marginal distributions for the variables of sentence and sex.

The remaining six numbers inside Table 10.1 are called joint frequencies. Each one indicates the number of units possessing the relevant characteristics of the two variables. According to Table 10.1, there are 225 convicted felons who are males who have received suspended sentences. In addition, there are 75 who are males in prison. There are ten females in jail. Thus, each number stands for the number of units with a given *combination* of characteristics.

Constructing Contingency Tables

There are certain rules researchers should follow when constructing contingency tables. These rules serve two purposes: (1) they assist researchers in communicating their findings as accurately as possible, and (2) they help readers understand these findings as completely as possible. By and large, these rules resemble those for constructing the frequency distributions discussed in Chapter 7.

First, a contingency table like Table 10.1 needs a title to indicate what data are found within it. This title should include the variables involved (sex and sentence) and the figures reported (frequencies, percents, or rates). It is sometimes appropriate to identify the locale of the data (King County Court, Washington) and when they were collected (1973). Finally, table titles should include any other information needed for properly interpreting the table. The title of Table 10.1 includes the information that all the units included are convicted *felons.*

Second, if the data are not the researchers' own, but come from some other study, this should be acknowledged and the source indicated at the foot of the table. In Table 10.1 the source of the data is given. This is done for the same reason that direct quotations are footnoted — to give proper credit to the work of others.

Third, the names of the variables and their categories must be spelled out in the table. Table 10.1 illustrates this requirement. Both variables are named (sex and sentence), as are their several categories (male, female, suspended, jailed, and imprisoned). This requirement guards against the inadvertent misreading of a contingency table.

The fourth and final rule concerns the proper placement of the two variables in the contingency table. A contingency table is usually constructed in order to investigate a particular research hypothesis. If a research hypothesis asserts that two variables are related, this might be investigated by constructing a contingency table. The fourth rule says that researchers should place their *independent* variable at the *top* of the contingency table and the *dependent* variable on the *left* side. Thus, the research hypothesis which led to the construction of Table 10.1 must have stated that a convicted felon's sentence (the dependent variable) is influenced by his or her sex (the independent variable). When a contingency table is examined to see if the frequencies in it are consistent with a research hypothesis, it is essential that researchers not confuse the independent and dependent variables. Such confusion can easily be avoided if this fourth rule is followed.

Reading Contingency Tables

In order to glean the most information from a contingency table, the following guidelines should be followed.

First, researchers should examine the marginal distributions (or marginals) and see what conclusions seem appropriate. For example, from Table 10.1 it is clear that: (1) most convicted felons are men (400 out of 500); (2) most convicted felons are given suspended sentences (310 out of 500); and (3) of those convicted felons who are incarcerated, most are sent to jail (110 out of 190).

Second, researchers should examine the joint frequencies, looking to see which cells of the table have the most units and which cells the fewest. Table 10.1, for example, suggests that: (1) of those convicted felons who are incarcerated, men outnumber women by about 10 to 1 (100 + 75 to 10 + 5), (2) of those convicted felons receiving a suspended sentence, men outnumber women by only about 5 to 2 (225 to 85), and (3) only a handful of the convicted felons are women sentenced to jail or prison (15 out of 500).

These are the major findings that investigators would most likely find by just reading Table 10.1. However, other noteworthy findings can be extracted from Table 10.1 by converting its frequencies into percentages. For this reason, it is usual for investigators to include percentage data in their contingency tables.

Percentages

There are three different ways to percentage a contingency table: (1) make the percentages in each *column* add to 100; (2) make the percentages in each *row* add to 100; or (3) make *all* of the percentages add to 100. These three alternatives are examined in reverse order.

Corner Percentages. When a contingency table is percentaged in such a way that all of the percentages add to 100, the percentages are called corner percentages. Corner percentages are calculated by dividing all of the frequencies (both marginal and joint) by the total number of units and then multiplying by 100. If Table 10.1 is converted into corner percentages, Table 10.2 results.

Table 10.2   Percentages of Convicted Felons by Sex and Sentence in King County Court, Washington, 1973

	Sex		
Sentence	Male	Female	Total
Suspended	45.0%	17.0%	62.0%
Jailed	20.0	2.0	22.0
Imprisoned	15.0	1.0	16.0
Total	80.0%	20.0%	100.0%

(N = 500)

Source: Modification of Table 7 in Roy Lotz and John Hewitt, "The Influence of Legally Irrelevant Factors on Felony Sentencing," *Sociological Inquiry* 47, No. 1, pp. 39-48.

Researchers do not use corner percentages very often because they are not particularly useful. In fact, not much more can be learned from the figures in Table 10.2 than can be learned from those in Table 10.1 because the two tables are nearly identical. In Table 10.1, the frequencies add to 500. In Table 10.2, the percentages add to 100. By corner percentaging Table 10.1, each frequency in Table 10.1 is divided by five to get the percentages in Table 10.2. Hence, the relationships among the percentages in Table 10.2 are identical to the relationships among the frequencies in Table 10.1. Thus, the six conclusions reached by examining Table 10.1 can also be reached by examining Table 10.2:

1. Most convicted felons are men (80 percent).
2. Most convicted felons are given suspended sentences (62 percent).
3. Of those convicted felons who are incarcerated (38 percent), most are sent to jail (22 percent).
4. Of those convicted felons who are incarcerated, men outnumber women by about 10 to 1 (20 + 15 percent to 2 + 1 percent).
5. Of those convicted felons receiving a suspended sentence, men outnumber women by only about 5 to 2 (45 percent to 17 percent).

6. Only a handful of the convicted felons are women sentenced to jail or prison (3 percent).

For merely describing a set of data, frequencies or corner percentages are usually sufficient, but researchers are often interested in causal relationships. They want to know if X is a cause of Y. Statistics can help assess causality. However, if contingency table analysis is used for this purpose, examining tables of frequencies or corner percentages is not sufficient. At the very least, other types of percentages must be studied as well.

Row Percentages. Row percentages are those which add to 100 across the rows of a contingency table. They are computed by dividing each joint frequency by its *row* marginal frequency and multiplying the result by 100. If Table 10.1 is converted into row percentages, Table 10.3 results.

Table 10.3   Percentages of Convicted Felons by Sex and Sentence, King County Court, Washington, 1973

Sentence	Sex		Total
	Male	Female	
Suspended	72.6%	27.4%	100.0% (N = 310)
Jailed	90.9	9.1	100.0 (N = 110)
Imprisoned	93.8	6.2	100.0 (N = 80)
Total	80.0%	20.0%	100.0% (N = 500)

Source: Modification of Table 7 in Roy Lotz and John Hewitt, "The Influence of Legally Irrelevant Factors on Felony Sentencing," *Sociological Inquiry* 47, No. 1, pp. 39-48.

Recall that the research hypothesis being investigated asserts that the sex of convicted felons affects the sentences they receive. The *first* row of Table 10.3 seems to support this hypothesis. In fact, it appears that men are more likely to receive suspended sentences than are women by a margin of nearly 3 to 1. However, this reasoning is faulty. The *bottom* row of Table 10.3 clearly shows that 80 percent of the sample are men. The fact that, of those receiving suspended sentences, only 72.6 percent are men actually shows that men are less likely to receive suspended sentences than are women. The reason for this seeming anomaly is quite simple. The research hypothesis calls upon the investigators to compare what happens to men at sentencing with what happens to women at sentencing. The row percentages in Table 10.3 are telling the investigators

how those given suspended sentences differ in terms of sex from those who
are jailed and from those who are imprisoned. Thus, the research hypothesis poses an answer to a question which the row percentages in Table
10.3 do not address.

   Column Percentages. Column percentages are those which add to 100
down the columns of a contingency table. They are computed by dividing
each joint frequency by its *column* marginal frequency and multiplying the
result by 100. If Table 10.1 is converted into column percentages, Table
10.4 results.

**Table 10.4   Percentages of Convicted Felons by Sex and Sentence,
King County Court, Washington, 1973**

	Sex		
Sentence	Male	Female	Total
Suspended	56.3%	85.0%	62.0%
Jailed	25.0	10.0	22.0
Imprisoned	18.7	5.0	16.0
Total	100.0%	100.0%	100.0%
	($N = 400$)	($N = 100$)	($N = 500$)

Source: Modification of Table 7 in Roy Lotz and John Hewitt, "The Influence
   of Legally Irrelevant Factors on Felony Sentencing," *Sociological Inquiry* 47, No. 1, pp. 39-48.

   These column percentages are those needed to address the research
hypothesis. They clearly show how male and female convicted felons
differ in terms of the sentences they receive. In other words, they show
what effect sex (the independent variable) has on sentence (the dependent
variable). Thus, researchers can easily reach the following conclusions by
examining Table 10.4:

1. Convicted felons who are women are much more likely than those
   who are men to receive a suspended sentence (85 percent to
   56.3 percent).
2. Convicted felons who are men are much more likely than those
   who are women to be sentenced to jail (25 percent to 10 percent).
3. Convicted felons who are men are much more likely than those
   who are women to be sentenced to prison (18.7 percent to 5
   percent).

The research hypothesis appears to be confirmed; men are more likely to be sentenced harshly than are women. *When researchers are interested in establishing a causal relationship, the contingency table should be percentaged so that the percentages in each category of the independent variable add to 100 percent.* When the independent variable is placed at the top of a contingency table, as in Table 10.1, this means that column percentages should be computed, as in Table 10.4. This is an extremely important principle with which everyone should be familiar.

Saving Space

When putting data in contingency tables, researchers often rely completely on tables of percentages. This is understandable because tables of frequencies often have little to offer to researchers interested in causal relationships. Thus, little is lost by not reporting the actual frequencies and some space is saved. In fact, if a study investigates *many* relationships, a great deal of space is saved by reporting only the percentaged tables.

From time to time, however, some readers will want to know from what frequencies the percentages were computed. There is a very simple way to accommodate such readers while still reporting only the tables of percentages. Consider a contingency table of corner percentages, such as Table 10.2. In this type of contingency table, all the percentages are based on the total number of units in the study. If the number of units is reported, interested readers can compute the actual frequencies for themselves. For example, in Table 10.2 the number of units is reported to be 500 ($N = 500$). Therefore, since 45 percent of the units are males given suspended sentences, the *number* of males given suspended sentences must be 45 percent of 500, or 225. Table 10.1 confirms this. In the same way, all of the frequencies in Table 10.1 can be computed from the corner percentages in Table 10.2 *as long as the total number of units is reported.*

Much the same thing is done with contingency tables of row or column percentages. Consider a table of column percentages, such as Table 10.4. In this type of contingency table, the percentages are based on the column marginal frequencies. If these marginal frequencies are listed, the remaining frequencies can be computed using the column percentages. For example, Table 10.4 reports the number of male convicted felons as 400. Therefore, since the *percentage* of male convicted felons sentenced to jail is 25 percent, the *number* of male convicted felons sentenced to jail must be 25 percent of 400, or 100. This is confirmed by Table 10.1. As long as the column marginal frequencies are given, the remaining frequencies can be computed from a contingency table of column percentages. Similarly, as long as the *row* marginal frequencies are given, the remaining frequencies can be computed from a contingency table of *row* percentages. Therefore, when researchers employ the simple expedient of indicating certain frequencies on their tables of percentages, interested readers will be able to compute tables of frequencies for themselves.

Establishing Causal Relationships

Suppose that a stratified random sample of 100 male convicted felons and 100 female convicted felons is drawn from the official records of a county court. Assume also that researchers are interested in the effect of sex on sentence and that they construct a contingency table and compute the appropriate column percentages, as shown in Table 10.5.

Table 10.5   Percentages of Convicted Felons by Sex and Sentence

Sentence	Sex Male	Female	Total
Suspended	40.0%	60.0%	50.0%
Jailed	30.0	20.0	25.0
Imprisoned	30.0	20.0	25.0
Total	100.0%	100.0%	100.0%
	($N = 100$)	($N = 100$)	($N = 200$)

Table 10.5 shows clearly that women are more likely than men to receive suspended sentences while men are more likely than women to be jailed or imprisoned. Does this demonstrate that sex affects sentence? No, it does not.

In Chapter 3 it was demonstrated that in order to confirm the hypothesis that X affects Y, one must do more than show that X and Y are related. The *rival* hypotheses which might account for this relationship must also be eliminated. Chapter 3 discussed several types of rival hypotheses, one of which is the following; X and Y are related only because they are both caused by a third variable (Z). In this case, the relationship between X and Y is said to be *spurious*. Now is the relationship between sex and sentence, as shown in Table 10.5, a spurious relationship? As was indicated in Chapter 3, this question can be answered only by identifying possible third variables and then checking to see if they affect the relationship between X and Y. For example, if women are charged with different types of crimes than are men, the sentences they receive might be affected. To consider this possibility, researchers must first divide the sample into subsamples based on the type of crime and then construct contingency tables for sex and sentence within each subsample. Suppose that they decide to distinguish between violent crimes and property crimes. After dividing their sample into these two subsamples, they can construct the subtables shown in Table 10.6.

Table 10.6   Percentages of Convicted Felons by Sex and Sentence, Controlling for Type of Crime

| | Violent Crime | | | Property Crime | | |
| | Sex | | | Sex | | |
Sentence	Male	Female	Total	Male	Female	Total
Suspended	12.0%	13.3%	12.3%	68.0%	68.2%	68.1%
Jailed	44.0	40.0	43.1	16.0	15.3	15.6
Imprisoned	44.0	46.7	44.6	16.0	16.5	16.3
Total	100.0%	100.0%	100.0%	100.0%	100.0%	100.0%
	($N = 50$)	($N = 15$)	($N = 65$)	($N = 50$)	($N = 85$)	($N = 135$)

These subtables suggest that the relationship between sex and sentence is spurious. In the *violent crime* subtable it is clear that women are no more likely than men to receive a suspended sentence ($13.3 \cong 12$ percent), and men are no more likely than women to be incarcerated ($88 \cong 86.7$ percent). The same statements apply when the *property crime* subtable is examined.

Then why do sex and sentence *appear* to be related in Table 10.5? The answer is fairly simple. According to Table 10.6, most of the female felons are convicted of property crimes (85 out of 100), while male felons are as likely to be convicted of violent crimes as property crimes (50 each). Thus, sex is related to type of crime. Further, Table 10.6 shows that persons convicted of property crimes were given more lenient sentences than those convicted of violent crimes. Hence, type of crime is related to sentence. Altogether, women are more likely than men to be convicted of crimes which the county court treats leniently. As a result, women are usually treated more leniently than men, not because of their sex, but because of the type of crime for which they have been convicted. Figure 10.1 illustrates the relationships between type of crime, sex, and sentence.

Figure 10.1   An Example of a Spurious Relationship

1. Sentencing for Female Convicted Felons

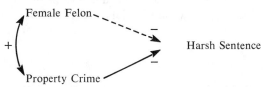

2. Sentencing for Male Convicted Felons

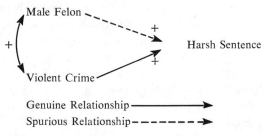

Genuine Relationship ─────────►
Spurious Relationship ─ ─ ─ ─ ─►

NOTE: Curved, double-headed arrows stand for symmetric relationships and no causality is implied. Straight, single-headed arrows stand for asymmetric relationships and causality is implied (of course, the claim may be spurious).

The Importance of Controls

By now, it should be clear that when a research hypothesis is investigated, it is not enough merely to examine the appropriate contingency table. The relationship in the table might be spurious. Researchers must identify rival hypotheses and eliminate them, one at a time, by controlling for those third variables which might be the *real cause* of the relationship in the contingency table. For many students of criminal justice, the discovery that relationships shown in contingency tables might be spurious rather than genuine is very disappointing, because it makes perfectly clear the vital role of personal judgment in criminal justice research. Contingency table analysis, like statistics in general, is a valuable tool, but it is no substutute for clear thinking. Thus, researchers must identify the rival hypotheses which need to be ruled out before the relationships in contingency tables can be relied upon with some confidence.

Unfortunately, one must do more than investigate potentially spurious relationships when using contingency table analysis; that is, it is not so simple as just deciding whether the relationship in a contingency table is either genuine or spurious. In fact, there are several ways in which the *real relationship* between X and Y can differ from the relationship in the contingency table. Two of these will be examined here: interaction and suppression.

Interaction

As was stated in Chapter 3, *interaction is present whenever the strength of the relationship between X and Y depends on the value of some third variable Z.* Clearly, when the relationship between X and Y depends on the value of Z, the investigators' findings will be mistaken if Z is ignored. The possibility of interaction requires that investigators identify variables which might potentially interact with X in terms of its effect on Y. When these rival hypotheses are ruled out, the investigators can place greater confidence in their findings concerning the relationship between X and Y. If these rival hypotheses are not ruled out, researchers must revise their original findings.

For instance, suppose that investigators draw a sample of 200 felons from the official records of a county court. They hypothesize that the severity of the sentence is related to a defendant's previous record of felony convictions. To investigate this possibility, Table 10.7 is constructed.

Table 10.7   Percentages of Those With and Without Previous Felony Convictions Given Various Sentences

Sentence	Previous Felony Conviction		Total
	Yes	No	
Suspended	40.0%	60.0%	50.0%
Jailed	30.0	20.0	25.0
Imprisoned	30.0	20.0	25.0
Total	100.0%	100.0%	100.0%
	(N = 100)	(N = 100)	(N = 200)

On the basis of Table 10.7, the research hypothesis appears to be supported. Of those convicted felons with a previous felony conviction, 60 percent are incarcerated. Of those convicted felons without a previous felony conviction, only 40 percent are incarcerated. Thus, those with a previous conviction are about 20 percent more likely to be sentenced to jail or prison than are those without such a conviction. However, might not the strength of the relationship between previous felony conviction (X)

and sentence (*Y*) depend on the type of crime (*Z*)? To test this possibility, investigators control for the type of crime, and Table 10.8 results.

Table 10.8   Percentages of Those With and Without Previous Felony Convictions Given Various Sentences, Controlling for Type of Crime

| | Violent Crime | | | Property Crime | | |
| | Previous Felony Conviction | | | Previous Felony Conviction | | |
Sentence	Yes	No	Total	Yes	No	Total
Suspended	40.0%	45.4%	43.6%	40.0%	77.8%	54.8%
Jailed	30.0	27.3	28.2	30.0	11.1	22.6
Imprisoned	30.0	27.3	28.2	30.0	11.1	22.6
Total	100.0%	100.0%	100.0%	100.0%	100.0%	100.0%
	(N = 30)	(N = 55)	(N = 85)	(N = 70)	(N = 45)	(N = 115)

The figures in Table 10.8 suggest that the strength of the relationship between previous felony conviction and sentence *does* depend on the type of crime. For those convicted of *violent crimes,* the presence of a previous conviction seems to have little effect on the sentence. With these cases, about 60 percent of those felons convicted of violent crimes are incarcerated regardless of whether there was a previous felony conviction. However, for those convicted of *property crimes,* the presence of a previous conviction seems to have a marked effect on the sentence. Here, while only 22.2 percent of those without a previous conviction are incarcerated, fully 60 percent of those with a previous conviction are incarcerated. Thus, of the felons convicted of property crimes, those with a previous conviction are about 38 percent more likely to be sentenced to jail or prison than those without a previous conviction. Therefore, this is an example of interaction: the effect of *X* (previous felony conviction) on *Y* (sentence) depends upon *Z* (type of crime). Specifically for violent crimes, the relationship between previous felony conviction and sentence is very weak. For property crimes, the relationship between previous felony conviction and sentence is very strong.

It should be noted that when the effect of *X* on *Y* depends on *Z*, then the effect of *Z* on *Y* must also depend on *X*. Consider the previous example. Suppose that investigators first look at the relationship between type of crime and sentence, as shown in Table 10.9.

Table 10.9   **Percentages of Those Convicted of Violent and Property Crimes Given Various Sentences**

Sentence	Type of Crime		Total
	Violent	Property	
Suspended	43.6%	54.8%	50.0%
Jailed	28.2	22.6	25.0
Imprisoned	28.2	22.6	25.0
Total	100.0%	100.0%	100.0%
	($N = 85$)	($N = 115$)	($N = 200$)

This table suggests that type of crime (X) has a modest effect on sentence (Y), but might not the strength of this relationship (between X and Y) depend on the presence of a previous felony conviction (Z)? To investigate this possibility investigators control for the presence of a previous felony conviction, as is shown in Table 10.10.

Table 10.10   **Percentages of Those Convicted of Violent and Property Crimes Given Various Sentences, Controlling for Previous Felony Conviction**

Sentence	Previous Felony Conviction			No Previous Felony Conviction		
	Type of Crime			Type of Crime		
	Violent	Property	Total	Violent	Property	Total
Suspended	40.0%	40.0%	40.0%	45.4%	77.8%	60.0%
Jailed	30.0	30.0	30.0	27.3	11.1	20.0
Imprisoned	30.0	30.0	30.0	27.3	11.1	20.0
Total	100.0%	100.0%	100.0%	100.0%	100.0%	100.0%
	($N = 30$)	($N = 70$)	($N = 100$)	($N = 55$)	($N = 45$)	($N = 100$)

Table 10.10 shows clearly that the strength of the relationship between type of crime and sentence does depend on the presence of a previous felony conviction. For felons with a previous conviction, the type of crime appears to have no effect on sentence. For felons without a previous conviction, the type of crime has a marked effect on sentence. This is an example of interaction: the effect of X (type of crime) on Y (sentence) depends on Z (previous felony conviction).

Whenever interaction is present, it can be said that the effect of X on Y depends on Z and that the effect of Z on Y depends on X. More simply, one can say that X and Z interact in terms of their effects on Y.

Suppression

Suppression is the *opposite* of spuriousness. A spurious relationship exists when X and Y appear to be related only because of the effects of a third variable Z. On the other hand, *suppression is present whenever X and Y appear to be unrelated only because their true relationship is suppressed (obscured) by the effects of a third variable Z.* The possibility of suppression means that researchers cannot just discard variables which appear to be unrelated when arrayed in a contingency table. Instead, they must identify third variables which might suppress this relationship and investigate them one at a time.

For example, suppose that researchers draw a stratified sample of 100 white convicted felons and 100 nonwhite convicted felons from the official records of a county court. They hypothesize that the severity of the sentence is related to a defendant's race. To investigate this possibility, Table 10.11 is constructed.

Table 10.11   Percentages of White and Nonwhite Convicted Felons Given Various Sentences

	Race of Felon		
Sentence	White	Nonwhite	Total
Suspended	50.0%	50.0%	50.0%
Jailed	25.0	25.0	25.0
Imprisoned	25.0	25.0	25.0
Total	100.0%	100.0%	100.0%
	($N = 100$)	($N = 100$)	($N = 200$)

Table 10.11 suggests that the investigators' research hypothesis is false. Of the white convicted felons, 50 percent receive suspended sentences and the other 50 percent are incarcerated. Exactly the same is true of nonwhite convicted felons. Thus, it appears that the race of convicted felons is unrelated to their sentence. However, it could be that some other variable is suppressing this relationship. Perhaps, the crimes for which whites and nonwhites are convicted differ. Specifically, perhaps the crimes for which they are convicted differ in terms of the race of the *victim*. If this is true, controlling for the race of the victim might demonstrate that there really is a relationship between the race of a convicted felon and the sentence handed down. Table 10.12 portrays the relationship between these two variables controlling for the race of the victim.

Table 10.12   Percentages of White and Nonwhite Convicted Felons Given Various Sentences, Controlling for the Race of the Victim

Sentence	White Victim			Nonwhite Victim		
	Race of Felon			Race of Felon		
	White	Nonwhite	Total	White	Nonwhite	Total
Suspended	42.9%	33.4%	40.0%	66.7%	57.2%	60.0%
Jailed	28.6	33.3	30.0	16.7	21.4	20.0
Imprisoned	28.5	33.3	30.0	16.6	21.4	20.0
Total	100.0%	100.0%	100.0%	100.0%	100.0%	100.0%
	$(N = 70)$	$(N = 30)$	$(N = 100)$	$(N = 30)$	$(N = 70)$	$(N = 100)$

After examining Table 10.12, it appears that there is a relationship between the race of a convicted felon and the sentence dispensed. When the victim is white, white felons are almost 10 percent more likely than nonwhite felons to receive a suspended sentence (42.9 − 33.4 ≅ 10 percent). Similarly, when the victim is nonwhite, white felons are about 10 percent more likely than nonwhite felons to receive a suspended sentence (66.7 − 57.2 ≅ 10 percent). In *both* subtables, white felons are more likely than nonwhite felons to be given suspended sentences. Why, then, when these two subtables are combined in Table 10.11, does the relationship between the race of a convicted felon and the sentence disappear? This is a perfectly good question. Here is the answer in three parts.

First, it has just been established that nonwhite felons are sentenced more harshly than white felons. Thus, the race of a convicted felon is related to the severity of the sentence. Second, Table 10.12 shows that the race of a *victim* is also related to the sentence handed down. Specifically, the *row* marginals in Table 10.12 show that when a victim is nonwhite, the felon's chances of receiving a suspended sentence are 20 percent higher than when a victim is white (60 − 40 = 20 percent). Finally, the *column* marginals in Table 10.12 show that nonwhite felons tend to victimize nonwhites (70 out of 100) while white felons tend to victimize whites (also 70 out of 100). Thus, most crime is intraracial — both the convicted felon and the victim are of the same race. Hence, there is a relationship between the race of a convicted felon and the race of his victim. The three relationships just discussed are diagrammed in Figure 10.2.

Figure 10.2   An Example of Suppression

1. Sentencing for Nonwhite Convicted Felons

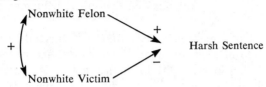

2. Sentencing for White Convicted Felons

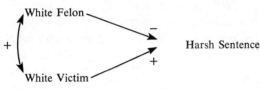

NOTE: Curved, double-headed arrows stand for symmetric relationships and no causality is implied. Straight, single-headed arrows stand for asymmetric relationships and causality is implied.

Figure 10.2 illustrates how the *race of a victim* obscures, or suppresses, the relationship between the *race of a convicted felon* and the *severity of the sentence*. On the one hand, nonwhite felons tend to be sentenced *more* harshly than white felons. On the other hand, however, they tend to victimize other nonwhites whose "victimizers," in turn, tend to be sentenced *less* harshly than others. The two tendencies cancel out so that, in the last analysis, nonwhite felons end up being sentenced no more harshly than white felons. Much the same thing happens with white felons, but in reverse. On the one hand, white felons tend to be sentenced *less* harshly than nonwhite felons. On the other hand, they tend to victimize other whites whose "victimizers," in turn, tend to be sentenced more harshly than others. Once again, the two tendencies cancel out so that in the last analysis, white felons end up being sentenced no less harshly than nonwhite felons.

Suppression is extremely difficult to detect. What is worse is that researchers often do not seem particularly interested in detecting it. Many studies whose purpose is to identify the various independent variables affecting a dependent variable are conducted as if there was no such thing as suppression. The studies begin with a long list of potential independent variables. Then each independent variable is related to the dependent variable, perhaps in a contingency table. If the relationship seems to be substantial, the independent variable is retained. If the relationship does not seem to be substantial, the independent variable is thrown out. In this way, the lengthy list of potential independent variables is quickly shortened to include only the "truly important" independent variables. One cannot help but wonder about the many interesting, but suppressed, relationships which are ignored in the course of this sort of research.

In addition to being difficult to detect, suppression is also misunderstood. Suppression is commonly reported to exist when the relationships in the various subtables are opposites of one another so that they somehow cancel out when the subtables are added together to form the original contingency table (Poister, 1978, p. 158; Williamson, 1977, p. 423). This is clearly not the case. In *both* subtables in Table 10.12, nonwhite felons are sentenced more harshly than white felons. It is *not true* that nonwhite felons are sentenced more harshly than white felons in some cases and less harshly in others so that when all cases are examined together no relationship is found. Suppression is not just the cancelling out in the entire sample of "equal-but-opposite" relationships in various subsamples. Suppression is the obscuring of a genuine relationship caused by the effects of a third variable.

A Note on the Importance of Controls

The possibility that the relationship in a contingency table might be spurious, influenced by interaction, or suppressed makes it essential that researchers know what they are doing. Only knowledgeable persons can suggest which variables need to be controlled. This task cannot be delegated to a statistician.

Finally, it should be pointed out that the problems caused by spuriousness, interaction, and suppression do not beset only contingency table analysis. Suppose that in all the examples used in this chapter, the dependent variable was the *length* of sentence, measured in months. Since all the independent variables are dichotomous, researchers could use one of the two-sample tests discussed in Chapter 9. Still they will have to worry about spuriousness, interaction, and suppression. If by using a two-sample test they find a statistically significant difference in the lengths of sentences given male and female felons, this difference might still be spurious; that is, it might still be true that men and women receive sentences of different lengths because they are convicted of different types of crimes. The fundamental point is this: *spuriousness, interaction, and suppression cannot be avoided by switching to another method of data analysis. They are caused by the social world criminal justice researchers study — not by the methods with which they study that world.*

A Hypothesis Test for Contingency Tables

Thus far, no mention has been made of hypothesis testing; that is, no effort has yet been made to determine whether a relationship found in a contingency table constructed from sampled data is characteristic of the population from which the sample is drawn. According to Tables 10.1 and 10.4, there was a relationship between the sex and sentence of convicted felons in King County Court, Washington, in 1973. Suppose that the 500 units studied are a random sample from the population of all felons convicted in that court during 1973. It is possible that the relationship between sex and sentence in the sample is *different* from the relationship between sex and sentence in the population. In the sample the females were sentenced less harshly than the males, but perhaps the females in the sample were sentenced less harshly than the rest of the females in the population. If so, there might be no relationship between sex and sentence in the *population,* Table 10.1 to the contrary notwithstanding. Perhaps the *males* in the sample were sentenced less harshly than the rest of the males in the population. If this is true, the relationship between sex and sentence in the population might be even stronger than the relationship in the sample. The point is that investigators have no good reason to expect a relationship found in sampled data to be a precise reflection of the relationship in the population. *A hypothesis test is needed.*

Fortunately, there is a hypothesis test designed to be used in this type of situation: the χ^2 (Chi square) test. The four steps involved when using the χ^2 test are listed in Figure 10.3.

Figure 10.3   Steps for Using the Chi Square Test

1. State the research and null hypotheses.
2. Set the permissible level of error.
3. Compute the χ^2 statistic.
4. Compare the χ^2 statistic with the appropriate χ^2 distribution.

The Research and Null Hypotheses

As stated earlier, the question is, Does the relationship between X and Y found in a contingency table also exist in the population? The research and null hypotheses for the Chi square test are:

H_o: There is no relationship between X and Y.

H_a: There is a relationship between X and Y.

Since these are nondirectional hypotheses, the Chi square test is a nondirectional test. In the example involving sex (X) and sentence (Y), the null hypothesis is rejected if *either* sex is found to be more harshly sentenced than the other (to a statistically significant degree). As far as the

Chi square test is concerned, it makes no difference which sex is sentenced more harshly than the other. Therefore, for this example the null and research hypotheses are:

H_o: There is no relationship between the sex and sentence of convicted felons.

H_a: There is a relationship between the sex and sentence of convicted felons.

Setting the Level of Error

When the Chi square test is used, the level of error is set with the same considerations in mind as was the case with the hypothesis tests discussed in Chapters 8 and 9. As before, the central issue is one's willingness to risk falsely rejecting a true null hypothesis.

Computing the Chi Square (X^2) Statistic

The test statistic for the Chi square test is computed by comparing the *observed* joint frequencies in a contingency table (called the *observed frequencies*) with the joint frequencies the null hypothesis leads investigators to *expect* in the contingency table (called the *expected frequencies*). If the observed frequencies are greatly different from the expected frequencies, investigators reject the null hypothesis in favor of the research hypothesis. If the observed frequencies are not too different from the expected frequencies, they attribute the minor differences to chance and do not reject the null hypothesis. What is needed is some method for comparing the observed frequencies with the expected frequencies in order to see how great the difference is between the two. This is what the Chi square statistic does.

The Expected Frequencies. Before the Chi square statistic is computed, the expected frequencies must be calculated. Examine the joint frequencies given in Table 10.13. If the null hypothesis is true, what should the joint frequencies in Table 10.13 look like? In other words, if the sex of convicted felons has no effect on their sentences, how many males and females should be given suspended sentences, sentenced to jail, or sentenced to prison? The answer to this question is easier than one might think. Notice that, altogether, 62 percent of those sentenced are given suspended sentences (310 out of 500). It stands to reason, therefore, that if sex has no effect on sentence (i.e., if the null hypothesis is true), then 62 percent of *each* sex should be given suspended sentences; that is, 62 percent of the females should get suspended sentences, and 62 percent of the males should get suspended sentences. If the null hypothesis

Table 10.13   Number of Convicted Felons by Sex and Sentence, King County Court, Washington, 1973

	Sex		
Sentence	Male	Female	Total
Suspended	225	85	310
Jailed	100	10	110
Imprisoned	75	5	80
Total	400	100	500

Source: Modification of Table 7 in Roy Lotz and John Hewitt, "The Influence of Legally Irrelevant Factors on Felony Sentencing," *Sociological Inquiry* 47, No. 1, pp. 39-48.

is true, 62 percent of the 100 females sentenced (62) should receive suspended sentences, and 62 percent of the 400 males sentenced (248) should be given the same sentence. Hence, the *expected* frequencies in the first row of the contingency table are 248 and 62, as shown in Table 10.14.

Table 10.14   Expected Number of Convicted Felons by Sex and Sentence, King County Court, Washington, 1973

	Sex		
Sentence	Male	Female	Total
Suspended	248	62	310
Jailed	88	22	110
Imprisoned	64	16	80
Total	400	100	500

By looking again at Table 10.13, it can immediately be seen that, altogether, 22 percent of the felons sentenced are jailed. If the null hypothesis is true, investigators should expect that 22 females (22 percent of 100) and 88 males (22 percent of 400) will be jailed, as shown in the second row of Table 10.14. Finally, investigators should expect 16 females and 64 males to be imprisoned (16 percent of 100 and 400, respectively), as shown in the third row of Table 10.14. These, then, are the expected frequencies associated with the observed frequencies found in Table 10.13.

There is another, faster way to calculate the expected frequencies. *To get the expected frequency associated with a given cell in a contingency table, multiply that cell's row marginal by its column marginal and divide this product by the total number of units.* Thus, the expected number of males given suspended sentences is:

310 (row marginal) • 400 (column marginal) ÷ 500 (total) = 248
The calculation of all the expected frequencies using this method is shown
in Figure 10.4.

**Figure 10.4   The Preferred Method for Computing Expected Frequencies
(Based on Table 10.13)**

1. The expected number of males given suspended sentences:
   310 • 400 ÷ 500 = 248
2. The expected number of females given suspended sentences:
   310 • 100 ÷ 500 = 62
3. The expected number of males sentenced to jail:
   110 • 400 ÷ 500 = 88
4. The expected number of females sentenced to jail:
   110 • 100 ÷ 500 = 22
5. The expected number of males sentenced to prison:
   80 • 400 ÷ 500 = 64
6. The expected number of females sentenced to prison:
   80 • 100 ÷ 500 = 16

This is the *preferred method* for computing the expected frequencies. The
earlier method, though easier to understand, involves two distinct steps:
(1) calculating the percentages for the row marginal distribution and (2)
taking those percentages of each column total. The preferred method
computes the expected frequencies in one quick step: row marginal times
column marginal divided by the total. It is faster and less prone to error
since fewer computational steps are involved.

  Computing χ^2. After the expected frequencies have been calculated,
the χ^2 statistic can be computed. The formula for χ^2 is:

$$\chi^2 = \Sigma \frac{(0 - E)^2}{E}$$

where: 0 = the observed frequency in a cell

   E = the expected frequency in that cell

Once the expected frequencies are known, χ^2 is relatively easy to calculate.
For each cell in a contingency table, three steps are involved: (1) the
expected frequency is subtracted from the observed frequency; (2) this
difference is squared; and (3) this square is divided by the *expected*
frequency. Once these steps have been carried out for each cell in the
table, they are added together to produce χ^2. As long as these steps are
followed in sequence, the correct value for χ^2 is easy to compute. Using
the sex-sentence example, Figure 10.5 shows how χ^2 is calculated.

Figure 10.5   Computing the χ^2 Statistic

Cell	O	E	O - E	$(O - E)^2$	$(O - E)^2/E$
1	225	248	-23	529	2.1331
2	85	62	23	529	8.5323
3	100	88	12	144	1.6364
4	10	22	-12	144	6.5455
5	75	64	11	121	1.8906
6	5	16	-11	121	7.5625

$$\chi^2 = 28.3004$$

By examining the formula for χ^2, it is easy to see how χ^2 measures the difference between the observed frequencies and the expected frequencies. If these two sets of frequencies are similar in value, the values of $O - E$ will be small, as will those of $(O - E)^2$; $(O - E)^2/E$; and χ^2 itself. When the observed joint frequencies are approximately what investigators expect (given the null hypothesis), then the χ^2 statistic will be small. On the other hand, if the observed frequencies differ greatly from the expected frequencies, the values of $O - E$; $(O - E)^2$; $(O - E)^2/E$; and χ^2 will be large. When the observed frequencies are markedly different from those the null hypothesis leads investigators to expect, then the χ^2 statistic will be large.

Comparing the χ^2 Statistic to the χ^2 Sampling Distribution

The logic of the χ^2 test is very straightforward. If the null hypothesis is true, the observed frequencies should resemble the expected frequencies and the χ^2 statistic will be small. However, due to chance, it is possible for the observed frequencies to differ substantially from the expected frequencies even when the null hypothesis is true. Such a substantial difference would, of course, result in a large χ^2 statistic. Ordinarily, when the null hypothesis is true, the χ^2 statistic will not be too large. The question is, How large is too large? That is, *how large a χ^2 statistic can investigators allow before rejecting the null hypothesis in favor of the research hypothesis?* The answer depends on two factors: (1) the level of error and (2) the degrees of freedom.

The level of error is set by investigators in light of the considerations noted earlier. The degrees of freedom depend only upon the number of rows and columns in the contingency table, not upon the size of the sample. Once the level of error and degrees of freedom are known, all that investigators need to do is consult the χ^2 sampling distribution table in order to find the boundary value which the χ^2 statistic must equal or exceed for the investigators to reject the null hypothesis. This process is nearly identical to that used with the one-sample and two-samples t tests discussed in Chapters 8 and 9. In both cases, the boundary value depends upon both the level of error and the degrees of freedom. In both cases, when the test statistic (i.e., t or χ^2) equals or exceeds the boundary value, the null hypothesis is rejected. Of course, the computation of both the test statistic and degrees of freedom for the χ^2 test differs from that for the t tests, but the tests are conducted in much the same way.

Although the level of error is set by investigators, the degrees of freedom must be computed. For the χ^2 test, the degrees of freedom are computed using the following formula:

$$df = (r - 1)(c - 1)$$

where: r = the number of rows in the contingency table

c = the number of columns in the contingency table

Thus, for Table 10.13, the number of degrees of freedom is:

$$df = (3 - 1)(2 - 1) = (2)(1)$$
$$= 2$$

Once the level of error and the degrees of freedom are known, the χ^2 test can be completed. The sampling distribution for the χ^2 statistic is found in Appendix E. The columns in this table correspond to the levels of error while the rows depend on the degrees of freedom. To find the boundary value, investigators enter this table at the column headed by the appropriate level of error and the row headed by the correct degrees of freedom. The boundary value is at the intersection of this column and this row.

For example, suppose that the investigators who constructed Table 10.13 set their level of error at .05 and calculate the degrees of freedom to be 2. To find the boundary value they turn to Appendix E and find the intersection of the second row and the column headed by .05. This boundary value is 5.991. Since (as shown in Figure 10.5) the χ^2 statistic is 28.30, which exceeds 5.991, the null hypothesis is rejected in favor of the research hypothesis. There is a relationship between the sex of convicted felons and the sentence they receive. This example is illustrated in Figure 10.6.

Researchers make frequent use of the χ^2 test. For example, Vito and Allen (1980), in their study of the success and failure of shock probation in Ohio, examined a number of factors which they thought explained why shock probation works in some cases and not in others. The relationship

Figure 10.6   Sampling Distribution for the χ^2 Statistic, 2 Degrees of Freedom, with the Critical Region (.05) Indicated

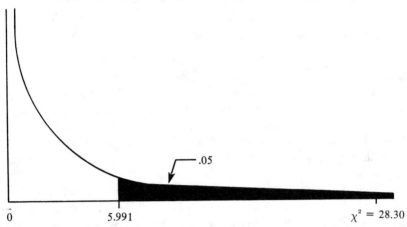

between each such factor and the success/failure of shock probation was investigated with the use of the χ^2 test. For example, one factor they studied was the age of the probationer. They set up a contingency table much like the one in Table 10.15 and computed the χ^2 statistic.

Table 10.15   Relationship Between Age and the Success of Shock Probation in Ohio, 1978

| | Age | | |
Shock Probation	21 and Under	Over 21	Total
Success	365	526	891
Failure	111	68	179
Total	476	594	1070

Source: Data from Gennaro F. Vito and Harry E. Allen, "Shock Probation In Ohio: Use of Base Expectancy Rates as an Evaluation Method," *Criminal Justice and Behavior* 7 (September, 1980), pp. 331-340.

The χ^2 statistic for Table 10.15 is 30.3414. Since the number of rows and columns are both equal to 2, the degrees of freedom are:

$$df = (2 - 1)(2 - 1) = (1)(1)$$
$$= 1$$

Suppose that Vito and Allen used the .05 level of error. Then, according to Appendix E, their critical value would have been 3.841. Since 30.3414 is greater than 3.841, the null hypothesis would be rejected. The con-

clusion would be that there is a relationship between the age of a probationer and the success of his treatment through shock probation.

Final Comments about the χ^2 Test

Since the χ^2 test is a commonly used test, it is also a commonly
misused test. Three errors are especially common. First, researchers
occasionally carry out the χ^2 test on a contingency table of percentages
rather than frequencies. In other words, rather than beginning with a
table like Table 10.13, they begin with tables like Tables 10.2, 10.3, and
10.4. *This is always wrong and should never be done.* The whole
rationale for the χ^2 test is to compare observed *frequencies* with expected
frequencies.

Second, from time to time the computational formula for the χ^2
statistic is misused. Two errors are common here. The first is to mistakenly divide $(O - E)^2$ by O rather than E. This is tantamount to using
the following faulty formula for χ^2:

$$\text{False } \chi^2 = \Sigma \frac{(O - E)^2}{O}$$

The second computational error is to mistakenly divide $O - E$ by E and
then square the result rather than first squaring $O - E$ and then dividing
by E. This is tantamount to using the following faulty formula for χ^2:

$$\text{False } \chi^2 = \Sigma \left(\frac{O - E}{E} \right)^2$$

Finally, the χ^2 test is occasionally misused by applying it in situations
where it is inadvisable to do so. In particular, the χ^2 test should not be
used when any of the *expected frequencies* are less than or equal to 5.
Oddly enough, this restriction is itself misunderstood. It is the expected
frequencies which must exceed 5, *not* the observed frequencies. The fact
that (according to Table 10.13) only five females were sentenced to prison
does not mean that it is inappropriate to use the χ^2 test on Table 10.13.
The important frequencies in this case are those in Table 10.14, and all
of them are well over 5. In many cases this restriction on the use of the
χ^2 test can be easily overcome. All that one needs to do is to recategorize
one, or both, variables. This will alter the marginal distribution(s) and,
therefore, the expected frequencies as well. For example, consider the
contingency table in Table 10.16.

**Table 10.16   Number of Male and Female Convicted Felons
Given Various Sentences**

	Sex		
Sentence	Male	Female	Total
Suspended	110	40	150
Jailed	5	5	10
Imprisoned	35	5	40
Total	150	50	200

The expected frequency for the number of females sentenced to jail is:

$$10 \cdot 50 \div 200 = 2.5$$

Since 2.5 is less than 5, it is inappropriate to apply the χ^2 test to the data in Table 10.16. However, if the jailed and the imprisoned are put into a single category called *incarcerated,* the result is Table 10.17.

**Table 10.17   Number of Male and Female Convicted Felons
Given Suspended Sentences and Incarcerated**

	Sex		
Sentence	Male	Female	Total
Suspended	110	40	150
Incarcerated	40	10	50
Total	150	50	200

Now all of the expected frequencies are well over 5 and the χ^2 test can be applied. Of course, it should be noted that Table 10.17 is different from Table 10.16. Hence, something is lost when two categories are combined into one in order to allow the χ^2 test to be used.

Measuring the Strength of a Relationship

Up to this point, almost nothing has been said about measuring the *strength* of the relationship in a contingency table because it seems so natural and easy to use column percentages for this purpose. For example, examine Table 10.8. Clearly, the relationship between previous felony conviction and sentence is stronger for those convicted of property crimes than those convicted of violent crimes. The column percentages support this conclusion. For felons convicted of property crimes, those with no previous felony convictions are almost 40 percent more likely to receive a suspended sentence than are those with such a previous conviction (77.8 − 40.0 = 37.8 ≅ 40 percent). For felons convicted of violent crimes, those with no previous felony convictions are only about 5 percent more likely to receive a suspended sentence than those with such a previous conviction (45.5 − 40.0 = 5.5 ≅ 5 percent). Researchers naturally interpret these *percentage differences* (40 percent and 5 percent) as measures of the strengths of these two relationships. As long as the contingency tables are relatively simple (just a few rows and columns), using percentage differences to measure the strength of relationships makes very good sense; percentage differences are both easy to compute and easy to interpret. What, though, should researchers do when they are confronted with a contingency table like Table 10.18?

Table 10.18   Percent of Felons Convicted of Several Types of Offenses Given Various Sentences

Sentence	Armed Robbery	Assault/ Battery	Grand Theft	Embezzle- ment	Total
Suspended	20.0%	50.0%	66.7%	80.0%	49.0%
Jailed	30.0	31.3	13.3	10.0	24.5
Imprisoned	50.0	18.7	20.0	10.0	26.5
Total	100.0%	100.0%	100.0%	100.0%	100.0%
	(N = 250)	(N = 400)	(N = 300)	(N = 50)	(N = 1000)

Type of Offense spans the Armed Robbery, Assault/Battery, Grand Theft, and Embezzlement columns.

After examining Table 10.18, two conclusions seem rather obvious. First, there certainly appears to be a relationship between the type of offense and the sentence. This is seen by comparing the percentages in each column with those in the other columns and computing the various percentage differences. Second, it is hard to say just how strong this relationship is. On the one hand, those convicted of armed robbery are sentenced much more harshly than those convicted of embezzlement. This suggests that the relationship between the type of offense and the sentence is a very strong one. On the other hand, those convicted of grand theft are sentenced only a little more harshly than those convicted of embezzlement, suggesting that the relationship between the type of offense and sentence is rather weak. Of course, one can compare other pairs of columns in Table 10.18, compute other percentage differences, and arrive at still other conclusions. Which of these conclusions is the correct one? Which is the most nearly correct one? These questions cannot easily be answered using percentage differences. In general, whenever the independent variable has more than two categories and, as a consequence, the contingency table has more than two columns, percentage differences are unsuitable as measures of the strength of a relationship. What is needed is a statistic that will measure the strength of relationship *in the entire contingency table, all at once.*

Misusing the χ^2 Statistic as a Measure of Relationship

Researchers are sometimes tempted to use the χ^2 statistic as a measure of the strength of a relationship. After all, the χ^2 statistic does measure how far the observed frequencies depart from the frequencies investigators expect to find when two variables are unrelated. Unfortunately, the χ^2 statistic does not measure the strength of a relationship very well. For example, consider Table 10.19.

Table 10.19   Number of Felons Convicted of Several Types of Offenses Given Various Sentences

	Type of Offense				
Sentence	Armed Robbery	Assault/ Battery	Grand Theft	Embezzle- ment	Total
Suspended	50	200	200	40	490
Jailed	75	125	40	5	245
Imprisoned	125	75	60	5	265
Total	250	400	300	50	1000

Table 10.19 contains the frequencies upon which the column percentages in Table 10.18 are based. The χ^2 statistic for Table 10.19 is 173.07. Using .01 as the level of error, with 6 degrees of freedom ($df = (3 - 1)(4 - 1) = (2)(3) = 6$) the critical value found in Appendix E is only 16.812. Since 173.07 is *much larger* than 16.812, researchers are tempted to conclude that there must be a *very strong* relationship between the type of offense and the severity of the sentence. However, *this reasoning is faulty.*

Suppose that all of the frequencies in Table 10.19 are multiplied by 10 to produce Table 10.20.

Table 10.20   Number of Felons Convicted of Several Types of Offenses Given Various Sentences

| | Type of Offense | | | | |
Sentence	Armed Robbery	Assault/ Battery	Grand Theft	Embezzle- ment	Total
Suspended	500	2000	2000	400	4900
Jailed	750	1250	400	50	2450
Imprisoned	1250	750	600	50	2650
Total	2500	4000	3000	500	10,000

Since *all* of the frequencies in Table 10.19 are multiplied by the same number, the column percentages based on Table 10.20 are identical to those based on Table 10.19. In particular, they are the column percentages found in Table 10.18. Since the column percentages are the same, it stands to reason that the strength of the relationship in Table 10.20 is equal to the strength of the relationship in Table 10.19. However, the χ^2 statistic for Table 10.20 is 1730.74, not 173.07. *The value of the χ^2 statistic depends upon the size of the sample as well as the strength of the relationship.* It is this property of the χ^2 statistic that disqualifies it as a measure of the strength of a relationship. In fact, with a large enough sample, even a weak relationship in a contingency table produces a very large χ^2 statistic.

Cramer's V

If it were not for the fact that the χ^2 statistic depends on the size of the sample, it could be used as a measure of the strength of a relationship (called *measure of relationship*). Hence, the χ^2 statistic does constitute a reasonable basis from which a satisfactory measure of relationship can be developed. In fact, several of the measures of relationship which have already been developed are based on the χ^2 statistic. The best of these appears to be Cramer's V. The formula for V is:

$$V = \sqrt{\chi^2/(N \cdot M)}$$

where: N = the sample size

M = either r − 1 or c − 1, whichever is smaller

Examine this formula for a minute. Notice that V avoids the dependence of the χ^2 statistic on the sample size by simply dividing χ^2 by N. As a consequence, V is not dependent on the size of the sample. This is a step in the right direction.

When χ^2 is divided by N, the resulting statistic is called *Phi square* (Φ^2):

$$\Phi^2 = \chi^2/N$$

Frequently, Φ^2 is itself used as a measure of relationship, but it has one major drawback. *It does not have a well-defined maximum.* Clearly, Φ^2's minimum value is .00, which occurs when χ^2 is .00. This, of course, indicates that X and Y are not related. However, Φ^2's maximum value depends on the number of rows and/or columns in the contingency table. Thus, Φ^2's maximum value for a contingency table with 3 rows and 4 columns (like Table 10.19) is not the same as its maximum value for a contingency table with 2 rows and 2 columns (like Table 10.15). This is very unfortunate because it greatly complicates the task of interpreting Φ^2. Suppose that investigators compute Φ^2 for some contingency table and get a value of .70. What does this mean? It is hard to answer this question intelligently without knowing the maximum value which Φ^2 can attain in a contingency table of the size studied. If the table has two rows and two columns, Φ^2's maximum value is 1.00. In this case, a Φ^2 of .70 suggests a strong relationship. If the table has three rows and three columns, Φ^2's maximum value is 2.00. Here, a Φ^2 of .70 suggests a moderate relationship, at best. Fortunately, V avoids this problem by dividing Φ^2 (or χ^2/N) by M ($r - 1$ or $c - 1$ whichever is smaller).

$$V = \sqrt{\Phi^2/M} = \sqrt{\chi^2/N/M} = \sqrt{\chi^2/(N \cdot M)}$$

By dividing by M, V's maximum value is always 1.00, regardless of the number of rows and/or columns in the contingency table. Therefore, V's major advantages as a measure of relationship are these:

1. Unlike χ^2, V is not dependent on the number of units, or the sample size.
2. Unlike Φ^2, V has well defined minima (.00) *and* maxima (1.00) which do not depend on the number of rows and/or columns in the contingency table.
3. V's value varies between .00 and 1.00 depending only on the strength of the relationship.

For these reasons, investigators are strongly advised to use V as a measure of relationship, especially when using nominal data.

In Figure 10.7, V is computed for four of the contingency tables introduced earlier.

Figure 10.7   Computing Cramer's V: Four Examples

The Computational Formula:

$$V = \sqrt{\chi^2/N \cdot M}$$

1. Using Table 10.13 $\chi^2 = 28.30$ $N = 500$ $r = 3$ $c = 2$

   $V = \sqrt{28.30/500 \cdot 1} = \sqrt{28.30/500} = .2379$

   $\cong .24$

2. Using Table 10.15 $\chi^2 = 30.34$ $N = 1070$ $r = 2$ $c = 2$

   $V = \sqrt{30.34/1070 \cdot 1} = \sqrt{30.34/1070} = .1684$

   $\cong .17$

3. Using Table 10.19 $\chi^2 = 173.07$ $N = 1000$ $r = 3$ $c = 4$

   $V = \sqrt{173.07/1000 \cdot 2} = \sqrt{173.07/2000} = .2942$

   $\cong .29$

4. Using Table 10.20 $\chi^2 = 1730.74$ $N = 10000$ $r = 3$ $c = 4$

   $V = \sqrt{1730.74/10000 \cdot 2} = \sqrt{1730.74/20000} = .2942$

   $\cong .29$

Clearly, once the χ^2 statistic is calculated, V is very easy to compute. The sample size and numbers of rows and columns are easily found by just looking at the table. Then, computing V is just a matter of multiplying, dividing, and taking the square root.

In general, Cramer's V is a very good measure of relationship for several reasons. First, it has the three desirable properties discussed earlier. Second, it is easy to compute. Third, it is very versatile. It can be used on contingency tables with any number of rows and columns. Moreover, it can be used when X and Y are both measured nominally, when one is measured nominally and the other ordinally, and when both are measured ordinally. However, *when X and Y are both measured ordinally, one may have reason to use measures of relationship other than Cramer's V.*

When Researchers May Not Want To Use Cramer's V. Suppose that some researchers are interested in the problem of social class discrimination in sentencing. Their research hypothesis is that social class and severity of sentencing are negatively related. In order to investigate this they draw a random sample of 800 convicted felons from the official records of a county court, and using level of education as a surrogate for social class, they construct Table 10.21.

Table 10.21   Relationship Between the Education of Convicted Felons and the Sentence Received

	Education				
Sentence	Some Elementary	Some Secondary	High School Graduate	High School Graduate Plus	Total
Suspended	33.3%	50.0%	60.0%	75.0%	48.1%
Jailed	33.3	33.3	25.0	15.0	30.0
Imprisoned	33.3	16.7	15.0	10.0	21.9
Total	100.0%	100.0%	100.0%	100.0%	100.0%
	($N = 300$)	($N = 300$)	($N = 100$)	($N = 100$)	($N = 800$)

The column percentages in Table 10.21 are consistent with the research hypothesis. The higher a convicted felon's social class, the more likely he/she is to receive a suspended sentence. The lower a convicted felon's social class, the more likely he/she is to be sentenced to prison. In addition, the Cramer's V for Table 10.21 is .21, which suggests a weak relationship between the level of education and the severity of sentencing.

However, suppose that the contingency table looked like Table 10.22 instead of Table 10.21.

Table 10.22   Relationship Between the Education of Convicted Felons and the Sentence Received

	Education				
Sentence	Some Elementary	Some Secondary	High School Graduate	High School Graduate Plus	Total
Suspended	33.3%	50.0%	75.0%	60.0%	48.1%
Jailed	33.3	33.3	15.0	25.0	30.0
Imprisoned	33.3	16.7	10.0	15.0	21.9
Total	100.0%	100.0%	100.0%	100.0%	100.0%
	($N = 300$)	($N = 300$)	($N = 100$)	($N = 100$)	($N = 800$)

Now the column percentages in Table 10.22 are consistent with the research hypothesis in all respects — except one. According to Table 10.22, felons with more than a high school education are sentenced *more* severely than those with just a high school degree. Generally, it appears as if higher levels of education are associated with less severe sentencing *up to a certain point*. After that point is reached, still higher levels of education are associated with more severe sentencing. This is not what is expected; but fortunately, the column percentages in Table 10.22 make it easy to see how these two variables are actually related. However, if researchers had relied solely on V, they would have been misled. The Cramer's V for Table 10.22 is .21 — exactly the same as for Table 10.21!

With a little thought, it is easy to understand what has happened here. Table 10.22 is identical to Table 10.21 *except that* the last two columns are interchanged. Clearly, since V gives the same result for both tables, it is insensitive to the interchanging of these two columns. In fact, V is insensitive to the interchanging of *any* columns in Tables 10.21 and 10.22. It is also insensitive to the interchanging of any *rows* in these tables. Far from being a shortcoming, this insensitivity of Cramer's V is a great asset. *Any measure of relationship which is to be used on nominal variables must give the same result no matter how the columns in the contingency table are ordered; that is, it must be insensitive to the interchanging of columns in a contingency table. This principle also applies to the rows of a contingency table.* By definition, there is no single correct way to order the several categories of a nominal variable. Hence, if the independent variable in a contingency table is nominal, there is no single correct way to order the columns in the table. If the dependent variable in a contingency table is nominal, there is no single correct way to order the rows in the table. Therefore, it follows that *any measure of relationship which gives different results depending upon how the columns and/or rows in a contingency table are ordered cannot be used when either variable in the table is measured nominally.*

For example, consider the two contingency tables in Figure 10.8.

Figure 10.8   **Two Tables Relating a Nominal Independent Variable to an Ordinal Dependent Variable**

First Table

Sentence	Type of Offense				
	Armed Robbery	Assault/ Battery	Grand Theft	Embezzle- ment	Total
Suspended	20.0%	50.0%	66.7%	80.0%	49.0%
Jailed	30.0	31.3	13.3	10.0	24.5
Imprisoned	50.0	18.7	20.0	10.0	26.5
Total	100.0%	100.0%	100.0%	100.0%	100.0%
	($N = 250$)	($N = 400$)	($N = 300$)	($N = 50$)	($N = 1000$)

Second Table

| | Type of Offense | | | | |
Sentence	Grand Theft	Armed Robbery	Embezzle- ment	Assault/ Battery	Total
Suspended	66.7%	20.0%	80.0%	50.0%	49.0%
Jailed	13.3	30.0	10.0	31.3	24.5
Imprisoned	20.0	50.0	10.0	18.7	26.5
Total	100.0%	100.0%	100.0%	100.0%	100.0%
	($N = 300$)	($N = 250$)	($N = 50$)	($N = 400$)	($N = 1000$)

These two tables are identical, except for the way the types of offense (categories of the independent variable) are ordered. Since the type of offense is a nominal variable, these two orderings are equally acceptable. Any conclusion which researchers derive from the first table can also be derived from the second table, and vice versa. For practical purposes, these two tables are identical. Certainly, one would not want to use a measure of relationship which gives one result for the first table and another result for the second table.

Now both variables in Tables 10.21 and 10.22 are measured ordinally. Thus, there is only one correct way to order the categories of education (the independent variable) and severity of sentence (the dependent variable). For this reason, Tables 10.21 and 10.22 are really two different tables, not just the same table arranged in two different formats as is the case with the tables in Figure 10.8. The point is this: a measure of relationship is needed which distinguishes between these two tables. Of the many such ordinal measures of relationship which are available, two of the most commonly used are gamma (γ) and tau$_c$ (τ_c).

Ordinal Measures of Relationship

These two measures of relationship have several things in common. First, γ and τ_c both measure the extent to which two particular patterns are present in a contingency table. Second, γ and τ_c both vary in the same interval: from -1.00 to $+1.00$. Third, γ and τ_c are both justified by the same rationale. However, γ and τ_c do differ in one very important respect: they almost always yield different results when computed for the same contingency table.

Patterns of Relationship. Suppose that the research hypothesis is: social class is negatively related to the severity of sentencing. Researchers are looking for a particular pattern of relationship between these two variables. They want to know the extent to which felons with higher levels of social class, or status, tend to get less severe sentences while felons with lower levels of social status tend to get more severe sentences. This is precisely what is meant by the research hypothesis: social class and the severity of sentencing are *negatively* related.

A second team of investigators might investigate the relationship between the number of previous felony convictions (number of convictions) and the severity of sentencing. Here, the research hypothesis is, the number of convictions is positively related to the severity of sentencing. This team of investigators is looking for a second pattern of relationship between two variables. They want to know the extent to which felons with several previous convictions receive more severe sentences while felons with relatively few previous convictions receive less severe sentences. This is just what the second research hypothesis means: the number of convictions is *positively* related to the severity of sentence.

Thus, γ *and* τ_c *measure the extent to which two ordinal variables are either negatively or positively related.* Other patterns of relationship are possible, but they are not detected by γ or τ_c. For example, in Table 10.22, the level of education and the severity of sentence are clearly related, but this relationship is neither negative nor positive. Instead, it is curvilinear. At first, more education is associated with *less* severity, but beyond a certain point, more education is associated with *more* severity. Still other patterns of relationship are possible. All of them will be ignored by both γ and τ_c.

As has already been indicated, γ and τ_c both vary between -1.00 and $+1.00$. They are also interpreted in much the same way. A value near .00 indicates that there is no relationship between X and Y. More precisely, it means that there is no negative or positive relationship between X and Y. (There might be a curvilinear relationship.) A negative value for γ or τ_c indicates that X and Y are negatively related. For example, investigators looking into the relationship between social status and the severity of sentencing expect to get negative values for γ and τ_c. On the other hand, a positive value for γ or τ_c means that X and Y are positively related. Clearly, positive values for γ and τ_c are anticipated by the investigators examining the relationship between the number of convictions and the severity of sentencing. Hence, the two patterns of relationship detected by γ and τ_c are identified by the sign of the two measures.

The Rationale for γ *and* τ_c. Both γ and τ_c are based on the concepts of *concordant and discordant pairs*. These two concepts are most easily defined with the aid of two examples. Suppose that investigators hypothesize that the number of convictions is positively related to the severity sentence. For the moment, assume that this research hypothesis is true. If the convicted felons are carefully examined *in pairs* (i.e., two at a time), the felon with more previous convictions should receive a *more* severe sentence than the other felon in the pair; or the felon with *fewer* previous convictions should receive a *less* severe sentence than the other felon in the pair. In other words, the investigators expect *concordant pairs*. They expect that, in any given pair, the felon with a *higher* score on the independent variable will also have a *higher* score on the dependent variable.

The other research hypothesis is that social status is negatively related to the severity of sentence. Suppose that this is true. If the convicted felons are carefully examined in pairs, the felon with *more* social status should receive a *less* severe sentence than the other felon in the pair; or the felon with *less* social status should receive a *more* severe sentence than the other felon in the pair. In other words, the researchers investigating this second research hypothesis expect *discordant pairs*. They expect that, in any given pair, the felon with a *higher* score on the independent variable will have a *lower* score on the dependent variable.

Here is how the concepts of concordant and discordant pairs provide the basis for both γ and τ_c. Suppose that each unit (e.g., felon) in a contingency table is paired with every other unit. Each such pair is carefully examined to see if it is either concordant or discordant. Once this is done, the numbers of concordant and discordant pairs are determined. There are three possibilities:

1. There are more concordant pairs than discordant pairs. This suggests that X and Y are positively related. The greater the difference between the numbers of concordant and discordant pairs, the stronger is the positive relationship between X and Y.

2. There are more discordant pairs than concordant pairs. This suggests that X and Y are negatively related. The greater the difference between the numbers of discordant and concordant pairs, the stronger is the negative relationship between X and Y.

3. The numbers of concordant and discordant pairs are approximately equal. This suggests that X and Y are neither positively nor negatively related.

Clearly, then, the first step in computing both γ and τ_c is to determine the numbers of concordant and discordant pairs.

Counting Concordant Pairs. Suppose that Table 10.23 is constructed by the investigators examining the relationship between the number of convictions and the severity of sentence.

Table 10.23   Relationship Between the Number of Previous Felony Convictions and the Severity of the Sentence

| | Number of Previous Felony Convictions | | | | |
Sentence	None	1	2 or 3	4 or More	Total
Suspended	90	70	40	10	210
Jailed	25	50	40	30	145
Imprisoned	10	30	45	60	145
Total	125	150	125	100	500

Since investigators hypothesize a positive relationship, they expect to find more concordant pairs than discordant pairs. How can they actually compute the number of concordant pairs in Table 10.23?

The easiest way to determine the number of concordant pairs is to begin with the 90 felons in the upper left-hand cell of Table 10.23. These 90 felons are in the *lowest* categories of *both* variables. They have no previous convictions and have received suspended sentences. *Each* of these 90 felons forms concordant pairs with *all* felons who have one or more previous convictions *and* who are in jail or prison. This latter group includes all felons in any of the six cells *below and to the right* of the cell with the 90 felons in it in Table 10.23. These six cells are indicated in Figure 10.9, Step One.

Figure 10.9   Computing Concordant Pairs (Based on Table 10.23)

Step One

| | Number of Previous Felony Convictions | | | | |
Sentence	None	1	2 or 3	4 or More	Total
Suspended	90	70	40	10	210
Jailed	25	50	40	30	145
Imprisoned	10	30	45	60	145
Total	125	150	125	100	500

Step Two

| | Number of Previous Felony Convictions | | | | |
Sentence	None	1	2 or 3	4 or More	Total
Suspended	90	70	40	10	210
Jailed	25	50	40	30	145
Imprisoned	10	30	45	60	145
Total	125	150	125	100	500

Figure 10.9   (continued)

Step Three

Number of Previous Felony Convictions

Sentence	None	1	2 or 3	4 or More	Total
Suspended	90	70	40	10	210
Jailed	25	50	40	30	145
Imprisoned	10	30	45	60	145
Total	125	150	125	100	500

Step Four

Number of Previous Felony Convictions

Sentence	None	1	2 or 3	4 or More	Total
Suspended	90	70	40	10	210
Jailed	25	50	40	30	145
Imprisoned	10	30	45	60	145
Total	125	150	125	100	500

Step Five

Number of Previous Felony Convictions

Sentence	None	1	2 or 3	4 or More	Total
Suspended	90	70	40	10	210
Jailed	25	50	40	30	145
Imprisoned	10	30	45	60	145
Total	125	150	125	100	500

Step Six

Number of Previous Felony Convictions

Sentence	None	1	2 or 3	4 or More	Total
Suspended	90	70	40	10	210
Jailed	25	50	40	30	145
Imprisoned	10	30	45	60	145
Total	125	150	125	100	500

There are 255 felons in these six cells. Since each of the first 90 felons forms concordant pairs with *all* 255 of the felons in these six cells, the total number of concordant pairs so far identified is:

$$90 \cdot 255 = 22,950$$

The second step in computing the number of concordant pairs is to move across the top row of Table 10.23, from the cell with 90 felons in it to the cell with 70 felons in it. These felons have one previous conviction and have received suspended sentences. Thus, each of these 70 felons forms concordant pairs with all felons who have two or more previous convictions and who are in jail or prison. This latter group includes all felons in any of four cells below and to the right of the cell with the 70 felons in it. These four cells are indicated in Figure 10.9, Step Two. There are 175 felons in these four cells. Since each of the 70 felons forms concordant pairs with all 175 felons in these four cells, the number of additional concordant pairs is:

$$70 \cdot 175 = 12,250$$

The next step is to move one more cell to the right in Table 10.23, to the cell with 40 felons in it. Each of these 40 felons forms concordant pairs with the 90 felons in the two cells below and to the right of their cell. These two cells are indicated in Figure 10.9, Step Three. Here, the number of additional concordant pairs is:

$$40 \cdot 90 = 3,600$$

The ten felons in the last cell in the first row of Table 10.23 do not form concordant pairs with anyone because there are no cells below and to the right of their cell. Therefore, the fourth step is to move to the cell with 25 felons, in the second row and first column of Table 10.23. Each of these 25 felons forms concordant pairs with all 135 felons in the three cells below and to the right of their cell. These three cells are indicated in Figure 10.9, Step Four. The number of concordant pairs added here is:

$$25 \cdot 135 = 3,375$$

Steps Five and Six follow in the same fashion, as indicated in Figure 10.9. The numbers of concordant pairs added by these two steps are 5,250 and 2,400, respectively. Step Six concludes the computations required to determine the total number of concordant pairs. These computations are all shown in Figure 10.10.

Figure 10.10   Summary of Concordant Pairs (Based on Table 10.23)

Step One

$$c_1 = 90(50 + 40 + 30 + 30 + 45 + 60) = 90 \cdot 255$$
$$= 22,950$$

Step Two

$$c_2 = 70(40 + 30 + 45 + 60) = 70 \cdot 175$$
$$= 12,250$$

Step Three

$$c_3 = 40(30 + 60) = 40 \cdot 90$$
$$= 3,600$$

Step Four

$$c_4 = 25(30 + 45 + 60) = 25 \cdot 135$$
$$= 3,375$$

Step Five

$$c_5 = 50(45 + 60) = 50 \cdot 105$$
$$= 5,250$$

Step Six

$$c_6 = 40 \cdot 60$$
$$= 2,400$$

Computing the Number of Concordant Pairs

$$C = 22,950 + 12,250 + 3,600 + 3,375 + 5,250 + 2,400$$
$$= 49,825$$

The total number of concordant pairs, denoted C, is 49,825.

Counting Discordant Pairs. Discordant pairs are counted in much the same way as concordant pairs. The process begins with the ten felons in the upper *right*-hand cell in Table 10.23. These ten felons are in the *highest* category of the independent variable and the *lowest* category of the dependent variable. They have four or more previous convictions and have received suspended sentences. *Each* of these ten felons forms discordant pairs with *all* felons who have three or fewer previous convictions *and* who are in jail or prison. This latter group includes all felons in any of the six cells *below and to the left* of the cell with ten felons in it. These six cells are indicated in Figure 10.11, Step One.

Figure 10.11   Computing Discordant Pairs (Based on Table 10.23)

Step One

Sentence	Number of Previous Felony Convictions				
	None	1	2 or 3	4 or More	Total
Suspended	90	70	40	10	210
Jailed	25	50	40	30	145
Imprisoned	10	30	45	60	145
Total	125	150	125	100	500

Figure 10.11   **(continued)**

Step Two

Sentence	Number of Previous Felony Convictions				
	None	1	2 or 3	4 or More	Total
Suspended	90	70	40	10	210
Jailed	25	50	40	30	145
Imprisoned	10	30	45	60	145
Total	125	150	125	100	500

Step Three

Sentence	Number of Previous Felony Convictions				
	None	1	2 or 3	4 or More	Total
Suspended	90	70	40	10	210
Jailed	25	50	40	30	145
Imprisoned	10	30	45	60	145
Total	125	150	125	100	500

Step Four

Sentence	Number of Previous Felony Convictions				
	None	1	2 or 3	4 or More	Total
Suspended	90	70	40	10	210
Jailed	25	50	40	30	145
Imprisoned	10	30	45	60	145
Total	125	150	125	100	500

Step Five

Sentence	Number of Previous Felony Convictions				
	None	1	2 or 3	4 or More	Total
Suspended	90	70	40	10	210
Jailed	25	50	40	30	145
Imprisoned	10	30	45	60	145
Total	125	150	125	100	500

Step Six

Sentence	Number of Previous Felony Convictions				
	None	1	2 or 3	4 or More	Total
Suspended	90	70	40	10	210
Jailed	25	50	40	30	145
Imprisoned	10	30	45	60	145
Total	125	150	125	100	500

There are 200 felons in these six cells. Hence, the number of discordant pairs identified so far is:

$$10 \cdot 200 = 2,000$$

The second step in computing the number of discordant pairs is to move across the first row of Table 10.23, from the cell with ten felons in it to the cell with 40 felons in it. These felons have two or three previous felony convictions and have received suspended sentences. Thus, each of these 40 felons forms discordant pairs with all felons who have fewer than two previous convictions and who are in jail or prison. This group includes all 115 felons in the four cells below and to the left of the cell with 40 felons in it. These four cells are indicated in Figure 10.11, Step Two. Hence, the number of additional discordant pairs is:

$$40 \cdot 115 = 4,600$$

Steps Three, Four, Five, and Six follow in the same fashion, as indicated in Figure 10.11. The numbers of discordant pairs added by these four steps are 2,450; 2,550; 1,600; and 500. All of the computations involved in counting the discordant pairs are shown in Figure 10.12.

Figure 10.12   Computing Discordant Pairs (Based on Table 10.23)

Step One

$$d_1 = 10(25 + 50 + 40 + 10 + 30 + 45) = 10 \cdot 200$$
$$= 2,000$$

Step Two

$$d_2 = 40(25 + 50 + 10 + 30) = 40 \cdot 115$$
$$= 4,600$$

Step Three

$$d_3 = 70(25 + 10) = 70 \cdot 35$$
$$= 2,450$$

Step Four

$$d_4 = 30(10 + 30 + 45) = 30 \cdot 85$$
$$= 2,550$$

Step Five

$$d_5 = 40(10 + 30) = 40 \cdot 40$$
$$= 1,600$$

Step Six

$$d_6 = 50 \cdot 10$$
$$= 500$$

Figure 10.12   (Continued)

Computing the Number of Discordant Pairs

$$D = 2,000 + 4,600 + 2,450 + 2,550 + 1,600 + 500$$
$$= 13,700$$

The total number of discordant pairs, denoted D, is 13,700.

A Note On Counting Concordant and Discordant Pairs. Concordant and discordant pairs are always counted in the way just described provided that one condition is met: *the two variables making up the contingency table must be arranged properly.* Specifically, the independent variable, at the top of the table, must have its lowest category on the left and its highest category on the right. The dependent variable, on the left-hand side of the table, must have its lowest category at the top and its highest category at the bottom. When this is done, the upper left-hand cell of the contingency table always contains units in the lowest categories of both variables; the upper right-hand cell always contains units in the highest category of the independent variable and the lowest category of the dependent variable. Once the contingency table is set up this way, the concordant and discordant pairs are counted as follows:

1. *Concordant Pairs.* Begin with the upper left-hand cell. Pair each unit in this cell with all units in cells below and to the right. Then move to the right across the first row of the table to the next cell and pair each unit in that cell with all units in cells below and to the right. Continue this process until all units have been properly paired.

2. *Discordant Pairs.* Begin with the upper right-hand cell. Pair each unit in this cell with all units in cells below and to the left. Then move to the left across the first row of the table to the next cell and pair each unit in that cell with all units in cells below and to the left. Continue this process until all units have been properly paired.

Computing γ. Once the numbers of concordant and discordant pairs (C and D, respectively), are counted, γ is easy to compute. The formula for γ is:

$$\gamma = \frac{C - D}{C + D}$$

Thus, as shown in Figure 10.13, the γ for Table 10.23 is .57.

Figure 10.13   Computing γ (Based on Table 10.23)

From Figures 10.13 and 10.15:

$C = 49,825$

$D = 13,700$

The computational formula:

$$\gamma = \frac{C - D}{C + D}$$

By substitution:

$$\gamma = \frac{49,825 - 13,700}{49,825 + 13,700} = \frac{36,125}{63,525} = .5687$$

$$\gamma \cong .57$$

A guide for interpreting both γ and τ_c is given in Figure 10.14.

Figure 10.14   A Guide for Interpreting Ordinal Measures of Relationship

+1.00 ←−−−−−− perfect positive relationship
.
.
.
+.80 ←−−−−−− strong positive relationship
.
.
.
+.50 ←−−−−−− moderate positive relationship
.
.
.
+.10 ←−−−−−− weak positive relationship
.
.
.
.00 ←−−−−−− no relationship
.
.
.
−.10 ←−−−−−− weak negative relationship
.
.
.
−.50 ←−−−−−− moderate negative relationship
.
.
.
−.80 ←−−−−−− strong negative relationship
.
.
.
−1.00 ←−−−−−− perfect negative relationship

According to this guide, there is a moderate positive relationship between the number of previous convictions and the severity of sentence.

γ is an extremely versatile measure of relationship. As long as the two variables composing a contingency table are both measured ordinally, γ is an appropriate measure to use. It may be used on contingency tables with *any* numbers of rows and columns, without exception.

However, in the eyes of some, γ does have one major drawback: it tends to *overestimate* the strength of a relationship. In effect, γ tends to be too *large*. This is best illustrated with an example. Suppose that the investigators examining the relationship between the number of convictions and the severity of sentence produce Table 10.24.

Table 10.24   Relationship Between the Number of Previous Felony Convictions and the Severity of the Sentence

Sentence	None	1	2 or 3	4 or More	Total
Suspended	125	75	0	0	200
Jailed	0	75	60	0	135
Imprisoned	0	0	65	100	165
Total	125	150	125	100	500

Number of Previous Felony Convictions

Since researchers are interested in the strength of this relationship, they compute γ, as shown in Figure 10.15.

Figure 10.15   Computing γ (Based on Table 10.24)

Step One: Compute C

$C = 125(75 + 60 + 0 + 0 + 65 + 100) + 75(60 + 0 + 65 + 100) +$
$0(0 + 100) + 0(0 + 65 + 100) + 75(65 + 100) + 60 \cdot 100$
$= 125 \cdot 300 + 75 \cdot 225 + 0 \cdot 100 + 0 \cdot 165 + 75 \cdot 165 + 60 \cdot 100$
$= 37,500 + 16,875 + 0 + 0 + 12,375 + 6,000$
$= 72,750$

Step Two: Compute D

$D = 0(0 + 75 + 60 + 0 + 0 + 65) + 0(0 + 75 + 0 + 0) + 75(0 + 0) +$
$0(0 + 0 + 65) + 60(0 + 0) + 75 \cdot 0$
$= 0 + 0 + 0 + 0 + 0 + 0$
$= 0$

Step Three: Compute γ

The computational formula:

$$\gamma = \frac{C - D}{C + D}$$

By substitution:

$$\gamma = \frac{72,750 - 0}{72,750 + 0} = \frac{72,750}{72,750}$$
$$= 1.00$$

This result ($\gamma = 1.00$) seems odd. According to Figure 10.14, this means that there is a perfect positive relationship between the number of convictions and the severity of sentence. Yet the frequencies in Table 10.24 make it clear that the relationship is *not* perfect, though it is quite strong. Some felons with one previous conviction are given suspended sentences while others are jailed. Similarly, of the felons with two or three previous convictions, some are jailed while others are imprisoned. Thus, the relationship is not a perfect one. It appears that γ has overestimated the strength of this relationship. It is primarily for this reason that some analysts prefer τ_c to γ as a measure of relationship for ordinal variables.

Computing τ_c. As will be explained in the following pages, the only difference between the formulas for γ and τ_c is in the denominator. The denominator for γ is $C + D$. This expression $(C + D)$ is, in effect, an estimate of the *total* number of pairs. It is produced by adding the number of discordant pairs to the number of concordant pairs. Some researchers argue that this simple procedure *underestimates* the total number of pairs. If γ's denominator is too small, γ will be too large. Rather than using $C + D$ as the denominator, the following expression is recommended by some investigators:

$$\tfrac{1}{2}\{N^2[(m - 1)/m]\}$$

where: N = the total number of units in the contingency table

m = the number of rows or columns in the table, whichever is smaller

Basically, this expression consists of two parts: $\tfrac{1}{2}(N^2)$ and $(m - 1)/m$. The first of these parts, $\tfrac{1}{2}(N^2)$, is an estimate of the number of pairs which can be formed from N objects.[1] The purpose of the second part, $(m - 1)/m$, is to adjust for the numbers of rows and columns in the contingency table.[2]

Therefore, the formula for τ_c is:

$$\tau_c = \frac{C - D}{\frac{1}{2}\{N^2[(m-1)/m]\}}$$

According to Figure 10.16, the value of τ_c for Table 10.23 is .43.

Figure 10.16   Computing τ_c (Based on Table 10.23)

Step One: Compute C and D

From Figures 10.10 and 10.12:
$C = 49,825$
$D = 13,700$

Step Two: Compute τ_c

The computational formula:

$$\tau_c = \frac{C - D}{\frac{1}{2}\{N^2[(m-1)/m]\}}$$

By substitution:

$$\tau_c = \frac{49,825 - 13,700}{\frac{1}{2}\{500^2[(3-1)/3]\}} = \frac{36,125}{\frac{1}{2}(250,000)(2/3)} = .4335$$
$$\cong .43$$

The value of γ for this same table is .57. This result is typical. τ_c *is always smaller than* γ, *and it is this which leads many to prefer it as a measure of relationship for ordinal variables.* For example, according to Figure 10.17, the value of τ_c for Table 10.24 is .87.

Figure 10.17   Computing τ_c (Based on Table 10.24)

Step One: Compute C and D

From Figure 10.18:
$C = 72,750$
$D = 0$

Step Two: Compute τ_c

The computational formula:

$$\tau_c = \frac{C - D}{\frac{1}{2}\{N^2[(m-1)/m]\}}$$

By substitution:

$$\tau_c = \frac{72,750 - 0}{\frac{1}{2}\{500^2[(3-1)/3]\}} = \frac{72,750}{\frac{1}{2}(250,000)(2/3)} = .8730$$
$$\cong .87$$

Recall that the value of γ for this table is 1.00. Since the variables in Table 10.24 are *not* perfectly related, τ_c's value of .87 seems more reasonable than γ's value of 1.00.

Like γ, τ_c is also a versatile measure of relationship. Since τ_c can be used on any contingency table on which γ is used, choosing between these two measures of relationship is largely a matter of personal preference. Although there is much to be said in favor of τ_c, γ is probably the most widely used measure of relationship for ordinal variables.

A Final Example. One research hypothesis discussed earlier is that the social status of convicted felons is negatively related to the severity of their sentences. Table 10.21 is a contingency table of column percentages which are relevant to this research hypothesis. Table 10.25 contains the frequencies from which these column percentages are computed.

Table 10.25   Relationship Between the Education of Convicted Felons and the Sentence Received

		Education			
Sentence	Some Elementary	Some Secondary	High School Graduate	High School Graduate Plus	Total
Suspended	100	150	60	75	385
Jailed	100	100	25	15	240
Imprisoned	100	50	15	10	175
Total	300	300	100	100	800

Both γ and τ_c for Table 10.25 are computed in Figure 10.18.

Figure 10.18   Computing γ and τ_c (Based on Table 10.25)

Step One: Compute C

$$
\begin{aligned}
C &= 100(100 + 25 + 15 + 50 + 15 + 10) + 150(25 + 15 + 15 + 10) + \\
&\quad 60(15 + 10) + 100(50 + 15 + 10) + 100(15 + 10) + 25 \cdot 10 \\
&= 100 \cdot 215 + 150 \cdot 65 + 60 \cdot 25 + 100 \cdot 75 + 100 \cdot 25 + 25 \cdot 10 \\
&= 21{,}500 + 9{,}750 + 1{,}500 + 7{,}500 + 2{,}500 + 250 \\
&= 43{,}000
\end{aligned}
$$

Figure 10.18   (Continued)

Step Two: Compute D

$$D = 75(100 + 100 + 25 + 100 + 50 + 15) + 60(100 + 100 + 100 + 50) +$$
$$150(100 + 100) + 15(100 + 50 + 15) + 25(100 + 50) + 100 \cdot 100$$
$$= 75 \cdot 390 + 60 \cdot 350 + 150 \cdot 200 + 15 \cdot 165 + 25 \cdot 150 + 100 \cdot 100$$
$$= 29,250 + 21,000 + 30,000 + 2,475 + 3,750 + 10,000$$
$$= 96,475$$

Step Three: Compute γ

$$\gamma = \frac{43,000 - 96,475}{43,000 + 96,475} = \frac{-53,475}{139,475} = -.3834$$
$$\cong -.38$$

Step Four: Compute τ_c

$$\tau_c = \frac{43,000 - 96,475}{\frac{1}{2}\{ 800^2 [(3-1)/3] \}} = \frac{-53,475}{\frac{1}{2}(640,000)(2/3)} = \frac{-53,475}{213,333.333} = -.2507$$
$$\cong -.25$$

Readers should examine Figure 10.18 very carefully to be sure that each step involved is understood.

Summary

Three measures of relationship are introduced in this chapter: Cramer's V, gamma (γ) and tau$_c$ (τ_c). The first of these measures (V) is used to investigate the relationship between *any* two categorical variables, but it is used most often when at least one of the two variables is measured nominally. The last two measures (γ and τ_c) are used only when both variables are measured ordinally *and* the research hypothesis posits a negative or a positive relationship between the two variables (as opposed to a curvilinear relationship).

Many other measures of relationship are available, but these three have at least two major advantages.[3] First, they are quite widely used, so, being familiar with them helps one read and evaluate the literature. Second, all three measures can be used on contingency tables with any number of rows and columns. A good many other measures of relationship are limited in this respect.

There is one more point to remember about measures of relationship. Researchers are often well advised *not* to use these measures. Quite frequently, the research hypothesis can be satisfactorily addressed using column percentages. When this is the case, the more complicated measures of relationship need not be used.

During the discussion of the χ^2 test and the measures of relationship, no mention was made about controlling for other variables. This omission should *not* be taken to mean that researchers can avoid the need for controls by simply using a hypothesis test or computing a measure of relationship. For example, when the χ^2 test is applied to Table 10.13, the null hypothesis (that sex and severity of sentence are not related) is rejected, but it is still quite possible that the relationship in Table 10.13 is spurious. The same point applies with regard to measures of relationship. For example, Cramer's V in Table 10.15 is only .17. This suggests a weak relationship. However, it could be that sex and severity of sentence are more strongly related and that some other variable is suppressing the relationship. *There is no way to get around the need to control for the possible effects of other variables.*

Notes

[1.] Actually, the number of pairs which can be formed from N objects is:

$$\tfrac{1}{2}(N)(N - 1)$$

However, when N is large (as it commonly is when contingency table analysis is used), the two expressions are almost identical:

$$\tfrac{1}{2}(N^2) \cong \tfrac{1}{2}(N)(N - 1)$$

[2.] For a lengthier discussion of τ_c and other similar measures of relationship, see Kendall (1948).

[3.] The list of such measures of relationship is so long that to just introduce them, let alone demonstrate them, is too ambitious a task for this text. Interested readers can get started by consulting Blalock (1980) or Siegel (1956).

Review Questions

1. Explain the meaning and significance of the following terms and ideas:
   a. contingency table
   b. corner, row, and column percentages
   c. rules for constructing contingency tables
   d. spuriousness
   e. interaction
   f. suppression
   g. the Chi square (χ^2) test
   h. Cramer's V

    i. concordant and discordant pairs

    j. gamma (γ)

    k. tau$_c$ (τ_c)

2. Suppose that researchers are interested in finding out if juveniles with more support from their parents are less likely to become delinquent. To investigate this, they gather information on 300 juveniles and construct the following contingency table.

Frequency of Delinquent Acts	Parental Support			Total
	Low	Medium	High	
None	35	78	97	210
Some	21	21	19	61
Many	16	11	2	29
Total	72	110	118	300

For the data in this contingency table, compute:

    a. the appropriate percentages for investigating the hypothesis

    b. the χ^2 statistic and conduct the χ^2 test on the research hypothesis at the .05 permissible level of error

    c. Cramer's V

    d. gamma (γ) and tau$_c$ (τ_c)

In your own words, state what conclusions you reach concerning the hypothesis on the basis of the percentages and statistics you have computed.

References

Blalock, Hubert. *Social Statistics,* 2nd rev. ed. New York: McGraw-Hill Book Co., 1980.

Kendall, M. G. *Rank Correlation Methods. London:* Griffin Publishing Co., 1948.

Poister, Theodore H. *Public Program Analysis: Applied Research Methods.* Baltimore: University Park Press, 1978.

Siegel, Sidney. *Nonparametric Statistics for the Behavioral Sciences.* New York: McGraw-Hill Book Co., 1956.

Vito, Gennaro F. and Harry E. Allen. "Shock Probation in Ohio: Use of Base Expectancy Rates as an Evaluation Method," *Criminal Justice and Behavior* 7 (1980) pp 331-340.

Williamson, John B., David A. Karp, and John R. Dalphin. *The Research Craft.* Boston: Little, Brown and Co., 1977.

Chapter 11
Analysis of Variance

Learning Objectives

After completing this chapter, the reader should be able to:

1. State the purposes for which analysis of variance (ANOVA) is used
2. Distinguish among one-way ANOVA, two-way ANOVA, and multi-way ANOVA
3. Understand the difference between independent samples and matched samples and relevance of the difference when ANOVA is used
4. Set up the nondirectional hypotheses used with ANOVA
5. Carry out one-way and two-way ANOVA

Introduction

In a sense, Chapters 8 and 9 constitute an introduction to this chapter. The one-sample tests discussed in Chapter 8 help researchers determine if the performance of a *single* group exceeds, or falls short of, an established standard of performance. The two sample tests discussed in Cahpter 9 help researchers decide whether or not *two* groups differ in some important respect. Chapter 11 carries this development one step further. Analysis of variance (ANOVA) is a statistical test designed to determine if *three or more* groups differ in some important respect. For example, a county court administrator might want to know if case disposition times vary substantially from courtroom to courtroom; or a state prison official might wonder if recidivism rates vary substantially from one prison to the next; or a police chief might like to know if ethnocentrism among police officers is affected by the training programs in which the officers have participated. In each example, a criminal justice administrator wants to compare several groups in terms of some important variable. The court administrator wants to compare several courtrooms in terms of their case disposition times; the prison official wants to compare several prisons in terms of their recidivism rates; the police chief wants to compare several training programs in terms of the ethnocentrism scores of the police officers who participate in those programs.

All three of these administrators could benefit from the use of ANOVA *if they have an inference problem*. Thus, if a court administrator draws a sample of cases from each courtroom and is going to base conclusions about *all* case disposition times on only those cases sampled, then there is an inference problem and the administrator could benefit by using ANOVA. If a state prison official draws a sample of all prisoners already released from the several prisons and bases his conclusions about *all* released prisoners on just those sampled, then he has an inference problem and could use ANOVA. Similarly, if a police chief plans to study a sample of police officers who have already gone through the various training programs *and* apply what is learned to *all* those who have undergone such training, then he has an inference problem and would be well advised to use ANOVA. As with all statistical tests, *ANOVA is used only when a sample is studied in order to learn something about the population from which it is drawn.*

An important feature of ANOVA is that there is no practical limit to the number of groups that can be compared. Thus, a court administrator can compare the case disposition times of three courtrooms or 33 courtrooms or 333 courtrooms. Furthermore, ANOVA can be used to compare the scores of a *single* group at several points in time, just as two-sample tests are used to compare a group's performance at two points in time (Chapter 9). For example, suppose that a new training program designed to reduce the ethnocentrism scores of police officers is conducted in two stages. Researchers might want to compare *three* sets of ethnocentrism scores for the officers undergoing training: their scores before the training, their scores after the first stage of the program, and their scores after the completion of the entire program. ANOVA could be used to determine if any significant change in ethnocentrism scores occurred in response to the program and, if so, during which stage.

Thus, ANOVA is a very valuable statistical test; all that is required is a collection of observations divided into three or more groups and interval or ratio level scores for each observation in the collection. If interval or ratio level scores cannot be secured, other statistical tests will have to be used.[1]

Variation

The two-sample tests discussed in Chapter 9 all had to do with determining whether or not two groups of scores differed significantly from one another. ANOVA has to do with determining whether or not three or more groups of scores *vary* significantly among themselves. Thus, the concept of *variation* is central to an understanding of ANOVA.

As previously noted (Chapter 7), any collection of scores will be seen to vary. If a collection of scores is divided into three or more groups, the *total* variation among the entire collection of scores can be divided into two parts: (1) variation *between* the scores of the several groups, and (2) variation among the scores *within* the several groups. For example, imagine investigators are examining the ethnocentrism scores of a *sample* of police officers. These ethnocentrism scores will vary. Some officers will have high scores, others will have low scores, and still others will have moderate scores. Suppose that this sample is divided into three groups based on the training the police officers had previously undergone. Even after this division, the ethnocentrism scores *within* each group will still vary. Among the group of officers who took training program A, some will have higher scores than others and some lower than others — just as one would expect. The same is true of those who completed training programs B and C. If the scores *within* each group vary, one can also expect that the scores *between* the groups will vary; that is, the scores of the officers who participated in program A will differ from the scores of those who completed programs B and C.

This sort of variation between the groups can arise only from two possible sources: (1) perhaps in the *population* of all police officers there are genuine differences in ethnocentrism depending upon previous training and the *sample* merely reflects these genuine differences or (2) perhaps in the population there are no differences in ethnocentrism depending upon previous training, but due to chance the three sample groups differ from one another. According to the first of these two possibilities, differences among the sample groups are said to be due to *genuine differences.* According to the second possibility, differences among the sample groups are said to be due to *sampling error.* If the variation between the sample groups is due to *sampling error,* the between-groups variation should be approximately equal to the within-groups variation. If the variation between groups is due to *genuine differences,* the between-groups variation should be greater than the within-groups variation. Therefore, *the greater the ratio of the between-groups variation to the within-groups variation, the more reasonable it is to conclude that the differences among the sample groups are due to genuine differences rather than sampling error.* ANOVA operationalizes this general principle.

Applying Analysis of Variance

Because of the effects of chance, researchers must do more than merely demonstrate that the ratio of between-groups variation to within-groups variation exceeds one. Instead, they must determine whether or not this ratio seems too large to be due to chance alone. ANOVA does just this. Figure 11.1 identifies the major steps in the use of ANOVA.

Figure 11.1   Steps to Follow when Using ANOVA

1. Decide which type of ANOVA to use.
2. Set the permissible level of error.
3. Compute the test statistic.
4. Compare the test statistic to the appropriate sampling distribution table.

Deciding Which Type of ANOVA to Use

ANOVA can be used in two ways: (1) to compare the scores of several groups or (2) to compare the scores of a single group at several points in time. The first way involves using *independent* samples since the observations in each group are independent of those in the other groups. The second way involves using *matched* samples since the observations in each "group" are matched with those in the other "groups." (Here, of course, the several "groups" are nothing more than the same units observed at different times.) With ANOVA, independent samples and matched samples have the same meanings and are derived in the same ways as when they are used with two-sample mean tests (Chapter 9).

Regardless of whether investigators are dealing with independent or matched samples, ANOVA always tests the same null and research hypotheses, namely:

$$H_o: \mu_1 = \mu_2 = \ldots = \mu_k$$
$$H_a: \text{Not } H_o$$

where: k = the number of groups
   μ_1 = the mean of the first population
   μ_2 = the mean of the second population
   .
   .
   .
   μ_k = the mean of the kth and last population

The null hypothesis asserts that all observations come from populations with the same mean — in effect, that all observations come from the same population. In the example involving case disposition times the null hypothesis would be that all courtrooms have the same mean case disposition time. In the example having to do with the ethnocentrism of police officers it would mean that all training programs produce officers with the same mean ethnocentrism score. Furthermore, with ANOVA the research hypothesis merely asserts that the null hypothesis is false. It does *not* specify which population means are presumed to be different from the remaining means. Thus, *with ANOVA only nondirectional tests are conducted.* There are *no* directional tests with ANOVA.[2]

Setting the Level of Error

As always, one must remember that as long as information from a sample is used to reach conclusions about a population, there is always the chance that a mistake will be made. There is no way to completely avoid this risk. What one must do is determine just how great a risk of making a Type I error is acceptable. (The basis for making this determination is discussed in Chapters 2 and 8.) Once this decision is made, ANOVA sees to it that the risk of making a Type II error is minimized.

Computing the Test Statistic

The test statistic used with ANOVA is a ratio of the between-groups variation to the within-groups variation. Here, the within-groups variation is taken as an *estimate* of what the between-groups variation should equal *if* the null hypothesis is true and the groups' sample means differ only because of chance. Hence, the test statistic is merely a ratio of the *observed* variation among the groups to an *estimate* of that variation based on the assumption that chance alone is responsible for the differences among the groups. Therefore,

$$\text{Test Statistic} = \frac{\text{Observed Between-Groups Variation}}{\text{Observed Within-Groups Variation}}$$

$$= \frac{\text{Observed Between-Groups Variation}}{\text{Estimated Between-Groups Variation}}$$

Thus, this test statistic has the same rationale as the test statistic used in the two-samples tests (Chapter 9). There the test statistic was described as the ratio between the observed difference between two sample means and the difference that would have occurred if chance alone were operating. In the following pages, the formulas for computing this test statistic are presented and illustrated with examples.

Mean Squares. So far, ANOVA's test statistic has been characterized as the ratio of the between-groups variation to the within-groups variation, but in most statistical literature this terminology is not used. Instead, the test statistic is identified as *the ratio of two mean squares.* Thus, the between-groups variation is replaced by the *mean square between-groups;* the within-groups variation is replaced by the *mean square within-groups.*

The ratio of the latter to the former is called an F ratio and is the test statistic used in ANOVA.

$$F = \frac{\text{Mean Square Between-Groups}}{\text{Mean Square Within-Groups}} = MS_b/MS_w$$

Each mean square is computed by dividing the appropriate *sum of squares* by the appropriate *degrees of freedom*. Thus, the mean square between-groups is equal to the sum of squares between-groups divided by the degrees of freedom between-groups. That is:

$$MS_b = SS_b/df_b$$

The mean square within-groups is equal to the sum of squares within-groups divided by the degrees of freedom within-groups, or:

$$MS_w = SS_w/df_w$$

In order to compute the F ratio, the two mean squares must be calculated, but before this can be done the two sums of squares and degrees of freedom must be calculated.

Sums of Squares: An important identity used in ANOVA states that the total sum of squares is equal to the sum of squares within-groups plus the sum of squares between-groups. Statistically, this is:

$$\Sigma\Sigma(X - \overline{X}_t)^2 = \Sigma\Sigma(X - \overline{X}_g)^2 + \Sigma\Sigma(\overline{X}_g - \overline{X}_t)^2$$

where: X = any observation in any one of the groups

$\overline{X}_g$ = the mean of the observations in any one of the groups

$\overline{X}_t$ = the mean of all the observations

This is abbreviated as follows:

$$TSS = SS_b + SS_w$$

Since these expressions are rather tedious to calculate, a shortcut is used. First, simplified computational formulas are used to compute *TSS* and SS_b, and then SS_w is computed by subtracting the former from the latter: $SS_w = TSS - SS_b$. Thus:

$$TSS = \Sigma X^2 - CT$$

and

$$SS_b = \frac{(\Sigma X_1)^2}{N_1} + \frac{(\Sigma X_2)^2}{N_2} + \ldots + \frac{(\Sigma X_k)^2}{N_k} - CT$$

where: X = any observation in any one of the groups

N = the total number of observations in all of the groups

X_i = any observation in group i (i = 1, 2, ..., k)

N_i = the number of observations in group i (i = 1, 2, ..., k)

CT = a special correction term, namely:

$$= \frac{(\Sigma X)^2}{N}$$

Although these expressions look rather formidable, they are much easier to use than one might think. Here is an illustration.

Suppose researchers are interested in knowing if training programs influence the ethnocentrism of their police officer graduates. To investigate this they identify three training programs and draw random samples of 12 graduates from police officers recently graduated from each training program. An ethnocentrism test is administered to all 36 officers. The scores are as found in Figure 11.2.

Figure 11.2   Ethnocentrism Scores by Training Program

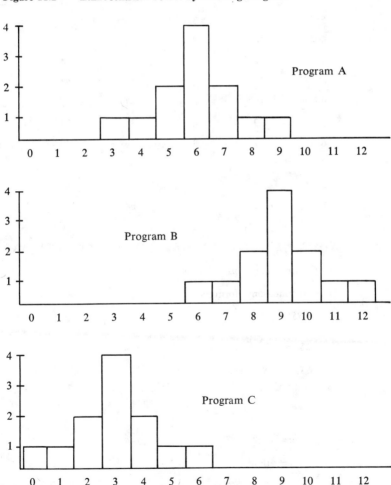

A brief examination of these ethnocentrism scores reveals a number of things. First, there is substantial variation *within* the three training program groups. Second, there is substantial variation *between* the scores of the three groups; but is this variation too great to be due to chance? ANOVA can be used to answer this question. Figure 11.3 illustrates the steps involved in calculating an *F* ratio for this example.

Figure 11.3   Computing the *F* Ratio: Independent Samples

Step 1: Prepare the Data

X_A	X_B	X_C	X_A^2	X_B^2	X_C^2
7	11	5	49	121	25
5	9	3	25	81	9
6	10	3	36	100	9
4	8	1	16	64	1
6	9	2	36	81	4
9	10	6	81	100	36
6	9	4	36	81	16
6	7	3	36	49	9
7	9	3	49	81	9
5	8	2	25	64	4
8	12	4	64	144	16
3	6	0	9	36	0

$\Sigma X_A = 72$ $\Sigma X_B = 108$ $\Sigma X_C = 36$ $\Sigma X_A^2 = 462$ $\Sigma X_B^2 = 1002$ $\Sigma X_C^2 = 138$

Step 2: Compute the Sums of Squares

The computational formulas:

$$TSS = \Sigma X^2 - \frac{(\Sigma X)^2}{N}$$

$$SS_b = \frac{(\Sigma X_A)^2}{N_1} + \frac{(\Sigma X_B)^2}{N_2} + \frac{(\Sigma X_C)^2}{N_3} - CT$$

$$SS_w = TSS - SS_b$$

By substitution:

$$TSS = (462 + 1002 + 138) - \frac{(72 + 108 + 36)^2}{36}$$

$$= 1602 - \frac{(216)^2}{36} = 1602 - 1296$$

$$= 306$$

$$SS_b = \frac{72^2}{12} + \frac{108^2}{12} + \frac{36^2}{12} - 1296 = \frac{5184 + 11664 + 1296}{12} - 1296$$

$$= \frac{18144}{12} - 1296 = 1512 - 1296$$

$$= 216$$

$$SS_w = 306 - 216$$
$$= 90$$

Step 3: Compute the Degrees of Freedom

The computational formulas:
$$df_t = N - 1$$
$$df_b = k - 1$$
$$df_w = N - k$$
By substitution:
$$df_t = 36 - 1$$
$$= 35$$
$$df_b = 3 - 1$$
$$= 2$$
$$df_w = 36 - 3$$
$$= 33$$

Step 4: Compute the Mean Squares

The computational formulas:
$$MS_b = SS_b / df_b$$
$$MS_w = SS_w / df_w$$
By substitution:
$$MS_b = 216/2$$
$$= 108$$
$$MS_w = 90/33$$
$$= 2.73$$

Step 5: Compute the F Ratio

The computational formula:
$$F = MS_b / MS_w$$
By substitution:
$$F = 108/2.73$$
$$= 39.60$$

A look at steps 1 and 2 shows that the sums of squares are not at all difficult to compute. All one has to do is sum the scores in each group, square the scores in each group and then sum them, and finally insert the several sums into the formulas for the sums of squares.

Degrees of Freedom: In order to compute the mean squares both the sums of squares and the degrees of freedom must be calculated first. In Chapter 8, the discussion of the t test indicated that the degrees of freedom for a sample of observations was equal to the size of the sample minus one. When that sample of observations is divided into several groups of observations, as it is with ANOVA, the degrees of freedom are divided into the degrees of freedom between-groups and the degrees of freedom within-groups — just as the total sum of squares is divided in two.

Total Degrees of Freedom = Degrees of Freedom Between-Groups
+ Degrees of Freedom Within-Groups

Statistically:

$$df_t = df_b + df_w$$

The formulas for df_b and df_w are found in Figure 11.3 and applied to the example problem.

Also found in Figure 11.3 are the mean squares and F ratio for the example. As can be seen from this figure, the mean squares are easily computed from the sums of squares and the degrees of freedom while the F ratio is easily computed from the mean squares.

Matched Samples. Suppose that researchers are especially interested in one particular training program. To test for its effectiveness in reducing ethnocentrism, they conduct the following study. A random sample of 12 police officers is selected and enrolled in the training program. The ethnocentrism of the 12 police officers is then measured three times: *before* the program, *halfway* through the program, and *after* the program. This produces three sets of 12 scores, just as with the preceding example. Since three sets of scores on the *same* 12 people are now available, the situation is quite different. With independent samples (the preceding example), the three sets of ethnocentrism scores could differ from one another in part because the three groups consisted of different people, no two of whom were identical. With matched samples, however, this possibility is eliminated. Furthermore, since there now are three ethnocentrism scores on each of the police officers, the within-groups variation can be divided into two parts: (1) variation due to deep-seated ethnocentric differences among the 12 officers and (2) variation due to sampling error alone. Because of this fact the calculation of the F ratio with matched samples differs from its calculation with independent samples. In the following sections, the latter example is used to illustrate how the F ratio is calculated with matched samples.

Sums of Squares: Since with matched samples the within-groups variation can be divided into *two* parts, the total sum of squares can now be divided into *three* parts: (1) the between-groups sum of squares, (2) the between-units (police officer) sum of squares, and (3) the error sum of squares. That is:

$$\Sigma\Sigma(X - \overline{X}_t)^2 = N\Sigma(\overline{X}_g - \overline{X}_t)^2 + k\Sigma(\overline{X}_u - \overline{X}_t)^2 + SS_e$$

where: X = any observation in any one of the groups

$\overline{X}_g$ = the mean of the observations in any one of the groups

$\overline{X}_u$ = the mean of the observations on any one of the units

$\overline{X}_t$ = the mean of all of the observations

SS_e = the error sum of squares

N = the number of units

k = the number of observations on each unit (the number of groups)

Or,

$$TSS = SS_g + SS_u + SS_e$$

where: SS_g = the between-groups sum of squares

SS_u = the between-units sum of squares

Fortunately, there exist simplified computational formulas for TSS, SS_g, and SS_u. SS_e is computed by subtracting SS_g and SS_u from TSS. These formulas are as follows:

$$TSS = \Sigma X^2 - CT$$

$$SS_g = \frac{(\Sigma X_{g1})^2}{N} + \frac{(\Sigma X_{g2})^2}{N} + \ldots + \frac{(\Sigma X_{gk})^2}{N} - CT$$

$$SS_u = \frac{(\Sigma X_{u1})^2}{k} + \frac{(\Sigma X_{u2})^2}{k} + \ldots + \frac{(\Sigma X_{uN})^2}{k} - CT$$

where: X = any observation in any one of the groups

X_{gi} = any observation in group i (i = 1, 2, . . . , k)

X_{uj} = any observation on unit j (j = 1, 2, . . . , N)

CT = a special correction term, namely:

$$= \frac{(\Sigma X)^2}{kN}$$

Again, although these simplified expressions seem complicated, the arithmetic operations involved are relatively easy. They merely involve addition, subtraction, multiplication, and division! The use of these expressions is illustrated in Figure 11.4.

Figure 11.4   Computing the F Ratio: Matched Samples

Step 1: Prepare the Data   B = Before   H = Half way   A = After

Unit	X_{gB}	X_{gH}	X_{gA}	ΣX_u	X_{gB}^2	X_{gH}^2	X_{gA}^2
1	11	7	5	23	121	49	25
2	9	5	3	17	81	25	9
3	10	6	3	19	100	36	9
4	8	4	1	13	64	16	1
5	9	6	2	17	81	36	4

Figure 11.4 **(continued)**

6	10	9	6	25	100	81	36
7	9	6	4	19	81	36	16
8	7	6	3	16	49	36	9
9	9	7	3	19	81	49	9
10	8	5	2	15	64	25	4
11	12	8	4	24	144	64	16
12	6	3	0	9	36	9	0
ΣX_{gi}	108	72	36	—	—	—	—
ΣX^2_{gi}	—	—	—	—	1002	462	138

Step 2: Compute the Sums of Squares

The computational formulas:

$$TSS = \Sigma X^2 - \frac{(\Sigma X)^2}{Nk}$$

$$SS_g = \frac{(\Sigma X_{g1})^2}{N} + \frac{(\Sigma X_{g2})^2}{N} + \ldots + \frac{(\Sigma X_{gk})^2}{N} - \frac{(\Sigma X)^2}{Nk}$$

$$SS_u = \frac{(\Sigma X_{u1})^2}{k} + \frac{(\Sigma X_{u2})^2}{k} + \ldots + \frac{(\Sigma X_{uN})^2}{k} - \frac{(\Sigma X)^2}{Nk}$$

$$SS_e = TSS - SS_g - SS_u$$

By substitution:

$$TSS = (1002 + 462 + 138) - \frac{(108 + 72 + 36)^2}{12 \cdot 3}$$

$$= 1602 - \frac{(216)^2}{36} = 1602 - 1296$$

$$= 306$$

$$SS_g = \frac{108^2}{12} + \frac{72^2}{12} + \frac{36^2}{12} - 1296 = \frac{11664 + 5184 + 1296}{12} - 1296$$

$$= \frac{18144}{12} - 1296 = 1512 - 1296$$

$$= 216$$

$$SS_u = \frac{23^2}{3} + \frac{17^2}{3} + \frac{19^2}{3} + \frac{13^2}{3} + \frac{17^2}{3} + \frac{25^2}{3} + \frac{19^2}{3} + \frac{16^2}{3} +$$

$$\frac{19^2}{3} + \frac{15^2}{3} + \frac{24^2}{3} + \frac{9^2}{3} - 1296$$

$$= \frac{529 + 289 + 361 + 169 + 289 + 625 + 361 + 256 + 361 + 225 + 576 + 81}{3}$$

$$- 1296$$

$$= 1374 - 1296$$

$$= 78$$

$$SS_e = 306 - 216 - 78$$

$$= 12$$

Figure 11.4   **(continued)**

Step 3: Compute the Degrees of Freedom

The computational formulas:
$$df_t = Nk - 1$$
$$df_g = k - 1$$
$$df_u = N - 1$$
$$df_e = (N - 1)(k - 1) = Nk - N - k + 1$$

By substitution:
$$df_t = 12 \cdot 3 - 1 = 36 - 1$$
$$= 35$$
$$df_g = 3 - 1$$
$$= 2$$
$$df_u = 12 - 1$$
$$= 11$$
$$df_e = 12 \cdot 3 - 12 - 3 + 1 = 37 - 15$$
$$= 22$$

Step 4: Compute the Mean Squares

The computational formulas:
$$MS_g = SS_g/df_g$$
$$MS_e = SS_e/df_e$$

By substitution:
$$MS_g = 216/2$$
$$= 108$$
$$MS_e = 12/22$$
$$= .55$$

Step 5: Compute the F Ratio

The computational formula:
$$F = MS_g/MS_e$$

By substitution:
$$F = 108/.55$$
$$= 196.36$$

Notice that the three groups of 12 scores in Figure 11.4 are identical to those in Figure 11.3; that is, the three ethnocentrism scores on 12 police officers in Figure 11.4 are numerically the same as the single ethnocentrism scores on three *groups* of 12 police officers in Figure 11.3. Thus, with this contrived example it is possible to see why calculating the *F* ratio for matched samples differs from calculating it for independent samples. The major difference is that in Figure 11.4 it makes sense to add the three ethnocentrism scores in each row since they belong to the same police officer (see the column headed ΣX_u). It would be nonsensical to do this for the scores in Figure 11.3. It is the variation in these row sums which provides the basis for computing the between-units sum of squares (Step 2 in Figure 11.4).

Several observations can be made about Figures 11.3 and 11.4. First, the total sum of squares is the same in both examples, as are the between-groups sum of squares. Second, when the between-units and error sums of squares from Figure 11.4 are added, the total is equal to the within-groups sum of squares from Figure 11.3. *Both of these observations always hold.* In other words, whether several sets of scores are treated as independent samples or as matched samples, the total and between-groups sums of squares will be unaffected. Matched samples merely serve to divide what would, in the case of independent samples, be the within-groups sum of squares into the between-units sum of squares and the error sum of squares.

The same observations can be made about the several degrees of freedom. The total degrees of freedom and the between-groups degrees of freedom are unchanged (Figure 11.3 and Figure 11.4). The within-groups degrees of freedom (Figure 11.3) are equal to the sum of the between-units degrees of freedom and the error degrees of freedom (Figure 11.4).

Notice that with matched samples the error mean square ($MS_e = SS_e/df_e$) is used as the denominator of the F ratio. This is why it is so important to recognize the difference between independent samples and matched samples. If one has matched samples, the resulting MS_e will almost inevitably be smaller than the MS_w based on independent samples. Hence, the F ratio will be larger and it will be easier to reject a false null hypothesis. In this case, the F ratio for matched samples is about five times larger than the F ratio for independent samples.

Comparing the Test Statistic with the Appropriate Sampling Distribution

Researchers are now ready to complete the ANOVA. If the F ratio is too large to be due to chance, the null hypothesis is rejected. The permissible level of error indicates how great a risk of falsely rejecting a true null hypothesis researchers are willing to run. If the calculated level of error is less than or equal to the permissible level of error, the null hypothesis is rejected. If it is not, the null hypothesis is not rejected. In this case, an F distribution table is used to make the decision about the null hypothesis. Like a t distribution table, an F distribution table is based on a sampling distribution — in this case, the sampling distribution of the F ratio. If the null hypothesis is true, and if many random samples are drawn from the population, and if the same ANOVA is performed with each sample, then a distribution of the resulting F ratios is called the sampling distribution of the F ratio. As shown in Figure 11.5, the sampling distribution of the F ratio resembles that of the χ^2 statistic in that it has only one tail.

Figure 11.5   The F Distribution Table at the .05 Level of Error with 2 and 30 Degrees of Freedom

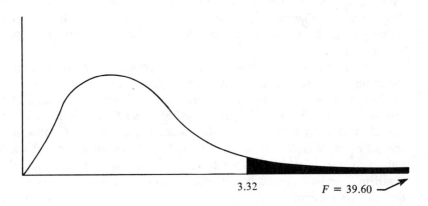

$$3.32 \qquad F = 39.60$$

Properly read, an F distribution table yields a boundary value which the calculated F ratio must equal or exceed in order to allow the null hypothesis to be rejected. This process is very much like using the t distribution table (Appendix C) to reach a conclusion when using certain one-sample or two-sample tests (Chapters 8 and 9). Thus, the final stage in applying ANOVA depends critically upon being able to read an F distribution table.

Actually, there is not just one F distribution table but rather a set of them — one for each permissible level of error. Appendix D contains two such tables: one for the .05 level of error and one for the .01 level of error. To locate the boundary value in such a table one needs two different degrees of freedom: (1) the degrees of freedom associated with the mean square in the numerator of the F ratio (df_1), and (2) the degrees of freedom associated with the mean square in the denominator of the F ratio (df_2). With independent samples the first degrees of freedom is $df_1 = df_b = k - 1$. The second degrees of freedom is $df_2 = df_w = N - k$. With matched samples the two degrees of freedom are (1) $df_1 = df_g = k - 1$, and (2) $df_2 = df_e = Nk - N - k + 1$.

Regardless of whether independent or matched samples are used, the *first* degrees of freedom $(k - 1)$ identifies the *column* of the F distribution table that the boundary value is in, while the *second* degrees of freedom,

$(N - k)$ or $(Nk - N - k + 1)$, identifies the *row* that the boundary value is in. Thus, the boundary value is located where this column and this row intersect in the table. For example, suppose that researchers have selected .05 as the permissible level of error. The degrees of freedom for the example involving independent samples are 2 and 33, respectively (Figure 11.3, Step 3). Looking at the intersection of column 2 and row 30 (there is no 33rd row) of the correct F distribution table, the boundary value is found to be 3.32. Since the calculated F ratio is 39.60 (Figure 11.3, Step 5) and it exceeds 3.32, the null hypothesis is rejected. (This is diagrammed in Figure 11.5.) Hence, it can be concluded that the three training programs do differ in their effect on the ethnocentrism of police officers.

Of course, the degrees of freedom and critical value are different for the example involving matched samples. According to Figure 11.4, Step 3, the two degrees of freedom are 2 and 22, respectively. Looking at the intersection of column 2 and row 22 of the same F distribution table, the boundary value is found to be 3.44. Since the calculated F ratio in this second example is 196.36 (Figure 11.4, Step 5) and it exceeds 3.44, the null hypothesis is rejected. Therefore, it can be concluded that the ethnocentrism scores of the 12 police officers do change as they pass through the training program.

Two-Way Analysis of Variance

In a way, what researchers are doing in these two examples is investigating the relationship between a categorical independent variable (training program) and an interval dependent variable (ethnocentrism). One-way ANOVA assesses whether this relationship is statistically significant. What can they do, though, if there are two categorical independent variables rather than just one? Two-way ANOVA is designed to deal with such a situation. If researchers have two categorical independent variables and a single interval or ratio dependent variable, two-way ANOVA can be used to determine whether the two independent variables have statistically significant effects on the dependent variable. The rationale for two-way ANOVA, like that for one-way ANOVA, rests on the important concept of variation.

Components of Variation

The test statistic used in one-way ANOVA is a ratio of two measures of variation. Specifically, the F ratio is a ratio of the *observed* between-groups variation to an *estimate* of that variation based on the assumption that the null hypothesis is true. Thus, if the null hypothesis is true, the observed and estimated between-groups variations should be about the same, and the F ratio should be approximately equal to one. If the null hypothesis is false, the observed between-groups variation should exceed its estimate and the F ratio should be greater than one. One-way ANOVA determines whether or not the F ratio exceeds one by an amount too great to be due to chance.

Simplifying things a bit, two-way ANOVA does for two independent variables what one-way ANOVA does for one independent variable. Two F ratios are calculated: one based on variation among the groups of observations formed by the first independent variable and one based on variation among the groups of observations formed by the second independent variable. Two-way ANOVA tests for the statistical significance of these two F ratios. Although the terminology is a little different from one-way ANOVA, the basic ideas are precisely the same.

It is easier to understand two-way analysis of variance if one arranges the data in a table like the one shown in Figure 11.6.

Figure 11.6   Two-Way Analysis of Variance Data Table

First Independent Variable, X_1

		X_{1a}	X_{1b}	• • •	X_{1k}	
	X_{2a}	N scores	N scores	• •	N scores	$\overline{X}_{ra}$
	X_{2b}	N scores	N scores	• •	N scores	$\overline{X}_{rb}$
Second Independent Variable, X_2	•	•	•	•	•	•
	•	•	•	•	•	•
	•	•	•	•	•	•
	X_{2l}	N scores	N scores	• •	N scores	$\overline{X}_{rl}$
		$\overline{X}_{ca}$	$\overline{X}_{cb}$	• • •	$\overline{X}_{ck}$	$\overline{X}_t$

In this figure, the scores in each of the categories of the first independent variable (X_1) are found in the *columns* of Figure 11.6. The scores in each of the categories of the second independent variable (X_2) are found in the *rows* of Figure 11.6. *Each* cell of this table contains N scores on the dependent variable. Hence, the total number of observations, or scores, is the number of cells times N, or $k \cdot l \cdot N$. The column means, $\overline{X}_{ca}$, $\overline{X}_{cb}$, . . . , $\overline{X}_{ck}$, are used to compute a *between-columns* mean square. That is:

$$\text{MS}_c = \text{SS}_c/\text{df}_c = l\Sigma(\overline{X}_{ci} - \overline{X}_t)^2/(k - 1)$$

where: SS_c = the between-columns sum of squares

df_c = the between-columns degrees of freedom

$\overline{X}_{ci}$ = the mean of the scores in the ith column
$\overline{X}_t$ = the mean of all of the scores
l = the number of rows
k = the number of columns

The row means, $\overline{X}_{ra}$, $\overline{X}_{rb}$, . . . , $\overline{X}_r$, are used to compute a *between-rows* mean square. In other words,

$$MS_r = SS_r/df_r = k\Sigma(\overline{X}_{rj} - \overline{X}_t)^2/(l - 1)$$

where: SS_r = the between-rows sum of squares
   df_r = the between-rows degrees of freedom
   $\overline{X}_{rj}$ = the mean of the scores in the jth row

The greater the ratio of the *between-columns* mean square to the error mean square (the greater the between-columns F ratio, F_c), the more likely one is to get a statistically significant result and to conclude that the *first* independent variable has an effect on the dependent variable. The greater the ratio of the *between-rows* mean square to the error mean square (the greater the between-rows F ratio, F_r), the more likely one is to get a statistically significant result and to conclude that the *second* independent variable has an effect on the dependent variable. Thus, the logic of two-way ANOVA is a direct extension of the logic of one-way ANOVA. Just how two-way ANOVA is actually carried out can be illustrated with an example.

Recall the first example concerning the effects of training programs on the ethnocentrism scores of police officers. In that example, three samples of 12 officers each were randomly selected from the graduation rosters of three different training programs and their ethnocentrism scores were examined with one-way ANOVA. It was concluded that the relationship was statistically significant — type of training program did affect ethnocentrism. Suppose, however, that investigators are curious about just what it is in the training programs that affects ethnocentrism. Is it the content of the programs which influences the ethnocentrism of the police officers? Could it perhaps be something about the instructors which has this effect? To investigate these possibilities, another study is conducted. First, police officers are placed into six groups based on two criteria: training program content (A, B, or C) and race of the training program instructor (white or nonwhite). Then random samples of six officers are selected from each of the six groups. The ethnocentrism scores of these 36 police officers are found in Figure 11.7.

Figure 11.7   Two-Way Analysis of Variance: Ethnocentrism Scores of Police Officers

Training Program Curriculum

		A	B	C	$\overline{X}_{rj}$
Race of Instructor	Nonwhite	6, 7, 8, 8, 9, 10	8, 9, 10, 10, 11, 12	1, 2, 3, 3, 4, 5	7
	White	4, 5, 6, 6, 7, 8	6, 7, 8, 8, 9, 10	5, 6, 7, 7, 8, 9	7
	$\overline{X}_{ci}$	7	9	5	$\overline{X}_t = 7$

When two-way ANOVA is applied to these scores, *two* tests of significance are being conducted. The first test involves this pair of hypotheses:

H_o: $\mu_{c1} = \mu_{c2} = \cdots = \mu_{ck}$

H_a: Not H_o

where: μ_{ci} = the mean of the population from which the scores in column i were drawn

In effect, the null hypothesis says that the scores in the columns come from populations with the same mean. The second pair of hypotheses is:

H_o: $\mu_{r1} = \mu_{r2} = \cdots = \mu_{rl}$

H_a: Not H_o

where: μ_{rj} = the mean of the population from which the scores in row *j* were drawn

In effect, this null hypothesis says that the scores in the *l* rows come from populations with the same mean. Thus, two-way ANOVA is very much like applying one-way ANOVA to the same scores *twice:* first, when the scores have been categorized by training program content, and second, when the scores have been categorized by the race of the instructor. In fact, the hypotheses tested by two-way ANOVA are precisely those which would be tested by using one-way ANOVA twice on the same scores. *The difference is that two-way ANOVA tests these same hypotheses more efficiently and also allows criminologists to test for interaction,* a topic discussed later in this chapter.

Computing the Test Statistic

Application of two-way ANOVA to the scores in Figure 11.7 leads to the calculation of two *F* ratios, as shown in Figure 11.8.

Figure 11.8   Two-Way Analysis of Variance: Computing the F Ratios

Step 1: Prepare the Data

	X_a	X_b	X_c	X_a^2	X_b^2	X_c^2
Nonwhite	6	8	1	36	64	1
	7	9	2	49	81	4
	8	10	3	64	100	9
	8	10	3	64	100	9
	9	11	4	81	121	16
	10	12	5	100	144	25

$\Sigma X_{na}=48$ $\Sigma X_{nb}=60$ $\Sigma X_{nc}=18$ $\Sigma X_{na}^2=394$ $\Sigma X_{nb}^2=610$ $\Sigma X_{nc}^2=64$

	X_a	X_b	X_c	X_a^2	X_b^2	X_c^2
White	4	6	5	16	36	25
	5	7	6	25	49	36
	6	8	7	36	64	49
	6	8	7	36	64	49
	7	9	8	49	81	64
	8	10	9	64	100	81

$\Sigma X_{wa}=36$ $\Sigma X_{wb}=48$ $\Sigma X_{wc}=42$ $\Sigma X_{wa}^2=226$ $\Sigma X_{wb}^2=394$ $\Sigma X_{wc}^2=304$

$\Sigma X_a=84$ $\Sigma X_b=108$ $\Sigma X_c=60$ $\Sigma X_a^2=620$ $\Sigma X_b^2=1004$ $\Sigma X_c^2=368$

$\Sigma X_n = 48 + 60 + 18 = 126$ $\Sigma X_w = 36 + 48 + 42 = 126$

Step 2: Compute the Sums of Squares

The computational formulas:

$$TSS = \Sigma X^2 - \frac{(\Sigma X)^2}{N \cdot k \cdot l}$$

$$SS_c = \frac{(\Sigma X_a)^2}{N \cdot l} + \frac{(\Sigma X_b)^2}{N \cdot l} + \frac{(\Sigma X_c)^2}{N \cdot l} - \frac{(\Sigma X)^2}{N \cdot k \cdot l}$$

$$SS_r = \frac{(\Sigma X_n)^2}{N \cdot k} + \frac{(\Sigma X_w)^2}{N \cdot k} - \frac{(\Sigma X)^2}{N \cdot k \cdot l}$$

$$SS_e = TSS - SS_c - SS_r$$

By substitution:

$$TSS = (620 + 1004 + 368) - \frac{(84 + 108 + 60)^2}{6 \cdot 3 \cdot 2}$$

$$= 1992 - \frac{(252)^2}{36} = 1992 - 1764$$

$$= 228$$

Figure 11.8   **(continued)**

$$SS_c = \frac{84^2}{12} + \frac{108^2}{12} + \frac{60^2}{12} - 1764$$

$$= \frac{22320}{12} - 1764 = 1860 - 1764$$

$$= 96$$

$$SS_r = \frac{126^2}{18} + \frac{126^2}{18} - 1764$$

$$= \frac{31752}{18} - 1764 = 1764 - 1764$$

$$= 0$$

$$SS_e = 228 - 96 - 0 = 228 - 96 = 132$$

Step 3: Compute the Degrees of Freedom

The computational formulas:

$$df_t = N \cdot k \cdot l - 1$$
$$df_c = k - 1$$
$$df_r = l - 1$$
$$df_e = df_t - df_c - df_r$$

By substitution:

$$df_t = 6 \cdot 3 \cdot 2 - 1 = 36 - 1$$
$$= 35$$
$$df_c = 3 - 1$$
$$= 2$$
$$df_r = 2 - 1$$
$$= 1$$
$$df_e = 35 - 2 - 1$$
$$= 32$$

Step 4: Compute the Mean Squares

The computational formulas:

$$MS_c = SS_c / df_c$$
$$MS_r = SS_r / df_r$$
$$MS_e = SS_e / df_e$$

By substitution:

$$MS_c = 96/2$$
$$= 48$$
$$MS_r = 0/1$$
$$= 0$$
$$MS_e = 132/32$$
$$= 4.13$$

Figure 11.8   (continued)

Step 5: Compute the F Ratios

The computational formulas:

$$F_c = MS_c/MS_e$$
$$F_r = MS_r/MS_e$$

By substitution:

$$F_c = 48/4.13$$
$$= 11.64$$
$$F_r = 0/4.13$$
$$= 0$$

As far as Step 1 is concerned, notice that the only arithmetic operations involved are addition and multiplication. First, for those police officers taught by nonwhites, the scores within each curricula type are added up, yielding ΣX_{na}, ΣX_{nb}, and ΣX_{nc}. Their scores are then squared and summed, yielding ΣX^2_{na}, ΣX^2_{nb}, and ΣX^2_{nc}. Then the same operations are performed on the scores of those officers taught by whites. Finally, the results for these two groups are totaled up, yielding X_a, X_b, ..., X^2_c These figures in Step 1 are the building blocks for the mean squares needed to apply two-way ANOVA. Once Step 1 is completed, the worst is over.

The remaining steps are relatively easy to complete, although the computational formulas for the mean squares look rather formiable — more so than they really are. The final results are two *F* ratios:

$$F_c = 11.64$$
$$F_r = 0$$

Comparing the Test Statistics to the Appropriate Sampling Distribution

The logic of ANOVA is really quite simple. If the two null hypotheses are correct, the two *F* ratios (F_c and F_r) should each be approximately equal to one. Thus, if either *F* ratio exceeds one by an amount too large to be due to chance, its null hypothesis is rejected. Otherwise, it is not. Several steps are involved. First, the appropriate *F* distribution table must be identified. This depends solely upon the permissible level of error. Second, from this table investigators must locate the two boundary values with which the two *F* ratios are to be compared. This location depends solely upon the degrees of freedom. The values are located exactly as they were for one-way ANOVA. Finally, if either *F* ratio equals or exceeds the boundary value from the table, the null hypothesis associated with that F ratio is rejected. These steps can be illustrated with the ethnocentrism example introduced earlier.

Suppose that investigators select the .05 level of error. This means that the .05 F distribution table found in Appendix D will be used. Further, each of the two F ratios (F_c and F_r) is a ratio of two mean squares:

$$F_c = MS_c/MS_e$$
$$F_r = MS_r/MS_e$$

Each of these three mean squares (MS_c, MS_r, and MS_e) has a degrees of freedom associated with it (df_c, df_r, and df_e, respectively). The boundary value for each F ratio is located in the F distribution table by going to the column headed by that F ratio's numerator degrees of freedom ($df_1 = df_c$ or df_r) and then going to the row headed by that F ratio's denominator degrees of freedom ($df_2 = df_e$). Figure 11.8, Step 3, shows that $df_c = 2$, $df_r = 1$, and $df_e = 32$. Thus, the boundary value for F_c is found in column 2 and row 30 (since the table has no 32nd row). It is equal to 3.32. According to Figure 11.8, Step 5, the value for F_c is 11.64. Since 11.64 is greater than 3.32, the first null hypothesis is rejected in favor of its alternative, namely:

$$H_o: \mu_{c1} = \mu_{c2} = \mu_{c3}$$
$$H_a: \text{Not } H_o$$

Thus, it can be concluded, that training program content has an effect on ethnocentrism.

The boundary value for F_r is found in column 1 and row 30 of the .05 F distribution table. It is equal to 4.17. Since the value for F_r is exactly zero, the second null hypothesis is not rejected.

$$H_o: \mu_{r1} = \mu_{r2}$$
$$H_a: \mu_{r1} \neq \mu_{r2}$$

Therefore, it is concluded that the race of the training program instructor has no effect on ethnocentrism.

Two-Way Analysis of Variance with Interaction

The conclusion that the race of the instructor has no effect on ethnocentrism seems a bit odd. According to Figure 11.7, the 18 police officers taught by nonwhite instructors have the same mean ethnocentrism score ($\overline{X}_{nw} = 7$) as the 18 taught by white instructors ($\overline{X}_w = 7$). This supports the conclusion that the race of the instructor is unrelated to ethnocentrism. However, *within* each type of training program (A, B, or C), the race of the instructor does seem to have an effect. For example, among the 12 officers taught with training program A, those taught by nonwhites have a mean ethnocentrism score of 8 while those taught by whites have a mean score of 6. Now the *overall* effect of the race of the instructor is an *average* of the effects of the race of the instructor within each type of training program. Thus, in this case, the effects in the three types of training programs *cancel out,* so that the overall effect of the race of the instructor vanishes.

Therefore, the race of the instructor does have an effect on eth-nocentrism, but the magnitude and direction of this effect depend upon the training program involved.

Similarly, Figure 11.7 shows that the magnitude and the direction of the effect of training program content on ethnocentrism depends upon the race of the instructor. For example, among those police officers taught by nonwhites, ethnocentrism is *lower* for those who use training program C than for those who used training program A. For those taught by whites, just the opposite is true. Therefore, one cannot talk unambiguously about the effects of training program content on ethnocentrism without first specifying the race of the instructor. Just as the effects of the race of the instructor depend upon the type of training program so also do the effects of the training programs depend upon the race of the instructor. In other words, the effect of each independent variable on the dependent variable depends upon the value of the other independent variable. That is, the effect of X_1 on Y depends upon the value of X_2; the effect of X_2 on Y depends upon the value of X_1. Whenever this happens, the two independent variables are said to *interact* in their effect on the dependent variable. In this example the race of the instructor and training program content *interact* in their effect on ethnocentrism.

Since the data in Figure 11.7 are based on a *sample* of police officers, it could be that this interaction is due solely to sampling error; that is, it could be that there is *no* interaction between race of the instructor and training program content in the population and that it appears in the sample only by chance. ANOVA can be used to help one decide whether this is true.

Interaction is tested for in two-way ANOVA in the following way. First, the error sum of squares (SS_e) is divided into an interaction sum of squares (SS_i) and a *new* error sum of squares (SS_e). Then, the error degrees of freedom (df_e) is likewise divided into df_i and a new df_e. From these four new computations (SS_i, SS_e, df_i, and df_e) two new mean squares are calculated:

$$MS_i = SS_i/df_i$$
$$MS_e = SS_e/df_e$$

Remember, this new MS_e will differ in value from the old MS_e. On the other hand, MS_c and MS_r are calculated just as they were with two-way ANOVA without interaction. Finally, three new F ratios are computed:

$$F_c = MS_c/MS_e$$
$$F_r = MS_r/MS_e$$
$$F_i = MS_i/MS_e$$

The statistical significance of each of these three F ratios is determined just as was done earlier. Another look at the ethnocentrism example illustrates how this is done. This is presented in Figure 11.9.

Figure 11.9   Two-Way Analysis of Variance with Interaction: Computing the F Ratios

Step 1: Prepare the Data

Done here precisely as was done with two-way analysis of variance without allowing for interaction. See Figure 11.8.

Step 2: Compute the Sums of Squares

The computational formulas:

$$TSS = \Sigma X^2 - \frac{(\Sigma X)^2}{N \bullet k \bullet l}$$

$$SS_c = \frac{(\Sigma X_a)^2}{N \bullet l} + \frac{(\Sigma X_b)^2}{N \bullet l} + \frac{(\Sigma X_c)^2}{N \bullet l} - \frac{(\Sigma X)^2}{N \bullet k \bullet l}$$

$$SS_r = \frac{(\Sigma X_n)^2}{N \bullet k} + \frac{(\Sigma X_w)^2}{N \bullet k} - \frac{(\Sigma X)^2}{N \bullet k \bullet l}$$

$$SS_i = \frac{(\Sigma X_{na})^2}{N} + \frac{(\Sigma X_{nb})^2}{N} + \frac{(\Sigma X_{nc})^2}{N} + \frac{(\Sigma X_{wa})^2}{N} + \frac{(\Sigma X_{wb})^2}{N}$$
$$+ \frac{(\Sigma X_{wc})^2}{N} - SS_c - SS_r - \frac{(\Sigma X)^2}{N \bullet k \bullet l}$$

$$SS_e = TSS - SS_c - SS_r - SS_i$$

By substitution:

$$TSS = (620 + 1004 + 368) - \frac{(84 + 108 + 60)^2}{6 \bullet 3 \bullet 2}$$

$$= 1992 - \frac{(252)^2}{36} = 1992 - 1764$$

$$= 228$$

$$SS_c = \frac{84^2}{12} + \frac{108^2}{12} + \frac{60^2}{12} - 1764$$

$$= \frac{22320}{12} = 1764 = 1860 - 1764$$

$$= 96$$

Figure 11.9   (continued)

$$SS_r = \frac{126^2}{18} + \frac{126^2}{18} - 1764$$

$$= \frac{31752}{18} - 1764 = 1764 - 1764$$

$$= 0$$

$$SS_t = \frac{48^2}{6} + \frac{60^2}{6} + \frac{18^2}{6} + \frac{36^2}{6} + \frac{48^2}{6} + \frac{42^2}{6} - 96 - 0 - 1764$$

$$= \frac{2304 + 3600 + 324 + 1296 + 2304 + 1764}{6} - (96 + 1764)$$

$$= \frac{11592}{6} - 1860 = 1932 - 1860$$

$$= 72$$

$$SS_e = 228 - 96 - 0 - 72 = 228 - (96 + 72) = 228 - 168$$

$$= 60$$

Step 3: Compute the Degrees of Freedom

The computational formulas:

$$df_t = N \cdot k \cdot l - 1$$
$$df_c = k - 1$$
$$df_r = l - 1$$
$$df_i = (k - 1)(l - 1)$$
$$df_e = df_t - df_c - df_r - df_i$$

By substitution:

$$df_t = 6 \cdot 3 \cdot 2 - 1 = 36 - 1$$
$$= 35$$
$$df_c = 3 - 1$$
$$= 2$$
$$df_r = 2 - 1$$
$$= 1$$
$$df_i = (3 - 1)(2 - 1) = 2 \cdot 1$$
$$= 2$$
$$df_e = 35 - 2 - 1 - 2 = 35 - 5$$
$$= 30$$

Step 4: Compute the Mean Squares

The computational formulas:

$$MS_c = SS_c / df_c$$
$$MS_r = SS_r / df_r$$
$$MS_i = SS_i / df_i$$
$$MS_e = SS_e / df_e$$

Figure 11.9   (continued)

By substitution:

$$MS_c = 96/2$$
$$= 48$$
$$MS_r = 0/1$$
$$= 0$$
$$MS_i = 72/2$$
$$= 36$$
$$MS_e = 60/30$$
$$= 2$$

Step 5: Compute the F Ratios

The computational formulas:

$$F_c = MS_c/MS_e$$
$$F_r = MS_r/MS_e$$
$$F_i = MS_i/MS_e$$

By substitution:

$$F_c = 48/2$$
$$= 24$$
$$F_r = 0/2$$
$$= 0$$
$$F_i = 36/2$$
$$= 18$$

From Figure 11.9 it can be seen that the basic calculations for two-way ANOVA with interaction are very simple. The major problem is just keeping track of them. According to Step 1 in Figure 11.8, one merely computes the following sums:

1. the sum of scores in each of the six cells of Figure 11.7 (i.e., $\Sigma X_{na}, \Sigma X_{nb}, \ldots, \Sigma X_{wc}$);
2. the sum of scores in each of the three columns of Figure 11.7 (i.e., $\Sigma X_a, \Sigma X_b,$ and ΣX_c);
3. the sum of scores in each of the two rows of Figure 11.7 (i.e., ΣX_n and ΣX_w);
4. the sum of all the scores (i.e., ΣX); and
5. the sum of the squares of all the scores (i.e., ΣX^2).

Then, in Step 2 these various sums are used to calculate the sums of squares. The rest is easy! All one needs to do is follow the remaining steps listed in Figure 11.9.

General Observations About Two-Way Analysis of Variance with Interaction

There are two important points to discuss concerning two-way ANOVA with interaction.

Effects on F_c and F_r. First, as can be seen by comparing Figures 11.8 and 11.9, allowing for interaction produces a new SS_e and a new df_e which are smaller than the old SS_e and the old df_e. *Typically,* this results in a new MS_e which is *smaller* than the old MS_e. When the new MS_e is smaller than the old MS_e, one result is larger values for F_c and F_r (since MS_c and MS_r remain unchanged).

$$F_c = MS_c/MS_e$$
$$F_r = MS_r/MS_e$$

Therefore, by allowing for interaction, one not only opens up the possibility of discovering a significant interaction effect but also *increases* the chances of discovering significant overall column and row effects when they exist in the population (i.e., the chances of finding significant values for F_c and F_r are increased).

Advantages of Two-Way Analysis of Variance with Interaction. Earlier it was noted that conducting two-way ANOVA is like conducting one-way ANOVA twice on the same data, except that it is more efficient. Now it can be seen that two-way ANOVA *with interaction* is still more powerful. First, it lets one test for a significant interaction effect between the two independent variables, something that would be impossible if one merely applied one-way ANOVA twice. Second, as was just demonstrated, it *ordinarily* increases the likelihood that one will discover significant overall effects for each independent variable on the dependent variable, if such effects exist in the population.

However, the advantages of two-way ANOVA (with or without interaction) do not come without cost. With one-way ANOVA researchers can have different numbers of units in the several categories of the independent variable. However, two-way ANOVA (with or without interaction) requires that the number of units in each cell of the data table be equal. When two-way ANOVA is attempted *without* the same number of scores in each cell, the calculations become much more complex and additional assumptions must be made.

How To Use Two-Way Analysis of Variance

Since using two-way ANOVA with interaction may well produce different results than using two-way ANOVA without interaction, one might wonder just when each type should be used. The answer is quite simple. First, researchers should perform two-way ANOVA allowing for interaction. If the interaction effect is statistically significant, they should proceed immediately to assess the statistical significance of the overall column and row effects. However, if the interaction effect is *not* statistically significant, they should perform two-way ANOVA without interaction and base their conclusions concerning the significance of the column and row effects on these latter calculations. The basic idea here is very straightforward. *If there is an interaction effect, then the column and row effects should be assessed in light of this fact. If there is not an interaction effect, then the column and row effects should be assessed in light of this fact.*

Independent Samples and Matched Samples

Recall that with one-way ANOVA investigators could proceed by analyzing the scores of several different groups of units or by analyzing several different scores for the same set of units. The former method was said to involve independent samples while the latter was said to involve matched samples. Both methods were illustrated with examples in the first part of this chapter. It is also possible to do two-way ANOVA on either independent samples or matched samples. However, all of the discussion of two-way ANOVA in this chapter has assumed the use of independent samples. For example, in the ethnocentrism example, the police officers using the three different training programs are different individuals and the officers taught by nonwhites are different individuals than those taught by whites. No matching is involved. Doing two-way ANOVA on matched samples is rather complicated and will not be covered in this text. However, if one has matched samples, using a version of two-way ANOVA which takes this into account has a major advantage: it makes it easier to reject false null hypotheses concerning column effects, row effects, and interaction effects. It clearly pays to know when one has matched samples and to use the appropriate variety of two-way ANOVA when this occurs.

Multi-Way Analysis of Variance

Earlier it was stated that one-way ANOVA enables investigators to assess the significance of the effect that a single categorical independent variable has on an interval dependent variable. Two-way ANOVA was observed to be a way to extend this idea to include two categorical independent variables. As it turns out, ANOVA can be extended to any number of categorical independent variables. Fortunately, multi-way ANOVA is basically a straightforward extension of two-way ANOVA. However, with additional independent variables the number of cells in the data table grows rapidly, thereby requiring more and more observations. This can be illustrated by imagining still another elaboration of the ethnocentrism example.

Earlier, investigators wanted to know about the effects of different training programs and race of the instructor on the ethnocentrism of police officers. Suppose that they now want to know if the size of the training program classes the officers attended has any effect on their ethnocentrism scores. If size of class is dichotomized and then included as a third independent variable, investigators will have to construct a data table with 12 cells in it. Thus, adding a third variable doubles the number of cells in the data table. If the investigators leave the number of observations in each cell unchanged, the total number of observations will be doubled. Furthermore, if size of class had three or more categories rather than just two, the number of observations necessitated by including this single additional variable would be even greater. As still more independent variables are added to the study, this difficulty is further aggravated. Therefore, investigators should keep in mind that conducting multi-way ANOVA may well require a good many observations.

Unfortunately, the complexities of multi-way ANOVA extend far beyond necessitating additional observations. If investigators carry out the three-way ANOVA introduced in the preceding paragraph, they will find it necessary to test for the statistical significance of *seven* effects! There are three overall effects to test: (1) training program content, (2) race of the instructor, and (3) size of the class. In addition, there will be four interaction effects to test: (1) the training program curricula-race of the instructor interaction effect, (2) the training program curricula-size of the class interaction effect, (3) the race of the instructor-size of the class interaction effect, and (4) the *joint* interaction effect among all three independent variables. If a fourth independent variable is added, a four-way ANOVA will require testing for fifteen effects: four overall effects and 11 interaction effects. Therefore, investigators must remember that using multi-way analysis of variance can become quite confusing because of the large number of overall and interaction effects. Readers interested in multi-way ANOVA should consult Ott (1977).

Summary

Analysis of variance (ANOVA) constitutes an extremely versatile tool in the hands of researchers. Its requirements are simple: (1) the data must be a random sample from some population; (2) the single dependent variable must be measured at the interval level; and (3) the independent variable(s) need only be measured categorically, at the nominal level. In exchange for these modest requirements, investigators receive a great deal. ANOVA enables them to: (1) test for the statistical significance of the effect of each independent variable on the dependent variable while controlling for the effects of the remaining independent variable(s), and (2) test for the statistical significance of one or more interaction effects on the dependent variable. Furthermore, ANOVA is not that difficult to carry out as long as one follows the four basic steps outlined in Figure 11.10.

Figure 11.10   Steps to Follow When Using Analysis of Variance

1. Decide which type of analysis of variance to use:
   a. One-way analysis of variance, two-way analysis of variance, or multi-way analysis of variance.
   b. Independent samples or matched samples.
2. Set the permissible level of error.
3. Compute the test statistic(s).
4. Compare the test statistic(s) to the appropriate sampling distribution table(s).

Notes

[1.] For a discussion of these alternative statistical tests, see Blalock (1980) or Siegel (1956).

[2.] Actually, there are a host of other hypothesis tests which may be conducted with ANOVA. For a discussion of these tests, see Guenther (1964) and Ott (1977).

Review Questions

1. Explain the meaning and significance of the following terms and ideas:
   a. between-groups variation and within-groups variation
   b. sums of squares
   c. degrees of freedom
   d. mean squares
   e. F ratio
   f. independent samples and matched samples
   g. one-way ANOVA and two-way ANOVA
   h. two-way ANOVA without interaction and two-way ANOVA with interaction

2. Suppose researchers want to investigate the effects of various policing strategies on the crime rate. They examine the effects of two independent variables: type of policing (X_1) and extent of policing (X_2). Their data (independent samples) are as follows (these scores are crime rates):

	Type of Policing		
	Beat Patrol	Auto Patrol	Auto Patrol plus Cars at Home
Low	7, 9	12, 19	13, 8
Moderate	9, 6	9, 8	6, 7
High	3, 4	6, 8	7, 5

   a. Perform one-way ANOVA on this data twice: (1) using type of policing as the independent variable and (2) using extent of policing as the independent variable. Is either effect significant?

   b. Perform two-way ANOVA with interaction on this data and two-way ANOVA without interaction if called for. Which effects are significant?

   c. Compare and contrast the findings using one-way ANOVA and two-way ANOVA.

3. Examine the data in question 2 from Chapter 9 using one-way ANOVA. How do the conclusions reached with ANOVA compare to those reached with the two-samples mean test?

4. Identify five research questions that one could investigate using ANOVA. Specify the dependent variable and the independent variable(s) and explain how the assumptions for the use of ANOVA are satisfied in each case.

References

Blalock, Hubert. *Social Statistics.* 2nd rev. ed. New York: McGraw-Hill Book Co., 1980.

Guenther, William. *Analysis of variance.* Englewood Cliffs, NJ: Prentice-Hall, Inc., 1964.

Ott, Lyman. *An Introduction to Statistical Methods and Data Analysis.* North Scituate, MA: Duxbury Press, 1977.

Siegel, Sidney. *Nonparametric Statistics for the Behavioral Sciences.* New York: McGraw-Hill Book Co., 1956.

Chapter 12
Correlation and Regression Analysis

Learning Objectives

After completing this chapter, the reader should be able to:

1. Describe and distinguish between simple correlation analysis and simple regression analysis
2. Construct scattergrams
3. Compute and properly interpret both correlation and regression coefficients
4. Identify the rationale for the best-fitting line
5. Describe multiple regression and correlation analysis
6. Describe the geometry of multiple regression and correlation analysis
7. Interpret multiple regression and correlation coefficients and beta coefficients and know when to use each
8. Understand and carry out the F test for the adequacy of the multiple regression equation
9. Explain how correlation and regression analysis might be used to address problems of interest to criminologists.

Introduction

Chapter 11 discussed the advantages of analysis of variance (ANOVA). One advantage given was that with ANOVA the independent variable(s) had only to be measured at the nominal level. What happens, though, if the independent variables are all measured at the interval level? Then the requirements of ANOVA are more than met. Applying ANOVA in such a situation would involve throwing away information because any statistical test which treats interval variables as if they were nominal variables does not take full advantage of the available information. This is just what ANOVA does — it treats all independent variables as nominal variables. Thus, if the research design more than meets the requirements for ANOVA, it makes good sense to use a more demanding statistical method. One such approach involves using correlation and regression. *Correlation and regression are complementary statistical methods designed for research which includes one interval dependent variable and one or more interval independent variables.* These statistical methods have a lot in common with ANOVA. Therefore, this chapter begins with a discussion of research involving one dependent variable and a single independent variable.

Simple Correlation and Regression: One Independent Variable

It is not difficult to identify research questions to which investigators might want to apply correlation and regression. For example, investigators interested in the relationship between the unemployment rate and the crime rate could use correlation and regression to relate the former to the latter. Investigators curious about variations in the rate of recidivism among offenders released from various penal institutions might use correlation and regression to investigate the relationship between rate of recidivism on the one hand and a measure of the quality of rehabilitation programs on the other. In both instances, investigators want to inquire into the relationship between an interval dependent variable and an interval independent variable. Specifically, they want to know how strong these relationships are. When both the independent and the dependent variables are measured at the interval level, there are *two* ways to define what is meant by a strong relationship: (1) a strong relationship might mean that the independent variable has a *marked effect* on the dependent variable, or (2) a strong relationship might mean that the dependent variable can be *accurately predicted* from the independent variable. Fortunately, correlation and regression analysis can be used to ascertain the strength of a relationship in both senses of the term. In particular:

1. *Correlation analysis* can be used to determine the strength of a relationship in the sense of one's ability to *accurately predict* the dependent variable from the independent variable.

2. *Regression analysis* can be used to determine the strength of a relationship when what one means is the *size of the effect* the independent variable has on the dependent variable.

This chapter explains how correlation and regression analysis is carried out and how the results it produces are interpreted.

The Scattergram

Before discussing correlation and regression, it is useful to introduce the scattergram. A scattergram is a graphic, or visual, display of the relationship between two interval variables in a body of data. It serves two major purposes. First, scattergrams help one "see" the relationship between the independent and the dependent variables. Thus, in a way scattergrams resemble the bar graphs, pie charts, and other visual data display methods discussed in Chapter 7. For this reason, researchers are always well advised to construct a scattergram before applying correlation and regression analysis. Also, scattergrams serve a second important purpose: they make it much easier to understand what correlation and regression are all about.

The scattergram closely resembles the Cartesian coordinate system. It consists of two perpendicular axes, one for each variable, and a set of data points (dots), one for each observation on the two variables. Figure 12.1 is a scattergram for two variables mentioned earlier, rate of recidivism and quality of rehabilitation programs.

There are a few simple rules for constructing scattergrams which, when followed, make them easier to understand. First, the independent variable (the quality of rehabilitation programs), is arrayed from left to right along the horizontal axis and is denoted by the letter X. The dependent variable (the rate of recidivism) is arrayed from bottom to top along the vertical axis and is denoted by the letter Y. Second, each axis is clearly marked in the units of its variable: The horizontal axis is marked in units of the quality of rehabilitation program; the vertical axis is marked in units of the rate of recidivism. Third, the data point for each observation is located directly above that observation's score on the independent variable, located on the horizontal axis, and directly to the right of that observation's score on the dependent variable, located on the vertical axis. For example, the leftmost data point in Figure 12.1 represents a penal institution whose score on the quality of rehabilitation programs is just 2 and whose rate of recidivism is .80.

There are 25 data points in Figure 12.1. Each one stands for a given penal institution. Its location depends upon that penal institution's scores on the two variables. The data upon which this scattergram is based are found in Table 12.1.

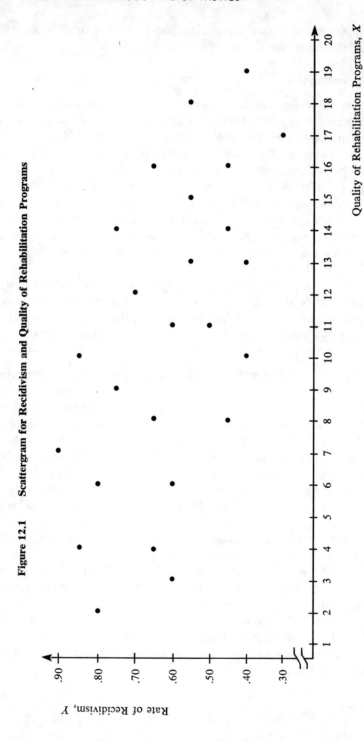

Figure 12.1   Scattergram for Recidivism and Quality of Rehabilitation Programs

Table 12.1   Recidivism and Rehabilitation Scores

Penal Institution	Rate of Recidivism	Quality of Rehabilitation
1	.90	7
2	.30	17
3	.80	6
4	.40	19
5	.60	11
6	.70	12
7	.50	11
8	.85	4
9	.65	8
10	.45	16
11	.55	13
12	.75	14
13	.45	8
14	.40	13
15	.85	10
16	.55	18
17	.60	6
18	.55	15
19	.75	9
20	.80	2
21	.60	3
22	.65	4
23	.40	10
24	.45	14
25	.65	16

With a little practice, it is easy to see how a scattergram can be quickly constructed from a set of scores on two interval variables.

Correlation Analysis

Once a scattergram has been constructed, it can be studied in order to see if the data points follow a pattern. *Analysts commonly use scatter-*

grams to see how closely the data points cluster around a straight line. Clearly, if the data points cluster closely around a straight line, it should be possible to predict the dependent variable from the independent variable with considerable accuracy. *The correlation coefficient, denoted r, measures the extent to which the data points fit a straight line.* In fact, it is sometimes called a measure of *linear* correlation. Thus, the correlation coefficient can be used to determine how accurately the dependent variable (*Y*) can be predicted from the independent variable (*X*). The calculations required to compute the correlation coefficient for the data in Table 12.1 are found in Figure 12.2.

Figure 12.2   Computing the Correlation Coefficient

Step 1: Prepare the data

Unit	Y	X	Y^2	X^2	XY
1	.90	7	.8100	49	6.30
2	.30	17	.0900	289	5.10
3	.80	6	.6400	36	4.80
4	.40	19	.1600	361	7.60
5	.60	11	.3600	121	6.60
6	.70	12	.4900	144	8.40
7	.50	11	.2500	121	5.50
8	.85	4	.7225	16	3.40
9	.65	8	.4225	64	5.20
10	.45	16	.2025	256	7.20
11	.55	13	.3025	169	7.15
12	.75	14	.5625	196	10.50
13	.45	8	.2025	64	3.60
14	.40	13	.1600	169	5.20
15	.85	10	.7225	100	8.50
16	.55	18	.3025	324	9.90
17	.60	6	.3600	36	3.60
18	.55	15	.3025	225	8.25
19	.75	9	.5625	81	6.75
20	.80	2	.6400	4	1.60
21	.60	3	.3600	9	1.80

Figure 12.2   (continued)

22	.65	4	.4225	16	2.60
23	.40	10	.1600	100	4.00
24	.45	14	.2025	196	6.30
25	.65	16	.4225	256	10.40
$\Sigma = 15.15$		266	9.8325	3402	150.25

Step 2: Compute r

The computational formula:

$$r = \frac{N\Sigma XY - (\Sigma X)(\Sigma Y)}{\sqrt{[N\Sigma X^2 - (\Sigma X)^2][N\Sigma Y^2 - (\Sigma Y)^2]}}$$

By substitution:

$$r = \frac{25(150.25) - 266(15.15)}{\sqrt{[25(3402) - 266^2][25(9.8325) - 15.15^2]}}$$

$$= \frac{3752.25 - 4029.90}{\sqrt{(85050 - 70756)(245.8125 - 229.5225)}}$$

$$= \frac{-273.65}{\sqrt{(14294)(16.29)}} = \frac{-273.65}{482.5446}$$

$$= -.57$$

These calculations are very straightforward. One merely squares the values of the dependent variable and the independent variable and then takes the product of the two variables to get the columns headed by Y^2, X^2, and XY, respectively, in Figure 12.2. Then one sums each of the five columns and inserts the resulting totals into the computational formula. The value which results is the correlation coefficient.

Interpreting the Correlation Coefficient. Interpreting the correlation coefficient is not difficult. In this example, the correlation coefficient is equal to $-.57$. The obvious question is, what does this mean? Several important points must be noted in the answer to this question.

The Sign of the Correlation Coefficient: First, the sign of the correlation coefficient indicates the *direction* of the relationship between the two variables. In this example the correlation is negative. This means that as the independent variable (quality of rehabilitation programs) increases, the dependent variable (rate of recidivism) decreases. Hence, the straight line about which the data points cluster in Figure 12.1 runs from the upper left to the lower right, much like that in Figure 12.3.

Figure 12.3   Moderate Negative Relationship (r = .40)

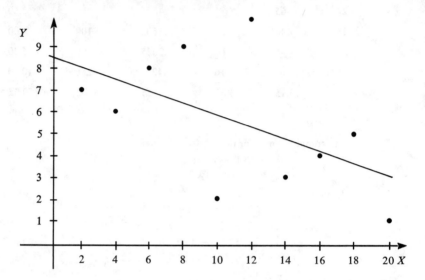

If the data points had been placed such that the straight line about which they clustered ran from the lower left to the upper right, then the relationship between X_1 and Y would have been a positive one, as in Figure 12.4.

Figure 12.4   Moderate Positive Relationship (r = .40)

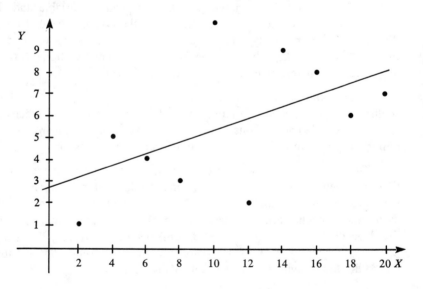

Thus, the sign of the correlation coefficient indicates the direction of the relationship between the independent and the dependent variables.

The Magnitude of the Correlation Coefficient: Second, the magnitude of the correlation coefficient, whether its sign is positive or negative, measures the degree to which the data points cluster along a straight line. The more closely the data points cluster along a straight line, the greater the magnitude of the correlation coefficient. Since the accuracy with which the dependent variable can be predicted from the independent variable is directly related to the extent to which the data points cluster around a straight line, this means that the magnitude of the correlation coefficient measures the accuracy with which Y can be predicted from X. The greater the magnitude of the correlation coefficient, the more accurately can Y be predicted from X.

Specifically, the correlation coefficient varies between negative one and positive one (-1.00 to $+1.00$). A value of zero (.00), indicates no relationship between the two variables. Hence, the independent variable would be of *no use* in predicting the dependent variable. On the other hand, a value of positive or negative one ($+1.00$ or -1.00) indicates a perfect relationship between the two variables. Here the independent variable could be used to predict the dependent variable *without error*. Of course, the correlation coefficient is not often *exactly* equal to zero or to (positive or negative) one. Instead, values close to zero indicate a weak relationship (as is Figs. 12.5. and 12.6), while values close to either positive or negative one indicate a strong relationship (as in Figs. 12.7 and 12.8).

Figure 12.5   Weak Negative Relationship ($r = -.15$)

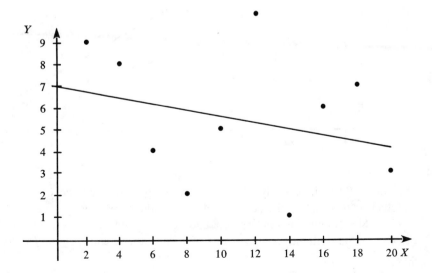

Figure 12.6   Weak Positive Relationship (r = .15)

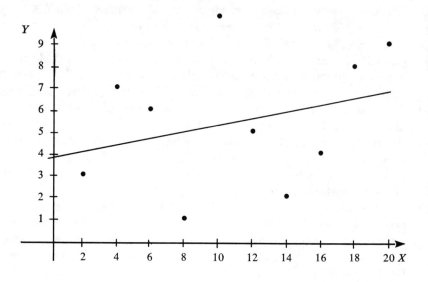

Figure 12.7   Strong Negative Relationship (r = −.70)

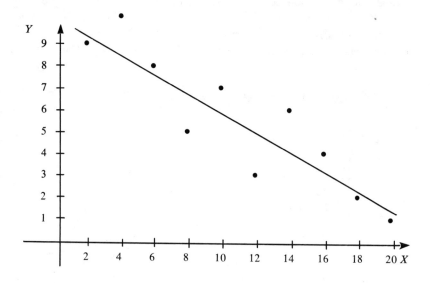

Widom (1979), in a study of women awaiting trial, used the correlation coefficient to measure the strength of the relationships among several attitudes. She found the relationship between *personal autonomy* and *self-esteem* to be quite strong (*r* = .60). On the other hand, *personal auton-*

omy and *femininity* were found to be almost completely unrelated (*r* = −.05). *Personal autonomy* and *feminism* were moderately related (*r* = .43), she reported. Figure 12.9 is a guide for making sense out of the magnitude of the correlation coefficient, but it must be used with considerable caution.

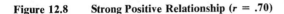

Figure 12.8   Strong Positive Relationship (*r* = .70)

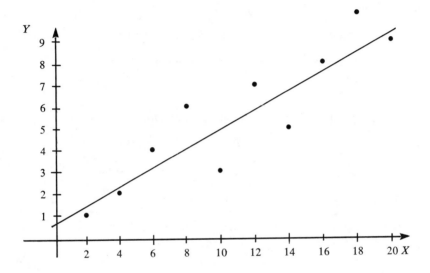

The Effect of Measurement Unreliability. In Chapter 4, the correlation coefficient was used to measure reliability. The larger the correlation coefficient, the more reliable the measurement; and the smaller the correlation coefficient, the less reliable the measurement. This has a considerable impact on the present use of the correlation coefficient as a measure of the strength of the relationship between two variables. If two variables are strongly related and are measured reliably, the correlation between them should be fairly close to positive one or negative one. However, if two variables are strongly related but are not reliably measured, the magnitude of the correlation between them will be diminished. *In general, lack of reliable measurement attenuates (makes smaller) the magnitude of the correlation coefficient.* Thus, the proper interpretation to be given to a correlation coefficient depends upon how reliably the two variables were measured. Regoli and Poole (1980) report a correlation of −.50 between role conflict and belief in self-regulation (for rural departments). Since Regoli and Poole are satisfied that both variables were measured reliably, they interpret this result to mean that role conflict and self-regulation are moderately related. If they had entertained serious doubts about the reliability of one or both variables, then a different interpretation would have been in order. In this case, a correlation of $-.50$ would have been evidence of a strong relationship between role conflict and belief in self-regulation. Generally speaking, in criminal justice research, the reliability of many variables is not as high as one might prefer. As a result, it is rare to compute correlation coefficients with values of either $+1.00$ or -1.00.

Figure 12.9   A Guide for Interpreting the Correlation Coefficient

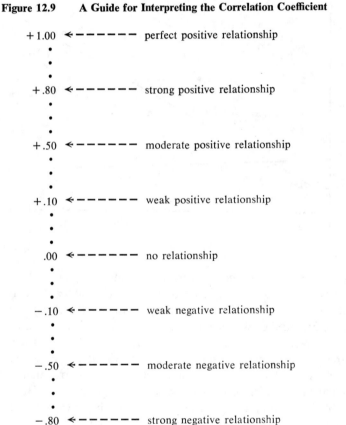

Explained Variation. Although the correlation coefficient has many virtues as a measure of the strength of a relationship, it also has shortcomings. In particular, some believe that the correlation coefficient does not lend itself to easy, straightforward interpretation. In fact, to many it is just a number which varies between -1.00 and $+1.00$ and whose value somehow measures the strength of a relationship. Fortunately, this uneasiness can be at least partially remedied. It turns out that the *square* of the correlation coefficient has a satisfying, easily grasped interpretation: when multiplied by 100, r^2 can be interpreted as the percentage of the variation in the dependent variable which is explained by the independent variable. Since the example correlation coefficient is $-.57$, its square is:

$$r^2 = (-.57) \cdot (-.57)$$
$$= .32$$
$$\text{thus, } 100 \cdot r^2 = 100 \cdot (.32)$$
$$= 32$$

Hence, it can be said that the quality of rehabilitation program explains about 32 percent of the variation in the rate of recidivism. To many this conclusion carries greater meaning than the mere assertion that the correlation coefficient is equal to $-.57$. This use of the square of the correlation coefficient is so popular that r^2 is called by its own name, *the coefficient of determination.*

Correlation and Causation. Throughout this chapter the correlation coefficient is interpreted as a measure of the accuracy with which the dependent variable can be predicted from the independent variable. *A substantial correlation does not prove that the dependent variable is caused by the independent variable.* A substantial correlation indicates only that the joint observations on the two variables (the data points) fit a pattern. As long as they fit a pattern, one variable can be used to predict the other. The fact that they fit a pattern does not necessarily mean that either variable causes the other. For example, Widom (1979) reported a substantial correlation between sense of personal autonomy and sense of self-esteem for women awaiting trial. This does not mean that sense of personal autonomy causes sense of self-esteem, or vice versa. It is investigators who label one variable "independent" and the other "dependent." Thus, even if one variable *is* a cause of the other, the correlation coefficient cannot be used to distinguish cause from effect. This can only be done by investigators using their professional judgment. The correlation coefficient merely measures how "predictable" the relationship is.

The Symmetry of the Correlation Coefficient. Careful readers might have noticed something interesting about the computational formula for the correlation coefficient in Figure 12.2 which states:

$$r = \frac{N\Sigma XY - (\Sigma X)(\Sigma Y)}{\sqrt{[N\Sigma X^2 - (\Sigma X)^2][N\Sigma Y^2 - (\Sigma Y)^2]}}$$

Clearly, the correlation coefficient will be unchanged by interchanging the scores for the independent and dependent variables. That is,

$$r = \frac{N\Sigma YX - (\Sigma Y)(\Sigma X)}{\sqrt{[N\Sigma Y^2 - (\Sigma Y)^2][N\Sigma X^2 - (\Sigma X)^2]}}$$

No matter which of two variables is labeled "dependent" or "independent," the value of the correlation coefficient stays the same. This is so because when two variables fit a pattern, *either* variable can be used to predict the other and with *equal* success.

Scale Free. The correlation coefficient has another interesting property — it is scale free. That is, the value of the correlation between two variables stays the same even if the *unit(s) of measurement* of one or both variables changes. For example, the correlation between the two variables in Figure 12.1 is −.57. If criminologists decided to measure recidivism as a *percent* rather than as a *proportion,* the correlation would be unaffected. Similarly, if their measure of the quality of rehabilitation programs was on a scale of one (1) to one-hundred (100) rather than one (1) to twenty (20), nothing would happen to the correlation coefficient. This is so because when the unit of measurement of a variable changes, the data points in the scattergram stay right where they are. The axes are merely recalibrated. Since the correlation coefficient measures the fit of the *data points* to a straight line, and since they have *not* moved, the correlation coefficient is unaffected.

This does *not* mean that the correlation coefficient is not influenced by *the way* the variables are measured. It clearly is. For example, it was just pointed out that the correlation coefficient is influenced by the reliability of the measured variables. Thus, the *quality* of measurement does make a difference, but the *units* of measurement have no effect on the value of the correlation coefficient.

Regression Analysis

Earlier it was noted that correlation analysis is used to measure the accuracy with which the dependent variable can be predicted from the independent variable. The correlation coefficient accomplishes this task by measuring the fit of the data points to a straight line. It was also noted earlier that regression analysis is used to measure the size of the effect the independent variable has on the dependent variable. The next several sections of this chapter are devoted to a discussion of regression analysis.

The Best-Fitting Line. Whereas correlation analysis is concerned with the fit of the data points to a straight line, regression analysis is concerned with certain properties of the straight line itself. Hence, it is now necessary to identify this straight line. Figure 12.10 is an exact duplicate of the

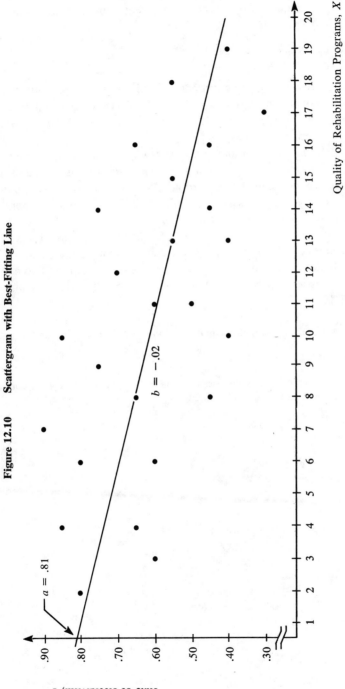

Figure 12.10   Scattergram with Best-Fitting Line

scattergram in Figure 12.1 except that a straight line has now been drawn through the data points.

The equation for such a straight line is,

$$\hat{Y} = a + b_1X$$

where X represents the independent variable and $\hat{Y}$ represents the pre-dicted values of the dependent variable (Y). $\hat{Y}$ is used here rather than Y because it is the *predicted* Y-values (the $\hat{Y}$-values) which lie in a straight line, not the actual Y-values.

The letters a and b represent values which identify the straight line. Specifically, *a is called the Y-intercept, or constant.* Its value is equal to the distance between the origin and the point where the straight line intersects the Y-axis, as is shown in Figure 12.10. On the other hand, *b is called the regression coefficient, or slope.* It stands for the rate of incline or decline of the straight line. Each pair of values for a and b identifies a unique straight line, and each straight line is defined by a unique equation with a particular pair of values for a and b. The constant (a) and regression coefficient (b) for the example data are calculated in Figure 12.11.

Figure 12.11   Computing the Regression Coefficient and Constant

Step 1: Prepare the Data

This step is carried out in exactly the same fashion as Step 1 for computing the correlation coefficient in Figure 12.2. The results were:

$$\Sigma Y = 15.15$$
$$\Sigma X = 266$$
$$\Sigma Y^2 = 9.8325$$
$$\Sigma X^2 = 3402$$
$$\Sigma XY = 150.25$$

Step 2: Compute b

The computational formula:

$$b = \frac{N\Sigma XY - (\Sigma X)(\Sigma Y)}{N\Sigma X^2 - (\Sigma X)^2}$$

By substitution:

$$b = \frac{25(150.25) - 266(15.15)}{25(3402) - 266^2}$$

$$= \frac{3752.25 - 4029.90}{85050 - 70756}$$

$$= \frac{-273.65}{14294}$$

$$= -.0191$$

$$\cong -.02$$

Figure 12.11   **(continued)**

Step 3: Compute a

The computational formula:

$$a = \frac{\Sigma Y - b\,(\Sigma X)}{N}$$

By substitution:

$$a = \frac{15.15 - (-.0191) \cdot (266)}{25}$$

$$= \frac{15.15 - (-5.0806)}{25} = \frac{20.2306}{25}$$

$$= .8092$$

$$\cong .81$$

Hence, the equation of the straight line for this data is,

$$\hat{Y} = .81 + (-.02)X$$

Notice that as was the case with the correlation coefficient, the computations required for the regression coefficient and the constant are not very difficult. The regression coefficient is calculated from the same sums as were used to calculate the correlation coefficient; only their arrangement in the computational formula is different. Calculation of the constant follows easily.

Identifying the Best-Fitting Line. Calculating the constant and the regression coefficient by use of the formulas found in Figure 12.11 amounts to deciding which straight line is to be drawn through the data points on the scattergram (Fig. 12.10). Different formulas would yield different results and, hence, different straight lines. One might ask, what is so special about the line identified by the formulas presented earlier? Why not use different formulas?

The major reason why these particular formulas are used is that the straight line they identify fits the data points in the scattergram better than any other straight line. Thus, the line they identify is the *best-fitting line*. Since the data points do not fall exactly on a straight line, the best-fitting line is only an approximation; that is, the best-fitting line misses the data points by an amount smaller than that by which other straight lines miss them. Specifically, the best-fitting line minimizes the sum of the squared vertical distances between the data points and the line. For this reason it is sometimes called the *least squares line*. There are other formulas for identifying the "best" straight line, but nearly all investigators who use regression methods calculate the constant and the regression coefficient in accordance with the formulas found in Figure 12.11[1].

Interpreting the Constant. It was stated earlier that the constant, *a*, stands for the distance from the origin to the point where the best-fitting line crosses the Y-axis. Actually this is somewhat oversimplified. The constant need *not* be a positive number. If it is *positive,* then the best-fitting line crosses the Y-axis *above* the origin, as shown in Figure 12.12.

Figure 12.12   Regression Equation with a Positive Constant

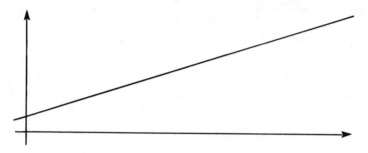

If it is *negative*, the straight line crosses the Y-axis *below* the origin, as shown in Figure 12.13.

Figure 12.13   Regression Equation with a Negative Constant

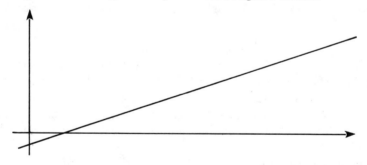

Thus, the sign of the constant is important as well as the *magnitude* of the constant. It is the magnitude of the constant which stands for the distance between the origin and the point where the best-fitting line intersects the Y-axis. Here the constant is .81 (Fig. 12.11). Thus, for the data points in Figure 12.10, the best-fitting line crosses the rate of recidivism-axis .81 units *above* the origin. Since the best-fitting line can be thought of as a *prediction* line, investigators would predict that a penal institution whose score on the quality of rehabilitation programs index was zero (0) would have a recidivism rate of .81. As a general rule, unless investigators are making projections, they do not use the constant. When they use regression methods, it is usually the regression coefficient which is of greatest interest.

Interpreting the Regression Coefficient. Earlier the regression co-efficient was said to stand for the rate of incline or decline of the best-fitting line. It is, moreover, the *sign* of the regression coefficient which indicates whether the line *inclines or declines* across the scattergram. In this respect, the sign of the regression coefficient conveys precisely the same information as the sign of the correlation coefficient. When the best-fitting line runs from the upper-left portion of the scattergram to the lower-right portion (as in Figs. 12.3, 12.5, and 12.7) then the regression coefficient, *b*, like the correlation coefficient, *r*, is negative. When the best-fitting line goes from the lower-left to the upper-right portions of the scattergram (as in Figs. 12.4, 12.6, and 12.8) then *b*, as well as *r*, is positive. Since the regression coefficient for the example data is negative ($-.02$), the best-fitting line for that data slopes from the upper-left portion of the scatter-gram to the lower-right portion, as shown in Figure 12.10.

The Magnitude of the Regression Coefficient. If the sign of the re-gression coefficient identifies the general direction in which the best-fitting line runs, it is the magnitude of the regression coefficient which indicates the "steepness" of the line's ascent or descent. The more steeply angled the straight line, the greater is the magnitude of the regression coefficient. Thus, the magnitudes of the regression coefficients in Figure 12.7 and 12.8 exceed those in Figures 12.3 and 12.4, which in turn exceed those in Figures 12.5 and 12.6. This is why the regression coefficient is so val-uable. In effect, *the regression coefficient tells investigators how big a change in the dependent variable is associated with a one unit change in the independent variable.* A large regression coefficient means that on the average a pronounced change in the dependent variable is likely to follow a one unit change in the independent variable. A small regression coef-ficient means that on the average only a slight change in the dependent variable is likely to follow a one unit change in the independent variable.

Not Scale Free. Since the regression coefficient indicates how big a change in the dependent variable is likely to follow a one *unit* change in the independent variable, it is clearly *not* a scale free measure of the strength of a relationship like the correlation coefficient. The units of measurement make a difference. For example, the regression coefficient for the example data was reported in Figure 12.11 to be $-.0191$. This means that on the average as the quality of rehabilitation programs in-creases one unit, the rate of recidivism drops about .02 (.0191) units. If the rate of recidivism is measured as a percent rather than as a proportion, the regression coefficient is -1.91. This new value for *b* is interpreted as follows: a one unit change in the quality of rehabilitation programs is on the average followed by a 2 (1.91) percent drop in the rate of recidivism. Since a drop of 2 units for a dependent variable measured on a 0 to 100 scale is equivalent to a drop of .02 units for a dependent variable measured on a .00 to 1.00 scale, nothing of *substance* has changed even if the regression coefficient has. This is illustrated in Figure 12.14.

Figure 12.14   Regression Analysis and Units of Measurement

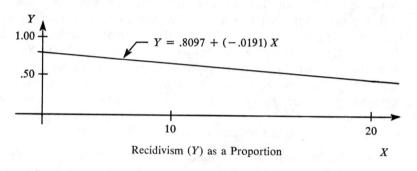

$$Y = .8097 + (-.0191) X$$

Recidivism (Y) as a Proportion

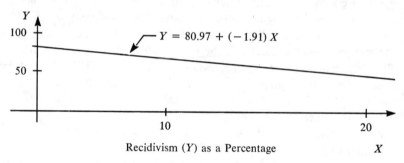

$$Y = 80.97 + (-1.91) X$$

Recidivism (Y) as a Percentage

The point of this discussion is that investigators must know what the units of measurement are before they can make sense out of a regression coefficient. Merely knowing that the regression coefficient equals $-.0191$ does them no good unless the units of measurement are also known. In this respect the regression coefficient differs greatly from the correlation coefficient which is scale free. However, there is a way to standardize the regression coefficient to make it scale free. This is discussed later in this chapter.

The Asymmetry of the Regression Coefficient. The regression coefficient differs from the correlation coefficient in one other important respect. Earlier it was observed that the correlation coefficient is a symmetric measure of the strength of a relationship. This means that no matter which of two variables is called the dependent variable and which the independent variable, the correlation coefficient remains the same. This is definitely *not* the case with the regression coefficient. Look carefully at the formula for the calculation of the regression coefficient:

$$b = \frac{N\Sigma XY - (\Sigma X)(\Sigma Y)}{N\Sigma X^2 - (\Sigma X)^2}$$

If the scores for the independent and dependent variables are interchanged, the resulting regression coefficient will change, too. That is:

$$b = \frac{N\Sigma YX - (\Sigma Y)(\Sigma X)}{N\Sigma Y^2 - (\Sigma Y)^2}$$

Clearly, these two regression coefficients will differ in value. This is illustrated with the example data in Figure 12.15.

Figure 12.15   Computing Both Regression Coefficients

Step 1: Prepare the data

From Figure 12.11:

$$\Sigma Y = 15.15$$
$$\Sigma X = 266$$
$$\Sigma Y^2 = 9.8325$$
$$\Sigma X^2 = 3402$$
$$\Sigma XY = 150.25$$

Step 2: Compute the first b

From Figure 12.11:

$$b = -.0191$$

Step 3: Compute the second b

The computational formula:

$$b = \frac{N\Sigma YX - (\Sigma Y)(\Sigma X)}{N\Sigma Y^2 - (\Sigma Y)^2}$$

By substitution:

$$b = \frac{25(150.25) - (15.15)266}{25(9.8325) - 15.15^2}$$

$$= \frac{3752.25 - 4029.90}{245.8125 - 229.5225}$$

$$= \frac{-273.65}{16.29}$$

$$= -16.7986$$

Here the first regression coefficient (where the rate of recidivism is the dependent variable) is $-.0191$. The second regression coefficient (where the quality of rehabilitation programs is the dependent variable) is -16.7986. These two regression coefficients are not even *approximately* equal. Thus, the regression coefficient is *asymmetric*. In the last analysis this means that for every two interval variables there are *two* best-fitting lines: one when the first variable is treated as if it were the dependent variable and another when the second variable is treated as if *it* were the dependent variable. It is extremely important that these two regression coefficients be distinguished.

As was indicated earlier, it is up to researchers to decide which of two variables is dependent and which is independent. It is often a difficult decision to make. For instance, suppose one assumes that the quality of rehabilitation programs (independent variable) affects the rate of recidivism (the dependent variable). Perhaps prison officials deliberately improved the quality of rehabilitation programs in those prisons with the highest rates of recidivism. This seems plausible. However, if it is true, the quality of rehabilitation programs should be treated as the *dependent* variable and the rate of recidivism as the independent variable, rather than the other way around. Which is which? Unfortunately, no statistical test can address this question. Only substantive knowledge can supply the answer.

Combining Correlation and Regression Analysis

A final point needs to be made concerning the joint use of correlation and regression analyses. In particular, it should be noted that correlation and regression are *complementary;* that is, although each method of analysis by itself reveals a good deal about the relationship between two variables, together they reveal more. As indicated earlier, the correlation coefficient measures the degree to which the data points of two variables lie along a straight line. When first examining the relationship between two interval variables, it makes sense to begin the inquiry with correlation analysis. Its use indicates whether the fitting of a straight line to the data offers much promise. If correlation analysis suggests that the data points do lie reasonably close to a straight line, regression analysis can be used to identify that line. If correlation analysis indicates that the data points do *not* lie at all close to any straight line, regression analysis need not be used at all. This is because of a simple fact: *if the relationship between two variables is not properly characterized in terms of a straight line, it makes little sense to identify and examine the straight line which characterizes their relationship best.* It is in this sense that correlation and regression are complementary: *correlation analysis indicates when regression analysis is appropriate.* Fortunately, this important partnership applies not only to the simple, two variable case but extends also to the more general, multivariate case.

Multiple Correlation and Regression Analysis

Suppose that researchers are trying to identify a second independent variable to introduce into their analysis. A number of possibilities occur to them almost immediately, but the variable which they choose is not so much a characteristic of a penal institution itself as it is a characteristic of an institution's inmate population. The second independent variable selected is the proportion of inmates in a penal institution who are *already* repeat offenders. These data are listed in Table 12.2.

Table 12.2   Recidivism, Rehabilitation, and Repeat Offender Scores

Penal Institution	Rate of Recidivism	Quality of Rehabilitation	Proportion of Repeat Offenders
1	.90	7	.80
2	.30	17	.50
3	.80	6	.65
4	.40	19	.35
5	.60	11	.50
6	.70	12	.70
7	.50	11	.50
8	.85	4	.80
9	.65	8	.55
10	.45	16	.55
11	.55	13	.65
12	.75	14	.60
13	.45	8	.60
14	.40	13	.45
15	.85	10	.55
16	.55	18	.60
17	.60	6	.60
18	.55	15	.45
19	.75	9	.75
20	.80	2	.60
21	.60	3	.55
22	.65	4	.60
23	.40	10	.55
24	.45	14	.50
25	.65	16	.70

The rationale for this selection seems obvious: researchers suspect that repeat offenders are more likely to recidivate than are first offenders. Therefore, penal institutions with high proportions of repeat offenders among their inmate populations are likely to have higher rates of recidivism than institutions with low proportions of repeat offenders. *Multiple regression analysis can be used to assess the accuracy of this hypothesis.*

Multiple Regression Analysis

Simple regression analysis fitted the following equation to a body of data:
$$\hat{Y} = a + bX$$
Multiple regression analysis merely extends this idea to include a second independent variable:
$$\hat{Y} = a + b_1X_1 + b_2X_2$$
With multiple regression analysis there are two regression coefficients, each of which tells researchers something about the effect of one independent variable upon the dependent variable. Although these regression coefficients and the constant can be computed by hand, the calculations are very tedious and errors are likely to be made. Therefore, one is well advised to use a computer for this purpose. In this example, when a computer is used to calculate the regression coefficients and constant, the results are:

$$a = .2193$$
$$b_1 = -.0108$$
$$b_2 = .8560$$

Rounding these figures off, the multiple regression equation is:
$$\hat{Y} = .22 + (-.01)X_1 + (.86)X_2$$
Earlier, the simple regression equation was identified as
$$\hat{Y} = .81 + (-.02)X$$
Clearly, both the constant and the regression coefficient for the quality of rehabilitation programs have changed. To explain why this has happened, it is necessary to look more carefully at what multiple regression analysis is and how its results should be interpreted.

The Geometry of Multiple Regression Analysis. The geometry of simple regression analysis is quite simple. First, there is a scattergram, a pair of perpendicular axes and a set of data points. Then a straight line is fitted to these data points. Finally, the regression coefficient and constant of the straight line are calculated and interpreted. Matters change considerably when an additional independent variable is included in the analysis. In this case there are *three* perpendicular axes (one for each variable) and the scattergram is a three dimensional figure. The scattergram in Figure 12.16 depicts the researchers' revised problem.

Figure 12.16   **A Scattergram in Three Dimensions:**
                     Data Points from the Researchers' Problem

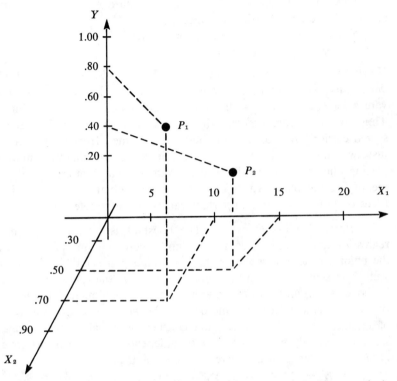

Here only two of the 25 data points are in place. As before, each is positioned to represent some penal institution's scores on the three variables. Thus, data point P_1 is that of a penal institution whose score on X_1 is 10, whose score on X_2 is .70, and whose score on Y is .80. Data point P_2 represents a penal institution whose scores on the same three variables are 15, .50, and .40, respectively. In precisely the same way, all 25 of the data points listed in Table 12.2 can be positioned in a three dimensional scattergram like that shown in Figure 12.16.

With *simple* regression analysis once the data points are plotted, the next step is to fit a straight line to the data points such that the sum of the squared vertical distances (from the data points to the line) is minimized. *Multiple* regression analysis applies the same principle. With multiple regression analysis, once the data points are plotted on a three dimensional scattergram, the next step is to fit a *plane* to the data points in such a way that the sum of the squared vertical distances from the data points to the *plane* is minimized. Hence, in multiple regression analysis the best-fitting *line* is replaced by the best-fitting *plane*. It is not easy to visualize a best-fitting plane. Fortunately, one does not really have to. The important point is this: *the best-fitting plane is drawn through data points in three dimensions just as the best-fitting line is drawn through data points in two dimensions,* namely, in such a way as to minimize the sum of the squared vertical distances.

Now, *all* planes have a formula of this form:

$$Y = a + b_1X_1 + b_2X_2$$

Hence, a *specific set of values* for a, b_1, and b_2 is associated with a *particular* plane. Multiple regression analysis involves finding the *optimal* values for a, b_1, and b_2 — the values which identify the best-fitting plane. Thus, for the researchers' data the regression coefficients and constant presented earlier, are those for the best-fitting plane. Hence, when there are just two independent variables, multiple regression analysis amounts to placing the data points in a three dimensional scattergram and then identifying the plane which best fits the data points. Now attention will focus on how these three important values are interpreted.

Interpreting the Constant. The constant is interpreted in multiple regression analysis much as it is in simple regression analysis. It identifies the point on the Y-axis where the best-fitting plane and the Y-axis intersect. The sign of the constant indicates whether that point of intersection is above the origin $(+)$ or below the origin $(-)$. Similarly, the magnitude of the Y-intercept measures the distance between the origin and the point of intersection. Substantively, the constant is equal to the Y-value researchers would predict when *both* independent variables are equal to zero. For instance, with the researchers' data:

$$\hat{Y} = .22 + (-.01)X_1 + (.86)X_2$$
$$= .22 + (-.01)0 + (.86)0$$
$$= .22$$

This is why the constant when multiple regression is used (.22) differs so greatly from the constant when simple regression is used (.81). With simple regression analysis the constant of .81 is the rate of recidivism researchers would predict if the quality of rehabilitation programs (X_1) is equal to zero. With multiple regression analysis, the constant of .22 is the rate of recidivism researchers would predict if *both* the quality of rehabilitation programs (X_1) *and* the proportion of repeat offenders (X_2) were equal to zero. Therefore, both the value and interpretation of the constant inevitably depend on which independent variables are included in the analysis.

Interpreting the Regression Coefficient. In simple regression analysis the regression coefficient is interpreted as follows:

1. Its sign indicates whether the independent variable and the dependent variable are positively $(+)$ or negatively $(-)$ related.

2. Its magnitude indicates how great a change in the dependent variable is associated with a one unit change in the independent.

In multiple regression analysis there are as many regression coefficients as there are independent variables. Each regression coefficient is interpreted in much the same way as is the single regression coefficient encountered in simple regression analysis. Thus, the sign of b_1 indicates whether X_1 and Y are positively or negatively related while the sign of b_2 conveys the same information concerning X_2 and Y. Interpreting the magnitudes of the two regression coefficients is a little more complicated, however. *In multiple regression analysis the magnitude of a regression coefficient indicates how large a change in the dependent variable is associated with a one unit change in one of the independent variables, assuming the other independent variable remains the same.* Thus, b_1 measures how much of a change in Y is associated with a one unit change in X_1, assuming X_2 does not change. At the same time, b_2 measures the change in Y associated with a one unit change in X_2, assuming X_1 does not change. This can be illustrated by looking at the researchers' multiple regression analysis results. The values for b_1 and b_2 are $-.01$ and $.86$, respectively. Thus, researchers would conclude that if the quality of rehabilitation programs is increased by one and the proportion of repeat offenders is kept the same, the rate of recidivism should drop about .01 units, or about 1 percent. Similarly, if the proportion of repeat offenders is increased by one and the quality of rehabilitation programs is held constant, the rate of recidivism should increase by .86 units, or about 86 percent. This appears to be an extremely large increase — but appearances are deceiving. Recall that the proportion of repeat offenders is measured on a scale of from .00 to 1.00. Thus, an increase of one would be from, say, .00 to 1.00 or from .35 to 1.35. This is clearly an enormous increase and, in the latter case, an impossible one since the proportion of inmates in a penal institution who are repeat offenders *cannot* exceed 1.00. Therefore, an increase in the proportion of repeat offenders of from, say, .40 to .50 would be an increase of one-tenth a unit or 10 percent. Hence, researchers would expect the rate of recidivism to increase by one-tenth of .86, or .086 units, or 8.6 percent. Thus, a 10 percent change in repeat offenders would be associated with an 8.6 percent change in recidivism, assuming that the quality of rehabilitation programs is held constant. Stated this way, the above conclusion seems quite reasonable. The initial confusion demonstrates how important it is to keep track of the various units of measurement when interpreting regression coefficients.

Beta Coefficients. When there are two or more independent variables, one naturally wonders which independent variable has the greatest effect on the dependent variable. Since regression coefficients measure such effects, it seems logical to use them to answer this sort of question. Thus, investigators might be expected to conclude that the proportion of repeat offenders has a greater effect on the recidivism rate than does the quality of rehabilitation programs, since .86 is greater than .01. Unfortunately *this reasoning is faulty*. The dependence of regression coefficients on the units of measurement renders them useless in determining the relative importance of the independent variables. The researchers' findings illustrate this point nicely. While a one unit change in the proportion of repeat offenders effects a .86 change in the rate of recidivism, a one unit change in the quality of rehabilitation programs effects only a .01 change (in each case assuming that the other independent variable remains the same). A one unit change in the proportion of repeat offenders (measured on a scale from .00 to 1.00) is an enormous change, while a one unit change in the quality of rehabilitation programs (measured on a scale from 0 to 20) is a relatively small change. Thus, the fact that .86 is greater than .01 merely confirms what was suspected all along: a huge change in the proportion of repeat offenders has a much greater effect on the recidivism rate than does a small change in the quality of rehabilitation programs. *What is needed is some way of determining what the effects on the rate of recidivism are when changes of the same size are made in both independent variables.* This is what beta coefficients are used for.

Beta coefficients (symbolized by B) are special types of regression coefficients (symbolized by b). Specifically, *if investigators standardize all of their variables before using multiple regression analysis, the resulting regression coefficients are called beta coefficients*. For this reason beta coefficients are sometimes called *standardized regression coefficients*. In effect, beta coefficients are scale free, regression coefficients.

The logic behind the beta coefficients is not very complex. The reason why investigators *cannot* use regression coefficients to compare the separate effects of two or more independent variables on the dependent variable is that the variables are measured in *different* units. However, if the variables are all measured in like units, regression coefficients *can* be used for this purpose.

To standardize variables means to measure them in the same, standard unit of measurement. Fortunately standardization does not require that investigators literally measure their variables a second time. Instead, standardization is done statistically by adjusting the original measurements, converting them into standardized measurements. This is all done on a computer, and will not be elaborated upon or demonstrated here.

Interpreting Beta Coefficients. Once the variables have all been standardized, multiple regression analysis can be used on the standardized variables. *When multiple regression analysis is performed on standardized*

*variables, the resulting beta coefficients are used to determine the relative
importance of the independent variables in terms of their effects on the
dependent variable.* Beta coefficients are interpreted just like regression
coefficients. They indicate how great a change in the dependent variable is
associated with a one unit change in one independent variable assuming
the other independent variable remains the same. Since all the variables
are now measured in the same standardized units, it is possible to compare the effect on Y of a one unit change in X_1 (namely, B_1) with the
effect on Y of a one unit change in X_2 (namely, B_2). Thus, if investigators
need to identify which of several independent variables has the greatest
effect on the dependent variable, beta coefficients should be computed and
compared.

Like regression coefficients, beta coefficients are ordinarily calculated
on a computer. The beta coefficients for the researchers' data are:

$$B_1 = -.3198$$
$$B_2 = .5637$$

Thus, the magnitude of the beta coefficient for the proportion of repeat
offenders ($B_2 \cong .56$) is clearly larger than the magnitude of the beta coefficient for the quality of rehabilitation programs ($B_1 \cong -.32$). Therefore, since B_2 is greater than B_1, it must be concluded that the proportion
of repeat offenders has a greater effect on the recidivism rate than does
the quality of rehabilitation programs. Notice, though, how much closer
in size the two beta coefficients are than the two regression coefficients
(.56 and $-.32$ rather than .86 and $-.01$, respectively). Thus, the beta
coefficients clearly show that the two independent variables are more
nearly equal in their effects on the rate of recidivism than the regression
coefficients would suggest.

Regoli and Poole (1980) used beta coefficients to measure the effects
of several professionalism subscales (their independent variables) on role
conflict in rural and urban police departments (their dependent variable).
For rural departments the largest coefficient found was for the self-
regulation subscale ($B = -.48$). They concluded that this "one-variable
. . . exerts the greatest direct effect." For urban departments three subscales had beta coefficients of *about* the same size. Thus, Regoli and Poole
(1980 p. 248) stated:

> The relative size of the beta coefficients for these three dimen-
> sions, belief in self-regulation ($B = -.28$), sense of calling to
> the field ($B = -.33$), and belief in autonomy ($B = -.28$),
> indicates that the magnitude of their direct effects on role con-
> flict are nearly equal.

The advantage of beta coefficients, then, is that they allow one to determine
which independent variable has the greatest effect on the dependent variable.

The Adequacy of the Multiple Regression Equation. Just as simple regression was complemented by correlation so also must multiple regression be complemented by some method for measuring how well the best-fitting plane actually fits the data points. When the data points do not really lie close to *any* plane, it makes little sense to spend time computing and interpreting the regression coefficients and constant which identify the plane which best fits the data points. Fortunately, *the multiple correlation coefficient (R) can be used to measure the fit of the best-fitting plane to the data points.*

The Multiple Correlation Coefficient. The best-fitting plane can be thought of as a *prediction* plane just as the best-fitting line was seen as a prediction line in the earlier discussion of simple regression and correlation. Hence, for each pair of values for the two independent variables, the multiple regression equation predicts a value for the dependent variable. If the best-fitting plane comes close to most of the data points, most of the predicted values will come close to the observed values of the dependent variable. Hence, one way to assess the fit of the best-fitting plane is to compare the predicted values with the observed values. The multiple correlation coefficient does this by simply *correlating* the predicted values and the observed values.

The multiple correlation coefficient is symbolized by the letter R and is best calculated on a computer. The multiple correlation coefficient for the researchers' data is $R = .7604$.

Interpreting the Multiple Correlation Coefficient. The multiple correlation coefficient varies in the interval between zero (.00) and positive one (+1.00). The lower its value, the farther away the data points are from the best-fitting plane. The higher its value, the closer the data points are to the best-fitting plane. Thus, the multiple correlation coefficient (R) is used in conjunction with multiple regression analysis very much like the correlation coefficient (r) is used in conjunction with simple regression analysis. A value close to 1.00 indicates a good fit.

The multiple correlation coefficient shares a few other important properties with the correlation coefficient. Both coefficients are scale free and, therefore, yield the same results regardless of the units of measurement used. In addition the value of both coefficients is attenuated by unreliability in the measurement of variables.

Finally, when the multiple correlation coefficient is squared and multiplied by 100, the resulting number is the percent of the variation in the dependent variable jointly explained by all of the independent variables together. For example, the value of the multiple correlation coefficient for the researchers' data is .76. Its square is:

$$R^2 = (.76) \cdot (.76)$$
$$= .58$$
$$\text{Hence, } 100 \cdot R^2 = 100 \cdot (.58)$$
$$= 58$$

Therefore, researchers can conclude that the quality of rehabilitation programs and the proportion of repeat offenders jointly explain about 58 percent of the variation in the rate of recidivism.

The square of the multiple correlation coefficient is used so frequently that it is known by a special name. It is called the *coefficient of determination*. Many users of multiple regression analysis consider the coefficient of determination (R^2) to be a more meaningful measure of the adequacy of the multiple regression equation than the multiple correlation coefficient itself. For example, Block (1979) uses multiple regression analysis to investigate the incidence of violent crime in 76 Chicago neighborhoods. Dealing with homicides, Block reports an R^2 of .73 in a multiple regression equation with five independent variables. Thus, these five independent variables explain 73 percent of the variation in homicide rates in the Chicago neighborhoods studied.

A Hypothesis Test for the Multiple Correlation Coefficient. Chapters 8, 9, and 11 made much of the fact that the data they dealt with were samples from larger populations. Why were these three chapters concerned solely with sample data? Each chapter dealt with a hypothesis test whose purpose was to determine if some conclusion concerning a sample was due only to chance or reflected a genuine truth about the population. Therefore, application of these hypothesis tests made sense only if the data examined were a sample from a population.

So far in this chapter, no mention has been made concerning the source of the data analyzed. This is because both correlation and regression can be applied to either population data or sample data. Thus, if the 25 penal institutions which are the object of the investigators' interests include *all* those existing in the region of the country being studied, correlation and regression analysis may be applied to these (population) data. On the other hand, investigators can also make use of correlation and regression if the 25 penal institutions are a random sample of all such institutions in the country. However, if the data are a sample from some larger population, an additional *inference* question arises: Do the findings based on the sample convey a truth concerning the population or are they just due to chance? For example, a multiple correlation analysis of sample data might conclude that several independent variables jointly explain a substantial percentage of the variation in the dependent variable. Does this sample conclusion hold in the population as well? Fortunately, there is a hypothesis test, based on the multiple correlation coefficient, which is designed to address this very question.

Earlier it was shown how the multiple correlation coefficient, by measuring the fit of the data points to the best-fitting plane, helps researchers evaluate the adequacy of the multiple regression equation. Like any other statistic, the multiple correlation coefficient can take on sample values different from its population value. Thus, a substantial multiple correlation coefficient computed from sample data is no guarantee that the several independent variables have a pronounced joint effect on the dependent variable in the population. Hence, a hypothesis test is clearly needed. The most widely used test is based on the multiple correlation coefficient and employs the following null and research hypotheses, where R symbolizes the value of the multiple correlation coefficient in the population:

$$H_o: R = 0$$
$$H_a: R > 0$$

The steps required for conducting this hypothesis test are listed in Figure 12.17.

Figure 12.17   Steps to Follow When Conducting a Hypothesis Test for the Multiple Correlation Coefficient

1. Set the permissible level of error.
2. Compute the test statistic.
3. Compare the test statistic to the appropriate sampling distribution table.

Setting the Level of Error. When testing for the significance of the multiple correlation coefficient, the level of error is set with the same considerations in mind as when ANOVA or a one-sample or two-samples test is being used. Recall that the level of error indicates how great a risk of falsely rejecting a true null hypothesis one is willing to run. As before, setting an extremely low level of error increases the risk of failing to reject a false null hypothesis.

Computing the Test Statistic. Like ANOVA, the hypothesis test for the multiple correlation coefficient employs the F ratio as a test statistic, but it is computed differently. Its computation is illustrated with the researchers' multiple correlation coefficient in Figure 12.18.

Figure 12.18   Computing the F Ratio for the Researchers' Multiple Correlation Coefficient

Step 1: Compute R

Earlier, it was stated that $R = .76$

Step 2: Compute the F ratio:

The computational formula:

$$F = \frac{R^2}{1 - R^2}\left(\frac{N - k - 1}{k}\right)$$

Where: k = the number of independent variables

By substitution:

$$F = \frac{.76^2}{1 - .76^2}\left(\frac{25 - 2 - 1}{2}\right) = \frac{.5785}{.4215} \cdot \left(\frac{22}{2}\right) = 1.3725 \cdot (11)$$

$$= 15.10$$

Notice that once the multiple correlation coefficient is computed, the F ratio follows easily.

Comparing the Test Statistic to the Appropriate Sampling Distribution Table. The hypothesis test is now ready to be completed. If the F ratio exceeds 1.00 by an amount too great to be due to chance, the null hypothesis will be rejected; if it does not, the null hypothesis will be retained. The question is, how large must the F ratio be before the null hypothesis is rejected? The answer is found in a table of the F distribution. Properly read, a table of the F distribution yields the lowermost boundary value which the F ratio must equal or exceed in order for the null hypothesis to be rejected.

To determine the lowermost boundary value, one first turns to the proper F distribution table, the table corresponding the level of error that has already been set (e.g., .05). (These tables are found in Appendix D.) To identify the exact boundary value in this F table, one needs to know two degrees of freedom: one to locate the *column* the boundary value is in, and one to locate the *row* the boundary value is in. The column degrees of freedom (df_1) is equal to the number of independent variables (k). In this case it would be 2. The row degrees of freedom (df_2) is equal to the size of the sample minus the number of independent variables minus one $(N - k - 1)$. Here this would be 25 minus 2 minus 1 or 22 $(25 - 2 - 1 = 22)$. The boundary value is located at the intersection of this column and this row. Thus, the researchers are interested in the intersection of column 2 and row 22. The value found in the F distribution table in Appendix D is 3.44. Since 15.10 is greater than 3.44, the researchers must reject the null hypothesis and conclude that in the population from which their sample was drawn, the proportion of repeat offenders and the quality of rehabilitation programs have a significant joint effect on the rate of recidivism.

The hypothesis test can be applied to the results from Block's (1979) study presented earlier. In Block's study:

$$R^2 = .73$$
$$N = 76$$
$$k = 5$$

Thus, the F ratio is:

$$F = \frac{.73}{1 - .73}\left(\frac{76-5-1}{5}\right) = \frac{.73}{.27} \cdot (14) = 2.7037 \cdot (14)$$
$$= 37.85$$

Further, the column degrees of freedom (k) is 5 while the row degrees of freedom $(N - k - 1)$ is 70. Using .05 as the level of error, the boundary value is 2.37. Since 37.85 is greater than 2.37 the null hypothesis is rejected. The five independent variables Block used do explain a substantial percentage of the variation in homicide rates in Chicago neighborhoods.

In addition to this hypothesis test for the adequacy of the multiple regression equation, several other hypothesis tests are commonly used with correlation and regression analysis. Those interested in such tests should consult Ott (1977).

Summary

The first half of this chapter introduced simple correlation and regression analysis and applied them to a problem of interest to criminologists: the effect of the quality of a penal institution's rehabilitation programs upon the rate of recidivism of the persons it discharges. First, the data points were plotted in a scattergram. Then a straight line was fitted to the data points. Correlation analysis measured the fit of the data points to the line while simple regression analysis measured the effect on the dependent variable caused by a one unit change in the independent variable.

The second half of this chapter extended the basic ideas of correlation and regression analysis to accommodate more than one independent variable and applied them to an extension of the researchers' problem. In multiple regression analysis, each regression coefficient measures the effects on the dependent variable caused by a one unit change in one independent variable, assuming the other independent variables remain the same. In addition, multiple regression analysis produces another type of coefficient, the beta coefficient. Beta coefficients are scale free, regression coefficients. They measure the effects of the independent variables on the dependent variable in terms of a common or standard unit of measurement. Thus, they have the distinct advantage of allowing one to make direct comparisons among the independent variables in terms of their effects on the dependent variable. On the other hand, regression coefficients measure the effects of the independent variables on the dependent variables *in terms of their natural units of measurements.* As a result, it is easier to assign substantive meanings to regression coefficients than it is to beta coefficients.

The multiple correlation coefficient measures the adequacy of the multiple regression equation. It is used to determine whether it is worthwhile to proceed with multiple regression analysis. A discussion of a hypothesis test based on the multiple correlation coefficient concluded the chapter.

Notes

[1.] For a discussion of other methods for calculating regression coefficients, see Feig (1978), Hocking (1976), Thisted (1978), and Vinod (1978).

Review Questions

1. Explain the meaning and significance of the following terms and ideas:
   a. correlation and regression analysis
   b. scattergram
   c. simple regression analysis and multiple regression analysis
   d. correlation coefficient, r
   e. regression coefficient, b
   f. constant, a
   g. correlation and causation
   h. explained variation
   i. coefficient of determination
   j. F test for the adequacy of the regression equation
2. Suppose researchers investigating the relationship between the crime rate (Y) and the unemployment rate (X_1) gather the following data:
   $$Y = 8, 7, 7, 12, 7, 10, 6, 16, 16, 9, 11, 5$$
   $$X_1 = 2, 6, 11, 9, 3, 7, 2, 21, 16, 10, 14, 6$$

a. Construct a scattergram for Y and X_1.

b. Compute r, r^2, a, and b and discuss the relationship between the crime rate and the unemployment rate they reveal.

c. Assume the data are a sample and conduct an F test to determine the adequacy of the regression equation.

d. *From the data,* does it appear that unemployment is a cause of crime?

e. What other variables might one investigate as possible causes of crime?

3. Distinguish between regression coefficients and beta coefficients. Under what circumstances should these two types of coefficients be used?

4. In what way does correlation analysis complement regression analysis?

References

Block, Richard. "Community, Environment, and Violent Crime." *Criminology* 17 (1979): 46-57.

Feig, Douglas G. "Ridge Regression: When Biased Estimation is Better." *Social Science Quarterly* 58 (1978): 708-716.

Hocking, R. R., Speed, F. M., and Lynn, M. J. "A Class of Biased Estimators in Linear Regression." *Technometrics* 18 (1976): 425-437.

Ott, Lyman. *An Introduction to Statistical Methods and Data Analysis.* North Scituate, MA: Duxbury Press, 1977.

Regoli, Robert and Poole, Eric. "Police Professionalism and Role Conflict: A Comparison of Rural and Urban Departments." *Human Relations* 33 (1980): 241-252.

Thisted, Ronald A. "Multicollinearity, Information, and Ridge Regression." Technical Report No. 66, Department of Statistics, University of Chicago, 1978.

Vinod, H. D. "A Survey of Ridge Regression and Related Techniques for Improvements Over Ordinary Least Squares." *Reviews of Economics and Statistics* 60 (1978): 121-131.

Widom, Cathy Spatz. "Female Offenders: Three Assumptions About Self-Esteem, Sex-Role Identity, and Feminism." *Criminal Justice and Behavior* 6 (1979): 365-382.

Chapter 13

Regression Analysis for Statistical Prediction

Learning Objectives

After completing this chapter, the reader should be able to:

1. Describe the following types of regression analysis: simple and multiple, linear and nonlinear
2. Identify and eliminate a high level of multicollinearity
3. Understand both polynominal and transformative regression equations
4. Interpret a coefficient of determination
5. Determine which of the various types of regression equations will provide the most precise statistical prediction
6. Calculate the value of the predicted dependent variable
7. Determine the range of the value of the predicted dependent variable.

Introduction

One of the best, if not the best, statistical methods that can be used to predict the value of a dependent variable is regression analysis. Such an analysis is founded on a simple axiom: a dependent variable, when correlated with independent variable(s), represents a basic pattern which can be used to predict the range of the values of the dependent variable that should occur if the trend continues.

A simplified, real-world example illustrates the basic idea behind regression analysis. Assume researchers want to predict the number of deaths resulting from traffic accidents that should occur on state highways next year if the trend continues and nothing drastic happens.

It should be obvious that the number of traffic fatalities in a state is related strongly to a variety of independent variables, such as the number of vehicles registered in a state, the number of highway miles in a state, and the number of licensed drivers in a state. As these variables increase, the number of traffic-related deaths also increases. As a consequence of such a relationship, these variables can be used to predict the number of traffic fatalities that should occur next year.

To predict the number of traffic fatalities, researchers need to gather data indicating the number of traffic fatalities, the number of registered motor vehicles, the number of highway miles, and the number of licensed drivers. These data must be gathered for time periods that correspond directly to the time periods for which the dependent variable data are collected. For instance, if data showing the number of traffic fatalities that occurred in 1979, 1980, 1981, and 1982 are gathered, then data showing the number of registered motor vehicles, the number of highway miles, and the number of licensed drivers that were recorded in 1979, 1980, 1981, and 1982 must also be collected. By regressing the independent variables on the dependent variable, researchers can predict the number of traffic deaths that probably should occur if the trend continues.

Review of Regression Analysis

Essentially there are two types of regression analysis: simple regression and multiple regression. Unfortunately, this dichotomy is not so simplistic as it appears, since each of these two types of regression is further divided into either linear regression or nonlinear regression. Figure 13.1 illustrates the types and variations of regression analysis.

Figure 13.1   Types and Variations of Regression Analysis

	Simple Regression	Multiple Regression
Linear Regression	One variable is used to project the dependent variable The data fall along a straight plane	More than one variable is used to project the dependent variable The data fall along a straight plane
Nonlinear Regression	One variable is used to project the dependent variable The data fall along a curved plane	More than one variable is used to project the dependent variable The data fall along a curved plane

Simple regression analysis uses a single, most important, independent variable to predict the value of the dependent variable. For instance, a simple regression analysis would use only the number of motor vehicles registered in a state to predict the number of traffic deaths. A *multiple regression analysis,* on the other hand, utilizes more than one independent variable to predict the value of the dependent variable. A multiple regression analysis would use not only the number of motor vehicles registered but it might also include variables such as the number of highway miles and the number of licensed drivers to predict the number of traffic fatalities.

A regression analysis, whether simple or multiple, is also either linear or nonlinear. A *linear regression* is one in which the data points fall along a straight plane. When regression analysis is *used to make statistical predictions,* the prediction line is called a plane, because the term *plane* indicates that the prediction consists of a range of values instead of one value. When regression analysis is *used to explain* which independent variable exerts the most influence on the dependent variables (as illustrated in the preceding chapter), the term *line* is used. A linear plane is either positive or negative. A *positive* linear plane occurs when an increase in the value of the variable(s) used to predict the dependent variable is associated with an increase in the value of the dependent variable. A *negative* linear plane occurs when an increase in the value of the independent variable(s) is associated with a decrease in the value of the dependent variable.

A *nonlinear regression* analysis is one in which the data points fall along a curved plane. A nonlinear plane, like a linear one, exists in two forms: the plane either curves up or it curves down. Figure 13.2 graphically depicts the four variations of simple regression planes.

It is important to note that one must ascertain the pattern of the data points in order to determine which type of regression analysis is most appropriate. Specifically, if the pattern of the data is linear, either simple linear regression or multiple linear regression must be used. On the other hand, if the pattern of the data points is nonlinear, either simple nonlinear or multiple nonlinear regression has to be used. With both linear and nonlinear regression the choice between simple and multiple modes depends upon the number of independent variables that are used to predict the value of the dependent variable. The reason that linear regression analysis is applied to linear patterns and nonlinear regression analysis is applied to nonlinear patterns is that such matches produce the most precise statistical prediction possible; that is, the one which produces the narrowest range of values.

A simple example illustrates this point. If researchers predict that 900 traffic fatalities should occur on a state's highways next year, and if the range of that prediction is ± 50 fatalities, the predicted number of traffic deaths is between 850 and 950 deaths. If they predict that 900 traffic fatalities should occur on a state's highways next year, and if the range of that prediction is ± 2 deaths, the predicted number of traffic fatalities is between 898 and 902 fatalities, a much more precise prediction.

Figure 13.2   Simple Linear and Nonlinear Planes

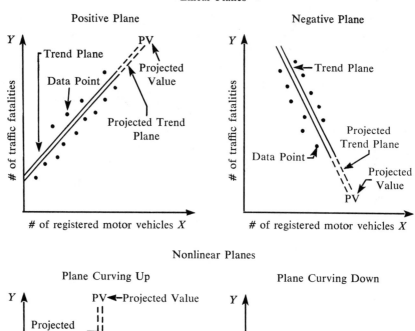

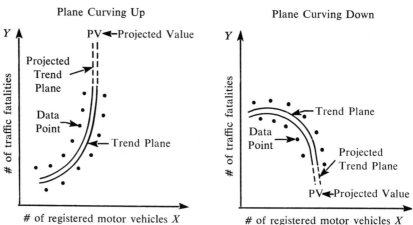

Regression analysis is a powerful statistical technique. However, as with all statistical techniques, one must cautiously interpret any statistical prediction, principally because the technique is totally insensitive to causal relationships. Reliance on substantive knowledge is necessary to insure that the independent variable(s) designated as being related to the dependent variable are in fact related.

The following procedural rules of thumb should help minimize, if not eliminate, any misapplications and/or misinterpretation that can occur when employing regression analysis to make statistical predictions:

1. Make sure that all the independent and dependent variables are either interval or ratio level data.
2. Do not predict the value of the dependent variables more than five time intervals (doing so many lead to unreliable predictions).
3. Realize that there always is some range associated with the value of the predicted dependent variable, and it should be as narrow as possible in order to increase the precision of a prediction.
4. Be certain that no drastic changes have occurred which could substantially affect the prediction.

Determining the Statistical Prediction Plane

The easiest and simplest way to determine the best-fitting statistical prediction plane is to follow a series of sequential steps which, when applied properly, help predict the most precise range of the value of the dependent variable. The steps employed in statistical prediction via regression analysis are presented in Figure 13.3

Figure 13.3   Steps Used to Make Statistical Predictions

1. Determine whether a high level of multicollinearity exists and, if so, eliminate it. (This step is necessary only when using multiple regression analysis.)
2. Ascertain which regression equation will provide the most precise value of the predicted dependent variable.
   — Examine the coefficient of determination.
3. Ascertain the value of the predicted dependent variable.
4. Determine the range of the value of the predicted dependent variable.

Ascertaining the Existence of a High Level of Multicollinearity and Eliminating It

A high level of multicollinearity exists when two or more independent variables are correlated strongly with each other. Multicollinearity does not exist when the independent variables correlate strongly with the dependent variable. (Such a correlation can and should exist.) Since multicollinearity occurs only between the independent variables, one needs only to check for the existence of high levels of multicollinearity when using multiple regression analysis.

A certain amount (level) of multicollinearity always exists because it is practically impossible to use variables which are statistically independent of each other. A low level of multicollinearity, however, does not affect the reliability of the regression coefficients, whereas the existence of a high level of multicollinearity does. In other words, multicollinearity must be eliminated only when the independent variables are *strongly* correlated with each other. As a rule of thumb, *a high level of multicollinearity exists when a coefficient resulting from the correlation of two independent variables is larger than* ± *.700* (Reinmuth, 1974, p. 44).

The simplest way to check for the existence of a high level multicollinearity is to compute a correlation coefficient for each possible pair of independent variables. These coefficients can then be arranged in a matrix and examined to see if high levels of multicollinearity exist. The size of the matrix obviously depends on the number of variables used to predict the value of the dependent variable. Figure 13.4 illustrates the correlation matrix for the three variables used to predict the number of traffic fatalities on state highways in the South. (Two of the variables, the number of motor vehicles registered and the number of licensed drivers, are multicollinear.)

Figure 13.4   Matrix of Correlation Coefficients Between Variables Used to Predict the Number of Traffic Fatalities

	Number of motor vehicles registered	Number of highway miles
Number of highway miles	.589	
Number of licensed drivers	.987	.571

the variables, number of motor vehicles registered and the number of licensed drivers are multicollinear

coefficient for correlation between number of highway miles and number of licensed drivers

The major reason for eliminating a high level of multicollinearity is that its existence destroys the accuracy and precision of a statistical prediction; that is, not much confidence can be placed in the regression coefficients used to predict the value of the dependent variable because the coefficients may not indicate accurately how much each independent variable contributes to the prediction. Stated more simply, the existence of a high level of multicollinearity affects the reliability of the predicted dependent variable value. Severe multicollinearity leads to:

1. regression coefficients which are so unreliable that they are meaningless,
2. impaired predictive accuracy, and
3. a standard error which is inordinately large (Gustafson, 1974, p. 138).

Essentially, there are two ways to eradicate multicollinearity: (1) eliminate all but one of the multicollinear variables and (2) multiply the multicollinear variables and use that product as a variable to predict the dependent variable. While the first method is by far the easier, the second is methodologically sounder since, when used properly, it enhances the predictive capability of the regression equation.

Eliminating the Multicollinear Variable(s). After the multicollinear variables are identified, all but one of them can be eliminated from the regression equation, inasmuch as removal of such a variable or variables will only slightly decrease the predictive power of the equation. Eliminating all but one of the variables is a particularly useful method, especially when they measure the same idea. For example, if a high level of multicollinearity exists between one variable which measures attitudes toward graduates of criminal justice programs and another variable measures attitudes toward graduates of law enforcement programs, the latter variable may be eliminated if both variables are measuring the same thing. Researchers, of course, must rely heavily on their substantive knowledge to decide which variable(s) can (and should) be dropped from the regression equation.

Employing Multiplicative Transformation. Another method used to eliminate a high level of multicollinearity is *multiplicative transformation,* a process which generates a new distinct variable by multiplying the values of the multicollinear variables together. For instance, the correlation matrix presented in Figure 13.4 indicates that one variable, the number of motor vehicles registered in a state, is highly collinear with another variable, the number of licensed drivers in a state. One way to eliminate this high level of multicollinearity is to multiply the values of those two variables and use that product as a variable in the regression equation instead of the values of each of the two multicollinear variables. This new variable, in other words, replaces the two original variables.

Although a multiplicative variable is artificial, it is exceedingly useful in predicting the value of the dependent variable, since such a variable represents the *combined effects* of two real variables. Since the new variable is a combination of real variables, the predictive power of the regression equation is not diminished. (When using multiplicative transformation, moreover, one does not have to decide which variable to eliminate.) Generally speaking, *one is strongly urged to use multiplicative transformation to eliminate a high level of multicollinearity.*

Determining Which Regression Equation Will Provide the Most Precise Predicted Value of the Dependent Variable

Unfortunately, there is no simple way to ascertain the pattern of the data, especially when more than one independent variable is used. The simplest way, therefore, to determine the pattern of the data is to utilize the following modified trial-and-error method: *one should first calculate various linear and nonlinear regression equations and then select the equation which yields the largest (strongest) coefficient of determination, provided that the level of error associated with the coefficient of determination is lower than the permissible level of error* (e.g., .10, .05, .01).

The first step in ascertaining which regression equation will provide the most precise statistical prediction is to calculate various linear and nonlinear regression equations. The three types of equations that generally are computed are linear, polynomial, and transformative. Figure 13.5 presents the formulas for multiple linear, polynomial, and two transformative equations.

Figure 13.5   Formulas for Multiple Linear, Polynomial, and Transformative Equations

Linear Equation:
$$\hat{Y} = a + b_1 X_1 + b_2 X_2 + \ldots + b_k X_k$$
Second Degree Polynomial:
$$\hat{Y} = a + b_1 X_1 + c_1 X_1^2 + b_2 X_2 + c_2 X_2^2 + \ldots b_k X_k + c_k X_k^2$$
Transformative Equations:

1. When the pattern of the data curves upward:
$$\sqrt{\hat{Y}} = a + b_1 X_1 + b_2 X_2 + b_3 X_3 + \ldots b_k X_k$$
   If the equation does not straighten the pattern enough, one should use:
$$\log \hat{Y} = a + b_1 X_1 + b_2 X_2 + b_3 X_3 + \ldots b_k X_k$$
2. When the pattern of the data curves downward:
$$\hat{Y} = a + b_1 \sqrt{X_1} + b_2 \sqrt{X_2} + b_3 \sqrt{X_3} + \ldots b_k \sqrt{X_k}$$
   If the equation fails to straighten the pattern enough, one should use:
$$\hat{Y} = a + b_1 \log X_1 + b_2 \log X_2 + b_3 \log X_3 + \ldots b_k \log X_k$$

Polynomial Equations. A polynomial regression equation uses the variables and the power(s) of the variable(s) to predict the dependent variable. Practically speaking, this means that polynomials are used to bend the plane until it conforms to the nonlinear pattern of the data. A second degree polynomial bends the plane once; a third degree polynomial bends the plane twice; and so forth. (There will always be one less bend than is indicated by the degree of the polynomial equation.) Solving the polynomial equations is relatively straightforward since the procedure is identical to solving linear equations. The variable value (X) and the square of the variable value (X^2) are merely substituted into the equation to predict the value of the dependent variable (e.g., if $X = 2$, then $X^2 = 4$).

Transformative Equations. Polynomial regression equations, especially third- and fourth-degree polynomials, are generally cumbersome to calculate. Consequently, it is far easier — and in many cases preferable — to use a *transformative equation.* Such an equation is one in which either the dependent variable (e.g., number of traffic fatalities) or the independent variable(s) is transformed mathematically; and those products, rather than the original data, are used to compute a regression equation. Basically, such data transformations rearrange a nonlinear pattern of the data in such a way that a linear regression equation can predict a precise range of the value of the dependent variable.

When transformative regression equations are used, the data must be transformed before the equation is computed. This task is quite simple, especially with the aid of a computer. For example, when using a transformative equation which utilizes the square root of Y $(\sqrt{Y})$, merely calculate the square root of each Y value (e.g., the square root of the number of traffic fatalities) and use those transformed values instead of the actual values (e.g., the actual number of traffic deaths) to compute the regression equation. When transformative equations which alter the X values are employed, identical mathematical functions are performed on the values of the variable(s) used to predict the dependent variable $(\sqrt{X}$ and log $X)$.

Unfortunately, researchers seldom know the pattern of the data prior to calculating a regression equation. Consequently, they have no alternative but to compute all these equations (linear, polynomial, and transformative) and then examine the coefficient of determination to see which regression equation will provide the most precise predicted value.

Examining the Coefficient of Determination. Once the regression equations are computed, one needs to see which equation has the largest coefficient of determination associated with it, since that equation *generally* is the one which will provide the most precise range of the predicted value.

The coefficient of determination, which is the square of the correlation between the dependent variable and the independent variable(s), is a statistic that indicates how well the statistical projection plane of a regression equation fits the pattern of the data.

As explained in Chapter 12, the coefficient of determination varies from the lowermost value of zero (indicating that the data are patternless and therefore cannot be used to make a precise prediction) to an uppermost value of 1.00 (suggesting that all the data fall within the plane and thus will lead to nearly perfect prediction). When a simple linear regression equation is used, the appropriate coefficient of determination is the square of a simple correlation (e.g., if $r = .77$, then $r^2 = .59$). When a multiple linear regression equation is employed, the appropriate coefficient of determination is the square of a multiple correlation (e.g., if $R = .80$, then $R^2 = .64$).

Regardless of which correlation coefficient is used, the larger the coefficient, the less likely is the data to vary from the plane and consequently the more precise is the statistical prediction. As a result, *one can assume that the regression equation which has the largest coefficient of determination associated with it is the appropriate equation, provided that the level of error associated with the coefficient of determination does not exceed the permissible level of error.*

Usually the level of error associated with the coefficient of determination is furnished by the computer solution. Sometimes, however, one must compute the level of error using information supplied in the computer printout. When such a computation is necessary, one should look at the Analysis of Variance (ANOVA) section of a computer printout. Figure 13.6 illustrates such a section.

Figure 13.6   Analysis of Variance

Due To	DF	Sum of Squares SS	Means of Squares MS = SS/DF	F Value
Regression	6	89498407	1416401	89.92
Residual	36	520010	15758	
Total	39	9018416		

To determine the level of error associated with the coefficient of determination, one calculates the F score by dividing the value found at the intersection of the headings, "Means of Squares" and "Regression" (1416401), by the value found at the intersection of the headings, "Means of Squares" and "Residual" (15758). The calculated F score for the data in Figure 13.6 is 89.9 ($1416401 \div 15758 = 89.9$). Next one ascertains the degrees of freedom associated with this regression. (The degrees of freedom associated with an F distribution is comprised of two dimensions.) The degrees of freedom are listed under the heading "DF" ($DF_1 = 6$ and $DF_2 = 36$).

Now say the permissible level of error had been set at .05. To see if the level of error associated with the coefficient of determination exceeds the permissible level of error, one enters the F distribution table in Appendix D. Using the F distribution table for $p = .05$, one proceeds across the column headings (df) until the column heading $df_1 = 6$ is reached and then proceeds down that column until it intersects the row which reads $df_2 = 36$ or the row which is closest to 36 without going beyond that figure. (In this example, $df_2 = 30$ is used.) At that intersection the number is 2.42. If the calculated F score (89.9) is *larger* than the lowermost value found in the F distribution table (2.42), the level of error associated with the coefficient of determination is small enough to have considerable confidence in the regression equation and its coefficient of determination. If the F score is not larger than the value found in the F distribution table, one should consider using another regression equation — one which has a similar, though somewhat smaller, coefficient of determination *and* a calculated level of error lower than the permissible level of error.

Ascertaining the Predicted Value of the Dependent Variable

Once one has determined which of the various regression equations best fits the underlying pattern of the data, ascertaining the predicted value is a relatively simple task: merely substitute the appropriate information into the selected regression equation. Assume that the average number of traffic fatalities that should occur in the Southern states next year is being predicted. Furthermore, suppose that three independent variables are used — the number of registered motor vehicles, the number of highway miles, and the number of licensed drivers — to make such a prediction.

However, as noted in Figure 13.4, two of the independent variables (the number of motor vehicles registered and the number of licensed drivers) are highly multicollinear. Assume, therefore, that this high level of multicollinearity is eliminated by multiplying the values of the two variables together and using this product to compute the regression equation (*multiplicative transformation*). The newly created variable, as well as the number of highway miles, is then used to calculate various linear, polynomial, and transformative regression equations to see which equation will provide the most precise prediction.

After the coefficients of determination and the regression coefficients for each of these regression equations are examined, it is determined that the following transformative equation will provide the most precise prediction:

$$\hat{Y} = a + b, \sqrt{X_1} + b_2 \sqrt{X_2}$$

where: $\hat{Y}$ = the value of the predicted dependent variable (e.g., the number of traffic deaths)

 a = the point at which the trend plane intersects the values of the dependent variable

 b_1 = the direction of and degree of change of the plane associated with the $\sqrt{X_1}$ value

 $\sqrt{X_1}$ = the value of the square root of the first independent variable (e.g., the product of the number of motor vehicles registered multiplied by the number of licensed drivers)

 b_2 = the direction of and degree change of the plane associated with the $\sqrt{X_2}$ value

 $\sqrt{X_2}$ = the value of the square root of the second independent variable (e.g., the number of highway miles).

Figure 13.7 illustrates an abridged version of the computer printout for the above equation.

Figure 13.7   Abridged Regression Output, with _T_ Values

Analysis of Variables

Variable	Coefficient	Standard Deviation of Coefficient	T Value
Constant	−445.8	253	−1.76
Number of Motor Veh. *	.450	.031	14.76
Number of High. Miles			
Number of Licensed Dr.	3.13	1.03	3.03

Standard Error = 142

with (40 − 3) = 37 Degrees of Freedom

Coefficient of Determination = 91.7 percent

Figure 13.7 **(continued)**

Analysis of Variance

Due To	DF	Sum of Squares	Mean Square $(MS - SS/DF)$
Regression	2	8271230	4135615
Residual	37	747186	20194
Total	9	9018416	4155809

X_1 Variable

(Number of Motor Veh. * Number of Licensed Dr.)	Standard Deviation of Predicted Y	Standardized Residuals
1771	28	1.14
2004	32	−.11
4057	53	−1.04
2478	44	1.33
1241	32	.34
2225	24	.58
1384	34	.92
2650	43	−1.99
1992	24	1.27
1175	34	.39

The printout indicates that the computed regression equation is as follows:
$$\hat{Y} = -445.8 + .45\sqrt{X_1} + 3.13\sqrt{X_2}$$

To calculate the average number of traffic fatalities that should occur, one will need to know for next year the average number of motor vehicles registered in Southern states, the average number of drivers licensed in Southern states, and the average number of highway miles in Southern states. Suppose the information in Figure 13.8 applies.

Figure 13.8   Information About Factors Used to Make Predictions

Average number of registered motor vehicles	2,739
Average number of highway miles	78,530
Average number of licensed drivers	2,585
Average number of traffic fatalities	1,152

When this information is substituted into the regression equation, it shows that the average number of traffic fatalities that should occur next year is approximately 1,627 fatalities.

$$\hat{Y} = -445.8 + .45\sqrt{X_1} + 3.13\sqrt{X_2}$$

where: $X_1 = (2739)(2585)$

$X_2 = 78530$

therefore: $\hat{Y} = -445.8 + .45\sqrt{(2739)(2585)} + 3.13\sqrt{77717}$

$= -445.8 + [(.45)(2660)] + [(3.13)(280)]$

$= -445.8 + 1197 + 876$

≈ 1627

Determining the Range of the Predicted Value of the Dependent Variable

Unfortunately the precision of these two predictions is somewhat misleading since it fails to take into account the range of the prediction. The exact range of the predicted value (1,627) can be determined by using the following formula (Ryan et. al., 1976, p. 164):

$$PV \pm PE \sqrt{SDY^2 + SE^2}$$

where: PV = the predicted value (e.g., the projected number of traffic deaths)

PE = the lowermost value of the critical region associated with the permissible level of error (e.g., .10, .05, or .01)

SDY^2 = the square of the estimated standard deviation of the predicted value

SE^2 = the square of the standard error

The first step in computing this formula is to determine the value associated with the elements of the formula. Since the average number of traffic deaths predicted for next year via multiple regression is 1,627 fatalities, $PV = 1627$. Next, PE must be ascertained. To do this, one must find out the degrees of freedom associated with the regression coefficients. The abridged computer printout shown in Figure 13.7 indicates that there are 37 degrees of freedom (located in the Analysis of Variables section of the printout). Since the permissible level of error was set at .05, one enters the t distribution table to ascertain the value associated with a .05 level of error when the degrees of freedom equal 37. To find this value, one looks at the t distribution table shown in Appendix C and reads across the row corresponding to 37 degrees of freedom (or the row which is closest to 37 without going beyond that figure) until that row intersects the column headed .05 level of error for a one-tailed test. The number at that intersection is 1.64; thus, $PE = 1.64$.

Now the estimated standard deviation of the predicted value must be ascertained. While there are several ways to hand calculate this estimated standard deviation, Ryan and his associates (1976, p. 164) suggest that the estimate can be approximated rather than hand calculated, inasmuch as an approximated estimate is much easier to determine and "good enough for most purposes."

To approximate the estimated standard deviation of the predicted value, one goes to the Analysis of Variables section of the computer print-out and looks for the heading "X_1 Variable." Proceed down that column until a value is found *that most closely approximates the X_1 value.* For next year's data the X_1 value is 2660 ($\sqrt{(2739)\ (2582)} = 2660$). One reads across the appropriate row until it intersects the column headed "Standard Dev. of Predicted Y." For next year's data the number at that intersection is 43.

Finally, the standard error of the estimate needs to be ascertained. This figure is the one associated with the heading "Standard Error" which is located in the Analysis of Variables section of the computer printout. The standard error of the estimate for the regression equation is 142; consequently, $SE = 142$.

By substituting this information into the formula, one can calculate the range of the predicted number of traffic fatalities. For next year the average number of traffic fatalities probably would fall between 1,383 and 1,871 deaths.

$$PV\ PE\ \sqrt{SDY^2 + SE^2}$$

where: $PV = 1627$

$\qquad PE = 1.64$

$\qquad SDY^2 = 43^2$

$\qquad SE^2 = 142$

Therefore,

$\qquad 1627 \pm 1.64 \sqrt{43^2 + 142^2}$

$\qquad 1627 \pm 1.64\ (148)$

$\qquad 1627 \pm 244$

$\qquad 1627 + 244 = 1871$

$\qquad 1627 - 244 = 1383$

(At this point, the reader is admonished to remember that this simplified real world example is only for illustrative purposes.)

Summary

Regression analysis is a powerful statistical technique which serves as the foundation for most statistical predictions. Such predictions are made by selecting the primary variable(s) associated with the dependent variable and using them as independent variable(s) to predict the dependent variable.

In the past regression analysis was used infrequently because it was time-consuming to calculate. However, with the rapid development of inexpensive computing systems, virtually every researcher has access to a computer which has the capability of calculating linear and nonlinear regression equations. Consequently, they need to know how to set up regression equations and to interpret computer-generated output.

The easiest way to interpret a computer output and thus determine which regression equation will furnish the most precise range of the value of the predicted value is to follow the sequential steps shown in Figure 13.4. To ascertain which regression equation to use, one should ask two questions:

1. How many independent variables are used to predict the value of the dependent variable?

2. Do the data fall on a linear or nonlinear plane?

Figure 13.9 provides guidelines for selecting the appropriate regression equation.

Figure 13.9   Determining Which Regression Equation to Use

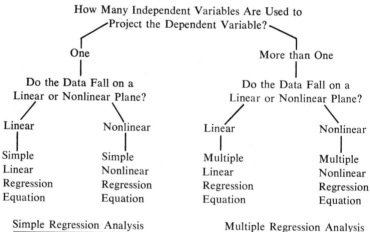

Regardless of which type of regression analysis is employed, the applicability of regression analysis is manifold, and the surface was just scratched in this chapter. Nevertheless, the processes and procedures discussed here serve as a foundation for the understanding and the further exploration of this powerful technique for predictive purposes.

Review Questions

1. Explain the meaning and significance of the following terms and ideas:
   a. simple regression analysis
   b. multiple regression analysis
   c. polynomial regression equation
   d. transformative regression equation
   e. nonlinear regression
   f. coefficient of determination
   g. standard deviation of the predicted Y
   h. multicollinearity.

2. Compute the following sets of scores:

X	Y	X^2	Y^2	XY
4	6	16	36	24
12	5			
16	9			
32	10			
3	5			
4	3			
5	2			

3. Discuss the steps involved in predicting the value of the dependent variable.

4. Explain the procedures used to determine the range of the predicted value of the dependent variable.

5. Why is it useful to check for the existence of a high level of multicollinearity before computing a regression equation?

6. Explain when and why researchers would determine the level of error associated with the coefficient of determination.

7. Predict for next year the amount of crime in the United States by regressing the crime rate for 1980 on the inflation rate, the per capita income, and the employment rate.

8. Suppose researchers are examining the effects of a youth services program designed to help persons between the ages of 16 and 24 who have been arrested for selling controlled substances. Two independent variables — the number of rearrests (X_1) and the age of the person (X_2) — are used to predict the effectiveness of the program ($\hat{Y}$). The following linear regression equation is the result:

$$\hat{Y} = 20 + .300X_1 + .050\,X_2$$
$$R^2 = .64$$

What does this equation tell an administrator?

References

Gustafson, Robert H. "The Role of Stratification in the Use of Multi-regression as Applied to Single-Family Residences." In *The Application of Multiple Regression Analysis in Assessment Administration.* Edited by International Association of Assessing Officers. Chicago: International Association of Assessing Officers, 1974.

Reinmuth, James E. "The Use of Multivariate Statistical Methods in Assessment Analysis, with Special Emphasis on the Problem of Multicollinearity." In *The Application of Multiple Regression Analysis in Assessment Administration.* Edited by International Association of Assessing Officers. Chicago: International Association of Assessing Officers, 1974.

Ryan, Thomas A. et al. *Minitab: Student Handbook.* North Scituate, MA: Duxbury Press, 1976.

Appendices

Appendix A

Table of Random Numbers

10 09 73 25 33	76 52 01 35 86	34 67 35 48 76	80 95 90 91 17	39 29 27 49 45
37 54 20 48 05	64 89 47 42 96	24 80 52 40 37	20 63 61 04 02	00 82 29 16 65
08 42 26 89 53	19 64 50 93 03	23 20 90 25 60	15 95 33 47 64	35 08 03 36 06
99 01 90 25 29	09 37 67 07 15	38 31 13 11 65	88 67 67 43 97	04 43 62 76 59
12 80 79 99 70	80 15 73 61 47	64 03 23 66 53	98 95 11 68 77	12 17 17 68 33
66 06 57 47 17	34 07 27 68 50	36 69 73 61 70	65 81 33 98 85	11 19 92 91 70
31 06 01 08 05	45 57 18 24 06	35 30 34 26 14	86 79 90 74 39	23 40 30 97 32
85 26 97 76 02	02 05 16 56 92	68 66 57 48 18	73 05 38 52 47	18 62 38 85 79
63 57 33 21 35	05 32 54 70 48	90 55 35 75 48	28 46 82 87 09	83 49 12 56 24
73 79 64 57 53	03 52 96 47 78	35 80 83 42 82	60 93 52 03 44	35 27 38 84 35
98 52 01 77 67	14 90 56 86 07	22 10 94 05 58	60 97 09 34 33	50 50 07 39 98
11 80 50 54 31	39 80 82 77 32	50 72 56 82 48	29 40 52 42 01	52 77 56 78 51
83 45 29 96 34	06 28 89 80 83	13 74 67 00 78	18 47 54 06 10	68 71 17 78 17
88 68 54 02 00	86 50 75 84 01	36 76 66 79 51	90 36 47 64 93	29 60 91 10 62
99 59 46 73 48	87 51 76 49 69	91 82 60 89 28	93 78 56 13 68	23 47 83 41 13
65 48 11 76 74	17 46 85 09 50	58 04 77 69 74	73 03 95 71 86	40 21 81 65 44
80 12 43 56 35	17 72 70 80 15	45 31 82 23 74	21 11 57 82 53	14 38 55 37 63
74 35 09 98 17	77 40 27 72 14	43 23 60 02 10	45 52 16 42 37	96 28 60 26 55
69 91 62 68 03	66 25 22 91 48	36 93 68 72 03	76 62 11 39 90	94 40 05 64 18
09 89 32 05 05	14 22 56 85 14	46 42 75 67 88	96 29 77 88 22	54 38 21 45 98
91 49 91 45 23	68 47 92 76 86	46 16 28 35 54	94 75 08 99 23	37 08 92 00 48
80 33 69 45 98	26 94 03 68 58	70 29 73 41 35	53 14 03 33 40	42 05 08 23 41
44 10 48 19 49	85 15 74 79 54	32 97 92 65 75	57 60 04 08 81	22 22 20 64 13
12 55 07 37 42	11 10 00 20 40	12 86 07 46 97	96 64 48 94 39	28 70 72 58 15
63 60 64 93 29	16 50 53 44 84	40 21 95 25 63	43 65 17 70 82	07 20 73 17 90
61 19 69 04 46	26 45 74 77 74	51 92 43 37 29	65 39 45 95 93	42 58 26 05 27
15 47 44 52 66	95 27 07 99 53	59 36 78 38 48	82 39 61 01 18	33 21 15 94 66
94 55 72 85 73	67 89 75 43 87	54 62 24 44 31	91 19 04 25 92	92 92 74 59 73
42 48 11 62 13	97 34 40 87 21	16 86 84 87 67	03 07 11 20 59	25 70 14 66 70
23 52 37 83 17	73 20 88 98 37	68 93 59 14 16	26 25 22 96 63	05 52 28 25 62
04 49 35 24 94	75 24 63 38 24	45 86 25 10 25	61 96 27 93 35	65 33 71 24 72
00 54 99 76 54	64 05 18 81 59	96 11 96 38 96	54 69 28 23 91	23 28 72 95 29
35 96 31 53 07	26 89 80 93 54	33 35 13 54 62	77 97 45 00 24	90 10 33 93 33
59 80 80 83 91	45 42 72 68 42	83 60 94 97 00	13 02 12 48 92	78 56 52 01 06
46 05 88 52 36	01 39 09 22 86	77 28 14 40 77	93 91 08 36 47	70 61 74 29 41

Random Numbers (continued)

```
32 17 90 05 97   87 37 92 52 41   05 56 70 70 07   86 74 31 71 57   85 39 41 18 38
69 23 46 14 06   20 11 74 52 04   15 95 66 00 00   18 74 39 24 23   97 11 89 63 38
19 56 54 14 30   01 75 87 53 79   40 41 92 15 85   66 67 43 68 06   84 96 28 52 07
45 15 51 49 38   19 47 60 72 46   43 66 79 45 43   59 04 79 00 33   20 82 66 95 41
94 86 43 19 94   36 16 81 08 51   34 88 88 15 53   01 54 03 54 56   05 01 45 11 76

59 58 00 64 78   75 56 97 88 00   88 83 55 44 86   23 76 80 61 56   04 11 10 84 08
38 50 80 73 41   23 79 34 87 63   90 82 29 70 22   17 71 90 42 07   95 95 44 99 53
30 69 27 06 68   94 68 81 61 27   56 19 68 00 91   82 06 76 34 00   05 46 26 92 00
65 44 39 56 59   18 28 82 74 37   49 63 22 40 41   08 33 76 56 76   96 29 99 08 36
27 26 75 02 64   13 19 27 22 94   07 47 74 46 06   17 98 54 89 11   97 34 13 03 58

91 30 70 69 91   19 07 22 42 10   36 69 95 37 28   28 82 53 57 93   28 97 66 62 52
68 43 49 46 88   84 47 31 36 22   62 12 69 84 08   12 84 38 25 90   09 81 59 31 40
48 90 81 58 77   54 74 52 45 91   35 70 00 47 54   83 82 45 26 92   54 13 05 51 60
06 91 34 51 97   42 67 27 86 01   11 88 30 95 28   63 01 19 89 01   14 97 44 03 44
10 45 51 60 19   14 21 03 37 12   91 34 23 78 21   88 32 58 08 51   43 66 77 08 83

12 88 39 73 43   65 02 76 11 84   04 28 50 13 92   17 97 41 50 77   90 71 22 67 69
21 77 83 09 76   38 80 73 69 61   31 64 94 20 96   63 28 10 20 23   08 81 64 74 49
19 52 35 95 15   65 12 25 96 59   86 28 36 82 58   69 57 21 37 98   16 43 59 15 29
67 24 55 26 70   35 58 31 65 63   79 24 68 66 86   76 46 33 42 22   26 65 59 08 02
60 58 44 73 77   07 50 03 79 92   45 13 42 65 29   26 76 08 36 37   41 32 64 43 44

53 85 34 13 77   36 06 69 48 50   58 83 87 38 59   49 36 47 33 31   96 24 04 36 42
24 63 73 87 36   74 38 48 93 42   52 62 30 79 92   12 36 91 86 01   03 74 28 38 73
83 08 01 24 51   38 99 22 28 15   07 75 95 17 77   97 37 72 75 85   51 97 23 78 67
16 44 42 43 34   36 15 19 90 73   27 49 37 09 39   85 13 03 25 52   54 84 65 47 59
60 79 01 81 57   57 17 86 57 62   11 16 17 85 76   45 81 95 29 79   65 13 00 48 60

03 99 11 04 61   93 17 61 68 94   66 08 32 46 53   84 60 95 82 32   88 61 81 91 61
38 55 59 55 54   32 88 65 97 80   08 35 56 08 60   29 73 54 77 62   71 29 92 38 53
17 54 67 37 04   92 05 24 62 15   55 12 12 92 81   59 07 60 79 36   27 95 45 89 09
32 64 35 28 61   95 81 90 68 31   00 91 19 89 36   76 35 59 37 79   80 86 30 05 14
69 57 26 87 77   39 51 03 59 05   14 06 04 06 19   29 54 96 96 16   33 56 46 07 80

24 12 26 65 91   27 69 90 64 94   14 84 54 66 72   61 95 87 71 00   90 89 97 57 54
61 19 63 02 31   92 96 26 17 73   41 83 95 53 82   17 26 77 09 43   78 03 87 02 67
30 53 22 17 04   10 27 41 22 02   39 68 52 33 09   10 06 16 88 29   55 98 66 64 85
03 78 89 75 99   75 86 72 07 17   74 41 65 31 66   35 20 83 33 74   87 53 90 88 23
48 22 86 33 79   85 78 34 76 19   53 15 26 74 33   35 66 35 29 72   16 81 86 03 11

60 36 59 46 53   35 07 53 39 49   42 61 42 92 97   01 91 82 83 16   98 95 37 32 31
83 79 94 24 02   56 62 33 44 42   34 99 44 13 74   70 07 11 47 36   09 95 81 80 65
32 96 00 74 05   36 40 98 32 32   99 38 54 16 00   11 13 30 75 86   15 91 70 62 53
19 32 25 38 45   57 62 05 26 06   66 49 76 86 46   78 13 86 65 59   19 64 09 94 13
11 22 09 47 47   07 39 93 74 08   48 50 92 39 29   27 48 24 54 76   85 24 43 51 59

31 75 15 72 60   68 98 00 53 39   15 47 04 83 55   88 65 12 25 96   03 15 21 92 21
88 49 29 93 82   14 45 40 45 04   20 09 49 89 77   74 84 39 34 13   22 10 97 85 08
30 93 44 77 44   07 48 18 38 28   73 78 80 65 33   28 59 72 04 05   94 20 52 03 80
22 88 84 88 93   27 49 99 87 48   60 53 04 51 28   74 02 28 46 17   82 03 71 02 68
78 21 21 69 93   35 90 29 13 86   44 37 21 54 86   65 74 11 40 14   87 48 13 72 20
```

Random Numbers (continued)

98 08 62 48 26	45 24 02 84 04	44 99 90 88 96	39 09 47 34 07	35 44 13 18 80
33 18 51 62 32	41 94 15 09 49	89 43 54 85 81	88 69 54 19 94	37 54 87 30 43
80 95 10 04 06	96 38 27 07 74	20 15 12 33 87	25 01 62 52 98	94 62 46 11 71
79 75 24 91 40	71 96 12 82 96	69 86 10 25 91	74 85 22 05 39	00 38 75 95 79
18 63 33 25 37	98 14 50 65 71	31 01 02 46 74	05 45 56 14 27	77 93 89 19 36
74 02 94 39 02	77 55 73 22 70	97 79 01 71 19	52 52 75 80 21	80 81 45 17 48
54 17 84 56 11	80 99 33 71 43	05 33 51 29 69	56 12 71 92 55	36 04 09 03 24
11 66 44 98 83	52 07 98 48 27	59 38 17 15 39	09 97 33 34 40	88 46 12 33 56
48 32 47 79 28	31 24 96 47 10	02 29 53 68 70	32 30 75 75 46	15 02 00 99 94
69 07 49 41 38	87 63 79 19 76	35 58 40 44 01	10 51 82 16 15	01 84 87 69 38
09 18 82 00 97	32 82 53 95 27	04 22 08 63 04	83 38 98 73 74	64 27 85 80 44
90 04 58 54 97	51 98 15 06 54	94 93 88 19 97	91 87 07 61 50	68 47 66 46 59
73 18 95 02 07	47 67 72 52 69	62 29 06 44 64	27 12 46 70 18	41 36 18 27 60
75 76 87 64 90	20 97 18 17 49	90 42 91 22 72	95 37 50 58 71	93 82 34 31 78
54 01 64 40 56	66 28 13 10 03	00 68 22 73 98	20 71 45 32 95	07 70 61 78 13
08 35 86 99 10	78 54 24 27 85	13 66 15 88 73	04 61 89 75 53	31 22 30 84 20
28 30 60 32 64	81 33 31 05 91	40 51 00 78 93	32 60 46 04 75	94 11 90 18 40
53 84 08 62 33	81 59 41 36 28	51 21 59 02 90	28 46 66 87 95	77 76 22 07 91
91 75 75 37 41	61 61 36 22 69	50 26 39 02 12	55 78 17 65 14	83 48 31 70 55
89 41 59 26 94	00 39 75 83 91	12 60 71 76 46	48 94 97 23 06	94 54 13 74 08
77 51 30 38 20	86 83 42 99 01	68 41 48 27 74	51 90 81 39 80	72 89 35 55 07
19 50 23 71 74	69 97 92 02 88	55 21 02 97 73	74 28 77 52 51	65 34 46 74 15
21 81 85 93 13	93 27 88 17 57	05 68 67 31 56	07 08 28 50 46	31 85 33 84 52
51 47 46 64 99	68 10 72 36 21	94 04 99 13 45	42 83 60 91 91	08 00 74 54 49
99 55 96 83 31	62 53 52 41 70	69 77 71 28 30	74 81 97 81 42	43 86 07 28 34
33 71 34 80 07	93 58 47 28 69	51 92 66 47 21	58 30 32 98 22	93 17 49 39 72
85 27 48 68 93	11 30 32 92 70	28 83 43 41 37	73 51 59 04 00	71 14 84 36 43
84 13 38 96 40	44 03 55 21 66	73 85 27 00 91	61 22 26 05 61	62 32 71 84 23
56 73 21 62 34	17 39 59 61 31	10 12 30 16 22	85 49 65 75 60	81 60 41 88 80
65 13 85 68 06	87 64 88 52 61	34 31 36 58 61	45 87 52 10 69	85 64 44 72 77
38 00 10 21 76	81 71 91 17 11	71 60 29 29 37	74 21 96 40 49	65 58 44 96 98
37 40 29 63 97	01 30 47 57 86	56 27 11 00 86	47 32 46 26 05	40 03 03 74 38
97 12 54 03 48	87 08 33 14 17	21 81 53 92 50	75 23 76 20 47	15 50 12 95 78
21 82 64 11 34	47 14 33 40 72	64 63 88 59 02	49 13 90 64 41	03 85 65 45 52
73 13 54 27 42	95 71 90 90 35	85 79 47 42 96	08 78 98 81 56	64 69 11 92 02
07 63 87 79 29	03 06 11 80 72	96 20 74 41 56	23 82 19 95 38	04 71 36 69 94
60 52 88 34 41	07 95 41 98 14	59 17 52 06 95	05 53 35 21 39	61 21 20 64 55
83 59 63 56 55	06 95 89 29 83	05 12 80 97 19	77 43 35 37 83	92 30 15 04 98
10 85 06 27 46	99 59 91 05 07	13 49 90 63 19	53 07 57 18 39	06 41 01 93 62
39 82 09 89 52	43 62 26 31 47	64 42 18 08 14	43 80 00 93 51	31 02 47 31 67

Source: The RAND Corporation, *A Million Random Digits,* Free Press, Glencoe, Ill., 1955, pp. 1-3, with the permission of the publisher.

Appendix B

Normal Distribution (z) Table

Z	.00	.01	.02	.03	.04	.05	.06	.07	.08	.09
0.0	.0000	.0040	.0080	.0120	.0159	.0199	.0239	.0279	.0319	.0359
0.1	.0398	.0438	.0478	.0517	.0557	.0596	.0636	.0675	.0714	.0753
0.2	.0793	.0832	.0871	.0910	.0948	.0987	.1026	.1064	.1103	.1141
0.3	.1179	.1217	.1255	.1293	.1331	.1368	.1406	.1443	.1480	.1517
0.4	.1554	.1591	.1628	.1664	.1700	.1736	.1772	.1808	.1844	.1879
0.5	.1915	.1950	.1985	.2019	.2054	.2088	.2123	.2157	.2190	.2224
0.6	.2257	.2291	.2324	.2357	.2389	.2422	.2454	.2486	.2518	.2549
0.7	.2580	.2612	.2642	.2673	.2704	.2734	.2764	.2794	.2823	.2852
0.8	.2881	.2910	.2939	.2967	.2995	.3023	.3051	.3078	.3106	.3133
0.9	.3159	.3186	.3212	.3238	.3264	.3289	.3315	.3340	.3365	.3389
1.0	.3413	.3438	.3461	.3485	.3508	.3531	.3554	.3577	.3599	.3621
1.1	.3643	.3665	.3686	.3718	.3729	.3749	.3770	.3790	.3810	.3830
1.2	.3849	.3869	.3888	.3907	.3925	.3944	.3962	.3980	.3997	.4015
1.3	.4032	.4049	.4066	.4083	.4099	.4115	.4131	.4147	.4162	.4177
1.4	.4192	.4207	.4222	.4236	.4251	.4265	.4279	.4292	.4306	.4319
1.5	.4332	.4345	.4357	.4370	.4382	.4394	.4406	.4418	.4430	.4441
1.6	.4452	.4463	.4474	.4485	.4495	.4505	.4515	.4525	.4535	.4545
1.7	.4554	.4564	.4573	.4582	.4591	.4599	.4608	.4616	.4625	.4633
1.8	.4641	.4649	.4656	.4664	.4671	.4678	.4686	.4693	.4699	.4706
1.9	.4713	.4719	.4726	.4732	.4738	.4744	.4750	.4758	.4762	.4767
2.0	.4773	.4778	.4783	.4788	.4793	.4798	.4803	.4808	.4812	.4817
2.1	.4821	.4826	.4830	.4834	.4838	.4842	.4846	.4850	.4854	.4857
2.2	.4861	.4865	.4868	.4871	.4875	.4878	.4881	.4884	.4887	.4890
2.3	.4893	.4896	.4898	.4901	.4904	.4906	.4909	.4911	.4913	.4916
2.4	.4918	.4920	.4922	.4925	.4927	.4929	.4931	.4932	.4934	.4936
2.5	.4938	.4940	.4941	.4943	.4945	.4946	.4948	.4949	.4951	.4952
2.6	.4953	.4955	.4956	.4957	.4959	.4960	.4961	.4962	.4963	.4964
2.7	.4965	.4966	.4967	.4968	.4969	.4970	.4971	.4972	.4973	.4974
2.8	.4974	.4975	.4976	.4977	.4977	.4978	.4979	.4980	.4980	.4981
2.9	.4981	.4982	.4983	.4984	.4984	.4984	.4985	.4985	.4986	.4986
3.0	.4986	.4987	.4987	.4988	.4988	.4988	.4989	.4989	.4989	.4990
3.1	.4990	.4991	.4991	.4991	.4992	.4992	.4992	.4992	.4993	.4993

Source: Harold O. Rugg, *Statistical Methods Applied to Education,* Houghton Mifflin Company, Boston, 1917, appendix table III, pp. 389-390, with the permission of the publisher.

Appendix C

Student's t Distribution Table

df	Level of Error for one-tailed test					
	.10	.05	.025	.01	.005	.0005
	Level of Error for two-tailed test					
	.20	.10	.05	.02	.01	.001
1	3.078	6.314	12.706	31.821	63.657	636.619
2	1.886	2.920	4.303	6.965	9.925	31.598
3	1.638	2.353	3.182	4.541	5.841	12.941
4	1.533	2.132	2.776	3.747	4.604	8.610
5	1.476	2.015	2.571	3.365	4.032	6.859
6	1.440	1.943	2.447	3.143	3.707	5.959
7	1.415	1.895	2.365	2.998	3.499	5.405
8	1.397	1.860	2.306	2.896	3.355	5.041
9	1.383	1.833	2.262	2.821	3.250	4.781
10	1.372	1.812	2.228	2.764	3.169	4.587
11	1.363	1.796	2.201	2.718	3.106	4.437
12	1.356	1.782	2.179	2.681	3.055	4.318
13	1.350	1.771	2.160	2.650	3.012	4.221
14	1.345	1.761	2.145	2.624	2.977	4.140
15	1.341	1.753	2.131	2.602	2.947	4.073
16	1.337	1.746	2.120	2.583	2.921	4.015
17	1.333	1.740	2.110	2.567	2.898	3.965
18	1.330	1.734	2.101	2.552	2.878	3.922
19	1.328	1.729	2.093	2.539	2.861	3.883
20	1.325	1.725	2.086	2.528	2.845	3.850
21	1.323	1.721	2.080	2.518	2.831	3.819
22	1.321	1.717	2.074	2.508	2.819	3.792
23	1.319	1.714	2.069	2.500	2.807	3.767
24	1.318	1.711	2.064	2.492	2.797	3.745
25	1.316	1.708	2.060	2.485	2.787	3.725
26	1.315	1.706	2.056	2.479	2.779	3.707
27	1.314	1.703	2.052	2.473	2.771	3.690
28	1.313	1.701	2.048	2.467	2.763	3.674
29	1.311	1.699	2.045	2.462	2.756	3.659
30	1.310	1.697	2.042	2.457	2.750	3.646
40	1.303	1.684	2.021	2.423	2.704	3.551
60	1.296	1.671	2.000	2.390	2.660	3.460
120	1.289	1.658	1.980	2.358	2.617	3.373
∞	1.282	1.645	1.960	2.326	2.576	3.291

Source: Table III of R. A. Fisher and F. Yates, *Statistical Tables for Biological, Agricultural and Medical Research* (1948 ed.), published by Oliver & Boyd, Ltd., Edinburgh and London, by permission of the publishers.

Appendix D

F Distribution Table

$$p \leq .05$$

df_1 / df_2	1	2	3	4	5	6	8	12	24	∞
1	161.4	199.5	215.7	224.6	230.2	234.0	238.9	243.9	249.0	254.3
2	18.51	19.00	19.16	19.25	19.30	19.33	19.37	19.41	19.45	19.50
3	10.13	9.55	9.28	9.12	9.01	8.94	8.84	8.74	8.64	8.53
4	7.71	6.94	6.59	6.39	6.26	6.16	6.04	5.91	5.77	5.63
5	6.61	5.79	5.41	5.19	5.05	4.95	4.82	4.68	4.53	4.36
6	5.99	5.14	4.76	4.53	4.39	4.28	4.15	4.00	3.84	3.67
7	5.59	4.74	4.35	4.12	3.97	3.87	3.73	3.57	3.41	3.23
8	5.32	4.46	4.07	3.84	3.69	3.58	3.44	3.28	3.12	2.93
9	5.12	4.26	3.86	3.63	3.48	3.37	3.23	3.07	2.90	2.71
10	4.96	4.10	3.71	3.48	3.33	3.22	3.07	2.91	2.74	2.54
11	4.84	3.98	3.59	3.36	3.20	3.09	2.95	2.79	2.61	2.40
12	4.75	3.88	3.49	3.26	3.11	3.00	2.85	2.69	2.50	2.30
13	4.67	3.80	3.41	3.18	3.02	2.92	2.77	2.60	2.42	2.21
14	4.60	3.74	3.34	3.11	2.96	2.85	2.70	2.53	2.35	2.13
15	4.54	3.68	3.29	3.06	2.90	2.79	2.64	2.48	2.29	2.07
16	4.49	3.63	3.24	3.01	2.85	2.74	2.59	2.42	2.24	2.01
17	4.45	3.59	3.20	2.96	2.81	2.70	2.55	2.38	2.19	1.96
18	4.41	3.55	3.16	2.93	2.77	2.66	2.51	2.34	2.15	1.92
19	4.38	3.52	3.13	2.90	2.74	2.63	2.48	2.31	2.11	1.88
20	4.35	3.49	3.10	2.87	2.71	2.60	2.45	2.28	2.08	1.84
21	4.32	3.47	3.07	2.84	2.68	2.57	2.42	2.25	2.05	1.81
22	4.30	3.44	3.05	2.82	2.66	2.55	2.40	2.23	2.03	1.78
23	4.28	3.42	3.03	2.80	2.64	2.53	2.38	2.20	2.00	1.76
24	4.26	3.40	3.01	2.78	2.62	2.51	2.36	2.18	1.98	1.73
25	4.24	3.38	2.99	2.76	2.60	2.49	2.34	2.16	1.96	1.71
26	4.22	3.37	2.98	2.74	2.59	2.47	2.32	2.15	1.95	1.69
27	4.21	3.35	2.96	2.73	2.57	2.46	2.30	2.13	1.93	1.67
28	4.20	3.34	2.95	2.71	2.56	2.44	2.29	2.12	1.91	1.65
29	4.18	3.33	2.93	2.70	2.54	2.43	2.28	2.10	1.90	1.64
30	4.17	3.32	2.92	2.69	2.53	2.42	2.27	2.09	1.89	1.62
40	4.08	3.23	2.84	2.61	2.45	2.34	2.18	2.00	1.79	1.51
60	4.00	3.15	2.76	2.52	2.37	2.25	2.10	1.92	1.70	1.39
120	3.92	3.07	2.68	2.45	2.29	2.17	2.02	1.83	1.61	1.25
∞	3.84	2.99	2.60	2.37	2.21	2.09	1.94	1.75	1.52	1.00

Source: Table V of R. A. Fisher and F. Yates, *Statistical Tables for Biological, Agricultural and Medical Research* (1948 ed.), published by Oliver & Boyd, Ltd., Edinburgh and London, by permission of the publishers.

F Distribution Table (continued)

$$p \le .01$$

df_1 / df_2	1	2	3	4	5	6	8	12	24	∞
1	4052	4999	5403	5625	5764	5859	5981	6106	6234	6366
2	98.49	99.01	99.17	99.25	99.30	99.33	99.36	99.42	99.46	99.50
3	34.12	30.81	29.46	28.71	28.24	27.91	27.49	27.05	26.60	26.12
4	21.20	18.00	16.69	15.98	15.52	15.21	14.80	14.37	13.93	13.46
5	16.26	13.27	12.06	11.39	10.97	10.67	10.27	9.89	9.47	9.02
6	13.74	10.92	9.78	9.15	8.75	8.47	8.10	7.72	7.31	6.88
7	12.25	9.55	8.45	7.85	7.46	7.19	6.84	6.47	6.07	5.65
8	11.26	8.65	7.59	7.01	6.63	6.37	6.03	5.67	5.28	4.86
9	10.56	8.02	6.99	6.42	6.06	5.80	5.47	5.11	4.73	4.31
10	10.04	7.56	6.55	5.99	5.64	5.39	5.06	4.71	4.33	3.91
11	9.65	7.20	6.22	5.67	5.32	5.07	4.74	4.40	4.02	3.60
12	9.33	6.93	5.95	5.41	5.06	4.82	4.50	4.16	3.78	3.36
13	9.07	6.70	5.74	5.20	4.86	4.62	4.30	3.96	3.59	3.16
14	8.86	6.51	5.56	5.03	4.69	4.46	4.14	3.80	3.43	3.00
15	8.68	6.36	5.42	4.89	4.56	4.32	4.00	3.67	3.29	2.87
16	8.53	6.23	5.29	4.77	4.44	4.20	3.89	3.55	3.18	2.75
17	8.40	6.11	5.18	4.67	4.34	4.10	3.79	3.45	3.08	2.65
18	8.28	6.01	5.09	4.58	4.25	4.01	3.71	3.37	3.00	2.57
19	8.18	5.93	5.01	4.50	4.17	3.94	3.63	3.30	2.92	2.49
20	8.10	5.85	4.94	4.43	4.10	3.87	3.56	3.23	2.86	2.42
21	8.02	5.78	4.87	4.37	4.04	3.81	3.51	3.17	2.80	2.36
22	7.94	5.72	4.82	4.31	3.99	3.76	3.45	3.12	2.75	2.31
23	7.88	5.66	4.76	4.26	3.94	3.71	3.41	3.07	2.70	2.26
24	7.82	5.61	4.72	4.22	3.90	3.67	3.36	3.03	2.66	2.21
25	7.77	5.57	4.68	4.18	3.86	3.63	3.32	2.99	2.62	2.17
26	7.72	5.53	4.64	4.14	3.82	3.59	3.29	2.96	2.58	2.13
27	7.68	5.49	4.60	4.11	3.78	3.56	3.26	2.93	2.55	2.10
28	7.64	5.45	4.57	4.07	3.75	3.53	3.23	2.90	2.52	2.06
29	7.60	5.42	4.54	4.04	3.73	3.50	3.20	2.87	2.49	2.03
30	7.56	5.39	4.51	4.02	3.70	3.47	3.17	2.84	2.47	2.01
40	7.31	5.18	4.31	3.83	3.51	3.29	2.99	2.66	2.29	1.80
60	7.08	4.98	4.13	3.65	3.34	3.12	2.82	2.50	2.12	1.60
120	6.85	4.79	3.95	3.48	3.17	2.96	2.66	2.34	1.95	1.38
∞	6.64	4.60	3.78	3.32	3.02	2.80	2.51	2.18	1.79	1.00

F Distribution Table (continued)

$$p \le .001$$

df_1 df_2	1	2	3	4	5	6	8	12	24	∞
1	405284	500000	540379	562500	576405	585937	598144	610667	623497	636619
2	998.5	999.0	999.2	999.2	999.3	999.3	999.4	999.4	999.5	999.5
3	167.5	148.5	141.1	137.1	134.6	132.8	130.6	128.3	125.9	123.5
4	74.14	61.25	56.18	53.44	51.71	50.53	49.00	47.41	45.77	44.05
5	47.04	36.61	33.20	31.09	29.75	28.84	27.64	26.42	25.14	23.78
6	35.51	27.00	23.70	21.90	20.81	20.03	19.03	17.99	16.89	15.75
7	29.22	21.69	18.77	17.19	16.21	15.52	14.63	13.71	12.73	11.69
8	25.42	18.49	15.83	14.39	13.49	12.86	12.04	11.19	10.30	9.34
9	22.86	16.39	13.90	12.56	11.71	11.13	10.37	9.57	8.72	7.81
10	21.04	14.91	12.55	11.28	10.48	9.92	9.20	8.45	7.64	6.76
11	19.69	13.81	11.56	10.35	9.58	9.05	8.35	7.63	6.85	6.00
12	18.64	12.97	10.80	9.63	8.89	8.38	7.71	7.00	6.25	5.42
13	17.81	12.31	10.21	9.07	8.35	7.86	7.21	6.52	5.78	4.97
14	17.14	11.78	9.73	8.62	7.92	7.43	6.80	6.13	5.41	4.60
15	16.59	11.34	9.34	8.25	7.57	7.09	6.47	5.81	5.10	4.31
16	16.12	10.97	9.00	7.94	7.27	6.81	6.19	5.55	4.85	4.06
17	15.72	10.66	8.73	7.68	7.02	6.56	5.96	5.32	4.63	3.85
18	15.38	10.39	8.49	7.46	6.81	6.35	5.76	5.13	4.45	3.67
19	15.08	10.16	8.28	7.26	6.61	6.18	5.59	4.97	4.29	3.52
20	14.82	9.95	8.10	7.10	6.46	6.02	5.44	4.82	4.15	3.38
21	14.59	9.77	7.94	6.95	6.32	5.88	5.31	4.70	4.03	3.26
22	14.38	9.61	7.80	6.81	6.19	5.76	5.19	4.58	3.92	3.15
23	14.19	9.47	7.67	6.69	6.08	5.65	5.09	4.48	3.82	3.05
24	14.03	9.34	7.55	6.59	5.98	5.55	4.99	4.39	3.74	2.97
25	13.88	9.22	7.45	6.49	5.88	5.46	4.91	4.31	3.66	2.89
26	13.74	9.12	7.36	6.41	5.80	5.38	4.83	4.24	3.59	2.82
27	13.61	9.02	7.27	6.33	5.73	5.31	4.76	4.17	3.52	2.75
28	13.50	8.93	7.19	6.25	5.66	5.24	4.69	4.11	3.46	2.70
29	13.39	8.85	7.12	6.19	5.59	5.18	4.64	4.05	3.41	2.64
30	13.29	8.77	7.05	6.12	5.53	5.12	4.58	4.00	3.36	2.59
40	12.61	8.25	6.60	5.70	5.13	4.73	4.21	3.64	3.01	2.23
60	11.97	7.76	6.17	5.31	4.76	4.37	3.87	3.31	2.69	1.90
120	11.38	7.31	5.79	4.95	4.42	4.04	3.55	3.02	2.40	1.56
∞	10.83	6.91	5.42	4.62	4.10	3.74	3.27	2.74	2.13	1.00

Appendix E

Chi Square Distribution Table
Level of Error

df	0.10	0.05	0.025	0.01	0.005
1	2.71	3.84	5.02	6.63	7.88
2	4.61	5.99	7.38	9.21	10.60
3	6.25	7.81	9.35	11.34	12.84
4	7.78	9.49	11.14	13.28	14.86
5	9.24	11.07	12.83	15.09	16.75
6	10.64	12.59	14.45	16.81	18.55
7	12.02	14.07	16.01	18.48	20.3
8	13.36	15.51	17.53	20.1	22.0
9	14.68	16.92	19.02	21.7	23.6
10	15.99	18.31	20.5	23.2	25.2
11	17.28	19.68	21.9	24.7	26.8
12	18.55	21.0	23.3	26.2	28.3
13	19.81	22.4	24.7	27.7	29.8
14	21.1	23.7	26.1	29.1	31.3
15	22.3	25.0	27.5	30.6	32.8
16	23.5	26.3	28.8	32.0	34.3
17	24.8	27.6	30.2	33.4	35.7
18	26.0	28.9	31.5	34.8	37.2
19	27.2	30.1	32.9	36.2	38.6
20	28.4	31.4	34.2	37.6	40.0
21	29.6	32.7	35.5	38.9	41.4
22	30.8	33.9	36.8	40.3	42.8
23	32.0	35.2	38.1	41.6	44.2
24	33.2	36.4	39.4	43.0	45.6
25	34.4	37.7	40.6	44.3	46.9
26	35.6	38.9	41.9	45.6	48.3
27	36.7	40.1	43.2	47.0	49.6
28	37.9	41.3	44.5	48.3	51.0
29	39.1	42.6	45.7	49.6	52.3
30	40.3	43.8	47.0	50.9	53.7
40	51.8	55.8	59.3	63.7	66.8
50	63.2	67.5	71.4	76.2	79.5
60	74.4	79.1	83.3	88.4	92.0
70	85.5	90.5	95.0	100.4	104.2
80	96.6	101.9	106.6	112.3	116.3
90	107.6	113.1	118.1	124.1	128.3
100	118.5	124.3	129.6	135.8	140.2

Source: *Applied Regression Analysis and Other Multivariable Methods* by David G. Kleinbaum and Lawrence L. Kupper, 1978, Wadsworth, Inc. Reprinted by permission of the publisher, Duxbury Press.

Appendix F

Distribution Table for a Sign Test

n	Level of Error for One-Tailed Test		
	.025	.01	.005
	Level of Error for Two-Tailed Test		
	.05	.02	.01
6	1	—	—
7	2	0	—
8	4	2	0
9	6	3	2
10	8	5	3
11	11	7	5
12	14	10	7
13	17	13	10
14	21	16	13
15	25	20	16
16	30	24	19
17	35	28	23
18	40	33	28
19	46	38	32
20	52	43	37
21	59	49	43
22	66	56	49
23	73	62	55
24	81	69	61
25	90	77	68

Source: Table I of F. Wilcoxon, *Some Rapid Approximate Statistical Procedures,* rev. ed. New York: American Cyanamid Company, 1964, with permission of publisher.

Appendix G

Distribution Table for a Mann-Whitney Test
Small Samples

Probabilities associated with values as small as observed values of U in the Mann-Whitney test (small samples)

$N_2 = 3$

U \\ N_1	1	2	3
0	.250	.100	.050
1	.500	.200	.100
2	.750	.400	.200
3		.600	.350
4			.500
5			.650

$N_2 = 4$

U \\ N_1	1	2	3	4
0	.200	.067	.028	.014
1	.400	.133	.057	.029
2	.600	.267	.114	.057
3		.400	.200	.100
4		.600	.314	.171
5			.429	.243
6			.571	.343
7				.443
8				.557

$N_2 = 5$

U \\ N_1	1	2	3	4	5
0	.167	.047	.018	.008	.004
1	.333	.095	.036	.016	.008
2	.500	.190	.071	.032	.016
3	.667	.286	.125	.056	.028
4		.429	.196	.095	.048
5		.571	.286	.143	.075
6			.393	.206	.111
7			.500	.278	.155
8			.607	.365	.210
9				.452	.274
10				.548	.345
11					.421
12					.500
13					.579

$N_2 = 6$

U \\ N_1	1	2	3	4	5	6
0	.143	.036	.012	.005	.002	.001
1	.286	.071	.024	.010	.004	.002
2	.428	.143	.048	.019	.009	.004
3	.571	.214	.083	.033	.015	.008
4		.321	.131	.057	.026	.013
5		.429	.190	.086	.041	.021
6		.571	.274	.129	.063	.032
7			.357	.176	.089	.047
8			.452	.238	.123	.066
9			.548	.305	.165	.090
10				.381	.214	.120
11				.457	.268	.155
12				.545	.331	.197
13					.396	.242
14					.465	.294
15					.535	.350
16						.409
17						.469
18						.531

Source: H. B. Mann and D. R. Whitney, "On a Test of Whether One or Two Random Variables is Stochastically Larger than the Other," *Annals of Mathematical Statistics* 18 (1947): 52-54; with permission of the publisher.

Distribution Table for a Mann-Whitney Test
Small Samples
(continued)
$N_2 = 7$

N_1 U	1	2	3	4	5	6	7
0	.125	.028	.008	.003	.001	.001	.000
1	.250	.056	.017	.006	.003	.001	.001
2	.375	.111	.033	.012	.005	.002	.001
3	.500	.167	.058	.021	.009	.004	.002
4	.625	.250	.092	.036	.015	.007	.003
5		.333	.133	.055	.024	.011	.006
6		.444	.192	.082	.037	.017	.009
7		.556	.258	.115	.053	.026	.013
8			.333	.158	.074	.037	.019
9			.417	.206	.101	.051	.027
10			.500	.264	.134	.069	.036
11			.583	.324	.172	.090	.049
12				.394	.216	.117	.064
13				.464	.265	.147	.082
14				.538	.319	.183	.104
15					.378	.223	.130
16					.438	.267	.159
17					.500	.314	.191
18					.562	.365	.228
19						.418	.267
20						.473	.310
21						.527	.355
22							.402
23							.451
24							.500
25							.549

Distribution Table for a Mann-Whitney Test
Small Samples
(continued)

$N_2 = 8$

U \ N₁	1	2	3	4	5	6	7	8	t	Normal
0	.111	.022	.006	.002	.001	.000	.000	.000	3.308	.001
1	.222	.044	.012	.004	.002	.001	.000	.000	3.203	.001
2	.333	.089	.024	.008	.003	.001	.001	.000	3.098	.001
3	.444	.133	.042	.014	.005	.002	.001	.001	2.993	.001
4	.556	.200	.067	.024	.009	.004	.002	.001	2.888	.002
5		.267	.097	.036	.015	.006	.003	.001	2.783	.003
6		.356	.139	.055	.023	.010	.005	.002	2.678	.004
7		.444	.188	.077	.033	.015	.007	.003	2.573	.005
8		.556	.248	.107	.047	.021	.010	.005	2.468	.007
9			.315	.141	.064	.030	.014	.007	2.363	.009
10			.387	.184	.085	.041	.020	.010	2.258	.012
11			.461	.230	.111	.054	.027	.014	2.153	.016
12			.539	.285	.142	.071	.036	.019	2.048	.020
13				.341	.177	.091	.047	.025	1.943	.026
14				.404	.217	.114	.060	.032	1.838	.033
15				.467	.262	.141	.076	.041	1.733	.041
16				.533	.311	.172	.095	.052	1.628	.052
17					.362	.207	.116	.065	1.523	.064
18					.416	.245	.140	.080	1.418	.078
19					.472	.286	.168	.097	1.313	.094
20					.528	.331	.198	.117	1.208	.113
21						.377	.232	.139	1.102	.135
22						.426	.268	.164	.998	.159
23						.475	.306	.191	.893	.185
24						.525	.347	.221	.788	.215
25							.389	.253	.683	.247
26							.433	.287	.578	.282
27							.478	.323	.473	.318
28							.522	.360	.368	.356
29								.399	.263	.396
30								.439	.158	.437
31								.480	.052	.481
32								.520		

Appendix H
Distribution Table for a Mann-Whitney Test
Large Samples

Critical values of U for a one-tailed test at $\alpha = .05$ or for a two-tailed test at $\alpha = .10$

N_1 \ N_2	9	10	11	12	13	14	15	16	17	18	19	20
1											0	0
2	1	1	1	2	2	2	3	3	3	4	4	4
3	3	4	5	5	6	7	7	8	9	9	10	11
4	6	7	8	9	10	11	12	14	15	16	17	18
5	9	11	12	13	15	16	18	19	20	22	23	25
6	12	14	16	17	19	21	23	25	26	28	30	32
7	15	17	19	21	24	26	28	30	33	35	37	39
8	18	20	23	26	28	31	33	36	39	41	44	47
9	21	24	27	30	33	36	39	42	45	48	51	54
10	24	27	31	34	37	41	44	48	51	55	58	62
11	27	31	34	38	42	46	50	54	57	61	65	69
12	30	34	38	42	47	51	55	60	64	68	72	77
13	33	37	42	47	51	56	61	65	70	75	80	84
14	36	41	46	51	56	61	66	71	77	82	87	92
15	39	44	50	55	61	66	72	77	83	88	94	100
16	42	48	54	60	65	71	77	83	89	95	101	107
17	45	51	57	64	70	77	83	89	96	102	109	115
18	48	55	61	68	75	82	88	95	102	109	116	123
19	51	58	65	72	80	87	94	101	109	116	123	130
20	54	62	69	77	84	92	100	107	115	123	130	138

Source: D. Auble, "Extended Tables for the Mann-Whitney Statistic," *Bulletin of the Institute of Educational Research at Indiana University* 1, no. 2 1953). Adapted and abridged from tables 1, 3, 5, and 7 with permission of the publishers.

Distribution Table for a Mann-Whitney Test
Large Samples
(continued)

Critical values of U for a one-tailed test at $\alpha = .01$ or for a two-tailed test at $\alpha = .02$

N_1 \ N_2	9	10	11	12	13	14	15	16	17	18	19	20
1												
2					0	0	0	0	0	0	1	1
3	1	1	1	2	2	2	3	3	4	4	4	5
4	3	3	4	5	5	6	7	7	8	9	9	10
5	5	6	7	8	9	10	11	12	13	14	15	16
6	7	8	9	11	12	13	15	16	18	19	20	22
7	9	11	12	14	16	17	19	21	23	24	26	28
8	11	13	15	17	20	22	24	26	28	30	32	34
9	14	16	18	21	23	26	28	31	33	36	38	40
10	16	19	22	24	27	30	33	36	38	41	44	47
11	18	22	25	28	31	34	37	41	44	47	50	53
12	21	24	28	31	35	38	42	46	49	53	56	60
13	23	27	31	35	39	43	47	51	55	59	63	67
14	26	30	34	38	43	47	51	56	60	65	69	73
15	28	33	37	42	47	51	56	61	66	70	75	80
16	31	36	41	46	51	56	61	66	71	76	82	87
17	33	38	44	49	55	60	66	71	77	82	88	93
18	36	41	47	53	59	65	70	76	82	88	94	100
19	38	44	50	56	63	69	75	82	88	94	101	107
20	40	47	53	60	67	73	80	87	93	100	107	114

Critical values of U for a one-tailed test at $\alpha = .001$ or for a two-tailed test at $\alpha = .002$

N_1 \ N_2	9	10	11	12	13	14	15	16	17	18	19	20
1												
2												
3									0	0	0	0
4		0	0	0	1	1	1	2	2	3	3	3
5	1	1	2	2	3	3	4	5	5	6	7	7
6	2	3	4	4	5	6	7	8	9	10	11	12
7	3	5	6	7	8	9	10	11	13	14	15	16
8	5	6	8	9	11	12	14	15	17	18	20	21
9	7	8	10	12	14	15	17	19	21	23	25	26
10	8	10	12	14	17	19	21	23	25	27	29	32
11	10	12	15	17	20	22	24	27	29	32	34	37
12	12	14	17	20	23	25	28	31	34	37	40	42
13	14	17	20	23	26	29	32	35	38	42	45	48
14	15	19	22	25	29	32	36	39	43	46	50	54
15	17	21	24	28	32	36	40	43	47	51	55	59
16	19	23	27	31	35	39	43	48	52	56	60	65
17	21	25	29	34	38	43	47	52	57	61	66	70
18	23	27	32	37	42	46	51	56	61	66	71	76
19	25	29	34	40	45	50	55	60	66	71	77	82
20	26	32	37	42	48	54	59	65	70	76	82	88

Index